MARKETING MANAGEMENT IN AFRICA

This book focuses on strategies for developing consumer markets in Africa using concepts and techniques from marketing, entrepreneurship, and project management. The authors argue that entrepreneurial activity in Africa is rapid, but limited, and requires a structured approach to drive success.

Beginning with an introductory chapter that frames the socio-economic and technological developments in Africa, readers are introduced to the conceptual model that provides this structured approach in four logical parts:

- The creative stage
- Entrepreneurial and enterprise activities
- Understanding consumer behavior and market segments
- A project management-based framework.

This multidisciplinary approach is supplemented with many examples and cases from a variety of sectors including health care, wind and solar power, and mobile technology. Through these, readers are able to understand how the model is implemented in reality to drive innovative economic and social development. *Marketing Management in Africa* will prove a valuable companion to any student of marketing or entrepreneurship with a particular interest in Africa.

George Tesar is Professor Emeritus of Marketing and International Business at Umeå University, Sweden, and Professor Emeritus at the University of Wisconsin–Whitewater, USA.

Steven W. Anderson is Professor of Chemistry at the University of Wisconsin–Whitewater, USA.

Hassimi Traore is Associate Professor of Chemistry at the University of Wisconsin–Whitewater, USA.

Jens Graff is a retired academic and author of six textbooks in business administration. He was previously an Associate Professor at Woosong University, Korea.

MARKETING MANAGEMENT IN AFRICA

Edited by George Tesar, Steven W. Anderson, Hassimi Traore, and Jens Graff

First published 2018
by Routledge
711 Third Avenue, New York, NY 10017

and by Routledge
2 Park Square, Milton Park, Abingdon, Oxon, OX14 4RN

Routledge is an imprint of the Taylor & Francis Group, an informa business

© 2018 Taylor & Francis

The right of George Tesar, Steven W. Anderson, Hassimi Traore, and Jens Graff to be identified as the authors of the editorial material, and of the authors for their individual chapters, has been asserted in accordance with sections 77 and 78 of the Copyright, Designs and Patents Act 1988.

All rights reserved. No part of this book may be reprinted or reproduced or utilized in any form or by any electronic, mechanical, or other means, now known or hereafter invented, including photocopying and recording, or in any information storage or retrieval system, without permission in writing from the publishers.

Trademark notice: Product or corporate names may be trademarks or registered trademarks, and are used only for identification and explanation without intent to infringe.

Library of Congress Cataloging-in-Publication Data
A catalog record for this book has been requested

ISBN: 978-1-138-71438-0 (hbk)
ISBN: 978-1-138-71439-7 (pbk)
ISBN: 978-1-315-23136-5 (ebk)

Typeset in Bembo
by Apex CoVantage, LLC

This book is dedicated to:

my Sluníčko

Elaine

my late mother Awa Diarra, my late mother Nassara Traore and my late mother Fanta Pelede, my late brothers Nourou Traore and Issa Hema, my late sisters Aminata Traore, Mamou Traore, Maimouna Traore, and Sanata Hema, my late niece Mariam Coulibaly, my late nephew 'Vieux' Coulibaly (Coul), with special acknowledgment to my wife, Lauren, and my daughter, Myriama

my wife, Svetlana

CONTENTS

List of figures	*x*
List of tables	*xii*
List of contributors	*xiii*
Preface	*xx*
Introduction	1

PART I
Environmental Issues and Macro Marketing · 19

SECTION A: ENVIRONMENT · 19

1 Foreign Aid on Economic Growth in Africa: Does Its
Effect Vary From Low- to Middle-Income Countries? · 21
Aye Mengistu Alemu and Jin-Sang Lee

2 Fishing in Dangerous Waters? How Narratives of 'Piracy'
and 'Security' Shaped Development Initiatives in the
Somaliland Fishery Sector · 40
Amanda Møller Rasmussen and Stig Jensen

viii Contents

SECTION B: MARKETING 71

3 Stimulation of Entrepreneurship in African Markets
Using Cluster Theory 73
Jens Graff

4 Social Marketing and Health Care 91
George Tesar

5 Business to Business Marketing Implications for Smaller
Enterprises in Africa 106
George Tesar

PART II
Micro Marketing 117

SECTION A: FINANCE 117

6 ICT-Facilitated Financial Service Deliveries in Africa 119
John Kuada

7 Mobile Transactions: A Powerful Channel to Drive
Financial Inclusion. Evidence From Kenya: M-Pesa Model 132
Mario Testa and Marco Pellicano

8 The Mobile Money Revolution 146
Jan-Erik Jaensson

9 Financing Behavior of Entrepreneurial Ventures in Tanzania 159
Tumsifu Elly

SECTION B: CONSUMPTION 173

10 Advancing Water Purification Technology and Delivery in
Africa 175
Steven W. Anderson

11 Understanding Consumer Buying Behavior in Africa 207
John Kuada and Andreea I. Bujac

Contents **ix**

12 Factors Determining the Rise of Modern Food Retailing
in East Africa: Evidence From Tanzania   224
Felix Adamu Nandonde and John Kuada

SECTION C: AGRICULTURE   241

13 Understanding the Role of Business Development
Services in Developing Agribusiness SMEs in Tanzania   243
Lola-Bona Vincent Lema and Daniel Wilson Ndyetabula

14 The Role of ICT Products in Agricultural and
Agribusiness Value Chain Development in Tanzania:
The Case of Tanga Fresh Limited   290
*Abdallah Mmeta Yongolo, Anna Andrew Temu, and Daniel
Wilson Ndyetabula*

15 Fruit-Drying Process to Enhance Agricultural
Productivity in Sub-Saharan Africa   315
Hassimi Traore

Integration   *329*
Bibliography   *333*
Webpages   *336*
Index   *339*

FIGURES

1.1	The Relationship Between Foreign Aid and GDP Growth in Ethiopia (Low Income)	29
1.2	The Relationship Between Foreign Aid and GDP Growth in Tanzania (Low Income)	29
1.3	The Relationship Between Foreign Aid and GDP Growth in Mozambique (Low Income)	30
1.4	The Relationship Between Foreign Aid and GDP Growth in Botswana (Upper Middle-Income)	30
1.5	The Relationship Between Foreign Aid and GDP Growth in Morocco (Lower Middle-Income)	31
7.1	Access Strand Over the Years 2006–2016	135
7.2	Frequency of Use of Financial Service	136
7.3	Percentage of ICT Access by Region, 2015	137
7.4	Percentage of Individuals Using the Internet by Development Status and Region, 2015	137
7.5	Safaricom Financial Performance	139
7.6	Working Model of M-Pesa	140
8.1	The Business Model	149
9.1	Distribution of Cases by Business Type	162
9.2	Financing Options by Cases	163
10.1	Profit/Loss Estimate for Grundfos LIFELINK in Katitika, Kenya	189
10.2	Cyanuric Acid (Abbreviated as H_3Cy)	192
11.1	Number of Articles Published Between 1996 and 2016	209
13.1	Chain of Actors in BDS Facilitation	250
13.2	Experiential Learning Cycle	254
13.3	Analytical Framework	255

13.4	Organization Structure of PIL	261
13.5	SCF Application Process Flowchart	265
13.6	The Relationship Between SMEs, BDS Providers, and SCF Project	267
13.7	The General Approach Taken by BDS Providers	269
14.1	Map of Tanzania Showing the Study Areas	296
14.2	Relationship Between TFL and Vodacom M-Pesa System in Milk Value Chain	299
14.3	Roles of ICT in Agribusiness Value Chain Development	303
14.4	Income Use by Respondents	306

TABLES

1.1	List of Countries Included in the Study	24
1.2	Explanatory Variables of Economic Growth, Expected Signs, and Data Sources	28
1.3	Partial Correlation of Economic Growth With the Independent Variables	32
1.4	System GMM Estimation for the Effect of Foreign Aid and Other Variables on Economic Growth	33
3.1	The Recommended Activities Would Strengthen the Porter Diamond	86
7.1	Classification of the Access Strand	135
10.1	Components of the LIFELINK System	184
10.2	Sensor Hand Pump Study Summary	196
12.1	List of International Retail Companies Operating in East Africa as of the End of 2015	228
12.2	Supermarkets Operating in Tanzania as of the End of 2015	229
12.3	A List of Supermarkets That Participated in the Investigation	230
12.4	Determinant Factors for the Rise of Modern Food Retailing	232
13.1	BDS Categories With Examples of Services	250
13.2	Company Overview Used for Case Study Selection	258
13.3	BDS Ranking on the SMEs Problematic Areas	268
14.1	The E-Payment System Versus the Traditional Cash Payment System	301
14.2	Demographic and Socio-Economic Characteristics	302
14.3	ICT Products That Promote Agribusiness Value Chain	304
14.4	Dairy Business Capital Source and Experience in Milk Business	305
14.5	Income Saving and Expenditure	306
14.6	Level of Awareness and Use of the MMPS	307
14.7	Perceptions on Access and Use of ICT Products	308
15.1	Burkina Faso Mango Prices by Quality and Market	325

CONTRIBUTORS

Aye Mengistu Alemu is an associate professor of Economics at SolBridge International School of Business, Daejeon, South Korea. Dr. Aye's specific research interests include addressing issues related to institutional economics, international trade, foreign aid, economic growth, and developing and emerging economies. The geographical focus of Dr. Aye's research has been mainly East Asia and Africa. Dr. Aye has published more than 21 research papers in internationally accredited peer-reviewed journals. He presented his research findings at various international conferences in Asia, Europe, Africa, Australia, United States, and Latin America. He received his PhD degree in Development Economics from Ritsumeikan Asia Pacific University (Japan), MA degree in International Political Economy from University of Tsukuba (Japan), MSc degree in Economics from University of Wales (United Kingdom), and BSc degree in Statistics and Mathematics from Addis Ababa University (Ethiopia).

Steven W. Anderson is Professor of Chemistry at the University of Wisconsin-Whitewater, where he lectures on topics in chemistry, specializing in organic chemistry. He has published results of his research in the *Journal of the American Chemical Society*, the *Journal of Organic Chemistry*, and the *Journal of Chemical Education*, among others. He was involved in the development of an integrated science and business major, an interdisciplinary program between the College of Business and Economics and the College of Letters and Sciences. Subsequently, he served as the second Coordinator of the Program for 5 years. He served as a coeditor of two editions of a textbook addressing strategic technology management and has published case studies focused on the integration of science and business. Professor Anderson has received a number of grants from a variety of sources including the National Science Foundation and the American Chemical Society. He

xiv Contributors

earned his doctorate in Organic Chemistry from Northern Illinois University, his MS in Organic Chemistry from Marquette University, and his Bachelor's degree in Chemistry from Carthage College. He has consulted with numerous companies including PPG Industries, Serigraph Inc., and Olmarc Packaging Company. Professor Anderson currently directs the Chemistry internship program.

Andreea I. Bujac is an assistant professor in the Department of Business and Management, International Business Centre at Aalborg University. She received her PhD in International Marketing from Aalborg University in 2014 and her MSc in International Business Economics from Aalborg University in 2010. Her primary research interests are in the field of consumer marketing. Specifically, she is interested in branding, consumer behavior, country-of-origin effects, and consumer ethnocentrism. She is the coauthor of a paper entitled 'Relationships Between Brand Perception, Ideology and Consumer Ethnocentrism in Post-Communist Romania,' which was published in the *Journal of Euromarketing* in 2014.

Tumsifu Elly is Senior Lecturer at the University of Dar es Salaam. He has accumulated extensive knowledge and experience in research, consultancy, and teaching for more than 17 years. He has wide experience in management sciences, entrepreneurship, livelihoods, and agribusiness. Specifically, Dr. Elly has been researching and publishing on engendering agribusiness entrepreneurship, rural entrepreneurship, landscape labeling, certification, firm capabilities and competitive advantage, and sources and access to information. He researched tourism-agriculture linkages for sustainable development, internationalization process of firms in Africa, impact of ICT investment on tourism export, and change management in the opening up for ICT, among others. He has undertaken consultancy activities on the following: Livelihoods Enhancement Analytical work for the Productive Social Safety Net—Demand Side Analysis (The World Bank), 'Landscape Labeling in Mbeya: Advancing an Agroecological Market Innovation' (EcoAgriculture Partners), 'Participatory Land Use Planning to Support Tanzanian Farmer and Pastoralist Investment' (EcoAgriculture Partners), 'Agricultural Information Needs and Sources of the Rural Farmers in Tanzania: A Case of Iringa Rural District' (BSU), and Market Assessment and Company mapping for Wekeza Youth Employment Strategy to inform job placement and apprenticeship (International Rescue Committee).

Jens Graff is a senior academic retired from the Danish University College system, author of six textbooks in business administration, and an accomplished researcher. He was an Associate Professor at SolBridge International School of Business at Woosong University in Korea and lectured at other international universities. He is a recognized expert in course and program development. He conducted a number of program development feasibility studies in Asia. Professor Graff facilitated several start-ups, mentored promising entrepreneurs, and consulted with a number of enterprises, also serving on their boards. His research interests are in the field of international business, marketing strategy, entrepreneurial behavior, and experimental learning; he has presented results of his research at many international academic and professional conferences. Dr. Graff holds a doctoral degree (PhD) in International Business from Umeå University in Sweden. He currently resides in Denmark.

Jan-Erik Jaensson has been involved extensively in research, consultancy, and management in Sweden and in Tanzania. Out of these engagements, he has researched and published on market orientation, customer satisfaction, innovation, entrepreneurial orientation, and tourist business development. He has also been engaged in research capacity building at the University of Dar es Salaam Business School and at the Open University of Tanzania for decades. Furthermore, he is the Chief Editor of the *Pan-African Journal of Business Management* (*PAJBM*) and the Vice-President for Communication and PR at the International Academy of African Business and Development (IAABD), and a reviewer for many international academic journals. He was a CEO of a Regional Tourist Board, 'Swedish Lapland Tourism,' in charge of the tourism development for 25% of the Swedish surface for 6 years. He started cooperation between the tourism companies about international marketing activities through a strategic marketing plan. Furthermore, he invented and developed the brand 'Swedish Lapland' domestic and international. He is currently employed in the Department of Marketing and Entrepreneurship, Faculty of Business Management at the Open University of Tanzania.

Stig Jensen is Associate Professor and former Director at the Centre of African Studies (CAS), University of Copenhagen. He holds a MA in Political Science from Copenhagen University and a PhD in Geography from the Department of Social and Spatial Changes, Roskilde University. He is affiliated with several national and international educational and research networks in the following capacities: council member at African Studies in Europe (AEGIS) and the Programme and Research Council at the Nordic Africa Institute; steering committee member of Sustainable Science Centre, Developing Countries Initiative, and Summer University Initiative, all at Copenhagen University. He has comprehensive experience with consultancy and advisor roles in different settings, including as a member of the evaluation team of DANIDA's bilateral Programme for Enhancement of Research Capacity in Developing Countries (ENRECA). He has extensive fieldwork experience from Africa, Asia, and South America.

John Kuada is Professor of International Management at Aalborg University, Department of Business and Management, Denmark. He holds two doctorate degrees: PhD from Copenhagen Business School, and Dr. Merc from Aalborg xvi Contributors

University. He has extensive experience as a business consultant and training advisor in areas of management, marketing, and cross-border inter-firm relations in Europe and Africa. He is author and/or editor of approximately 18 books on management and internationalization of firms and has written over 100 articles in refereed scholarly and professional journals on a wide range of international business issues including entrepreneurship, international marketing, intercultural management, leadership, and strategy. He serves on the editorial review boards of a number of marketing/management journals focusing on business and management in Africa and Asia. He is the founder and editor of *African Journal of Economic and Management Studies* (published by Emerald).

Jin-Sang Lee is a professor at the State University of New York, Korea. He has worked in the United Kingdom, Ethiopia, and Korea. He specializes in international development and cooperation, African economies, and education and science and technology Official Development Assistance (ODA). He holds his undergraduate degree from the University of Glasgow, an MSc from Lancaster University, and a PhD from the University of Strathclyde, United Kingdom.

Lola-Bona Vincent Lema is a retail account manager of CRDB Bank in Tanzania. She holds a Master of Science degree in Agricultural Economics from Copenhagen University. She has a special interest in agribusiness management, especially financial management in agribusiness firms. She reads and writes extensively about agribusiness management.

Abdallah Mmeta Yongolo is a research assistant in the Department of Agricultural Economics and Agribusiness at the School of Agricultural Economics and Business Studies, Sokoine University of Agriculture. With his background in rural development and agribusiness management, he has done expensive work in agribusiness value chain analyses. His research interests are in agribusiness information communication technologies.

Felix Adamu Nandonde is an assistant lecturer in Marketing at Sokoine University of Agriculture, Morogoro, Tanzania. He graduated with a PhD in Business Economics from Aalborg University in Denmark, has an MSc from Newcastle University, United Kingdom, and a Bachelor of Business Administration from Mzumbe University, Tanzania. He teaches undergraduate courses: Business Communication and Business Strategy and Management Strategy for MBA Evening. He also teaches International Marketing of Agribusiness Products for MBA-Agribusiness. His research works has appeared in *Journal of African Business*, *Africa Management Review*, *Ethiopian Journal of Business and Economics*, *Journal of Business Research*, *British Food Journal*, *Journal of Language, Technology & Entrepreneurship in Africa*, and *International Journal of Retail & Distribution Management*. He has published five book chapters with IGI Global, Springer International, and De Gruyter publishers. Mr. Nandonde has authored a handbook of business communication skills with Mzumbe Book Project, Morogoro, Tanzania. Before joining academia, he worked with National Bank of Commerce (NBC) in 1997, Tanzania Limited as a Sales Consultant in Business Banking. Mr. Nandonde has presented papers in various international conferences: Makerere Business School (Uganda), AIB-SSA at RIARA Business School (Kenya), York School of Management (United Kingdom), Aarhus Business School and Aalborg University (Denmark). He is a member of the Academy of International Business, Association for Business Communication, and Africa Academy of Management.

Daniel Wilson Ndyetabula has worked as an academic member of staff in the Department of Agricultural Economics and Agribusiness since 2008. He has conducted a wide range of research and supervised graduate student researches. He also serves as the Coordinator of Postgraduate Studies in the School of Agricultural Economics and Business Studies (SAEBS), Sokoine University of Agriculture (SUA). He is on the team of researchers at SUA that developed and popularized the SUGECO program 'Growing Innovative Entrepreneurs Through Action Research in the Agribusiness Value Chains.' He has in the past served as Visiting Scholar at the University of Wisconsin-Whitewater (United States) for research work on triggering cues for agribusiness value chain development. He has extensive knowledge in agribusiness economics, more specifically in agribusiness finance, agribusiness project and investment appraisal, and agribusiness value chain analyses. His primary research interests are in the areas of value chain financing, investments in sustainable agricultural intensification, and agribusiness value chain analysis.

Marco Pellicano has been a Full Professor of Strategic Management since 2001 at the Department of Management and Innovation Systems of the University of Salerno (Italy). He has written several academic essays and scientific articles on corporate governance, mostly regarding relational and systemic approaches in strategic dynamics. He is an expert of corporate social responsibility and has been the Scientific Coordinator of the Social Report of the University of Salerno since 2007. He is also interested in other academic issues, such as the competitive dynamics of local systems.

Amanda Møller Rasmussen holds an MA in African Studies from Copenhagen University and a MA in Social Anthropology of Development from the School of Oriental and African Studies. Her research interests are focused within the Horn of Africa and include development, fisheries, and the economic, social, and cultural flows between the local and the global.

Anna Andrew Temu is a senior lecturer in the Department of Agricultural Economics and Agribusiness. She received her MSc in Agricultural Economics from

xviii Contributors

the University of Guelph, Canada, and her PhD in Agricultural Economics and Agribusiness Development from the University of Illinois, Urbana-Champaign in the United States. Since 1986, she has worked as academic member of staff and has been teaching and conducting research at the Sokoine University of Agriculture. She has authored and coauthored several academic papers and supervised master's and PhD students.

George Tesar is Professor Emeritus of Marketing and International Business at Umeå University in Umeå, Sweden, and Professor Emeritus at the University of Wisconsin-Whitewater. He is an Adjunct Professor at Aalborg University in Denmark. Professor Tesar is a coauthor of several books on applications of marketing and recently coauthored a book on innovative applications of marketing management in African context. Professor Tesar has a doctorate from the University of Wisconsin-Madison and an MBA from Michigan State University. He is a mechanical engineer with several years of industry experience. He served on several boards and is professionally active as a consultant training academics, executives, and managers in technology transfer, internationalization, and foreign market entry strategies. He is a founding member of the Product Development and Management Association, a professional association focusing on technology transfer and new product development. He is active in international student and faculty exchanges and a member of the Fulbright Association. Professor Tesar lectures abroad extensively.

Mario Testa is Assistant Professor of Business Management at the University of Salerno (Italy). He obtained his degree in Business Administration in 2002 cum laude, discussing a thesis on business strategy. He was awarded a scholarship to study abroad, focusing on business ethics issues at the Center for Business Ethics of Bentley University (United States). He received his PhD in Marketing and Communications in 2006, and since then he has been Research Fellow at the Department of Business Studies and Research of the Faculty of Economics and at the Department of Industrial Engineering of the Faculty of Engineering at University of Salerno developing research projects on Corporate Governance and Green Energy. In 2010, he worked for some months in Kenya at the non-governmental organization Terre Solidali, where he was a consultant on training in project cycle management for members of the Somali agriculture and livelihoods cluster. His passion for developing countries is further highlighted by experiences as a Visiting Researcher at Nairobi University (Kenya) and Makerere University of Kampala (Uganda). He has written around 30 scientific publications mostly on the following research fields: corporate social responsibility, green economy, and organizational behavior.

Hassimi Traore is Associate Professor of Chemistry at the University of Wisconsin-Whitewater, where he lectures on Chemistry with expertise in

Physical Chemistry. He has a doctorate in Chemistry, a master's degree in Applied Math from the University of Iowa, and a master's degree from University of Ouagadougou in Burkina Faso (West Africa). He has published results of his research in Elsevier, in *Australian Journal of Chemistry* and the *Journal de la Société Ouest-Africaine de Chimie*. He is the recipient of several science grants, including a National Science Foundation grant, with which he established a modeling laboratory at University of Wisconsin-Whitewater. He has also served as a grant reviewer for National Science Foundation and is professionally active as a consultant for the Higher Learning Commission. He is actively working with international students and served as coordinator in an exchange program between University of Wisconsin-Whitewater and l'IUT de Marseille (France). In addition, Dr. Traore does non-profit work to benefit his country of birth, Burkina Faso, and is currently collaborating on a development project in collaboration with faculty from Purdue University.

PREFACE

This publication focuses on aspects of marketing management in the current African context. The objective is to outline and illustrate how marketing management can be used to stimulate economic and social development. Marketing management plays an important role in economic and social development aided by various forms of telecommunication activities and the Internet. The combination of marketing management and greater communication and information-gathering capabilities enable growth of consumer markets. The growth and restructuring of consumer markets change how consumers purchase and consume products and services and how they structure new personal and public lifestyles. We call this approach development of *social and economic public space* that motivates dynamic socio-economic growth.

The authors attempt to bring together a theoretical foundation of marketing management as an invaluable tool of entrepreneurship combined with the scientific method of inquiry. We have tried to examine marketing management and the sciences in the context of the Internet and widely available telecommunication capabilities. In many African countries, the Internet and telecommunication capabilities generate numerous social and economic activities. Our observations and experiences indicate that many such activities lack a decision-making structure and scientific framework. New and dynamic entrepreneurs start small enterprises but often fail due to a lack of structure or scientific understanding of their potentially idealistic initiatives.

Several of our doctoral students at Umeå University in Sweden and Aalborg University in Denmark, from various African countries, frequently searched for better ways for their mostly young entrepreneurs to succeed in new ventures. Long discussions with these doctoral students led us to better understand some of the social and economic obstacles that limit entrepreneurial success. However, in spite of the obstacles, the doctoral students generally succeeded and found new ways to assure new and aspiring entrepreneurs that they could succeed if they understood how to make skilled decisions and use scientific principles in their undertakings.

Some of us at the University of Wisconsin-Whitewater tried for years to combine managerial approaches with applying scientific principles to problems faced by entrepreneurs. Combining the scientific method to solving problems in marketing management motivated undergraduate and graduate students alike to think about the problems faced by entrepreneurs in dynamic social and economic environments. A number of students interested in combining managerial decision making with a strong scientific foundation came from African countries and returned as aspiring entrepreneurs.

Our principal interest is to combine marketing management approaches with a strong scientific foundation for emerging entrepreneurship in African economies. We are also interested in how entrepreneurship is driven by opportunities via the Internet and telecommunication capabilities. The Internet and telecommunication capabilities help entrepreneurs bypass many traditional institutions that administer established commercial operations. New entrepreneurial initiatives create a new dynamic social and economic public space leading to socioeconomic growth.

Our expectations are that this publication will help outline and illustrate relationships between marketing management and the sciences that are needed to strengthen the foundation of entrepreneurial activities in various African countries. African countries are by no means homogeneous; on the contrary, they are different, perhaps even singular, in how they manage or administer social and economic public space and plan for the future. This publication can be a useful resource for students, academic researchers, entrepreneurs, and practicing managers in their endeavors to find new and better ways to initiate start-ups and manage for a better future.

We thank our colleagues and students for their support and cooperation in our attempts to understand the new entrepreneurial dynamics in using marketing management and scientific approaches to solve problems in what we call a new social and economic public space in the African setting. Thank you.

INTRODUCTION

Marketing is becoming indispensable for educators and managers of large global enterprises to understand culturally different markets and consumers. In their views, marketing is seen more and more as a social discipline. Two fundamental philosophies drive the marketing discipline: (1) consumers are central to all activities of an enterprise, and (2) profit is a reward offered by satisfied consumers. Managers who subscribe to these central notions of marketing believe that marketing functions within an environment that guides their missions and market initiatives. Marketing is relatively less known among smaller enterprises and entrepreneurs as a social discipline and is generally applied as a series of managerial tools and techniques used to position their products and services in consumer-driven and competitive markets.

Marketing management is the application of marketing tools and technique; it employs scientific, technological, and managerial marketing resources. Marketing management is accountable for identifying marketing opportunities for enterprises within the context of their missions. Marketing managers are responsible for interpreting what consumers, as members of societies, want to consume, what lifestyles they want to lead, and how they want to relate to their environments. Marketing management provides a framework for planning—for an enterprise to succeed, it must plan what initiatives it will undertake, what resources it will allocate to each initiative, and how it will manage its markets. Marketing management also provides approaches intended to build the organizations needed to implement plans—every initiative most likely requires a creative new organization to manage identified markets. Marketing management guides the use of marketing tools and techniques configured as strategies to reach markets, market segments, and consumers. Marketing management is also responsible for controlling marketing initiatives ranging from identifying fundamental opportunities to determining levels of consumer satisfaction and profitability.

2 Introduction

For incipient and growing enterprises in African countries, marketing management is a new phenomenon, but marketing management is emerging as a competitive force in entrepreneurial initiatives due to the influx of entrepreneurs returning from studies or training abroad. This is primarily because marketing management emphasizes problem solving and the decision-making responsibilities of marketing managers. The ability to solve problems and make decisions is the foundation for structural stability of enterprises. Marketing managers set the marketing objectives, policies, plans, and programs needed to systematically allocate the resources available to an enterprise.

The marketing management framework is built on fundamental beliefs that managers accept constant change; place consumers at the center of all initiatives; build an integrated system around all marketing activities; and consider scientific, technological, and other inputs as theoretical constructs and findings in managing the marketing effort. Marketing management has emerged as a discipline closely aligned with the sciences, technology, and other social disciplines. This realization often leads to entrepreneurial activities among marketing managers and stimulates their innovative activities that eventually lead to formation of a social and economic public space. Creating a social and economic public space, within which active and passive creation and consumption take place, consists of a series of visible activities directly related to private and public consumption of products and services.

Creating a social and economic public space is necessary in order to provide a platform for socio-economic growth closely aligned with entrepreneurial startups; growth of small and medium-sized enterprises; introduction of supply providers; and components, material, and equipment needed by entrepreneurs and small and medium-sized enterprises. Thus, marketing management is perceived as the tools and techniques necessary to systematically introduce change into an economy challenged by social and economic conditions. Many African economies recognize that often entrepreneurial initiatives will not survive without the marketing discipline and marketing management.

The financial and social resources spent for economic and social development in Africa are enormous. An appraisal of recent development efforts by donor countries to Africa such as Canada, Denmark, Sweden, and the United States clearly suggests that random and uncoordinated economic and social development efforts based on large-scale projects are marginally productive. Projects often fail completely from the start, or shortly thereafter, primarily due to lack of administrative structures, systemic failures, or cultural misunderstandings. Although projects appear distinctively structured and adequately funded, they often lack the collective organizational initiatives to succeed and grow. More precisely, economic and social developmental attempts lack the organizational momentum to successfully function in economically and socially unstable countries with unstable entrepreneurial climates and markets.

Economic and Social Developments

Entrepreneurial initiatives in many African countries have increased over the past 10 years or so; they cut across levels of technology, consumption patterns, and public and private lifestyles. Some entrepreneurial initiatives represent innovations aimed at consumer markets, whereas others are suitable for public consumption. Innovations introduced by entrepreneurs include generation of wind and solar power that contribute to the development of additional small and medium-sized peripheral enterprises. Introduction of environmentally responsive and energy-efficient appliances used for cooking, laundry, and small home refrigeration contribute to less air pollution. The availability of on-demand 24-hour health care services saves lives. Innovations such as these contribute to environmental improvements in both the private and public sectors.

These developments, along with many others, are possible because of scientific advancement, technological innovation, and engineering improvements such as telecommunication capabilities, regional and local Internet availability, and access to personal computers. New technology brings new ways of doing things, stimulates creative thinking, and improves social and economic productivity. Under such conditions, entrepreneurship thrives, new innovative products and services stimulate new markets, and consumers improve their lifestyles.

The combination of social, economic, technological, and market innovations has led to new approaches in macro and micro social and economic development in several African countries. The tendency in many countries is to move from large-scale, externally funded projects to small-scale, internally shaped entrepreneurial initiatives. Entrepreneurs tend to find their own resources and undertake activities that donors of large-scale capital likely would never sponsor. Many entrepreneurs endure and grow into successful small enterprises; others even expand into larger enterprises with customers and clients abroad.

Although many new entrepreneurial initiatives may be arbitrarily structured and marginally managed, they function in a social and economic space that in some African countries is unstable. In order to become stable and prosper in the future, these entrepreneurial initiatives need scientifically based creativity, decision-making skills, and sound marketing management philosophies. Some African countries such as Tanzania, Ghana, and Zambia have found ways to stimulate development of small projects, help entrepreneurs find start-up capital, form industrial clusters, and have formed university-based advisory centers to assist entrepreneurial start-ups in their early stages.

Not all recent economic and social developments can be attributed to growing entrepreneurial initiatives; other forces are active as well. A significant number of African entrepreneurs have university education in either management or the sciences. Some received their educations abroad, whereas others attended local universities and others had internships or participated in student exchange programs.

4 Introduction

Many returning students brought innovative ideas and plans for start-ups; some even brought the necessary equipment for a start-up. It is not clear what education or training is best suited for start-ups in various African countries, but it is apparent that many recent entrepreneurial experiences result from exposure to different economic and social climates.

The importance of the educational experiences of entrepreneurs lies in their ability to apply their experiences, both domestic and abroad, to the economic and social situations in their personal environments. More specifically, their ability to identify entrepreneurial opportunities and implement them despite obstacles and administrative hurdles. Over the past few years, some entrepreneurial initiatives have transitioned into viable enterprises marketing locally relevant products and services. These initiatives include software development, food processing enterprises, and financial management and money transaction operations, among others.

Many of the entrepreneurial initiatives are closely aligned with wider social developments and lifestyle changes. Consumers are becoming more informed and educated. They are transitioning from street markets to small retail shops and even to larger grocery store chains. Younger consumers do not follow the shopping patterns of their elders; they prefer to shop in larger stores, frequent recently available large box discount stores, and buy their groceries in stores that offer a greater selection of products. The changes in consumer buying habits are strengthening the positions of retailing institutions, including Internet-based entities, and changing consumer markets.

Major Drivers of Change

The economic and social changes described previously would not have been possible without the rise in entrepreneurial efforts and new technological capabilities. The introduction of telecommunication, rapid acceptance of mobile or cellular telephones by individuals of all ages, and the ability to accept telephone-based communication as a universal platform drives many of the economic and social changes. Telecommunication allows consumers to function in previously unknown or economically not feasible markets for them. Telecommunication capabilities combined with health care services, personal financial management and payment capabilities, and additional capabilities such as purchasing small amounts of clean drinking water are changing the lifestyles of many consumers.

Internet availability further contributes to major economic and social changes. The Internet provides a window for many African entrepreneurs, consumers, and the public into the world around them. Although there are regions of African countries with limited availability computers and Internet connections, mostly due to lack of electricity, these obstacles are being overcome by introduction of solar or wind energy that offer the potential for Internet connectivity and use of personal computers.

Where Internet connections are available, new information sources are available, and individuals can more easily communicate with others—entrepreneurs can solicit help from other entrepreneurs, and consumers can compare products, services, and even lifestyles. What is more important is the use of the Internet for educational purposes; especially for education in rural and remote areas. The combination of innovative solar cells integrated into students' backpacks and the availability of laptop computers offer totally new educational experiences for students. Students can literally charge their backpacks during the day and do their homework or share their computers with adults in the evening.

Telecommunication and the Internet have additional benefits for economic and social development across the African landscape—they lead to development of appropriate local technology. Development of appropriate technology is important for the continuity of social and cultural history. Indigenous technology carries with it standards and norms as pillars of stability and social and economic cohesiveness. Exogenous technology, especially technology that is substantially different from indigenous technology, brings social and economic disturbance and discontinuity.

New technology developed internally or externally needs to meet local conditions. The more successful entrepreneurs understand this and identify technological opportunities on the basis of their perception of continuity from previous technological trends. Entrepreneurial success also depends on the ability to empirically verify that the new technological advance introduced by an entrepreneur is compatible with previous generation technology and requires minimal education or training to use it. Most forms of scientific management introduced by high technology focused entrepreneurs are based on systematically developed and tested scientific approaches.

For example, major changes in cooking among rural households, such as moving away from organic fuels that pollute to cleaner fuels such as natural gas, or in some cases, electricity simplify day to day living conditions, speed up cooking time and leave more productive time for other activities. Since the new cleaner fuels are centrally distributed and require minimal education or training for users, fuel-gathering concerns have been reduced, and the time necessary for cooking preparation and the cooking times themselves have been reduced. The new devices needed to convert from traditional to new cooking methods also require new cooking appliances, which, in turn, may require some education to demonstrate their optimal use. The entire process of converting from old polluting fuels to new non-polluting processes provides entrepreneurial opportunities.

It is increasingly apparent that entrepreneurial small-project formation leading to social and economic development is driven by telecommunication capabilities and the Internet thus changes the technological climate of many social and economic constituencies and consumers. Structure and scientifically based applications are frequently missing from entrepreneurial initiatives. Both are integral parts of marketing management approaches and frameworks. Consequently, the most important component of a start-up is its marketing management philosophy.

6 Introduction

Marketing Management Approaches and a Framework

Successful African entrepreneurs point out that many start-ups need more than a marketing management philosophy; these start-ups need sound marketing management practices and techniques based on established scientific knowledge. In its fundamental definition, a marketing management philosophy does not differentiate on the basis of size—it applies equally to small and large enterprises. It is a system of activities that range from collecting information needed to formulate the mission of an enterprise, establishing its role in the external environment, organizing and managing resources, identifying markets, and selecting competitors. The role of marketing management is to identify marketing opportunities within the framework of entrepreneurial abilities, systematically select and act on optimal opportunities, design and market products and services, satisfy consumers, and control the entire marketing effort.

Marketing management functions on both macro and micro marketing levels. Macro marketing managers are concerned with how the entire marketing process interacts with the environment outside its proprietary marketing systems. Macro marketing activities function within boundaries set by a society, regions, or nation. Macro marketing activities include setting guidelines for acceptable technological limits, lifestyles of individuals, economic policies and conditions, and social constraints. Marketing managers obtain information from these sources to construct managerial philosophies, identify market opportunities, and set performance and ethical standards. They also try to determine the level of risk posed by the external forces they face.

Decisions by marketing managers within the marketing framework of an enterprise are considered part of micro marketing activities. Micro marketing decisions are influenced by external forces or macro marketing forces. Micro marketing activities include all activities ranging from collecting information about consumers, markets, competitors, or anything else needed to deliver value to consumers and generate profits for an enterprise. Marketing managers' micro marketing decisions are influenced by environmental forces, either as broad societal guidelines or trends that significantly influence micro marketing initiatives. Decisions made by marketing managers concerning products and services, marketing strategies, determining competitive positions or other considerations are proprietary, strategic, and strictly internal to each enterprise.

Marketing management decision making increasingly relies on decision-making approaches taken from the sciences and based on the scientific method of inquiry. Decisions are made on information systematically obtained by research methods based on participatory, observation, or experimental research methodologies. Most scientific inquiries today are based partially or completely on a combination or all these research methods. Most marketing initiatives are based on sound qualitative or quantitative information including identification of markets, development of consumer profiles, and assessment of consumption behavior.

Marketing strategies are formulated on the basis of managerial decisions made on information collected using scientific research approaches.

The soundness and rigor of information generated by scientifically based marketing research allow marketing managers to model many marketing events and approaches. For example, they can model how a particular marketing strategy will trigger consumer responses to new products using specific promotional or distribution channels. Competitive models can be built to predict and plot market positions of competitors and even predict, by generating probabilities, how competitors will respond to various market challenges.

Managers of high technology start-ups suggest that entire start-up, their development, and the control process of designing a successful venture can be modeled. The entire enterprise development process, including solicitation of venture capital, organization development, staffing issues, and many other components of a start-up are known and can be modeled. Many high technology enterprises, especially ventures with a scientific foundation, can be professionally managed from their beginnings, in contrast to ventures initiated and managed by entrepreneurs with minimal managerial skills. High technology entrepreneurs also suggest that computer-based models can be designed to manage entrepreneurial ventures on a day-to-day basis with only occasional executive or managerial intervention. Even the control mechanisms needed to monitor enterprise performance can be modeled, because most needed inputs such as inventory or stock can be automated. Each part, component, or material needed to produce a product or render a service can be electronically tracked. The output side of an enterprise can also be modeled and the three modules integrated into a comprehensive control model connected to standard financial and accounting procedures.

Macro Marketing Management Approaches

Macro marketing management has two fundamental aspects: (1) collecting information from the environmental forces that directly impact the social behavior of an enterprise, and (2) an enterprise's communication with society. Conventionally, regardless of its nature and size, an enterprise functions at the discretion of society. Its society creates the space in which an enterprise forms its initiatives, manages market transactions, and grows. An enterprise responds to forces created by the collective actions of the society that sets the norms of social behavior, economic performance, technological sophistication, and lifestyles of its citizens—including consumers. From a broader perspective, an enterprise's society sets the standards and norms for its actions.

Conversely, as information feedback, an enterprise informs its society about its actions and contributions. By its overt and covert behaviors, an enterprise indicates how socially responsible it is and how it connects with positive and negative societal changes. Expectations are that an enterprise will function within acceptable standards and norms and will not deviate from them, although some may

8 Introduction

be set arbitrarily by culture or tradition, whereas others are promulgated as laws. Notions of social responsibility, approaches to economic and social development, or introduction of new technology all fit within the context of macro marketing and shape the marketing activities of enterprises.

From a marketing management perspective, macro marketing forces (1) set the level and nature of technology, (2) impact lifestyles based on the market behavior of consumers, (3) influence consumption patterns based on available product and service offerings, and (4) affect levels of economic well-being and social coexistence. Marketing managers' decisions correspond to the interaction of societal forces and structure their entrepreneurial actions accordingly.

Micro Marketing Management Approaches

Micro marketing management in an enterprise represents all the controllable variables related to the entire marketing effort. Marketing initiatives begin among top decision makers and reach to the individuals responsible for incremental functions within the enterprise. Every member of an enterprise must focus on the needs and wants of consumers and is responsible, on some level, for the satisfaction of consumers, because consumers who are satisfied with the products or services offered by an enterprise will purchase the product or service again.

An enterprise selects the markets in which it wants to function, identifies the segments for its unique products or services, and develops profiles of the consumers it wants to nurture on the basis of its mission. Enterprises, even start-ups, need to understand their markets and consumers before they develop and market products or services. Although a product or service development process may begin with an entrepreneur's initial idea, any idea must be tested in the market. There are marketing research techniques well suited for such testing—focus group discussions, personal interviews, and Internet-based surveys, among others. It is possible to collect information directly from individuals essential for micro marketing decisions even in the most remote regions of the world.

Micro marketing management includes (1) forming marketing strategies, (2) determining levels of consumer satisfaction, (3) analyzing consumer behavior, and (4) monitoring the dynamics of consumption behavior. These are controllable, to a certain degree, and subject to strategic decision making. Marketing managers need to understand how consumers behave in highly dynamic and competitive markets. Marketing research methods available to managers today, mostly due to telecommunication capabilities and the Internet, can be viewed as a continuous flow of information from consumers to enterprises.

Marketing and Enterprise Formation

Marketing practices today are essential prerequisites to forming new ventures, entrepreneurial start-ups, or actual small enterprises. Although some entrepreneurs would state that they simply do not have enough information to map out the entire entrepreneurial undertaking, if they seek venture financing, they will need to produce a viable business plan before they even get considered for funding. Consequently, a business plan in its general form represents the marketing framework for an entrepreneurial initiative, and it should not be difficult to integrate all the necessary marketing management approaches. Entrepreneurs face a great deal of risk and need to reduce their risk by using systematic approaches to marketing activities from the beginning of each venture.

Objective of This Publication

The objective of this publication is to illustrate how marketing management can be used in developing small-scale enterprises in an African setting. Approaches to economic and social development in many African countries are changing rapidly and moving from large-scale, externally funded projects to small-scale, internally funded projects. Entrepreneurial initiatives are growing. Many recent entrepreneurial start-ups clearly indicate deficiencies in managerial approaches, especially deficiencies in using marketing management philosophies. A significant number of entrepreneurs responsible for recent start-ups did not consider the needs and wants of consumers, potential markets, or the implications of their initiatives on the public. Many of them failed.

Marketing management philosophies provide theoretical and conceptual foundations for entrepreneurial initiatives and also provide structure and a decision-making framework. Entrepreneurs need to understand the macro aspects of marketing management as well as the micro marketing controllable aspects of marketing activities. More specifically, marketing management, based on scientific approaches to research, helps entrepreneurs as marketing managers identify the appropriate tools and techniques needed to develop products and services, introduce them in the market, and monitor their market performance.

Predictions can be made about many initial start-ups on the basis of what is known about marketing management combined with the latest technologies such as telecommunication capabilities and the Internet. Potential success can be verified by building computer-based models depicting the intent of a venture and its eventual dynamics. The potential dynamics of a venture can be modeled and its probability of success evaluated in economically and socially challenged countries, even though available information may be limited.

The attached conceptual framework introduces some of the required assumptions. The framework is designed to identify the macro and micro marketing dynamics in which enterprises function in many African countries. The framework is provided for smaller enterprises striving for managerial, organizational, and marketing stability. Along with a system of managerial decision making, it has four components: (1) the creative stage of human capital, (2) the entrepreneurial and enterprise marketing management effort, (3) the consumption behavior of

10 Introduction

individual consumers and market segments, and (4) the economic, social, and environmental benefits. Each component relates directly to the proposed process of how small projects introduced by entrepreneurs are structured within and outside of markets and how they collectively contribute to economic and social development—and creation of social and economic public space.

We also collected a number of discussion papers representing different views on economic and social development. These are divided into three categories: (1) macro challenges in the emerging entrepreneurial climate across Africa, (2) examples of entrepreneurial initiatives driving consumer markets that are changing African lifestyles, and (3) examples of functioning entrepreneurial activities in specific areas of markets, economies, and small-scale enterprises. The conceptual model that follows is largely based on research described in the contributions or gathered directly from sources familiar with issues related to entrepreneurial initiatives across Africa.

There are many examples of projects introduced by a generation of young African entrepreneurs; they include development of appropriate solar and wind technology, processes utilizing water chemistry, and the use of mobile telephones for banking transactions. Through social marketing practices, young African entrepreneurs are able to provide clean drinking water in rural areas even in remote regions of Africa. In medicine, Internet use enables medical professionals in remote areas to analyze emergencies quickly by communicating with qualified specialists located in major city hospitals or in countries abroad. These types of services require a combination of professionals, telecommunication engineers, and marketing managers to facilitate the necessary supply and demand conditions and market structures. Most of all, entrepreneurs with vision and skills are needed to develop the necessary opportunities and networks to facilitate such initiatives.

Framework

The central focus of this framework is on applying marketing management as a set of entrepreneurial tools and techniques in economic and social development and the subsequent creation of social and economic public space that lead to socio-economic growth. Marketing management approaches can be applied by large international enterprises as well as among smaller ones. The underlying philosophy is that consumers are the focal point of all marketing operations. Marketing opportunities originate with consumers and form markets. Marketing managers identify and evaluate opportunities within the context of their enterprise missions, resources, and competitive markets; they develop products and services to meet consumer needs and wants and deliver them in the most efficient and effective ways to selected consumers. The purpose is to support and improve consumers' lifestyles and stabilize social and economic well-being. Consumer-focused enterprises utilize marketing management as their operational and strategic philosophy.

Macro and micro components of marketing management are conceptualized to coordinate macro and micro marketing activities in order to satisfy consumers and contribute to the overall external entrepreneurial environments in which enterprises function. Macro marketing management is a two-way process— managers seek information from the environment, process that information, and identify the most suitable opportunities. In return, these managers are responsible for contributing to and improving the social and economic climate that determines the entrepreneurial environment in which they function. Micro marketing activities are partly based on the managerial philosophy and ability to correctly identify opportunities and fully realize them.

The framework begins with entrepreneurs seeking marketing opportunities in a singular environment, generally a single country environment, for developing products or services lacking in that environment for various social, economic, or technological reasons. Entrepreneurs tend to tolerate high levels of risk and are willing to take chances; often they do not have the necessary tools and techniques to help them understand the level of risk they face. The conceptual framework that follows is based on marketing management philosophy and designed to provide a better understanding of how entrepreneurial risk can be reduced or eliminated. The framework focuses specifically on rapidly emerging entrepreneurs in an African setting, their small-scale start-ups, and the stages of social and economic challenges they face on both macro and micro marketing levels.

Creative Stage of Human Capital

The first part of the conceptual framework focuses on individual entrepreneurial efforts. Although each entrepreneur is creative and executes ideas differently, perceives the world through a different set of perceptual filters, implements a set of preferences, and forms attitudes, it is possible to identify some commonalities and generalize about what the creative process encompasses. From a theoretical point of view, entrepreneurs generate ideas either inductively or deductively. Both types generate ideas that potentially lead to new products or services.

Some entrepreneurs have a broad view of the world and generate ideas inductively. They see or experience relationships that interact in unusual ways and study those relationships and interactions. Entrepreneurs with scientific backgrounds construct scientific experiments; those who lack a scientific background devise their own experiments. Others have a relatively narrow view of the world, see things only the way they are, and generate ideas deductively; they deduce relationships on the basis of what they see and experience. This type of entrepreneur converts deduced relationships into opportunities.

Marketing opportunities generated by entrepreneurs potentially make market contributions and create value for consumers. Entrepreneurs must consider various issues before consumers can realize any social economic or psychological value. Before any product or service is fully developed and introduced in a market,

12 Introduction

it must be scientifically tested to determine its feasibility as a safe and viable product or service for consumers' consumption processes. Scientific verification sometimes is beyond entrepreneurial abilities and tends to be in the realm of an individual entrepreneur's normative judgment. There must be a match between the scientific ability to accept a product or service and the scientific feasibility of a product or service proposed by an entrepreneur.

Even if a match exists between the scientific ability to accept a product or service and the scientific feasibility to potentially deliver the product or service to consumers, an entrepreneur may not have the skills to develop the product or service and deliver it to the market. Many entrepreneurs fail early in their attempts. The relationship between scientific feasibility and the entrepreneurial skill to introduce innovations is critical and needs systematic empirical verification. Empirical verification consists of qualitative and quantitative assessment of the entrepreneur's initial idea and the value it will produce as a contribution to consumers and markets.

The final creative stage of human capital leads to value-creating activities and market contributions by entrepreneurs motivated to significantly contribute directly or indirectly to social and economic development. Because value creation leading to market contributions is complicated and an individually driven unstructured process, to a certain degree, entrepreneurs need guidelines—they need structure and a decision-making framework. Innovative value-creating activities increase the need for additional creative skills, and thus stimulate further creation of human capital.

Entrepreneurial and Enterprise Marketing Management Efforts

The second part of the conceptual model is concerned with marketing management at the entrepreneurial and enterprise levels. Marketing management provides the structural and decision-making support entrepreneurs need to professionalize their efforts in creating value for consumers and markets. For enterprises, marketing management provides an operational and strategic philosophy. On either level, marketing management helps marketing managers understand how to disperse products and services directly to consumers throughout markets. More specifically, marketing management tools and techniques assist in formulation of marketing strategies deployed by entrepreneurs and enterprises to disperse the value they create as products and services. Entrepreneurs create value through their enterprises and disperse created value through markets to consumers.

Various conditions need to exist before the actual dispersion of created value can happen. These conditions vary in each environment or country. The entrepreneurial reliability and marketing conditions need to be examined in the context of social and economic public space. It is not normal within the context of marketing to release a product or offer a service that is not acceptable to the social and economic public space, or more precisely acceptable to consumer markets. It is equally difficult to market a product or a service for which the right conditions do not exist in the market. Entrepreneurs and enterprises must assure markets and consumers that the products or services they intend to disperse throughout the social and economic public space will have a constructive impact and contribute to social and economic growth and stability.

In the African socio-economic climate, there are two determinants of growth and stability: (1) technological acceptance of products and services, and (2) appropriate marketing approaches for reaching consumers. Innovative products and services must fit within consumer tolerances for new technology. If technologically new or improved products and services are to serve consumers, they have to be understood and consumers must be able to use them as intended without any difficulties. Consumers may not be willing to use technologically new products or services if they have to learn how to use them. For example, replacing paper notes or coins with electronic currency may be a hardship for older individuals who are not able to use mobile telephones.

Entrepreneurs and enterprises must have suitable marketing tools and techniques to introduce and market even products or services that are technologically compatible with consumers' needs. There must be a direct match between the reasons why products or services are created and the consumers for whom they are intended. This matching process is the responsibility of the entrepreneurs who create the products or services and the marketing managers of the entire marketing management process. If there is no match between products or services and intended consumers, their social and economic value will not be properly dispersed and may negatively impact future markets and consumers.

Checks and balances are needed to ensure a correct match between technologically new products and services and intended consumers; the technological ability of the market and consumers must be determined with appropriate margins or tolerances for acceptance of innovative technology. Upgrades and replacements are common in technologically changing markets. The question is, how flexible are the markets and consumers in their abilities to accept the next level of technology?

Social awareness is another aspect of dispersing value and creating products and services. Society must be aware of technologically new products and services in order for them to create social and economic value. A general awareness of products and services sets social and economic value—markets and consumers must be able to purchase products and services freely and the public must know about them. Directly or indirectly, technologically new products and services must have social and economic value for all members of the public.

If technologically new products or services are economically feasible, marketing managers still face important challenges: Do profitable markets for them exist, and are consumers willing and able to purchase them? If a significant percentage of the public cannot afford technologically new products or services, they are not economically feasible and consumers may not purchase them.

14 Introduction

Consumption Behavior of Consumers and Market Segments

Assuming that technologically new products and services deliver social and economic value to markets and consumers, entrepreneurs and enterprises must consider the consumption value of the new products and services and the consumption behavior associated with them. The consumption value of technologically new products and services is measured by positive or negative reactions of the consumers who consume them. However, consumption is a collective behavior; the collective consumption of products and services forms consumer lifestyles, and aggregate lifestyles manifest themselves as market segments. Marketing managers frequently try to identify market segments on the basis of several demographic, economic, social, or even socio-psychological factors but may not be successful. Naturally occurring market segments based on consumption behavior and lifestyles are easier to identify, especially for high technology products or services.

Technologically new products and services with high consumption value may change collective social and economic behavior and significantly alter individual lifestyles. For example, introduction of solar energy into a rural area previously without electricity changes not only consumption behavior, but also individuals' lifestyles substantially. Marketing managers need to consider how individual consumers consume products and services and their behavior after they stop consuming the products or services.

Aside from services, many new products, regardless of where they are marketed, have a finite life. Wherever consumers are—rural areas, remote parts of countries, or major urban areas—eventually there will be product residuals. Product residuals materialize because products no longer match consumers' needs or consumers lose interest in them. More technologically advanced products generate more complex residuals. Marketing managers are becoming more concerned about post-consumption behavior of consumers and how they dispose of product residuals.

For example, disposal of televisions, computers, or other electronic appliances is an enormous problem in mature markets and will soon become a worldwide problem regardless of how socially or economically challenged a market is. As electricity becomes more available and ownership of electronic appliances grows, product residuals will become an acute problem.

In order to manage this phenomenon, individual post-consumption behavior must be monitored. Individual consumers need options for dealing with post-consumption challenges. At the same time, post-consumption is also a collective issue. The public, consumer groups, and marketing managers need to determine the actual technological, social, and economic values of individual products and the values of their residuals. From a broader perspective, the technological, social, and economic value of technologically new products and services depends on how they fit within the entire social and economic public space and how they contribute to socio-economic growth.

Economic, Social, and Environmental Benefits

Marketing management philosophy has evolved over distinct stages: (1) production, (2) product, (3) sales, (4) marketing, and is currently focused on (5) social marketing. The social marketing philosophy focus of marketing management applies equally to macro and micro marketing initiatives. Entrepreneurs, enterprises of all sizes, and even government-owned organizations and public agencies in advanced markets subscribe, in theory, to social marketing as the central operational philosophy of marketing management. The social marketing philosophy as implemented through marketing management policies and strategies suggests that marketing initiatives are formulated not only to satisfy consumers and provide platforms for consumers' lifestyles, but also for society's benefit.

Regardless of the intent of marketing initiatives, consumers today are concerned about consumption issues that directly impact their well-being and also are concerned about the environment in which they reside and consume products and services. Conservation of resources, elimination of pollution, water management, and organic agriculture, among other private and public concerns, drive individual consumption of products and services. The introduction of small-scale experiments such as sun drying herbs, fruit, and other locally grown agricultural products, in a number of African countries, demonstrate broad social awareness of these concerns. Similar examples are found in combinations of marketing and scientific initiatives: water purification has enormous impact on individuals' quality of life, improves public health, and reduces health care issues. Generating electricity in remote rural areas with solar cells to power computers, use the Internet, or communicate with the outside world benefits individuals and social groups. Improved quality of life incrementally increases personal and social values.

Incremental increases in personal and social values are directly connected to and provide a foundation for economic, social, and environmental benefits. These benefits are by-products of entrepreneurial initiatives guided by marketing management philosophy; however, they would not be possible without technological innovations such as telecommunication, computers, and the Internet. Entrepreneurs' abilities to connect consumers' needs and wants with new technological innovations by developing realistic and acceptable solutions help societies live better and healthier lives.

African entrepreneurs clearly contribute to incremental increases in personal and social values by their marketing initiatives. Many economic and social development specialists believe a structured approach to guide the efforts of new African entrepreneurs and suitable tools and techniques to implement their initiatives would help them be even more successful in their initiatives. We believe that marketing management provides the best conditions within which dynamic

16 Introduction

entrepreneurship can flourish. When marketing management philosophies are combined with the sciences and utilize scientific approaches to problem solving, they are even more effective in improving private and public lives.

Recent Developments: Research and Illustrations

We include the following case and research studies to illustrate recent developments across Africa in marketing management, entrepreneurship, and scientific innovation due to advances in telecommunication and the Internet. The case studies and research findings are divided into two major parts: (1) entrepreneurial issues and macro marketing, and (2) micro marketing. Each part is further subdivided on the basis of the specific developments presented. Part I consists of environmental and broad macro marketing issues. Part II focuses on micro marketing and the developments in financial management,consumption, and agriculture.

The first two essays in Part I concern environmental issues and discuss the complexity of economic, social, political, and foreign policy forces that impact the social and economic public space in which marketing management and entrepreneurs attempt to function. These forces create extremely hostile conditions in several African countries and prevent scientific innovation from taking place. Although technological developments such as telecommunication and the Internet are available, they are not necessarily used for social and economic development. The predominant emphasis in some African countries is still on large projects organized and managed by foreign enterprises that limit the growth of indigenous small start-ups and enterprises. There is also evidence of antisocial behavior that completely prevents socially and economically acceptable development of any entrepreneurial initiatives in a limited number of African countries.

The three additional essays in Part I examine various macro marketing management options available to entrepreneurs and marketing managers in various African socio-economic environments. The essays propose alternative approaches to entrepreneurial initiatives and levels of involvement in rapidly changing markets. Many consumer and business to business markets are growing and becoming increasingly more complex. Newly established smaller enterprises need to cooperate as they become dependent on each other for auxiliary services. Industrial clusters bring small and medium-sized enterprises together for more efficient and effective productivity capacity. Growing markets need additional support to further growth. The health care market, for example, is expanding rapidly mostly due to scientific and technological developments and is considered a framework for a variety of entrepreneurial initiatives. Business to business marketing is essential for supplying entrepreneurial start-ups along with small and medium-sized enterprises with necessary material, parts, and components needed to produce products and services.

The financial and financial management topics discussed in the first section of Part II illustrate how technological advances, especially in telecommunication and the Internet, change consumer purchasing and consumption behavior. These changes play a significant role in marketing management on the enterprise level, even generating venture capital; they are changing marketing strategies and the approaches to forming new enterprises and markets. The use of so-called mobile money in some African economies is ahead of other countries in the world.

Telecommunication and the Internet are changing the consumption of products and services by African consumers. More palatable and healthier products and services are available at nominal cost to consumers—clean drinking water, for example. Consumers are becoming better informed and educated about how to shop, what products or services to select, and how to consume them. Consumers are changing where they shop and how they prepare the groceries they purchase. The entire field of retailing is changing and marketing managers need to keep up with consumers.

The developments among consumers are particularly evident in agriculture. Agriculture and agricultural products and services play a fundamental role in social and economic development. Agricultural activities, especially in rural areas, include enormous entrepreneurial opportunities. Agricultural enterprises cooperate by forming clusters, many in remote areas, and building completely new value chains for rural and urban consumers. Some agricultural enterprises expand abroad by exporting products and developing brand name recognition. Entrepreneurs are finding innovative agricultural opportunities in drying fruit, tea, and herbs—for which major demand abroad is growing.

PART I

Environmental Issues and Macro Marketing

Section A: Environment

1

FOREIGN AID ON ECONOMIC GROWTH IN AFRICA

Does Its Effect Vary From Low- to Middle-Income Countries?

Aye Mengistu Alemu and Jin-Sang Lee

Introduction

The role of foreign aid in the growth process of developing countries has been a topic of intense debate. It is estimated that Africa has received more than one trillion US dollars during the last 50 years.[1] However, many countries are still underdeveloped and depend on foreign aid to run themselves, indicating that this aid has not been effective.

The issue of aid effectiveness was brought vigorously to the fore in 2005 when the Paris Declaration (PD) was endorsed by Organisation for Economic Co-operation and Development (OECD) Development Assistance Committee (DAC) members. Despite continuous aid to African countries, some of them became worse off than they were in the early 1960s. From a recipient country's point of view, aid should be short term when the country suffers a shock internally or externally. Likewise, many low-income countries in Africa do not have great opportunities for foreign direct investment (FDI) because they receive limited attention from multinational companies (MNCs). In such cases, most low-income African countries mainly tend to have foreign aid, at least to provide their population with basic services such as education, health, roads, and so forth, and possibly to build institutional capacity to govern their countries. Foreign aid to low-income countries may also flow in in various forms such as cash, projects, programs, education and training, technical assistance, and others.

Middle-income countries in Africa have a substantial quantity of natural resources that are economical and act as a 'pulling' factor for FDI. However, the majority of low-income African countries has very low levels of economic infrastructure such as transportation and basic services as well as low levels of human capacity in terms of elementary and secondary enrollment ratios as well as vocational and technical training opportunities. These economic and social environments make it difficult for low-income African countries to achieve economic development. Consequently, most of the low-income African countries are heavily dependent upon foreign aid, which is mostly channeled through humanitarian aid such as food and emergency needs, with only a small portion being utilized for economic infrastructure. However, empirical studies on foreign aid and economic growth in developing countries have generated mixed results that make it difficult to draw policy recommendations. *The main objective of this study is, therefore, to investigate the effects of foreign aid on economic growth in low-income and non–low-income African countries.*

Literature Review

Theoretically, the main role of foreign aid in stimulating economic growth is to supplement domestic sources of finance such as savings, thus increasing the amount of investment and capital stock. As Morrissey[2] points out, there are a number of mechanisms through which aid can contribute to economic growth, including (1) increased investment, in physical and human capital; (2) increased capacity to import capital goods or technology; (3) lack of indirect effects that reduce investment or savings rates; and (4) transfer of technology that increases the productivity of capital and promotes endogenous technical change.

There are four strands of literature on the role of foreign aid on economic growth. The first studies claim that foreign capital inflow is necessary and sufficient for economic growth in less developed countries. Also, it has been confirmed that there is a positive relationship between aid and economic growth because it not only augments domestic resources but also supplements domestic savings, assists in closing the foreign exchange gap, creates access to modern technology and managerial skills, and allows easier access to foreign markets, ultimately leading to economic growth.[3,4,5,6] By the same token, Pallage and Robe[7] noted that foreign aid is a major source of economic growth for developing countries, especially in Africa, where it averages 12.5% of the gross domestic product and establishes by far the most important source of foreign capital. Under such circumstances, foreign aid has the potential to play a key role in boosting developing countries' economic growth as well as reducing poverty. Similarly, Addison et al.[8] examined the trends of official development assistance (ODA) to Africa over the period 1960 to 2002 and concluded that foreign aid does, in fact, promote growth and reduce poverty. It also has a positive impact on the public sector, contributing to higher public spending and lower domestic borrowing. Burnside and Dollar[9] also examined the effect of aid on economic growth, using standard cross-country panel regressions that included an interaction term of aid with a policy index and found that aid has a positive impact on growth in developing countries as long as these countries have sound macroeconomic policies.

The second group of studies assert that external capital has significant negative effects on the economic growth of recipient countries. According to this view, foreign aid is fully consumed; it substitutes rather than complements domestic resources, assists import of inappropriate technology, distorts domestic income distribution, and encourages a bigger, inefficient, and corrupt government in developing countries.[10,11]

The third view is that foreign aid has no impact on economic growth.[12] This view is shared by Moyo,[13] who argues that aid has not helped to improve social and economic conditions in Africa for several reasons: (1) sectors that are critical and important to the development of the country have rarely been allocated any resources, and less than 6.5% of development aid or assistance received by developing countries over the years has been allocated to areas that are critical to accelerated growth and economic development, such as education, health care, infrastructure, energy, agriculture, technology, and the environment; (2) the debt and aid resources have been stolen and corruptly squandered by government officials to enrich themselves, their families, and their friends instead of being directed to the productive sectors of the national economy; (3) during the Cold War, the policies of the developed countries favored African countries that were friendly with them, and as a result, official development assistance (ODA) was usually quite unpredictable and could not be depended on for making long-term development plans. In addition, many of the Western donors often attached conditions to aid that made its effective use for development difficult; and (4) in many instances, aid was driven by interest groups in the developed countries to sell their products, services, and technologies that were not suitable for African development because they were often obsolete and inappropriate for African conditions.

The fourth view is that the relationship between foreign aid and economic growth may depend on the quality of the recipient country's institutions and economic policies, that is, integrated monetary, fiscal, and trade policies.[14,15] McGillivray et al.[16] suggested four different views from positive and negative perspectives and emphasized political conditions and institutional capacity. According to Mbaku,[17] African countries failed to use aid efficiently because they lacked competent laws and institutions to use received aid appropriately and effectively. Kosack[18] examined the impact on the human development index, but only in democratic countries. He found that aid has a negative impact in autocratic countries but a positive impact on the human development index and growth in democratic ones.

However, it must be borne in mind that regional differences in the effects of foreign aid among the recipient countries are inevitable. Effects could be influenced by income levels or levels of socio-economic development of recipient countries. Ekanayake and Chatrna[19] analyzed 83 recipient countries in Asia, Africa, and Latin America and the Caribbean, using panel data series for foreign aid, and concluded that foreign aid brought mixed impact on the economic growth of recipient countries. Latin American and the Caribbean countries especially experienced adverse effects on economic growth, whereas African countries showed positive effects. De Ree and Nillesen[20] studied the impact of foreign aid on civil conflict in sub-Saharan Africa but found no evidence that foreign aid has an impact on civil conflicts. Some studies show different evidence: negative effects in the short term but positive ones in the long term. For example, Moreira[21] carried out a study of the impact of economic growth at the macro-level using a cross-country regression model and examined the short- and the long-term results. The long-term effects were found to be better than those in the short term. Juselius et al.[22] also found that the impact of foreign aid was positive in the long term.

Methodology

Scope of the Study

Though often spoken of as a single, homogenous group, African countries are remarkably diverse and heterogeneous in historical, political, social, economic, linguistic, cultural, and geographical terms. The region includes both middle-income, lower middle-income, upper middle-income and higher-income economies, some with large and some with small populations, some with a store of natural resources and those with virtually none. Thus, it is important to examine in detail whether the effect of foreign aid on economic growth in Africa has been uniform. Accordingly, African countries have been categorized into low-income and non–low-income countries on the basis of the World Bank's classification (low-income: Gross National Income (GNI) per capita $\leq$ \$1,005; lower-middle income economies: \$1,006 $\leq$ GNI per capita $\leq$ \$3,975; upper-middle income African economies: \$3,976 $\leq$ GNI per capita $\leq$ \$12,275; and higher-income economies: GNI per capita $\geq$ \$12,276; see Table 1.1).

Specifications of Model

This section discusses the model specifications to examine the relationships between foreign aid and economic growth. The empirical model for estimating

TABLE 1.1 List of Countries Included in the Study

Low-Income Africa (19 Countries)	Non–Low-Income Africa (20 Countries)
Benin, Burkina Faso, Burundi, Chad, Democratic Republic of Congo, Ethiopia, Gambia, Guinea Bissau, Kenya, Malawi, Madagascar, Mali, Mauritania, Mozambique, Rwanda, Sierra Leone, Tanzania, Togo, Uganda	*Higher-income economies* Equatorial Guinea *Upper-middle economies* Algeria, Libya, Botswana, Gabon, Mauritius, Seychelles, South Africa, Tunisia *Lower-middle economies* Angola, Congo Republic, Cote d'Ivoire, Cape Verde, Egypt, Ghana, Morocco, Namibia, Nigeria, Senegal, Zambia

the impact of foreign aid on economic growth is based on previous growth literature and other empirical studies. Therefore, in deriving our empirical model for estimating the aid-growth relationship, we posit that:

$$\Delta Y_{it} = f\left(PC_{it}, HC_{it}, NR_{it}, Z_{it}\right) \tag{1}$$

Where ΔY_{it} denotes economic growth in real per capita GDP of country i at time t, PC_{it} is a vector of physical capital sources of country i at time t, HC_{it} is a vector of human capital of country i at time t, NR_{it} is a vector of natural resources of country i at time t, and Z_{it} is a vector of other growth-determining policy and institutional variables as explained in the empirical literature. The endogenous growth model in particular emphasizes the importance of capital (both physical and human) as well as policy and institutional factors in promoting economic growth. On this basis, our model can be specified as follows:

$$\Delta Y_{it} = \alpha + \beta PC_{it} + \eta\, HC_{it} + \delta NR_{it} + \gamma Z_{it} + \mu_t \tag{2}$$

Where ΔY_{it} is economic growth in real per capita, PC_{it}, HC_{it}, $NR_{it,}$ and Z_{it} are already mentioned previously, μ_t is the error term. On the other hand, critical capital sources for economic growth of developing countries comprise foreign aid, domestic investment (DI), and foreign direct investment (FDI).

$$\text{Hence, } PC = f\left(Aid, DI, FDI\right) \tag{3}$$

Where 'Aid' denotes foreign aid, which is net official development assistance (ODA) as a share of GDP, DI denotes domestic investment which is gross capital formation (GCF) as a share of GDP, and FDI represents the share of foreign direct investment to GDP. Similarly, we can break human capital (HC) down into two components: (1) education, which is captured by enrollment ratio, and (2) health, which is estimated by life expectancy.

$$\text{Hence, } HC = f\left(education, health\right) \tag{4}$$

$$\text{Natural resources } (NR) = f\left(oil\ exports,\ ores\ and\ metals\ exports,\ arable\ land\ ratio\right) \tag{5}$$

$$Z = f\left(Policy,\ Institutional\right) = f(degree\ of\ openness,\ exchange\ rate,\ inflation\ index,\ economic\ freedom,\ quality\ of\ infrastructure) \tag{6}$$

Thus, substituting (3), (4), (5), and (6) in (2), produces our refined model as:

$$\Delta Y_{it} = \alpha + \beta_1 \text{Aid}_{it} + \beta_2 \text{DI}_{it} + \beta_3 \text{FDI}_{it} + \beta_4 \text{SER}_{it} + \beta_5 \text{LXP}_{it} + \beta_6 \text{OIL}_{it}$$
$$+ \beta_7 \text{ORE}_{it} + \beta_8 \text{OPEN}_{it} + \beta_9 \text{EXCH}_{it} + \beta_{10} \text{INF}_{it} + \beta_{11} \text{EFRD}_{it} \qquad (7)$$
$$+ \beta_{12} \text{INFR}_{it} + \beta_{13} \text{LOCK}_{it} + \mu_t$$

Choice of Explanatory Variables

Foreign Aid: The relationship between foreign aid and economic growth is not conclusive, as discussed in detail elsewhere in this chapter. The traditional justification for foreign aid is that it eases the resource constraints of developing economies, especially on the supply side.[23] In this view, therefore, foreign aid is regarded as a positive coefficient on economic growth.

FDI Inflow: The neoclassical approach assumes that FDI promotes economic growth by introducing valuable capital and technology into recipient countries. Moreover, FDI is one of the main avenues for the movement of technology, management know-how, and modern business methods across national borders. Therefore, the rationale for increased efforts to attract more FDI stems from the belief that FDI has several positive impacts on economic growth through productivity gains, technology transfers, the introduction of new processes, managerial skills, know-how in the domestic market, employee training, international production networks, and access to markets to bring about structural change and sustainability.

Domestic Investment: Using the Solow model as a predictor, the investment ratio is a key determinant of economic growth regardless of a country's level of development.[24] Investment ratio depends on the saving ratio. The neoclassical growth models of Solow[25] and Swan[26] also predict that an exogenously higher value of I/Y raises the steady-state level of output per effective worker as well as the growth rate. Thus, domestic capital is expected to influence economic growth significantly.

Human Capital: Endogenous growth theory considers human capital as the major determinant of economic growth. In fact, it is the role of human capital that prevents the marginal product of capital from falling and thereby countries get richer.[27] However, right up until the second half of the 1990s, the role of human capital was linked to education, although a few authors had already recognized the importance of other factors such as health. Mankiw et al.[28] first considered not only education but also health in a broader analysis of human capital. Human capital in this study refers to both education and health as will be explained.

Human capital, particularly that attained through *education*, has been emphasized as a critical determinant of economic progress,[29] and growth rates are affected by ideas and invention, which in turn are related to the stock of human capital, either through research and development activities or through the absorptive capacity of technology. According to Habiyaremye and Ziesemer,[30] there are three different views that explain how education affects the production process and contributes to economic performance. First, education has the effect of increasing labor efficiency. Second, educated workers are able to perform complex tasks and are, therefore, not substitutable by unskilled workers. Third, the education and skills of workers generate more output. Applied to the case of developing countries, these views suggest that educated workers help the country to absorb, implement, and diffuse foreign technology and stimulate economic growth.

Likewise, *health*, as a form of human capital, should be envisaged as a property that may be improved through investment in resources. Barro and Sala-i-Martin[31] examined the relationship between economic growth and health and confirmed that good health is a crucial component of overall well-being. Similarly, López-Casasnovas[32] argued that good health raises levels of human capital and has positive impacts on individual productivity and economic growth. As Sen[33] points out, life expectancy implies an intrinsic capability on which personal welfare depends. Thus, the health variable is often captured by the life expectancy of individuals.

Initial GDP per capita: Barro and Lee[34] have carried out an empirical analysis for a panel of around 100 countries from 1960 to 1990, and the findings strongly support the general notion of conditional convergence. The main implication from this study was, therefore, that poorer countries can achieve faster growth per capita provided that other variables remain constant.

Population Growth: On the one hand, it is believed that population growth enlarges the labor force and, therefore, has a positive impact on economic growth. A large population also provides a large domestic demand for goods and services, provided that it has purchasing power. On the other hand, a large population growth is not only associated with food problems but also imposes constraints on the development of savings, foreign exchange, and human resources. Thus, the net relationship between a greater population and economic growth depends on whether the return to human capital and expansion of knowledge is greater than the diminishing returns of natural resources. Thus, the effect of population growth on economic growth is ambiguous.[35]

Exchange Rate: In theory, the depreciation of the local currency exchange rate against the US dollar should represent a window of opportunity to boost exports. Thus, it has been hypothesized that a depreciating and stable exchange rate is positively linked to economic growth.

Inflation: A high rate of inflation increases the uncertainty of business and hence is harmful to economic growth. It raises the cost of capital and inhibits capital investment. Andersen and Gruen[36] and Fischer[37] find that, on average, a one-percentage-point rise in the rate of inflation can cost an economy more than one-tenth of a percentage point in its growth rate. Indeed, Fischer[38] regards the inflation rate as the best single indicator of macroeconomic policies that may indicate the overall ability of the government to manage the economy. Hence, it can be hypothesized that a low and stable inflation rate promotes economic growth and efficiency in the long term.

Openness: Endogenous growth models predict that the openness of an economy could positively influence economic growth, because the flow of goods and investment across borders through international trade could be an effective means of diffusion of technology at the international level. Overall, the openness to trade can play an important role in raising the long-term sustainable rate of productivity growth.[39]

Quality of Infrastructure: A study by Canning and Bennathan[40] indicates that infrastructure, particularly telecommunications infrastructure, significantly increases economic growth. Thus, infrastructure is expected to contribute strongly to economic growth.

Economic Freedom: The economic freedom variable aims to capture the freedom to choose and supply resources, completion in business, and the right to secure the property rights of individuals. As a result, economic freedom in a country is expected to promote economic growth via stimulating capital accumulation.

Natural Resources: The effect of natural resources such as oil, ores, and arable land on economic growth is also a debatable issue. However, there is an increasing consensus that this depends on how it is managed. If natural resources and their revenue are carefully managed, it would be a blessing; if not, however, it would be a curse. Thus, the effect of natural resources on economic growth is ambiguous.

Lack of Access to the Sea: Almost one-third (or 15) of Africa's 53 countries are landlocked and have no access to the sea. The prevailing view is that being landlocked causes a disadvantage in economic development. Collier[41] (2002) argues that a landlocked status is one of the four key factors preventing the poorest countries from growing and reaping the benefits of globalization. However, in recent years, there has been an accelerated economic growth in many landlocked African countries including Ethiopia, Uganda, Rwanda, and Zambia. Thus, the dichotomous dummy variable that captures lack of access to the sea is expected to have an ambiguous effect on economic growth. Based on the theoretical explanations discussed earlier, the independent variables and their expected relationships with economic growth are summarized in Table 1.2.

TABLE 1.2 Explanatory Variables of Economic Growth, Expected Signs, and Data Sources

Variable	+/-	Data Sources
Initial Gross Domestic Product per Capita (GDP/C)	–	World Development Index (WDI)
Foreign Aid	+	World Development Index (WDI)
FDI Inflow	+	World Development Index (WDI)
Gross Fixed Capital Formation (GFCF)/GDP	+	World Development Index (WDI)
Oil Exports (% of total exports)	+	www.geodatasource.com
Ores and Metal Exports (% of exports)	+	World Development Index (WDI)
Arable Land Ratio	+	World Development Index (WDI)
Population (in mill)	+	World Development Index (WDI)
Degree of Openness	+	World Development Index (WDI)
Quality of Infrastructure	+	World Development Index (WDI)
Secondary School Enrollment Ratio	+	WDI database
Life Expectancy	+	WDI database
Exchange Rate	+	WDI database
Inflation Index	–	WDI database
Economic Freedom Index	+	Heritage Foundation Index
Landlocked (1 = landlocked and 0 = otherwise)	–	Various sources

Results

The Trend of Foreign Aid and Economic Growth in Africa

The following diagrams show the trends of foreign aid and economic growth in selected low-income African countries such as Ethiopia, Tanzania, and Mozambique on the one hand, and Botswana and Morocco from the middle-income group on the other hand. Accordingly, Figures 1.1, 1.2, and 1.3 highlight a similar pattern of relationship between foreign aid and economic growth performance in Ethiopia, Tanzania, and Mozambique, respectively. On the other hand, we can find

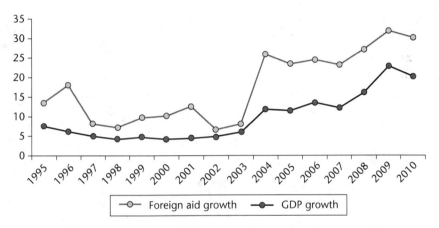

FIGURE 1.1 The Relationship Between Foreign Aid and GDP Growth in Ethiopia (Low Income)

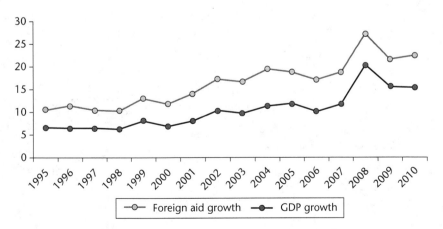

FIGURE 1.2 The Relationship Between Foreign Aid and GDP Growth in Tanzania (Low Income)

inconsistent patterns of relationship between foreign aid and economic growth in Botswana and Morocco as shown in Figures 1.4 and 1.5, respectively. Thus, with this guiding information, it is important to investigate further the exact relationship between foreign aid and economic growth in Africa both at aggregate and disaggregated levels, based on the degree of economic development.

The Correlation Between Economic Growth and Independent Variables

Before we move on to the regression analysis, it is worth examining the correlations that exist between economic growth and foreign aid. In other words, the

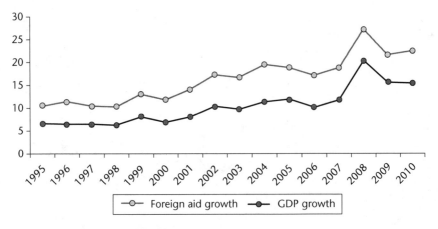

FIGURE 1.3 The Relationship Between Foreign Aid and GDP Growth in Mozambique (Low Income)

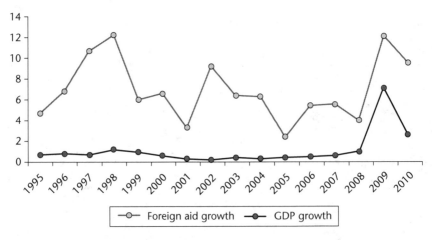

FIGURE 1.4 The Relationship Between Foreign Aid and GDP Growth in Botswana (Upper Middle-Income)

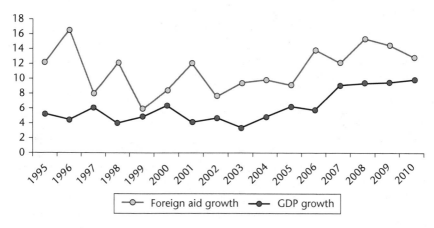

FIGURE 1.5 The Relationship Between Foreign Aid and GDP Growth in Morocco (Lower Middle-Income)

correlation coefficients of each variable determine the nature and strength of the relation between each factor and economic growth. Accordingly, correlation analysis not only helps to clarify relations among variables but also often suggests directions for experimental research such as regression analysis. Table 1.3 shows that there is a direct correlation between foreign aid and economic growth.

Similarly, the correlation analysis reveals that initial income per capita is negatively correlated with economic growth. On the other hand, the evidence shows that the ratio of GFCF/GDP, oil exports/total exports, degree of openness, life expectancy, and quality of infrastructure are positively correlated with economic growth in Africa.

Regression Results

One of the most significant results from the full sample as well as the middle-income Africa subsample is initial GDP/C (level of development of a given country at the beginning of 1995) is found to be a strong negative determinant of economic growth. More specifically, the coefficient of the initial GDP/C variable was estimated at −0.001, implying that convergence occurs at the rate of 0.1 per year. On the other hand, no significant evidence was found for low-income African countries to converge at this point. However, though it was not significant, the negative sign of the coefficient suggests some indications of convergence in the region.

Our main variable of interest—aid per capita—has been found to be a statistically significant factor of economic growth for only low-income African countries, not for the middle-income African subsample. It is obvious that low-income African countries are heavily dependent upon foreign aid for supplementing their

TABLE 1.3 Partial Correlation of Economic Growth With the Independent Variables

Variable	Correlation	Significance
Initial GDP/C	−0.157	0.000★★★
Foreign Aid	0.068	0.090★
FDI Inflow	0.036	0.390
GFCF/GDP	0.309	0.000★★★
Oil Exports (% of total exports)	0.197	0.000★★★
Ores and Metal Exports (% of exports)	0.012	0.784
Arable Land Ratio	0.036	0.389
Population (in mill)	0.035	0.396
Degree of Openness	0.076	0.069★
Quality of Infrastructure	0.086	0.040★★
Secondary School Enrollment Ratio	0.004	0.931
Life Expectancy	0.099	0.018★★
Exchange Rate	0.001	0.981
Inflation Index (consumer price index)	−0.051	0.221
Economic Freedom Index	−0.001	0.970
Landlocked (0 = landlocked and 1 = otherwise)	0.0551	0.189

basic needs and even to support government budget. In these countries, most foreign aid amounts were not spent on areas related to economic growth. Moreover, some low-income African countries are effectively using foreign aid for education and health care, and these would enhance economic growth in the long term.

On the other hand, the FDI variable has been found to be statistically significant at the 5% level for the middle-income African subsample, but not for the low-income one. For instance, the result in Table 1.4 (column 3) implies that a 1% increase in FDI inflow would result in a 0.1% increase in economic growth in middle-income African countries. Thus, while foreign aid has a strongly positive impact on economic growth in low-income African countries, it is the FDI inflow that has resulted in a significant impact on economic growth for middle-income African countries. The probable explanation is perhaps that low-income countries have few options of financial resources and this eventually enables them to create a better macroeconomic management system and also to utilize foreign aid in a very efficient way. Donors also give smaller amounts of aid to middle-income African countries than to low-income ones.

Likewise, the empirical analysis indicates that a one-percentage increase in the ratio of fixed capital formation to total GDP will increase economic growth by 12.4% and 12.4% for middle-income and low-income African countries, respectively. Natural resource variables such as the ratio of oil exports to total exports were found to be statistically significant for only middle-income African countries but not for low-income ones. This is perhaps because most of the middle-income African countries are currently oil exporters, whereas many of the low-income African countries are not.

TABLE 1.4 System GMM Estimation for the Effect of Foreign Aid and Other Variables on Economic Growth

Independent Variables	Africa	Middle-Income Africa	Low-Income Africa
Initial GDP/C	−.001★★★	−.001★★★	−.001
	(.0002)	(.0002)	(.001)
Foreign Aid	.0003	.0001	.002★★★
	(.0002)	(.0002)	(.001)
FDI Inflow	.001★★	.001★★	.001
	(.0002)	(.0002)	(.0012)
GFCF/GDP	.144★★	.124★	.124★★
	(.063)	(.079)	(.055)
Oil Exports (% of total exports)	.131★★★	.127★★★	.112
	(.047)	(.051)	(.098)
Ores and Metal Exports (%) of Exports)	.008	.003	.007
	(.014)	(.029)	(.014)
Arable Land Ratio	.008	.103	.039★★
	(.019)	(.066)	(.021)
Population (in mill)	.028★	.002	.029
	(.015)	(.019)	(.025)
Degree of Openness	.042★★	.075★★★	.005
	(.018)	(.026)	(.016)
Quality of Infrastructure	.067	.310★	.435
	(.107)	(.194)	(.561)
Secondary School Enrollment Ratio	.028	.115★★	.080★★★
	(.023)	(.049)	(.028)
Life Expectancy	.099★	.037	.148★
	(.056)	(.081)	(.083)
Exchange Rate	−.0001	−.0004	.0002
	(.0003)	(.001)	(.0004)
Inflation Index (consumer price index)	−.001	−.001	−.020★★★
	(.0013)	(.002)	(.004)
Economic Freedom Index	.014	−.024	.075
	(.045)	(.077)	(.052)
Landlocked (0 = landlocked; 1 = otherwise)	1.407	1.638	−.302
	(.871)	(1.606)	(.728)
Constant	2.329	−3.407	6.217
	(4.355)	(8.102)	(94.948)
P-value for Hansen Test	0.36	0.27	0.18
Number of groups	39	20	19
Observations per group	15	15	15
Number of observations	585	300	285

On the other hand, no evidence was found for the minerals and ores variable to induce economic growth in a significant way in both subsamples. Interestingly, however, the arable land ratio has been found to be a very important factor in stimulating economic growth mainly in low-income African countries. This result is consistent with the current situation that low-income African countries, particularly those with ideal climates and arable land density, have recently achieved economic growth mainly driven by the high price in agricultural commodities. Accordingly, the result confirms that a 1% increase in the arable land ratio for low-income African countries would increase economic growth approximately by 3.9%.

Theoretically, the effects of population growth on economic growth are disputable. In line with this, no evidence has been found that population growth is a significant factor for growth in income per capita, both in middle-income and low-income countries. The degree of openness of a country has been found to be an influential factor in economic growth in middle-income African countries but not in low-income ones. The empirical evidence shows that a 1% increase in trade openness would result in about a 7.5% increase in economic growth for middle-income African countries. This implies that openness to trade can enhance productivity by enabling more efficient allocation of resources, by providing greater opportunities to exploit economies of scale and by exposing the domestic economy to greater competitive pressures. Moreover, infrastructure has been found to be a crucial factor in speeding up economic growth only in middle-income African countries, whereas no significant evidence was found in low-income African countries because infrastructural development is still at the infant stage in such countries.

The *education* aspect of human capital has been captured by the level of secondary school enrollment ratio, whereas the *health* aspect of human capital is captured by life expectancy variable. Accordingly, it has been found that education is very critical both in middle-income and low-income African countries in their efforts to induce sustainable and faster economic growth. By the same token, the life expectancy variable was found to be statistically significant at the 10% level, for the full sample as well as the low-income African subsample, implying that a healthy labor force is crucial for sustainable economic growth. On the other hand, no evidence was found that the exchange-rate variable significantly affected economic growth, both in the full sample as well as the subsamples. This result is similar to other previous empirical studies, which recorded mixed results for the role of exchange-rate policy on economic growth. Inflation has a mixed effect on economic growth both in the full sample as well as the subsamples. For instance, inflation is negatively associated with and statistically significant only for the low-income African subsample, whereas it is statistically insignificant for middle-income African countries. Generally, low, single-digit level of inflation does not seem to have a significantly negative effect on economic growth. However, a high level of inflation (as happened in Zimbabwe in 2008–2009) would damage the prospects of savings, investment, and economic growth.

The economic freedom variable aimed to capture the freedom to choose and supply resources, completion in business, and the right to secure property rights of individuals. All these tend to motivate economic growth via stimulating capital accumulation. However, the empirical results found no evidence that economic freedom affected economic growth in Africa at this point. Lastly, the dummy variable that captured the state of being 'landlocked' was not statistically significant either.

Conclusion

The impact of foreign aid on economic growth is an ongoing issue for discussion. The impact of foreign aid was found to be closely related to the socio-economic environment and political situation of recipient countries. In order to find empirical analysis of the impact of aid on economic growth, this study attempted to use different variables related to economic output. It used data from major African countries by dividing them into low-income and middle-income countries according to the level of income per capita. The results revealed that the middle-income countries tended to experience a greater impact on their economic growth from FDI as well as from the revenue they generated from the export of natural resources (mainly oil exports), whereas the low-income countries were significantly affected mainly by foreign aid.

Thus, this study shows that the criticism of foreign aid is flawed, at least in the case of low-income African countries. In fact, foreign aid has played a critical role in stimulating economic growth through supplementing domestic sources of finance such as savings, and thus increasing the amount of investment and capital stock in low-income African countries.

Notes

1 Dambisa Moyo, *Dead Aid: Why Aid Is Not Working and How There Is a Better Way for Africa* (New York: Farrar, Straus, and Giroux, 2009).
2 Oliver Morrissey, "Does Aid Increase Growth?" *Progress in Development Studies* 1, no. 1 (2001): 37–50.
3 Carl-Johnson Dalgaard, Henrik Hansen, and Finn Tarp, "On the Empirics of Foreign Aid and Growth," *Economic Journal* 114, no. 496 (2004): 191–216.
4 Craig Burnside and David Dollar, "Aid, Policies, and Growth," *American Economic Review* 90, no. 4 (2000): 847–868.
5 Henrik Hansen and Finn Tarp, "Aid Effectiveness Disputed," *Journal of International Development* 12, no. 3 (2000): 375–398.
6 Karuna Gomanee, Sourafel Girma, and Oliver Morrissey, "Aid and Growth in Sub-Saharan Africa: Accounting for Transmission Mechanisms," *Journal of International Development* 17, no. 8 (2005): 1055–1075.
7 Stéphane Pallage and Michel A. Robe, "Foreign Aid and the Business Cycle," *Review of International Economics* 9, no. 4 (2001): 641–672.
8 Tony Addison, George Mavrotas, and Mark McGillivray, "Aid to Africa: An Unfinished Agenda," *Journal of International Development* 17, no. 8 (2005): 989–1001.

9 Burnside and Dollar, "Aid, Policies, and Growth."
10 Peter Boone, "Politics and the Effectiveness of Foreign Aid," *European Economic Review* 40, no. 2 (1996): 289–329.
11 William Easterly, "Can Foreign Aid Buy Growth?" *Journal of Economic Perspectives* 17, no. 3 (2003): 23–48.
12 Paul Mosley, John Hudson, and Sara Horrell, "Aid, the Public Sector and the Market in Less Developed Countries," *The Economic Journal* 97, no. 387 (1987): 616–641.
13 Moyo.
14 Burnside and Dollar, "Aid, Policies, and Growth," 847–868.
15 Mark McGillivray et al., "Controversies Over the Impact of Development Aid: It Works; It Doesn't; It Can, but That Depends...," *Journal of International Development* 18, no. 7 (2006): 1031–1050.
16 Ibid.
17 John Mukum Mbaku, *Institutions and Development in Africa* (Trenton, NJ: Africa World Press, 2004).
18 Stephen Kosack, "Effective Aid: How Democracy Allows Development Aid to Improve the Quality of Life," *World Development* 31, no. 1 (2003): 1–22.
19 E.M. Ekanayake and Dasha Chatrna, "The Effect of Foreign Aid on Economic Growth in Developing Countries," *Journal of International Business and Cultural Studies* 3 (2010): 140–155.
20 Joppe De Ree and Eleonora Nillesen, "Aiding Violence or Peace? The Impact of Foreign Aid on the Risk of Civil Conflict in Sub-Saharan Africa," *Journal of Development Economics* 88, no. 2 (2009): 301–313.
21 Sandrina Berthault Moreira, "Evaluating the Impact of Foreign Aid on Economic Growth: A Cross-Country Study," *Journal of Economic Development* 30, no. 2 (2005): 25–48.
22 Katarina Juselius, Niels Framroze Møller, and Finn Tarp, "The Long-Run Impact of Foreign Aid in 36 African Countries: Insights from Multivariate Time Series Analysis," United Nations University World Institute for Development Economics Research, Helsinki, WIDER Working Paper 51/2011, accessed August 29, 2017, www.wider.unu.edu/publication/long-run-impact-foreign-aid-36-african-countries-0
23 Jonathan Munemo, Subhayu Bandyopadhyay, and Arabinda Basistha, "Foreign Aid and Export Performance: A Panel Data Analysis of Developing Countries," in *Theory and Practice of Foreign Aid (Frontiers of Economics and Globalization, Volume 1)*, ed. Subhayu Bandyopadhyay (Bingley, UK: Emerald Group Publishing Limited, 2006), 421–433.
24 Robert M. Solow, "A Contribution to the Theory of Economic Growth," *The Quarterly Journal of Economics* 70, no. 1 (1956): 65–94.
25 Ibid.
26 Trevor W. Swan, "Economic Growth and Capital Accumulation," *Economic Record* 32, no. 2 (1956): 334–361.
27 Robert E. Lucas, "On the Mechanics of Economic Development," *Journal of Monetary Economics* 22, no. 1 (1988): 3–42.
28 N. Gregory Mankiw, David Romer, and David N. Weil, "A Contribution to the Empirics of Economic Growth," *The Quarterly Journal of Economics* 107, no. 2 (1992): 407–437.
29 Robert J. Barro and Jong-Wha Lee, "International Data on Educational Attainment: Updates and Implications," *Oxford Economic Papers* 53, no. 3 (2001): 541–563.
30 Alexis Habiyaremye and Thomas Ziesemer, "Absorptive Capacity and Export Diversification in Sub-Saharan African Countries," UNU-MERIT, 2006. United Nations University/Maastricht University UNU-MERIT, Maastricht, *Working Paper 2006-2030* (June 2006), accessed August 29, 2017, www.merit.unu.edu/publications/working-papers/abstract/?id=2707
31 Robert J. Barro and Xavier Sala-i-Martin, *Economic Growth*, 2nd ed. (Cambridge, MA: The MIT Press, 2004).

32 Guillem López-Casasnovas, Berta Rivera, and Luis Currais, eds., *Health and Economic Growth: Findings and Policy Implications* (Cambridge, MA: MIT Press, 2005).
33 Amartya Sen, "Mortality as an Indicator of Economic Success and Failure," *The Economic Journal* 108, no. 446 (1998): 1–25.
34 Barro and Lee, "International Data," 541–563.
35 Robert J. Barro, *Determinants of Economic Growth: A Cross-Country Empirical Study* (Cambridge: MIT Press, 1997).
36 Palle Schelde Andersen and David W.R. Gruen, "Macroeconomic Policies and Growth," Economic Research Department, Reserve Bank of Australia, Sydney, *RDP 9507* (1995).
37 Stanley Fischer, "The Role of Macroeconomic Factors in Growth," *Journal of Monetary Economics* 32, no. 3 (1993): 485–512.
38 Ibid.
39 Claudia Dobre, "The Relation Between Openness to Trade and Economic Growth," *Analele Ştiinţifice ale Universităţii "Alexandru Ioan Cuza" din Iaşi. Ştiinţe* economice, no. 55 (2008): 237–247, accessed September 24, 2013, www.ceeol.com.
40 David Canning and Esra Bennathan, "The Social Rate of Return on Infrastructure Investments," The World Bank, Policy Research Working Paper WPS2390 (July 31, 2000), accessed August 31, 2017, http://documents.worldbank.org/curated/en/261281468766808543/The-social-rate-of-return-on-infrastructure-investments.
41 Paul Collier, "Primary Commodity Dependence and Africa's Future," The World Bank, Working Paper 28111 (April 25, 2002), accessed August 31, 2017, http://documents.worldbank.org/curated/en/514531468740135280/Primary-commodity-dependence-and-Africas-future.

Bibliography

Addison, Tony, George Mavrotas, and Mark McGillivray. "Aid to Africa: An Unfinished Agenda." *Journal of International Development* 17, no. 8 (2005): 989–1001.

Alemu, Aye Mengistu, and Jin-Sang Lee. "Foreign Aid on Economic Growth in Africa: A Comparison of Low and Middle-Income Countries." *South African Journal of Economic and Management Sciences* 18, no. 4 (2015): 449–462.

Andersen, Palle Schelde, and David W.R. Gruen. *Macroeconomic Policies and Growth.* Economic Research Department, Reserve Bank of Australia, 1995.

Barro, Robert J. *Determinants of Economic Growth: A Cross-Country Empirical Study.* Cambridge, MA: MIT Press, 1997.

Barro, Robert J., and Jong-Wha Lee. "International Data on Educational Attainment: Updates and Implications." *Oxford Economic Papers* 53, no. 3 (2001): 541–563.

Barro, Robert J., and Xavier Sala I. Martin. *Economic Growth,* 2nd ed. Cambridge, MA: MIT Press, 2004.

Boone, Peter. "Politics and the Effectiveness of Foreign Aid." *European Economic Review* 40, no. 2 (1996): 289–329.

Burnside, Craig, and David Dollar. "Aid, Policies, and Growth." *American Economic Review* 90, no. 4 (2000): 847–868.

Canning, David, and Esra Bennathan. "The Social Rate of Return on Infrastructure Investments." Policy Research Working Paper WPS2390, July 31, 2000, The World Bank. Accessed August 31, 2017. http://documents.worldbank.org/curated/en/26128Z1468766808543/The-social-rate-of-return-on-infrastructure-investments

Chenery, Hollis B., and Alan M. Strout. "Foreign Assistance and Economic Development." *American Economic Review* 56, no. 4 (1996): 6–19.

Collier, Paul. "Primary Commodity Dependence and Africa's Future." Working Paper 28111, April 25, 2002, The World Bank. Accessed August 31, 2017. http://documents.worldbank.org/curated/en/514531468740135280/Primary-commodity-dependence-and-Africas-future.

Dalgaard, Carl-Johnson, Henrik Hansen, and Finn Tarp. "On the Empirics of Foreign Aid and Growth." *Economic Journal* 114, no. 496 (2004): 191–216.

De Ree, Joppe, and Eleonora Nillesen. "Aiding Violence or Peace? The Impact of Foreign Aid on the Risk of Civil Conflict in Sub-Saharan Africa." *Journal of Development Economics* 88, no. 2 (2009): 301–313.

Dobre, Claudia. "The Relation Between Openness to Trade and Economic Growth." *Analele Ştiinţifice ale Universităţii "Alexandru Ioan Cuza" din Iaşi. Ştiinţe economice*, no. 55 (2008): 237–247. Central and Eastern European Online Library. Accessed September 24, 2013. www.ceeol.com/.

Easterly, William. "Can Foreign Aid Buy Growth?" *Journal of Economic Perspectives* 17, no. 3 (2003): 23–48.

Ekanayake, E.M., and Dasha Chatrna. "The Effect of Foreign Aid on Economic Growth in Developing Countries." *Journal of International Business and Cultural Studies* 3 (2010): 140–155.

Fischer, Stanley. "The Role of Macroeconomic Factors in Growth." *Journal of Monetary Economics* 32, no. 3 (1993): 485–512.

Gomanee, Karuna, Sourafel Girma, and Oliver Morrissey. "Aid and Growth in Sub-Saharan Africa: Accounting for Transmission Mechanisms." *Journal of International Development* 17, no. 8 (2005): 1055–1075.

Gupta, Kanhaya L., and M. Anisul Islam. *Foreign Capital, Savings and Growth: An International Cross-Section Study*. Dordrecht: Reidel Publishing Company, 1983.

Habiyaremye, Alexis, and Thomas Ziesemer. "Absorptive Capacity and Export Diversification in Sub-Saharan African Countries," United Nations University/Maastricht University UNU-MERIT, Maastricht, Working Paper 2006–2030 (June 2006). Accessed August 29, 2017. www.merit.unu.edu/publications/working-papers/abstract/?id=2707.

Hansen, Henrik, and Finn Tarp. "Aid Effectiveness Disputed." *Journal of International Development* 12, no. 3 (2000): 375–398.

Islam, Anisul. "Foreign Aid and Economic Growth: An Econometric Study of Bangladesh." *Journal of the History of Economic Thought* 24, no. 5 (1992): 541–544.

Juselius, Katarina, Niels Framroze Møller, and Finn Tarp. "The Long-Run Impact of Foreign Aid in 36 African Countries: Insights from Multivariate Time Series Analysis." WIDER Working Paper 51/2011. Helsinki: United Nations University World Institute for Development Economics Research. Accessed August 29, 2017. www.wider.unu.edu/publication/long-run-impact-foreign-aid-36-african-countries-0.

Kosack, Stephen. "Effective Aid: How Democracy Allows Development Aid to Improve the Quality of Life." *World Development* 31, no. 1 (2003): 1–22.

López-Casasnovas, Guillem, Berta Rivera, and Luis Currais. *Health and Economic Growth: Findings and Policy Implications*. Cambridge, MA: MIT Press, 2005.

Lucas, Robert E. "On the Mechanics of Economic Development." *Journal of Monetary Economics* 22, no. 1 (1988): 3–42.

Mankiw, N. Gregory, David Romer, and David N. Weil. "A Contribution to the Empirics of Economic Growth." *The Quarterly Journal of Economics* 107, no. 2 (1992): 407–437.

Mbaku, John Mukum. *Institutions and Development in Africa*. Trenton, NJ: Africa World Press, 2004.

McGillivray, Mark, et al. "Controversies Over the Impact of Development Aid: It Works; It Doesn't; It Can, but That Depends. . . ." *Journal of International Development* 18, no. 7 (2006): 1031–1050.

Moreira, Sandrina Berthault. "Evaluating the Impact of Foreign Aid on Economic Growth: A Cross-Country Study." *Journal of Economic Development* 30, no. 2 (2005): 25–48.

Morrissey, Oliver. "Does Aid Increase Growth?" *Progress in Development Studies* 1, no. 1 (2001): 37–50.

Mosley, Paul. "Aid, Savings and Growth Revisited." *Oxford Bulletin of Economics and Statistics* 42, no. 2 (1980): 79–95.

Mosley, Paul, John Hudson, and Sara Horrell. "Aid, the Public Sector and the Market in Less Developed Countries." *The Economic Journal* 97, no. 387 (1987): 616–641.

Moyo, Dambisa. *Dead Aid: Why Aid Is Not Working and How There Is a Better Way for Africa.* New York: Farrar, Straus, and Giroux, 2009.

Munemo, Jonathan, Subhayu Bandyopadhyay, and Arabinda Basistha. "Foreign Aid and Export Performance: A Panel Data Analysis of Developing Countries." In *Theory and Practice of Foreign Aid*, 421–433. Ed. S. Lahiri. Bingley, UK: Emerald Group Publishing Limited, 2006.

Pallage, Stéphane, and Michel A. Robe. "Foreign Aid and the Business Cycle." *Review of International Economics* 9, no. 4 (2001): 641–672.

Sen, Amartya. "Mortality as an Indicator of Economic Success and Failure." *The Economic Journal* 108, no. 446 (1998): 1–25.

Solow, Robert M. "A Contribution to the Theory of Economic Growth." *The Quarterly Journal of Economics* 70, no. 1 (1956): 65–94.

Swan, Trevor W. "Economic Growth and Capital Accumulation." *Economic Record* 32, no. 2 (1956): 334–361.

The World Bank, Policy Research Working Paper WPS2390 (July 31, 2000). Accessed August 31, 2017. http://documents.worldbank.org/curated/en/261281468766808543/The-social-rate-of-return-on-infrastructure-investments.

2

FISHING IN DANGEROUS WATERS?

How Narratives of 'Piracy' and 'Security' Shaped Development Initiatives in the Somaliland Fishery Sector

Amanda Møller Rasmussen and Stig Jensen

Introduction: Fishing for Pirates in Somaliland[1]

On a warm and moist morning in November 2014, Amanda Møller Rasmussen was sitting in an uncomfortable plastic chair at the Danish fishery NGO FairFishing's[2] head office in Berbera, a coastal city in the Sahil region of Somaliland. Due to its location in a natural sandslip, and of it having one of the few operational ports in the country, Berbera is a big economic asset for the Somaliland government. As it also hosts the largest population of Somaliland fishermen, it was a natural choice for a Danish NGO focusing on developing the Somaliland fishery sector. Together with a Danish consultant hired by the NGO and the translator 'Mohammed,' Rasmussen had arranged two focus group interviews that morning with Somaliland boat owners and company agents. Although a 'boat-owner' or 'company agent' does not necessarily refer to a man who occupies himself by spending time on the sea, but rather refers to the ownership of a fishing vessel or company, these men had experiences with fisheries on both land and sea, and many were, or had been, fishermen. For two hours that morning, the boat owners came and went during the interview, discussing the fishery landscape and talking openly about both challenges and changes to the fishery industry in 2014. Since the fishery industry in Somaliland has traditionally consisted of small artisan fishing communities or subsistence foot-fishermen, supplying the markets of Berbera, Hargeisa, and Burco, with little to no local or foreign investment,[3] the boat owners explained how they saw the presence of the Danish development project as necessary for continued prosperity of the fishery industry. They particularly stressed the need for a continuance of development revenue. As Rasmussen had noticed during her 3.5-month fieldwork with the Danish NGO, the development professionals and volunteers had stressed the importance of their project in relation to combating the issue of piracy, especially in funding applications, and she asked the boat owners how they had experienced this issue. Since FairFishing had branded their project as an anti-piracy initiative—while stressing on the one hand the potential risk of Somali fishermen becoming pirates and on the other hand the potential solution to piracy through developing the fishery occupation into a more economically viable solution for the men occupied by pirate activities—she was surprised by the confusion of the boat owners. Similarly to what she would later experience in her engagements and interviews with persons connected to the fishery sector, none of the boat owners saw piracy as a particular threat to their occupation or the sector in general. In fact, none of the boat owners saw any particular link between piracy and fisheries—not in the sense that Somaliland fishermen were in danger of becoming pirates, were particularly harassed by pirates, or that the Somaliland fishery sector should be a particular important factor in addressing the regional issue of piracy. Not even those who had been fishermen since before the civil war in 1991 agreed that piracy was a problem in Somaliland. In fact, as the men had little to say about piracy, they lost interest in the question after a few minutes. Instead, they used the focus group interviews as an opportunity to highlight the challenges of the lack of infrastructure and foreign illegal, unregulated, and unreported fishing (IUU). These issues were highlighted because they saw Rasmussen and the consultant as a link to the fishery NGO by whose presence their businesses had benefited, and because they, on a larger scale, hoped, or even expected, that the attention of international development organizations would accumulate future development projects and revenue.[4]

A couple of days later, Rasmussen recalls riding in the back seat of the NGO's local office's black SUV on the road between Berbera and Hargeisa. On her way, she and the consultant discussed what they should write about the NGO's anti-piracy objective in the impact assessment, since the people they had talked to did not have much to say about piracy. The potential on-shore remedy for piracy outside the Horn of Africa had attracted donations and popularity among the development community and public in Denmark. In fact, Mærsk Line, a global container unit and the biggest operation of the A.P. Møller–Mærsk Group, had paid for the same impact assessment, which Rasmussen assisted with, under, among other, assumptions that the project was believed to be an anti-piracy remedy. As Rasmussen would later discover, a lot of funding had been allocated to the sector on a similar premise. When the consultant asked her to dig deeper into this theme and write a short literature review about Somali piracy upon arrival in Copenhagen, Rasmussen thought that would be an easy matter, especially since she had been presented this linkage several times in Denmark. She felt that *everyone* talked about the linkage between Somali piracy and fisheries, of which the following quotation from an article by one of FairFishing's development professionals is an example:

> [Translated by authors] Since most pirates are being recruited from Somali fishery communities along the coast, it is important to build the capacity and infrastructure of the fisheries, as well as a coastguard and a fishery

control. These will in turn terminate the international illegal fishery, which risk coming back, when the pirates end their business.[5]

However, if Rasmussen was, indeed, right that this anti-piracy project objective and its project was deemed successful by both global and local actors, why then did the interviewees not recognize the same importance of the linkage between the issue of piracy and the fishery sector?

Just a few days after returning to the cool offices of FairFishing in Copenhagen, Rasmussen started to inquire among the volunteers at FairFishing. They explained to her how their project was rather connected with a general strengthening of the fishermen's gear, techniques, and possibilities. They explained how this, by multiplication effect, would increase the general living conditions in the area. They told her that by strengthening the sector, both fishermen, their communities, and the general Somaliland society, would be better off economically, hence reducing the incitement to piracy and other criminal activities. Although such an explanation sounded plausible, Rasmussen noticed how the linkage between piracy and fisheries was continuously stressed in the NGOs communication—especially on social media and in funding applications. When she started to inquire once again, questioning why the linkage of piracy and fishermen seemed more alive in funding documents than in the sea navigated by Somaliland fishermen, she was met with the same explanations on 'security issues' and an accusation of focusing too much on the piracy theme. Although this was not the last time Rasmussen would run into this specific rationalization of this connection, it was, in the end, brushed over easily in the impact assessment.[6]

A year and a half later, on a warm, late afternoon in April 2016, Rasmussen was sitting in the Hargeisa office of an official from the Somaliland Ministry of Fisheries and Marine Resources. She had returned to Somaliland to map out the fishery development actors and their social linkages and to follow the success of the 'fishery-piracy narrative.' A narrative that in the last 1.5 years seemed to be successfully sustained and even more thriving in 2016 than 2014 on social media and among the development professionals. This resulted in a great influx of interest, culminating in more and more development projects focusing on the fishery sector. For the NGO FairFishing, the volunteers had started to tour around Denmark, lecturing on how to make pirates into fishermen.[7] At the same time, the NGO had received its largest donation from the European Union (EU), to duplicate its project in Somalia. Since her first visit in Somaliland, the fishery development sector in Somaliland had increased into a multi-stakeholder field with a handful of international actors and investments totaling more than 26 million dollars since 2012.[8] The projects, and their volunteers and aid professionals, had successfully used reports and social media to stress the importance of their presence by referring to the continued linkage between piracy, insecurity, and fishery in the regions, among other ways. By a stroke of luck, Rasmussen's colleague had been able to set up a meeting to discuss obstacles and possibilities to Somaliland fisheries with an official from the ministry, and the official had been kind enough to meet with her. Sitting in a large room with an overworked fan, Rasmussen was with 'Abdul,' two men in their thirties, her colleague, and others who had business at the ministry, who came and went over the next hour. The meeting had been informative, people had laughed and the mood felt relaxed, up until the point when Rasmussen asked about issues of piracy. Being a bit confused at first, the men at the office told Rasmussen that her question was somewhat misplaced and silly. If she really was interested in the *Somaliland* fishery sector, she should be aware that piracy was rather an issue further south. They, however, acknowledged that there was somewhat of a link between fishery development and improved security in the region, since all development and growth would lead to a more stable region. Feeling a bit embarrassed and ridiculed, Rasmussen awkwardly asked, quite leadingly, how the ministry then felt about international NGOs linking piracy with fisheries in their reports. The official looked at her confused and asked her to elaborate on how they did so. After explaining how this linkage could be found in development reports or on the organizations' social media, the men talked quite freely on the fact that they did not know if the NGOs made this linkage, or why. They were plainly not that interested if the NGOs did so, since as the official pointed out close to the end of the interview, he believed that the organizations was, indeed, interested and successful in developing and attracting funding to the fishery sector—an achievement seen as more important than the words used to describe it.[9] Feeling confused, as if she had missed something in her inquiry, Rasmussen used the next couple of days to trace the linkage between piracy and fishery on social media, in reports, and in articles by the development professionals. She easily found such linkage on social media, in reports, and in general by the public media. In fact, quite confusingly, this narrative seemed more alive and well than ever. When, the next day, Rasmussen asked her colleague and another friend if the official really did not know this compelling narrative, they asked her:

> Why does it matter? As long as the fishery sector receives international attention, the officials, fishermen and the NGOs are happy. Why should they care if the western NGOs believe that there are pirates in Somaliland?[10]

The Political Sea That Surrounds Fishery Development

While at first glance these kinds of stories might seem as typical anecdotes about how international development professionals and volunteers misread the situation on the ground, we suggest that it is no coincidence that the 'fishery-piracy narrative' in its various formats continues to thrive. Rather than seeing the different types of stakeholders as homogenous groups with homogenous narratives, the success and continued usage of this narrative is a testimony to the various appropriations, mobilizations, and negotiations by a myriad of heterogonous local

44 Amanda Møller Rasmussen and Stig Jensen

and international actors who have been a part of successfully putting Somaliland fisheries and the sea—as spaces for intervention and crises—on the global agenda.

While Somaliland has experienced increasing interest from academics and development professionals in recent years, Somaliland fisheries, on the other hand, have seldom caught the attention of scholars or development policies. Rather, scholars have primarily engaged with this region on the basis of its agricultural and nomadic sectors, which are often associated with a Somali way of life. As a result, only marginal research has gone into the historical and contemporary trends among fishermen[11] and coastal communities. Perhaps for good reason, since the fishery sector is, in fact, relatively small, with currently only 1% of the Somaliland population estimated by the Somaliland government to be employed in small-scale fishing. However, in contrast to current development beliefs, there have always been fishermen in Somaliland. They and Somali fishermen in general have, however, lived on the margins of dominant nomadic culture.[12,13] However, in recent years, a new trend has surfaced, and the water that surrounds the Somali region, including the fishermen who occupy it, has experienced a surge of international attention.

This attention coincided with, on one hand, international media coverage of 'Somali piracy' and its proposed linkage to terror and instability in the region, which should be fought by patrolling the sea. On the other hand, it also accompanied an academic and political linkage between development solutions on shore to the global threat on sea.[14] Somali piracy and its attained discursive position as a global threat has, with its assumed linkage to fishermen and coastal communities, successfully channeled global interests and resources to the Somaliland fishery sector. At the moment, a myriad of actors—national navies, international organizations, NGOs, the United Nations, the private sector, and other regional and emerging global actors—are engaged in fighting piracy either on the sea or on the ground.

Particularly development organizations joined the cause of fighting piracy, which traditionally had engaged security and state actors. The development organizations argued that fishery development could help fight instability in the region and be a solution to piracy, since their focus of providing ice, infrastructure, financial schemes, training, and fishery co-ops would lead to economically viable possibilities for the fishermen who were at risk of becoming pirates. Under catchphrases such as 'Building Fisheries Instead of Pirate Bays,'[15] donor relationships, cooperation, and partnerships were established between development organizations and donor countries, as well as security actors and the private sector, especially the shipping industry. These relationships have, so far, successfully accumulated large amounts of funding and support. Especially, the organizations that linked their development projects with security needs have received finances and social backing, and the development professionals and their expertise have come to be seen as invaluable in the fight against piracy. The linkage between fishermen and pirates—and security and development—has showed itself quite persistent and has shaped both relationships and technologies in the sector.

It is this assumption, repeated by development professionals, scholars, and the global media, of an intimate relation between fishermen and pirates—where fishermen risk becoming pirates, and where pirates can be transformed into fishermen—that is the starting point of this chapter. We argue that the linkage between piracy and fisheries comes from a long interaction, claim making, and interdependency among development professionals, the donors, the Somali fishermen, and the global community. Both fishery practices and development—and piracy, for that matter—are dynamic practices that evolve in face of internal and external pressures and negotiations. We propose to investigate how the 'fishery-piracy narrative' linked a variety of actors and their surrounding networks and created the discursively field of fishery development in Somaliland. In the following pages, we outline how fishery development initiatives today differentiates from earlier initiatives due to their successful linkages and partnerships with security interests and private sector funding. We argue that while the 'fishery-piracy narrative' has been capable of translating a myriad of interests, it has more to do with the interpretations of events than with interventions that seek to 'make the Somali pirates into fishermen.'[16] At the same time, we investigate how the narrative functioned as a point of departure for different global and local practices that inhabited and governed the fishery development arena. Finally, we argue that fishery development in Somaliland—and its technologies and practices—must be understood in its nesting within a wider political economy of interdependence and 'success' in which development actors, local fishermen and politicians, national navies, donors, and the global media seek to secure their position and divert resources in ways that would sustain their interests. This becomes particularly important in light of recent changes in the region—with, for example, the Danish navy and NATO finishing their mission to combating piracy on the sea—and the resurgence of piracy. In other words, this chapter concerns itself with how a marginal arena, the Somaliland fishery sector, came to be of great importance on the global development agenda, by the linkages and de-linkages among the actors within the contested political sea that surrounds fishery development in the region.

History of Fishery Development in Somaliland—Sunken Projects and New Currents

Historically fishery development projects in Somaliland share the important characteristic of working with a sector that has received only little development attention. A major reason is that even though there always have been fishing communities along the northern Somali coast, these communities existed on the margins of a dominant nomadic culture.[17,18] Today, only an estimated 765 fishermen[19] are active in the Salal, Awdal, Sahil, and Sanaag region, out of an estimated coastal population of 20,000.[20] Although fisheries in this region have received scarce scholarly attention, it becomes clear from the scarce literature that Somali culture has an historical and inhabited aversion toward fishing and fish eating.[21] Similarly to many other cultures in the world, fishermen have often been treated as 'outcasts' on the lower end of the social hierarchy, with little recognition of their history, tradition, or knowledge. In like manner, they have often lacked the social, economic, or cultural capital to demand the same political rights as the dominant Somali nomads or pastoralists.[22] During Rasmussen's research in Somaliland, it became apparent that this aversion still exists to some degree. Although it is slowly changing, being a fisherman today is not considered a particularly 'good job.' At the same time, it is perceived as hazardous, since the occupation is dangerous, economically insecure, hard work, and often involves long periods of being away from one's family. Perhaps as a result of this social aversion, there is a shared belief among development professionals, Somaliland politicians, and the global public that the Somaliland fishery sector and fishery tradition is somewhat 'non-existent,' since it does not employ a large amount of artisanal or industrial fishermen.[23]

In spite of the Somaliland fishery sector being relatively small, there have been efforts to develop the sector since colonial times. Admittedly, there is a major methodological obstacle in tracing these initiatives, since they, on one hand, have been few in number and quickly lost interests and hence investments. On the other hand, there is a lack of differentiation in accounts of fisheries and development initiatives in Somalia/Somaliland. Since the demarcation between Somalia/Somaliland has changed over time, so have records in regards to fisheries. Although a genealogy would be beneficial to current studies of fisheries in the Somali region, a short review must suffice for this chapter.

Fishery Projects That Hit a Snag

A few development initiatives that focused on the fishery sector were launched during the British Protectorate. Traditionally, most of the development funding spent under British colonial rule was spent on initiatives focusing on agriculture and livestock. Nonetheless, since the Protectorate had observed the successful fisheries in Aden and Somalia, the Protectorate tried to jump-start local fishery activities on several occasions. These efforts included the purchase of dhows, the contracting of a fishery officer, and the training of fishermen in commercial fishing as well as the opening of a small canning factory.[24] These efforts exercised the logic of modernization, that is, the idea that fisheries could be developed from 'traditional' low-scale fishing into 'modern' commercial fishing. All the same, these efforts were quickly deemed unsuccessful, as only a few Somalis showed interest in becoming fishermen, thus the initial plans to establish fishery co-ops were never fulfilled.[25]

It took until Siad Barre's coup d'état in 1969 before fishery development once more became a popular venture. In accordance to the Soviet Union and later Italian funded project of 'Scientific Socialism,' the sea went from a space of subsidence to a source of profit.[26] Throughout the 1970s, these efforts, to a smaller or bigger degree in Somaliland, included the launching of deep-sea trawling fleets, the building of fish factories and processing plants, and information about fish consumption through public outreach.[27] Although most of the development efforts from the Ministry of Fishery and Marine Transport were focused to the South, even the initiative to arrange small numbers of traditional fishermen in cooperatives reached the North. These fishing cooperatives were assigned technical and financial assistance.[28] Additionally, as a reaction to the droughts in 1974 and 1976, new fishery settlements were built along the coast to encourage drought affected people to take up fishing.[29] The government also built fishing hubs in Zeila and Berbera as well as a cold storage in the latter.[30] These efforts should be seen within the development techno-politics of the 1970s, which focused on bringing traditional lifestyle into modernity.[31] However, these initiatives were short lived in terms of investments. As for the drought re-settlement programs, only a very small number of the previous nomads took up fisheries.[32] Instead, the sea as a source for revenue showed itself to be more profitable in issuing fishery licenses to foreign fishing fleets, which often resulted in Somalis working alongside, or for, foreign vessels.[33]

Once again, Somaliland fisheries were out of fashion until the 1980s, where aid organizations like the Danish International Development Agency (DANIDA), Food and Agriculture Organization (FAO), the United Nations Capital Development Fund (UNCDF), and the World Bank became involved intermittently in efforts to develop the artisanal fisheries and capacities of coastal cities.[34,35] The focus in the 1980s was on rapid economic growth and markets demands. The UNCDF supported the development of artisanal fishery cooperatives around Berbera,[36] whereas DANIDA built a freezing facility in 1986. DANIDA's initiative was part of the wider World Bank NECFISH initiative. Also, FAO built smaller freezing facilities[37] and collected data on the fisheries' resources with funding from the Norwegian Agency for Development Cooperation (NORAD). However, as a result of the civil war in the end of the 1980s and the beginning of the 1990s, all of these facilities were destroyed, and fishery development fell into the background, as aid was focused on humanitarian efforts.

Current Development Projects—A Different Kettle of Fish?

Historically, a prevalent trait of fishery development in Somaliland has thus been its noticeably lack of continuous attention from its donors and development projects. Since the civil war and up until 2012, fishery development was out of fashion. However, with the newfound interest in the sea outside the Horn of Africa, this has changed.[38] This happened as new NGOs emerged in Somaliland with funding from primarily the private sector. Save the Children Denmark and the Danish NGO FairFishing were some of the first organizations to arrive in Berbera. Both NGOs had received their funding particularly from the shipping industry, to remove the incitement to piracy. Subsequently, more and more development organizations became interested in developing the Somaliland fishery sector in the period 2012–2017.[39] While these initiatives also focused on providing the fishermen with training, gear, and infrastructure so that fisheries in the region could become commercially and economically viable occupations, they differentiate from earlier initiatives primarily in two ways. On one hand, there is an increased focus on entrepreneurship and market strategies. Whether it be the American NGO Shuraako[40] providing microloans to the fishermen, the Danish NGO FairFishing establishing a treatment facility and fishery cooperate, the DANIDA- and DFID-funded Somaliland Development Fund (SDF) focusing on the fishery value chain,[41] or the World Bank focusing on creating jobs through supporting the value chain, or through the Somaliland Business Fund, which matches funds in a loan scheme, they all rest on the assumption that breaking up traditional uses of the sea by new skills, technologies, and credit will provide the inherent entrepreneur fishermen access to the market. This access will then, in turn, let the fishermen overcome scarcity through a realization of market exchange, which, in turn, will lead to more employment and investment in the sector. Simultaneously, on the other hand, there is an increased interlacing of development and security. Fishing development became popular again around the same time as political and academic discourses began to theorize a correlation between security and development in the beginning of 2012.[42] At the moment, all of the development initiatives in the fishery sector entwine, to a lesser or greater extent, their project into a greater effort of stabilizing the region. Underpinning this logic is the idea that, if the sector is provided with infrastructure, knowledge, and investment—the sector becomes economically viable and attracts more investment, thus employment—as a result, addressing the issues of insecurity and crime in the region.[43] Especially the issue of 'Somali Piracy'—that is, the consensual global interpretation[44] of a global threat that often involves ideas about a failed, dangerous, and uncontrollable Somalia,[45] where fishermen are both desperate and poor—has received a great deal of international attention. While Somaliland has remained mostly free from pirates,[46] phrases like 'make Somali pirates into fishermen' have successfully attracted large amounts of funding, gear, and development professionals, mainly to the northern part of the region. The underpinning logic presumes that fishery and piracy are connected because both occupations are on the sea and within an economic cycle where the economic viability of fisheries and piracy are the main factor in why fishermen become pirates, and vice versa—thus curable by market-oriented interventions. The underlying assumption is that piracy is a product of insufficient economic opportunities and poor fishermen, which can easily be fixed by providing the fishermen accessibility to the market. It is within this market and security logic that the Somaliland fishermen are cast as poor fishermen, potential pirates, and potential entrepreneurs—all at the same time.

Fishing for New Partnerships

Perhaps the biggest difference in regards to previous attempts to jump-start the Somaliland fishery sector is the actors involved, directly or through donations, in developing the sector. Previously, the development initiatives involved donor countries, international agencies and, to some extent, the Somali state. Today, however, the landscape also includes, among others, NGOs, national navies, and private sector donors (especially from the shipping industry). When looking at the funding routes of the fishery development organizations, it is apparent that many of the initiatives have received their funding from the EU or less traditional donors—that is, the private sector, and especially the shipping industry.[47] These donors were attracted to the NGO's promise of combating the global threat of piracy—an issue high on the agenda of both the shipping industry and the EU, which has two naval forces patrolling the Somali waters. Through promises of easy-fix capacity building, an influx of new technologies, and the microloans, the development professionals' promises to turn pirates into fishermen.

With new partnerships and donor relationships came new strategies. In her fieldwork, Rasmussen experienced how the development professionals articulated the previous attempts of interventions as 'failed' in the sense that the projects were short lived and never realized the 'untapped potential' of the fishery sector. It was important to the development professionals that their projects—and their new security and market-oriented strategies and partnerships—was different than the projects of the 1980s and 1990s.[48,49] Especially, the Danish NGO FairFishing criticized DANIDA's previous and more 'traditional' interventions on its social media and public appearances.[50] These perceived 'failures' of previous projects created the momentum for more market-oriented solutions, and their claimed 'novelty' was helpful in attracting funding.

As a result of these interactions with previous projects and the current trends within evaluation of development projects, the projects are shorter and focus more on calculable outputs—such as the amount of ice produced, the loans provided, or the fish landed—that are easily weighed and measured. It is within this context of creating new partnerships by branding one's project as new, and the negotiations between development professionals and their private sector donors, that we must understand fishery development today. The market-oriented focus relies on an assumption that the expansion of the sector will always benefit the fishermen. However, this risks overlooking the existing challenges of demand as well as the social context of power and exploitation in which real-world exchanges are subsumed.[51] In the context of the Somaliland fishery development, this becomes particularly clear in the obsession with the production of ice and local investment, which overshadows questions of security for the crew fishermen, labor rights, assets, debt, and the loss of markets, which for the most vulnerable fishermen— the subsistence foot-fishermen who traditionally have sold to the nearby hotels risks—can be devastating, as they risk losing their income because they do not have the economic and social capital to compete with the new and larger companies.[52] Scholars like David Harvey, for instance, demonstrate the importance of reflecting on how forms of accumulations are linked with, or provoke, dispossession.[53] Inherent in the idea of an 'untapped fisherman potential'—to both become pirates or entrepreneurs—is the assumption that the market transcends the political landscape within which the fishermen operates. It ignores important questions of who can actually access these new technologies and possibilities and who are excluded from them. In a broader sense, it risks ignoring what will happen to the sector and scarce market—or environment—if more and more people become fishermen. Further, since poverty becomes articulated as complications for accessing the market, the poor are cast as the 'abnormal,' and the issues of 'insecurity,' ignoring that, as Maia Green points out: "Very often it is not among the poor that we should be looking for those relations which have contributed to the poverty of others."[54] At the same time, the market-oriented development seems to miss out the important economic and social distinctions between the fishermen. Naturally, boat owners, skippers, crew fishermen and subsistence foot-fishermen do not have the same needs. Likewise, they do not have the same capitals to address or engage with the fishery development projects. Rather, it is the strongest players within the fishery sector—often the boat owners—who have the time, resources, and social capital to attend participatory fishery meetings, buy the newly provided gear, and pay back loans.[55] Simply providing access to markets does not automatically create opportunities for the poor, because the inequality to access the market or development aid stands in the way. As pointed out by Anna Tsing "markets are made in the friction of political and cultural circumstances"[56] and in the case of the fishery landscape this meant that especially the stronger players (the haves) in the fishery landscape could enforce their property rights and negotiate their interests against the weaker players (the have-nots). Importantly, the local conditions that separated stronger and weaker players were not addressed by development projects and became somewhat institutionalized through the politically managed question of access and prioritization. Such issues are the backside of the market-oriented focus, even if such a focus has directed foreign investment to the sector.

Fishy Pirates: Salt-Water Robin Hoods or Marauding Fishermen?

So far, we have demonstrated that two emerging trends are prevalent within the fishery development sector in Somaliland today: that is the focus on the market and security as well as the larger and more heterogenic development and donor landscape, which resulted in the Somaliland fishery sector—a sector with only marginal, if any, influence on a global scale—becoming a space of intervention and investment among the global community. In this process, the fishermen were, within the logics of marketization and security, cast as both potential pirates and entrepreneurs, informed by the proposed solutions of the development projects. This context is important to understand why fishery development became a priority. However, to fully understand how development projects based on these assumptions are formed by, and inform, the narratives, we should look to the functionality of these narratives and the communities that surrounds them.

Building Fisheries Instead of Pirate Bays—A Project in Somaliland[57]

This 2016 Twitter update from the corporate social responsibility team at Mærsk Line is an example of how the linkage between Somaliland fisheries and piracy in the region are stressed among one of the larger donors. Mærsk Line has, on numerous occasions, funded the Danish NGO FairFishing's initiatives (and, in 2012, the initiative of Save the Children Denmark) on the basis that those projects could, by strengthening the capacity, skill, and infrastructure of the fishery sector, decrease, or even eliminate, piracy in the region. A premise, which Mærsk, as a shipping company, has a great interest in. What we term the 'fishery-piracy narrative' is particularly interesting when noting the fact that while Somaliland has remained mostly free of pirates, the funding attracted by this narrative have primarily gone to Somaliland fisheries. However, this linkage between piracy and Somaliland fisheries is not unique to Mærsk or to the development initiatives it has funded. Rather, the linkage between fisheries and piracy—or fisherman and pirate—was a recurring theme in the documents of the fishery development projects, especially in funding documents and reports, as well as on social media and the organizations' homepages.[58] FairFishing, for example, has perhaps been the most vocal NGO in terms of its project's anti-piracy potential. The usage of a 'fishery-piracy narrative,' however, was contextual. The NGO highlighted their perception of the fishermen as being poor and thus tempted by piracy, only in funding applications to donors with security interests—like the shipping industry. An example would be this passage from a funding application directed toward Mærsk:

> [Translated by authors] The communities along the Somaliland coast have historically been isolated, poor and tempted by piracy. In the long run, it is necessary to give people an alternative [to piracy] via fishery.[59]

On the other hand, the NGO downplayed the linkage in other applications directed toward for example DANIDA.[60] Up until recently, a large amount of FairFishing's funding and donations were donated by the shipping industry.

A core function of the 'fishery-piracy narrative' was its articulation of crisis. On one hand, it used the underlying global assumption and engagement with the Somali region as characterized by failure, danger, and poverty.[61] On the other hand, it assumes that, since the Somaliland fishery sector is believed by the development professionals to be lacking both skills, infrastructure, and capital, it is thus in need of the expertise and solutions that the development projects bring to Berbera. By stressing the linkage between piracy and fishery—between issues of security and development solutions—the narrative creates a language of crisis[62] that invents a space to intervene in (the fishery sector) and a threatening persistent consequence (the global threat of piracy) if this is not addressed immediately. As previous attempts are cast as 'unsuccessful' and the development professionals are cast as 'experts'—in the sense that they provide the knowledge and possibilities for transformation—the development professionals use the language of crises and 'Somali Piracy's' high priority on the global security agenda to cement the importance and legitimacy of their intervention, and thus their raison d'être. An example of this is how the World Bank, in a recent publication, stresses how the market-oriented development initiatives are the *only* solution to combat piracy in Somalia:

> It is recognised that a key part of the long-term solution is to provide alternative economic opportunities in the coastal communities, in particular for the youth. **Fisheries offer one of the only such opportunities,** so that while the fisheries outcome of a development assistance project may be less than optimal its contribution to countering future piracy may be significant.
>
> *[Highlight by authors]*[63]

When the development professionals use the 'fishery-piracy narrative' and its inherent language of crisis, they cast themselves as invaluable experts and their projects as of high trade value to a myriad of actors—such as maritime corporations, naval actors, security firms, international organizations, and donor countries—all somehow invested in combating piracy. When organizations like Save the Children Denmark states 'efforts on land are needed to improve young people's living conditions and thus remove the incentive to turn to piracy,'[64] the organization creates a linkage between efforts on land (most often in Somaliland, and especially in Berbera) and the crime on sea, thus successfully recasting piracy from a solely crime-based problem on sea to involve pre-crime development solution on land.[65]

A Fishery Expert's Tale

Stories are important. The ways we talk, write, and think about development have real effects.[66] Christian Bueger, for instance, in his work on how pirates use the narratives on Somali piracy, demonstrates how

> Narratives are crucial for the repertoire constituting a practice and providing coherence to it. They are outcome as well as representative of the constant negotiation of a common enterprise. Telling and re-telling stories are a core activity in any practice.[67]

The fishery development arena in Somaliland, that is, a space(s) wherein different actors strategically negotiate, struggle, cooperate, mobilize social relations, and deploy discursive means to further their interests, is relatively small, in the sense that only a handful of organizations work with the fishery sector. Most of the organizations use local staff for the daily project administration and fly in the development professionals for shorter period field visits. These experts often stay in one of three quite luxurious hotels—the Ambassador or the Maan soor in Hargeisa, or the Maan soor in Berbera—or rent a compound. Many of the development professionals have met on these hotels, either as they were staying there or since they dine in the restaurants used by foreigners. Some have also visited each other's projects or even cooperated on interventions. For the development professionals lucky enough to be seen as important in the fishery sector, there is also the possibility of participating in the monthly 'Fishery Meeting' at the Ministry of Fisheries and Marine Resources. It is, in fact, quite easy for the development professionals to bump into one another on their short trips to Somaliland, especially since many of the development professionals attend larger events, such as yearly investment forums, or the yearly Fair Fish Festival, or since the development professionals seldom go outside Hargeisa or Berbera, as other cities in Somaliland are hard to reach or even considered dangerous. Some of the development professionals also meet in their representative countries or at global events.[68,69]

The fact that most of the development professionals seldom went outside of Hargeisa or Berbera perhaps explains the centralization of development investment and projects to the fishery hub of Berbera. Anthony Bebbington, for instance, has highlighted how it is typical for NGOs to swarm toward the same areas. A major reason is that the attention of a development project often results in improved infrastructure, making it easier for other projects to join the race.[70,71] Another reason, as Rosalind Eyben illustrates, is that the professionals establish working and private relationships.[72] As Bebbington demonstrates elsewhere, such a 'spatialization of aid' favors some spaces at the expense of others in the process of linking this particular space to the global community. This could explain the tendency to focus on 'fishery-piracy narrative' in Somaliland—and especially Berbera—although, as mentioned previously, Somaliland has remained mostly free of pirates.

The development professionals did not give Rasmussen the impression that 'piracy' was an important theme among their peers. It did not seem as the issue was brought up during the monthly 'Fishery Meeting' or when the professionals met at the Ambassador or at field visits.[73,74] When Rasmussen asked 'John,' a development professional from an American fishery NGO, about how his project—a project that in its project documents had connected fisheries and piracy—related to piracy in the region, he answered:

> Maybe this [that there are pirates in Somaliland] is what they say in London. However, here there are no pirates.[75]

54 Amanda Møller Rasmussen and Stig Jensen

This answer was typical on the response Rasmussen got during her trip to Somaliland in 2016. She quickly became aware that the development professionals shared the perception that there were, in fact, no pirates in Somaliland. She was continuously reminded that Somaliland fishermen were hardworking and had no predisposed risk of becoming pirates or criminals, more so than any other in Somaliland. The development professionals rather stretched the linkage between growth, capacity building, and security in the region. Many argued that these development initiatives were rather a way to prevent *future* pirates or instability. For many of the development professionals (also the ones who did not emphasize piracy), it did not matter if the funding came from donors who linked their development initiatives with preemptive piracy initiatives, as long as the funding went into boosting the fishery sector:[76]

> That [making pirates into fishermen] is rubbish when they start of in Somaliland. . . . I think it was a bit misunderstood and perhaps the realities outpaced them. Some believed there would also come pirates from there [Somaliland], since the youth have nothing to do, and becomes more and more religious. When they have nothing to do, this becomes a source of revenue. However, then piracy was sorted out. So, perhaps they had expected piracy to become an issue or a risk, and then the circumstances changed.[77]

This extract comes from a development professional who worked for a donor country agency. Although his organization had not financially supported organizations that claimed to be a solution to the issue of piracy, he excused the other organizations. While he agreed that there were no pirates in Somaliland, which then cannot be transformed into fishermen on accordance of fishery projects in Somaliland, he did not counter the project's objective. During the interview, he actually even praised many of the different projects in Berbera—even if, as he made clear, the 'fishery-piracy narrative' was off.[78] This tendency was repeated among the different development organizations on the ground in Somaliland and on social media. The *piratization*[79] of one's project did not lead other organizations to discredit the project. Neither was the assumption countered in other documents. So far, no development organizations have officially countered the 'fishery-piracy narrative,' even if they behind closed doors believe it to be 'rubbish.' Rather, it seemed that everyone accepted the fact that such stories about piracy led to more funding opportunities.[80] At the same time, it showcased the ability of the development professionals to opt in and out of each other's understandings and narratives in efforts to promote their interests and legitimate their own role. As the 'fishery-piracy narrative' had proven itself quite successful in cementing larger amounts of funding, it could be risky to criticize these donor relationships, especially if the development professionals hoped to tap into the funding potential in the future. In other words, it seemed to be in everyone's interest to maintain a somewhat coherent representation of the development landscapes.

Fish or Cut Bait

Critical development scholars have time and again showcased that people participate in development on the most favorable terms they can obtain.[81] Spaces of interventions are spaces of negotiations, appropriation, mobilization, and rejection among both developers and beneficiaries. It is interesting that the fishermen in Berbera had not expressed any recognition toward the 'fishery-piracy narrative' when Rasmussen enquired in 2014; however, it is more interesting to see how the fishermen navigated these questions.

Before the development projects came to Somaliland, the fishermen navigated at the sea and in the local social arena. As a result of the sudden development interest, the fishermen were now forced to navigate among the fishery organizations as well. Being a part of one of the fishery projects meant to have advantage—whether this being the access to cheap ice, freezing facilities, or new gear. These new technologies, gear, and ice are important advantages when the fishermen compete over scarce markets and on the sea. Benedetta Rossi, for instance, demonstrates how there is always something to gain from a project, no matter how little. In fact, and perhaps even more important, there is always something to lose out on, when competing with one another.[82] In the case of the Somaliland fishermen, the advantages came only if the fishermen were favored by the development organizations to receive training, gear, or ice. This perhaps also explains why the fishermen do not feel the need to cement the lack of pirates in Somaliland, but rather appropriate the situation to promote their own interests. An example of this was the way the fishermen told Rasmussen how they benefited from the NGO FairFishing's project. When she inquired about the cooperation, she was told by one of the fishermen, 'No one should complain. I hope no one complains. FairFishing gave us ice when we needed it.'[83] This quote is typical to the answers she received during both of her stays in Somaliland. Both the fishermen and the people she met were pleased with the newfound attention and the possibilities it brought with it as well as the promises for the future.[84] It seemed that they cared less about how the funding was attached. However, it is important to acknowledge as pointed out by Sarah White, for instance, 'That people do not express other interest does not mean that they do not have them. It simply means that they have no confidence that they can be achieved.'[85] The fishermen were very realistically aware to what extent they could achieve benefits by virtue of being the recipient of these development projects even on this development rationale. They also led Rasmussen to believe that they also were aware of the consequences for their income if these projects went to other and more 'piracy prone' areas. But even if they raised these concerns, would the donors and development professionals—among whom many acknowledged that there were no pirates in Somaliland—change anything, or even listen, if the fishermen started to stress the fact that there were no pirates in Somaliland? Who would, in fact, benefit from such an objection? And what would be at risk for the fishermen?

Naturally, no one is interested in destroying a perceived economic possibility or perhaps even the risk of being put out of business. Even if a fisherman did not want to become part of the project, this was quite hard. Since the interventions transformed the sector and the markets, he would still need to navigate among the new realities. An example of this was one of the companies that sold ice previously to FairFishing's project. The company owner tried to make FairFishing aware that they were putting him out of business; however, his complaints was interpreted as being 'selfish,' and the organization did not believe him to be representative of the needs and interests of the fishery sector as a whole.[86] Whether this is actually the case is not important, because the power of interpretation lies with the NGO. They decide who in relation to their project speaks for the community and who does not. They choose among the fishermen who should be representatives on field visits. For the Gumaar Company, that meant being ignored. Only by transforming its business into focusing on boats and spare parts could the company survive. Since FairFishing also started to provide cheap gear and spare parts since 2015, we still need to see what this meant for a local company like 'Gumaar.' With stories like these, why should the fishermen take any chances in objecting to any objective, especially if they did not perceive it as disadvantageous to them?

Nothing Makes a Fish Bigger Than Almost Being Caught

The idea that Somali pirates can be transformed into fishermen is not, however, invented by the development professionals. Rather, as Brittany Gilmer demonstrates, pictures of Somali men wrapped in macawiis with AK-47s on boats came to symbolize not only the 21st century pirate archetype,[87] but also a global fear of piracy. The Somali Waters became synonymous with piracy, and the ideas of fragility, violence, and chaos were associated with Somalia by the global media and international actors.[88] The persistence of the 'fishery-piracy narrative' must be understood within this context.

On one hand, the lack of scholarly attention to Somaliland fisheries created a vacuum, where primarily development organizations produced data, reports, and policy papers on fisheries. The repeated linkage between pirates and fishermen in these reports[89] created a narrative that became stronger and stronger, as it was repeated and widely used. These reports—when circulated among the actors and referred to in newer reports—received a status as 'evidence' in the conceptual tool kit, which determined the parameters of thinkable interventions in the fishery sector.[90] At the same time, these documents and narratives informed and were informed by the same epistemic communities and scrutinized by donors with interests in securitizing the Somali waters.

On the other hand, these 'fishery-piracy narratives' was also repeated and utilized among different Somali communities. In recent literature, scholars have highlighted how piracy became linked with fisheries as a way of legitimizing and giving meaning to piracy among pirates,[91] as well as among the local communities in Somalia and Somaliland,[92,93] and the Diaspora.[94] In these versions, the Somali pirates are presented as poor and desperate fishermen and/or as a 'coast guard' against the illegal, unregulated, and unreported fishing practices and toxic waste dumping of foreign fleets that harm local fisheries. Among captured pirates, the narrative was also utilized to claim innocence in an effort to avoid judgment.[95] The narrative has been more or less successful on the ground in Somalia, following the shifting political and moral economy of maritime piracy.[96] Also the political elite in Somalia has utilized these narratives in various formats to promote political interests[97] and channel development revenue.

Finally, blurring the lines between fishermen and pirates has an important dimension that regards the governance of Somali waters and demarcation of territory. It is part of international actors' long engagement with the Somali region as a place of chaos and intervention. It constructs ideas about inclusion and exclusion in regards to the resources of the ocean, and in regards to the resources that are brought forward by fishery development and anti-piracy measures. However, at the same time, by articulating the waters as spaces for international intervention, they become discursive platforms from where the Somali government, the Diaspora, and local Somalis are able to produce claims and reestablish connections with the globalized world and market. By utilizing and appropriating these narratives and development logics' in various formats—and their many promises of outside intervention—more funding than ever had reached Somaliland. We expect this trend to continue if the 'fishery-piracy narrative' continues to be utilized and appropriated by local forces. In other words, the international actors' own narratives are being used strategically in an attempt to accentuate the need for outside development revenue and attention in a process that internationalizes and localizes the fishery sector—all at the same time.

In other words, the fishermen, the pirates, the Somali Diaspora, and political elite appropriated versions of the 'fishery-piracy narrative' and directed claims on the global community. Within the narratives' own premise that somehow the strengthening of the fishery sector could prevent piracy, fishermen were suddenly able to put claims onto development organizations and articulate their need for outside intervention—and funding. These claims articulated how the sector would fall back into the same situation *if* the development projects left the sector. Pirates in interviews also used this narrative.[98] This usage of the 'fishery-piracy narrative' for one's own interest can be seen in various arenas. In courtrooms, alleged pirates repeated the narrative in order to prove their innocence.[99] For the Diaspora and the political elite, the narrative became a platform to address issues of independence and the need of foreign funding.[100] Likewise, as pointed out by Christian Bueger, the usage of different piracy narratives also resulted in international counter-piracy actors to acknowledge the importance of other issues such as overfishing and toxic waste dumping.[101]

Particularly, the 'fishery-piracy narrative' became a way of interpreting Somaliland's fishery sector in a multitude of ways within a globalized world. By stressing

58 Amanda Møller Rasmussen and Stig Jensen

the need for intervention—and emphasizing the danger to global interests—funds and attention were given to Somaliland, an area, which as a result of its not acknowledged independence, has received only very small amounts of international aid. By using the development projects' and global actors' own narrative and construction of the Somali region, the narrative became a platform to reestablish linkages for people who have had only a very marginalized position in terms of economic, social, and juridical capital in a globalized world.

Perhaps the most central element to the 'fishery-piracy narrative' is its particular vagueness. Like a 'buzzword,' the narrative is a popular expression. It varies according to who utilizes it. Its vagueness produces a situation where no one could disagree with its goodness and rightness.[102] It is an alluring and symbolic discourse that is borne out of a moral conviction that provides the organizations with the legitimacy they need to ground their project.[103] How could a project that combats piracy be bad? At the same time, its fuzzy and interchangeable nature provides room for contestation and for a varied group of stakeholders— fishermen, pirates, development professionals, and donors—to appropriate their sometimes-conflicting political agendas.[104] This essence makes it possible for both security actors and development professional to somewhat agree on an objective, although they are informed by different logics and agendas. The fuzziness and positive connotations of fighting piracy on shore, however, camouflages their differences as being on the same page. In its many variations, it has thus worked to legitimize practices among a myriad of communities.

Importantly, this is not to pass judgment on whether the 'fishery-piracy narrative' is relevant to the fishery sector. There is no doubt that in the early 1990s, Somali fishermen were harmed and harassed by foreign trawlers, and that fishermen engaged in attacks on ships for a few thousand dollars.[105] Jatin Dua, for instance, in his outstanding and detailed ethnography in the Somali region, highlighted the historical and political dynamics of rent-seeking practices that initially formed early Somali piracy and showcased the complex underlying dynamics and influences of piracy practices and their negotiated meaning locally.[106,107] While it seems appealing to connect fishery and piracy, it seems important to highlight, as Ken Menkhaus stated, that 'in recent years, as piracy has expanded from being a localized practice to a wider trans-regional phenomenon, the majority of participants involved are no longer ex-fishermen and often have little if any maritime expertise.'[108] Rather, as Menkhaus and Dua demonstrate, the growing field of responses and actors also informs these practices.[109]

Inspired by Brittany Gilmer's question on whether one can accurately distinguish pirates from fishermen,[110] as a result of these narratives, we cement that the survival of the 'fishery-piracy narrative' is not dependent on whether there are any fishy pirates, salt-water Robin Hoods, or marauding fishermen—or all of the above at the same time. Rather, as we are going to explore in the next chapter, the narrative survives through the new partnerships, donor relationships, and the consensual tale among the epistemic networks that surrounds the fishery landscape.

Reeling in Donors and Support—Securitization of Development

In Berbera, there are an estimated 756 fishermen, many of whom are benefiting from one of the fishery projects. Those fishermen had high hopes of entering into projects to receive gear and funding.[111] If this is the case, why then do the organizations, which have fishermen willingly engage with their projects, need to stress a linkage between to security and piracy—why is the aim of developing the fishery sector not enough?

Latourian-inspired approaches to development studies have taught us that concepts, projects, and narratives become real only if they successfully translate the interests of actors and incorporate these into a network. David Mosse, for instance, demonstrates how 'success' and its counterpart 'failure' are the dogmas of development interventions.[112] Without the possibility of a successful future, there would never be a project to start with. However, documentation and success are both negotiated and produced within their respective networks,[113] in a process that includes competition as well as interdependency among the actors.[114] The development actors need to participate in negotiations with their development funding networks, their epistemic communities of fishery knowledge, and the fishermen on the ground. From all places, they need support either in the form of economic or social capital, which they achieve only if they successfully translate the interests of the network.[115] In other words, the fishery development projects in Somaliland receive funding and support only if they can translate the donors' and surrounding political and social landscape's interests into their project and can provide them with documentation of their success.

It [the interest in piracy] depends on the donor[116]

This was the answer Rasmussen was given when she asked a development professional why he was part of a project that focused on anti-piracy measures also in Somaliland, when he himself had agreed that there were, in fact, no pirates in Somaliland. This understanding permeated the sector. An example is of the Danish NGO FairFishing, who tried to receive state funding since its establishment in 2012. To the annoyance and confusion of the NGO, DANIDA chose to allocate their donations to the donor organized trust Somaliland Development Fund. As a result, the NGO, quite bitterly, attacked DANIDA (and their previous engagement in the sector) several times, in Danish television, in articles, and on social media. While DANIDA never officially reacted to the critique, Rasmussen met several development professionals that speculated to the NGOs partnership with the private sector, as well as their stressing of the 'fishery-piracy narrative,' as DANIDA's main reason. Importantly, in both email correspondences and on several field visits, development professionals from DANIDA and FairFishing met and discussed these projects, opening up for some sort of collaboration. However, in stark contrast to DANIDA is the funding the NGO received from the shipping sector. As already seen, these donor partnerships were established on the

60 Amanda Møller Rasmussen and Stig Jensen

objective of combating piracy on shore in Somaliland. Likewise, EU was also entranced by the NGO's success and donated 3 million euro. The example of FairFishing showcased the tension that surrounds the 'fishery-piracy narrative.' On one hand, it could help an organization attract funding, and on the other hand, it could risk scaring off other donors. As seen previously, the narrative—or perhaps narratives—was manifold in formation, usages, and de-usages. Looking at FAO, this becomes even clearer. Since 2012, FAO has been active in a myriad of projects in Berbera. Although FAO had not particularly stressed any security or piracy linkages to their projects, it was explained to Rasmussen during an interview with FAO development professional 'Paul' how the funding FAO had received from DANIDA and NORAD, among others, had ceased. While the development professional agreed that Somaliland did not have the same issues with piracy as did the South, he also explained that FAO had needed to become part of a biometrics-based ID-scheme funded by the Counter Piracy Trust Fund. This scheme was implemented so that, on one hand, the Ministry of Fisheries and Marine Resources could register data on the fishery activities (numbers of boats, vessels, villages, and fishermen). On the other hand, it was implemented in order for the fishermen to avoid being misidentified as pirates. He speculated on how the misidentifying issue could perhaps be a result of the increased focus on a linkage between piracy and fisheries; however, he felt that this was secondary to the important task of getting data about the fisheries, something that was last done when FAO made its 2005 country profile of Somali Fisheries.[117] For him, it seemed that the practice of linking up to different donors and networks in order to receive funding—and give their ideas legitimacy in exchange—was a rather natural way of forwarding one's own projects and interests. This seemed as a recurring trend among the development professionals in the sector.

In his work, Alnoor Ebrahim showcases how the relationship between the donors and NGOs are based on an interdependent and competitive relationship. In this relationship, the donor provides the NGO with economic capital in exchange for a 'successful' project, which functions as a conveyed symbolic resource in the form of a good reputation and feel-good associations.[118] Ebrahim stresses how both the NGO and the donor are dependent on these exchanges. It is through this process of interdependency that the boundaries of 'success' and 'failure' are bargained within the network. As David Mosse and David Lewis establish, a project or policy 'become real through the work of generating and translating interests, creating context by tying in supporters and so sustaining interpretations.'[119] Such policies function to mobilize support within their wider epistemic, social, and economical networks, rather than forming practice on the ground, and relies on the continuous translation of interests among actors with reason to support the project.[120]

In the case of the Somaliland fishery sector, the donors are donor countries and institutions who have their navies fighting pirates in Somali waters and, on the other hand, the shipping industry. On one hand, the 'fishery-piracy narrative' becomes a way of tapping into a shared global fear. It is a way for the development professionals to signal 'relevancy' and an 'expertise' that suddenly became highly demanded by military and government institutions.[121] Likewise, the narrative cast development professionals as invaluable players in combating piracy and made some NGOs that were very marginal in size and power into global 'do-gooders' who received not only funding, but also praise by the international community in their part-taking of securitizing the region. As Brittany Gilmer cites from one of her interviews: "Everyone knows there is a lot of money out there for combating piracy."[122]

On the other hand, the proposed market-oriented and security focus solutions paved the way for new actors, funding, and solutions to enter the Somaliland fishery sector. At the same time, it was a way for donors like Mærsk to showcase their social engagements. Thus, when the events of the Somali waters were translated into a question about security and piracy, it created a successfully channel for funding, support, and legitimacy for both the organizations and donors. Together with the silence from other stakeholders, they created an acceptable storyline for enough actors to uphold the success of the narrative. As a result of linking these development projects to the private and security sector, as seen earlier, the development professionals' interpretations of events in documents and on social media became 'securitized' and 'marketized.' These interpretations, however, risk blurring the actual relation between the fishery projects and fishery sector into a scenario where the fishermen become risks, rather than men with real skills, knowledge and desires. At the same time it risk erasing their agency as these proposed solutions are based on assumptions of poverty and danger, which are not recognized by the fishermen, but rather was a product of the global imagination, casting Somali men in a boat as potential pirates.[123] As the interventions in the sector are still relatively new, we have yet to see the effects of these interventions. Nonetheless, scholars like Brittany Gilmer have hinted in her work on the FAO ID-Scheme the tremendous consequences of branding Somali fishermen as 'potential pirates'—as the fishermen were met with suspicion and harassment.[124]

The underlying assertion between development, market, and security informed the sector in various ways. Martin Murphy argues that the global interest in Somali fisheries is doubtfully related to the insecurity and famine of the Somali people. Instead, it channeled global power dynamics and issues of global fears.[125] These fears tend to be structured around the interests of the powerful in the global imagination, and their consequences are, therefore, often ignored.[126] Security discourses have successfully appropriated development discourses, and vice versa, which for better or for worse, has led to important changes in how development organizations today work with the fishery sector.

Conclusion: A Small Fish in a Global Pond

The purpose of this diversion into the forms and functionality of the 'fishery-piracy narratives' is not only to bring light to the complex cultural dynamics of the fishery development arena and networks, but also to throw critical light on how narratives inform and become the center of interpretations of events. Rather than evaluating the narrative's epistemic value, we looked into its effects on the fishery sector. We found that the main accomplishment of the narrative was linking up a small and marginalized space with the global community's interests. Up until 2012, the private sector, international navies, or even the international organizations overlooked the Somaliland fisheries. Their interests came only as a result of the development actors' successful articulation of the linkage between piracy and fisheries. This made the development agenda relevant to the global community and made poverty reduction fundamental in combating piracy. On one hand, the narrative was successful in harnessing a wide amount of funding from the private sector and global actors into the Somaliland fisheries. On the other hand, it became a platform where different actors could address and put claims onto the global community. In this process, the narrative came to bear the rationale of marketization and securitization in its venture with the fishery arena. The narrative became real through its consistent translation of interests among local and global actors. We showcased how the narrative formed a type of consensus in which the 'fishery-piracy narrative' became a somewhat feel-good and unifying buzzword. It transformed a global disinterest into an interest based on discursive position of piracy as a 'global threat,' and with its vagueness, it was capable of hiding and translating various political interests from a myriad of actors. In a sense, it established a foregone narrative with a foregone conclusion.

Notes

1 Amanda Møller Rasmussen conducted the research for this chapter as a part of her MA theses at the Centre of African Studies, Copenhagen University (2015) and at the School of Oriental and African Studies (2016). In 2014, she was an intern at a Danish NGO and followed their activities for 3.5 months, including a shorter trip to their project site in Berbera. In 2016, she conducted a little less than 2 months of fieldwork in Hargeisa, following the 'fishery-piracy narrative' among the development actors and locally in Hargeisa. The interviews and participatory observation was supplemented with analysis of primary and secondary documents, including email correspondence, planning documents, and newspaper articles, which were gathered online and generously provided by some of the NGOs. Rasmussen has also used social media, reports, and documents to map and follow the development organizations' outputs and practices, including their references to other organizations. After agreement, all interviews, observations, and field notes have been anonymized.
2 FairFishing is a Danish NGO working to develop the fishery sector in Somaliland. The NGO has been active since 2012 and has focused primarily on building an ice cooling and treatment facility in Berbera. In 2016, the NGO received 3 million euro from the EU to duplicate its project in the South of Somalia.
3 Mark Bradbury, *Becoming Somaliland* (London: Progression, 2008), 11, 146.
4 Amanda Rasmussen, interview by author with boat owners and company agents, Berbera, November 24, 2014.
5 Kurt Bertelsen Christensen, "Fra Pirat til Fisker—Jamen, Hvordan?" *Jyllands Posten*, May 12, 2014, http://jyllands-posten.dk/debat/breve/article6714712.ece

Fishing in Dangerous Waters? **63**

6 Amanda Rasmussen, field notes, Copenhagen and Berbera, 2014.

7 AOF Nordsjælland, "Kursuskatalog efterår-vinter 2016," *Course Catalogue* (2016): 5.

8 This estimation was found during AMR's fieldwork and desk research for her MA dissertation at the School of Oriental and African Studies (2016). It is based on official budgets available for the development initiatives in the region. These numbers do not include the amount of resources put into any of the advocacy NGOs, the World Bank initiatives, and FAO. The number is, therefore, likely to be much higher.

9 Amanda Rasmussen, interview by author at the Ministry of Fisheries and Marine Resources, April 2016.

10 Amanda Rasmussen, field notes, Hargeisa, 2016.

11 'Fishermen' is the term used among the development professionals and the people Rasmussen interviewed in Somaliland, since fishing as the activity of going to the sea and catching fish are considered a man's profession. Women are rather linked up to the fishery sector through other activities, such as sewing fishing nets, as traders, and so forth. Although it is not the purpose of this chapter to discuss the conceptual framework behind the term 'fisherman,' the term is a complicated analytical term, as it risks blurring the lines between different types of fishermen—for example, foot-fishermen, crew, boat owners, and traders—the term was used in this article to stay true to the language used in interviews.

12 Martin Murphy, *Somalia: The New Barbary? Piracy and Islam in the Horn of Africa* (London: Hurst, 2011), 19.

13 Ioan Lewis, *Understanding Somalia and Somaliland*, 3rd ed. (London: Hurst & Company, 2011), 63.

14 Brittany Gilmer, *Political Geographies of Piracy* (New York: Palgrave Macmillan, 2014), 3.

15 Mærsk Line, Twitter post, October 27, 2015, https://twitter.com/MaerskLine/status/659041318719635456

16 FairFishing, "CISU Application, B" (2014): 1.

17 Murphy, 19.

18 Lewis, *Understanding Somalia and Somaliland*, 63.

19 It is not the purpose for this chapter to discuss the conceptual framework behind the concept of 'fisherman'; however, since the numbers come from an estimation by the World Bank and the Ministry of Fisheries and Marine Resources, it is important to acknowledge that they do not differentiate among who these fishermen are. It seems fair to estimate that the amount of people employed by the fishery sector is larger than 767, since the sector employs a variety of occupations—such as boat owners, skippers, crew members, traders, boat builders, net weavers, and so on, as well as people who are employed only in limitedly by the fishery sector.

20 Kieran Keheller, *Somalia Sustainable Fisheries Development Note Identifications of Areas for Possible World Bank Support. Policy Note*, Report no. AUS13836 (Africa: World Bank, 2016), 6, 29, 31.

21 Lewis, *Understanding Somalia and Somaliland*, 63.

22 Bradbury, 11.

23 Amanda Rasmussen, "Anything Fishy in Somaliland? Development and Small-Scale Fishermen in Berbera" (MA thesis, Copenhagen University, 2015), 42.

24 Brock Millman, *British Somaliland: An Administrative History, 1920–1960* (London & New York: Routledge, 2013), 239.

25 Millman, 239.

26 Jatin Dua, "A Sea of Trade and a Sea of Fish: Piracy and Protection in the Western Indian Ocean," *Journal of East African Studies* (2013): 362–364.

27 Dua, "A Sea of Trade and a Sea of Fish: Piracy and Protection in the Western Indian Ocean," 363.

28 Mohammed Yassin, "Somali Fisheries Development and Management" (Postgraduate, Oregon State University, 1981), 26.

29 Ahmed Gulaid, *Feasibility Report on The Fisheries Sector in Somaliland. Current Status, Opportunities and Constraints. Discussion Paper Consultant's Findings, April–June 2004* (Somalia: United Nations Development Programme, 2004), 7.

30 Somaliland Chamber of Commerce, Industry & Agriculture, *Fishing Sector—Somaliland Chamber of Commerce, Industry and Agriculture* (Somalia: Somaliland Chamber of Commerce, Industry & Agriculture, 2016).

31 Anna Tsing, *Friction: An Ethnography of Global Connection* (Princeton: Princeton University Press, 2005), 21.

32 Nina Fitzgerald, *Somalia: Issues, History and Bibliography* (New York: Nova Science Publisher Inc., 2002), 22–24.

33 Jatin Dua and Ken Menkhaus, "The Context of Contemporary Piracy: The Case of Somalia," *Journal of International Criminal Justice* 10, no. 4 (2012): 735.

34 World Bank, *Project Completion Report Somalia. Fisheries Exploration/Pilot Project Report Nr. 10983* (Somalia: World Bank, 1992).

35 World Bank, *Staff Appraisal. Fisheries Exploration/Pilot Project Report Report Nr. 4685-SO* (Somalia: World Bank, 1984).

36 Staffan Larsson and Jan Valdelin, *Manufacturing Fishing Vessels* (Stockholm: SIDA, 1986).

37 Niels Rohleder, "Alle Taler om The Livestock-Ban," *Information*, 1991, www.information.dk/27546.

38 Admitting Save the Children Denmark reached Berbera already in 2010, however, it seems accurate to highlight the 2012 since the actual influx of interest in fishermen, rather than youth, as a particular target group, did not happen until 2012.

39 In May 2016, these development organizations were active and directly engaged in developing the fishery sector in Somaliland: FairFishing, FAO, Oxfam, Shuraako, Somaliland Development Fund (SDF), World Bank, Horn of Africa Voluntary Youth Committee (HAVOYOCO), Save the Children Denmark, and STIDIT.

40 More information on the NGO Shuraako can be found at its homepage: http://shuraako.org/

41 More information on Somaliland Development Fund can be found at its homepage: www.somalilanddevelopmentfund.org/

42 Gilmer, *Political Geographies of Piracy*, 2.

43 Amanda Rasmussen, "A Tale of How Fishermen in Somaliland Became Pirates" (MA thesis, School of Oriental and African Studies, 2016).

44 Stig Jarle Hansen, "Debunking the Piracy Myth: How Illegal Fishing Really Interacts With Piracy in East Africa," *The RUSI Journal* 156, no. 6 (2011): 26.

45 Murphy, 1.

46 Peter Pham, "Putting Somali Piracy in Context," *Journal of Contemporary African Studies* 28, no. 3 (2010): 355.

47 Rasmussen, "A Tale of How Fishermen in Somaliland Became Pirates," Appendixes.

48 Amanda Rasmussen, field notes, Hargeisa, 2016.

49 Rasmussen, "Anything Fishy in Somaliland? Development and Small-Scale Fishermen in Berbera," 80.

50 FairFishing, Facebook post, May 8, 2014, www.facebook.com/fairfishing.org/posts/471852616281251

51 Marcus Taylor, "Displacing Insecurity in a Divided World: Global Security, International Development and the Endless Accumulation of Capital," *Third World Quarterly* 30, no. 1 (2009): 153.

52 Rasmussen, "Anything Fishy in Somaliland? Development and Small-Scale Fishermen in Berbera," 73.

53 David Harvey, "The 'New' Imperialism: Accumulation by Dispossession," *Social Register* 40 (2004).

54 Maia Green, "Representing Poverty and Attacking Representation: Perspectives on Poverty From Social Anthropology," *The Journal of Development Studies* 42 (2006): 1142.

Fishing in Dangerous Waters? **65**

55 Rasmussen, "Anything Fishy in Somaliland? Development and Small-Scale Fishermen in Berbera," 74–80.

56 Tsing, 21.

57 Mærsk Line.

58 Rasmussen, "A Tale of How Fishermen in Somaliland Became Pirates," 26, 38–40.

59 FairFishing, "Mærsk Application" (2014), 3.

60 FairFishing "DANIDA Application" (2013).

61 Murphy, 1.

62 Jonathan Crush, *Power of Development* (London and New York: Routledge, 1995), 10, 16.

63 Keheller, 17.

64 Oceans Beyond Piracy, "Industry Contributions to Somali Coastal Development," report (2014): 7.

65 Gilmer, *Political Geographies of Piracy*, 152.

66 James Ferguson, *The Anti-Politics Machine* (Minneapolis and London: University of Minnesota, 1990). Arturo Escobar, *Encountering Development: The Making and Unmaking of the Third World*, 2nd ed. (Princeton and Oxford: Princeton University Press).

67 Christian Bueger, "Practice, Pirates and Coast Guards: The Grand Narrative of Somali Piracy," *Third World Quarterly* 34, no. 10 (2013): 1815.

68 Amanda Rasmussen, field notes, Hargeisa, 2016.

69 Amanda Rasmussen, field notes, Copenhagen and Hargeisa, 2014.

70 Anthony Bebbington, "Global Networks and Local Development: Agendas for Development Geography," *Tjidschrift Voor Ecnomische En Sociale Geografie* 94, no. 3 (2002): 728.

71 Anthony Bebbington, "NGOs and Uneven Development: Geographies of Development Intervention," *Progress in Human Geography* 28, no. 6 (2004).

72 Rosalind Eyben, "The Sociality of International Aid and Policy Convergence," in *Adventures in Aidland: The Anthropology of Professionals in International Development*, ed. David Mosse (New York and Oxford: Berghahn, 2011).

73 Rasmussen, field notes, Copenhagen and Berbera, 2014.

74 Rasmussen, field notes, Hargeisa, 2016.

75 Amanda Rasmussen, interview with development professional 'John,' Hargeisa, March 2016.

76 Rasmussen, "A Tale of How Fishermen in Somaliland Became Pirates," 30–38.

77 Amanda Rasmussen, interview with development professional 'Eric,' Hargeisa, March 2016.

78 Amanda Rasmussen, interview with development professional 'Eric,' Hargeisa, March 2016.

79 Gilmer, *Political Geographies of Piracy*.

80 Rasmussen, "A Tale of How Fishermen in Somaliland Became Pirates," 35–36.

81 Sarah C. White, "Depoliticising Development: The Uses and Abuses of Participation," *Development in Practice* 6 (1996): 14.

82 Benedetta Rossi, "Aid Policies and Recipient Strategies in Niger" in *Brokers and Translator: The Ethnography of Aid and Development*, eds. David Mosse and David Lewis (Bloomfield: Kumarian Press, 2006), 45.

83 Amanda Rasmussen, interview by author with boat owners and company agents, Berbera, November 24, 2014.

84 Amanda Rasmussen, field notes, Berbera, 2016.

85 White, 6, 14.

86 Internal documents and emails among the development professional at the NGO FairFishing.

87 Gilmer, "Fishermen, Pirates, and the Politics of Aid: An Analysis of the Somali Fishermen Registration Programme," *Geoforum* 77 (2016): 108.

88 Murphy, 109.

89 Rasmussen, "A Tale of How Fishermen in Somaliland Became Pirates."

90 Green, "Calculating Compassion: Accounting for Some Categorical Practices in International Development," in *Adventures in Aidland: The Anthropology of Professionals in International Development*, ed. David Mosse (New York & Oxford: Berghahn, 2011), 37.
91 Bueger.
92 Hansen.
93 Pham.
94 Dua and Menkhaus, 763.
95 Gilmer, Brittany. "Fishermen, Pirates, and the Politics of Aid: An Analysis of the Somali Fishermen Registration Programme." *Geoforum* 77 (2016): 108.
96 Dua, "A Sea of Trade and a Sea of Fish: Piracy and Protection in the Western Indian Ocean," 365.
97 Bueger, 1824.
98 See, for example, Christian Bueger's research: "Practice, Pirates and Coast Guards: The Grand Narrative of Somali Piracy."
99 Gilmer, Brittany. *Political Geographies of Piracy*. New York: Palgrave Macmillan, 2014, 31–2.
100 Dua and Menkhaus, 763.
101 Bueger, 1824–1825.
102 Andrea Cornwall, "Introductory Overview—Buzzwords and Fuzzwords: Deconstructing Development Discourse," in *Deconstructing Development Discourse: Buzzwords and Fuzzwords*, eds. Andrea Cornwall and Deborah Eade (Warwickshire: Practical Action Publishing, 2010), 62–65.
103 Andrea Cornwall and Karen Brock, "What Do Buzzwords Do for Development Policy? A Critical Look at 'Participation', 'Empowerment' and 'Poverty Reduction'," *Third World Quarterly* 26 (2005): 1055.
104 Cornwall, 62–65.
105 Dua and Menkhaus, 753–755.
106 Jatin Dua, "Piracy and the Narrative of Recognition. The View From Somaliland," *Social Science Research Council* (2012).
107 Dua, "A Sea of Trade and a Sea of Fish: Piracy and Protection in the Western Indian Ocean."
108 Ken Menkhaus, "Dangerous Waters," *Survival* 51, no. 1 (2009), 22.
109 Menkhaus, 22.
110 Gilmer, Brittany. "Fishermen, Pirates, and the Politics of Aid: An Analysis of the Somali Fishermen Registration Programme." *Geoforum* 77 (2016), 109.
111 Rasmussen, "Anything Fishy in Somaliland? Development and Small-Scale Fishermen in Berbera," 86.
112 David Mosse, "Introduction: The Anthropology of Expertise and Professionals in International Development," in *Adventures in Aidland: The Anthropology of Professionals in International Development*, ed. David Mosse (New York and Oxford: Berghahn, 2011).
113 David Mosse, *Cultivating Development* (London and New York: Pluto Press, 2005), 158.
114 Alnoor Ebrahim, *NGOs and Organizational Change: Discourse, Reporting and Learning* (Cambridge: Cambridge University Press, 2003), 2, 156.
115 Ebrahim, 156.
116 Amanda Rasmussen, interview with development professional 'Paul,' Hargeisa, April 2016.
117 Ibid.
118 Ebrahim, 52, 63.
119 David Mosse and David Lewis, "Theoretical Approaches to Brokerage and Translation in Development," in *Brokers and Translator: The Ethnography of Aid and Development*, eds. David Mosse and David Lewis (Bloomfield: Kumarian Press, 2006), 13.
120 Mosse, *Cultivating Development*, 8, 17.
121 Gilmer, *Political Geographies of Piracy*, 67.

122 Gilmer, *Political Geographies of Piracy*, 146.
123 Rasmussen, "Anything Fishy in Somaliland? Development and Small-Scale Fishermen in Berbera."
124 Gilmer, "Fishermen, Pirates, and the Politics of Aid: An Analysis of the Somali Fishermen Registration Programme."
125 Murphy, 109.
126 Robin Luckham, "The Discordant Voices of Security," in *Deconstructing Development Discourse: Buzzwords and Fuzzwords*, eds. Andrea Cornwall and Deborah Eade (Warwickshire: Practical Action Publishing, 2010), 269–280.

Bibliography

Bebbington, Anthony. "Global Networks and Local Developments: Agendas for Development Geography." *Tijdschrift Voor Economische En Sociale Geografie* 94, no. 3 (2002): 297–309.

Bebbington, Anthony. "NGOs and Uneven Development: Geographies of Development Intervention." *Progress in Human Geography* 28, no. 6 (2004): 725–745.

Bradbury, Mark. *Becoming Somaliland*. London: Progressio, 2008.

Bueger, Christian. "Practice, Pirates and Coast Guards: The Grand Narrative of Somali Piracy." *Third World Quarterly* 34, no. 10 (2013): 1811–1827.

Cornwall, Andrea. "Introductory Overview—Buzzwords and Fuzzwords: Deconstructing Development Discourse." In *Deconstructing Development Discourse: Buzzwords and Fuzzwords*, 1st ed., 1–18. Eds. Andrea Cornwall and Deborah Eade. Warwickshire: Practical Action Publishing, 2010.

Cornwall, Andrea, and Karen Brock. "What Do Buzzwords Do for Development Policy? A Critical Look at 'Participation', 'Empowerment' and 'Poverty Reduction.'" *Third World Quarterly* 26, no. 7 (2005): 1043–1060.

Crush, Jonathan. *Power of Development*. London: Routledge, 1995.

Dua, Jatin. "Piracy and the Narrative of Recognition. The View From Somaliland." *Social Science Research Council* (2012).

Dua, Jatin. "A Sea of Trade and a Sea of Fish: Piracy and Protection in the Western Indian Ocean." *Journal of East African Studies* 7, no. 2 (2013): 353–370.

Dua, Jatin, and Ken Menkhaus. "The Context of Contemporary Piracy: The Case of Somalia." *Journal of International Criminal Justice* 10, no. 4 (2012): 749–766.

Duffield, Mark. "The Liberal Way of Development and the Development—Security Impasse: Exploring the Global Life-Chance Divide." Security *Dialogue* 41, no. 1 (2010): 53–76.

Ebrahim, Alnoor. *NGOs and Organizational Change: Discourse, Reporting and Learning*. Cambridge: Cambridge University Press, 2003.

Escobar, Arturo. *Encountering Development*. Princeton, NJ: Princeton University Press, 2012.

Eyben, Rosalind. "The Sociality of International Aid and Policy Convergence." In *Adventures in Aidland: The Anthropology of Professionals in International Development*. Ed. David Mosse. New York and Oxford: Berghahn, 2011.

Ferguson, James. *The Anti-Politics Machine*. Minneapolis: University of Minnesota Press, 1990.

Fitzgerald, Nina J. *Somalia: Issues, History and Bibliography*. New York: Nova Science Publisher Inc., 2002.

Gilmer, Brittany. "Fishermen, Pirates, and the Politics of Aid: An Analysis of the Somali Fishermen Registration Programme." *Geoforum* 77 (2016): 106–113.

Gilmer, Brittany. *Political Geographies of Piracy*. New York: Palgrave Macmillan, 2014.

Green, Maia. "Calculating Compassion: Accounting for Some Categorical Practices in International Development." In *Adventures in Aidland: The Anthropology of Professionals in International Development*, 33–56. Ed. David Mosse. New York and Oxford: Berghahn, 2011.

Green, Maia. "Representing Poverty and Attacking Representation: Perspectives on Poverty from Social Anthropology." *The Journal of Development Studies* 42 (2006): 1108–1129.

Gulaid, Ahmed. "Feasibility Report on the Fisheries Sector in Somaliland: Current Status, Opportunities and Constraints." Discussion Paper Consultant's Findings, April–June 2004. Somalia: United Nations Development Programme, 2004.

Hansen, Stig Jarle. "Debunking the Piracy Myth." *The RUSI Journal* 156, no. 6 (2011): 26–31.

Harvey, David. "The 'New' Imperialism: Accumulation by Dispossession." *Social Register* 40 (2004): 63–87.

Keheller, Kieran. "Somalia Sustainable Fisheries Development Note Identifications of Areas for Possible World Bank Support. Policy Note." Report no. AUS13836. Africa: World Bank, 2016.

Larsson, Staffan, and Jan Valdelin. *Manufacturing Fishing Vessels*. Stockholm: SIDA, 1986.

Lewis, Ioan. M. *Making and Breaking States in Africa*, 1st ed. Trenton, NJ: Red Sea Press, 2010.

Lewis, Ioan M. *Understanding Somalia and Somaliland*, 3rd ed. London: Hurst, 2011.

Li, Tania Murray. *The Will to Improve*. Durham, NC: Duke University Press, 2007.

Luckham, Robin. "The Discordant Voices of Security." In *Deconstructing Development Discourse: Buzzwords and Fuzzwords*, 269–280. Eds. Andrea Cornwall and Eade Deborah. Warwickshire: Practical Action Publishing, 2010.

Marchal, Roland. "Somali Piracy: The Local Contexts of an International Obsession." *Humanity: An International Journal of Human Rights, Humanitarianism, and Development* 2, no. 1 (2011): 31–50.

Maxwell, Daniel G., and Nisar Majid. *Famine in Somalia: Competing Imperatives, Collective Failures, 2011–2012*. New York: Oxford University Press, 2016.

Menkhaus, Ken. "Dangerous Waters." *Survival* 51, no. 1 (2009): 21–25.

Millman, Brock. *British Somaliland: An Administrative History, 1920–1960*. London and New York: Routledge, 2013.

Mosse, David. *Cultivating Development*. 1st ed. London and New York: Pluto Press, 2005.

Mosse, David. "Introduction: The Anthropology of Expertise and Professionals in International Development." In *Adventures in Aidland: The Anthropology of Professionals in International Development*, 1–31. Ed. David Mosse. New York and Oxford: Berghahn, 2011.

Murphy, Martin N. *Somalia: The New Barbary? Piracy and Islam in the Horn of Africa*. 1st ed. London: Hurst, 2011.

Oceans Beyond Piracy. "Industry Contributions to Somali Coastal Development." Report, 2014.

Pham, J. Peter. "Putting Somali Piracy in Context." *Journal of Contemporary African Studies* 28, no. 3 (2010): 325–341.

Rasmussen, Amanda. "Anything Fishy in Somaliland? Development and Small-Scale Fishermen in Berbera." Postgraduate, Centre of African Studies, Copenhagen University, 2015.

Rasmussen, Amanda. "A Tale of How Fishermen in Somaliland Became Pirates." Postgraduate, School of Oriental and African Studies, 2016.

Rohleder, Niels. "Alle Taler Om the Livestock-Ban." Information, 1991. www.information.dk/27546.

Rossi, Benadetta. "Aid Policies and Recipient Strategies in Niger." In *Brokers and Translator: The Ethnography of Aid and Development*, 27–50. Eds. David Mosse and David Lewis. Bloomfield: Kumarian Press, 2006.

Somaliland Chamber of Commerce, Industry & Agriculture. "Fishing Sector—Somaliland Chamber of Commerce, Industry and Agriculture." Somalilandchamber.com, 2016. www.somalilandchamber.com/?page_id=122.

Taylor, Marcus. "Displacing Insecurity in a Divided World: Global Security, International Development and the Endless Accumulation of Capital." *Third World Quarterly* 30, no. 1 (2009): 147–162.

Tsing, Anna. *Friction: An Ethnography of Global Connection*, 1st ed. Princeton: Princeton University Press, 2005.

Wedel, Janine. "Studying Through a Globalizing World." In *Ethnographies of Aid*, 1st ed., 149–174. Eds. Jeremy Gould and Henrik Marcussen. Roskilde University: IDS, 2004.

White, Sarah C. "Depoliticising Development: The Uses and Abuses of Participation." *Development in Practice* 6, no. 1 (1996): 6–15.

World Bank. "Project Completion Report Somalia. Fisheries Exploration/Pilot Project." Report Nr. 10983, Somalia: World Bank, 1992.

World Bank. "Staff Appraisal: Fisheries Exploration/Pilot Project Report." Report Nr. 4685-SO, Somalia: World Bank, 1984.

Yassin, Mohamed. "Somali Fisheries Development and Management." Postgraduate, Oregon State University, 1981.

Section B: Marketing

3

STIMULATION OF ENTREPRENEURSHIP IN AFRICAN MARKETS USING CLUSTER THEORY

Jens Graff

Introduction

Recent economic and social developments in some African countries suggest that the approaches to traditional large-scale projects related to economic development have not been effective over the years. Large-scale projects are often funded by large international organizations, a limited number of non-governmental organizations (NGOs) and, in some cases, national governments. Most of the projects, for various in-country reasons, were ineffective and inefficient even though they were proposed on the basis of the recommendations of internationally well-known economists.

Some African countries are turning to alternative approaches to stimulate economic and social development. Many of the more radical approaches are based on developments in telecommunications and the Internet, which provide platforms for rapid growth of a new class of entrepreneurs starting innovative smaller ventures. There appear to be different types of entrepreneurs actively developing products and services that directly benefit local markets and stimulate personal consumption.

The new young entrepreneurs frequently do not have the necessary managerial skills to successfully understand markets. They may have technological knowledge as it relates to computers and use of the Internet, but they lack marketing know-how. The growth of management philosophies, especially the growth of marketing management, offers these entrepreneurs platforms on which to build their commercial initiatives. Marketing management allows entrepreneurs to identify marketing opportunities and select those opportunities with the best potential for market acceptance, but most of all they can make optimal decisions within the context of marketing management philosophies. One recently

74 Jens Graff

emerged managerial tool used by entrepreneurs and marketing managers is the formation of regional industrial clusters. Regional industrial clusters help smaller enterprises cooperate on a variety of industrial initiatives that would be difficult to accomplish individually.

Many economists have been critical of the way aid programs through the United Nations and other donor institutions previously were designed. Too many intermediate entities in the receiving countries extracted the funding, and very little remained for the poor. Control was too inefficient. It was a concern for the supported industrialization programs in these countries.[1] In recent decades, however, more control mechanisms are built into the programs, and specific partner companies in the receiving countries get more direct support.

It is increasingly apparent today that African entrepreneurs start businesses triggered by the relatively high growth in many African economies. The penetration of microloans and the Internet has enhanced this development. They are entrepreneurial the African way, fulfilling needs in the community and basing their activities within local boundaries and local resources. Often, they establish micro companies, but when sales expand, their businesses expand too, and even produce for foreign buyers and thereby engage in exports.

The Danish foreign aid organization DANIDA introduced a so-called private sector program in 1993 (later named *B2B Program* and ultimately *Partnership Program* before it was put on hold in 2015) for establishing joint ventures between Danish companies and local companies with the aim of transferring know-how and technology to local companies. An exit strategy was built in so that after some years the local company would be the sole owner of the joint venture.

This type of program undoubtedly contributed to the development and economic growth of the receiving countries. The programs were thought of as linking private companies together in a joint venture and, in principle, covered all business sectors. The outcome has been uneven without much synergy. Riskær suggested involving the Danish Development Fund for Developing Countries (Investeringsfonden for Udviklingslande—IFU) at an early stage to get access to expertise in the area.[2]

Business economists believe that companies cooperating in industrial clusters are more productive and profitable because they create synergy. It is obtained by behaving in microcosms with supporting businesses and by producing companies with their suppliers and sub-suppliers nearby.[3]

It can be asked whether donor countries could direct their funds more effectively toward creating businesses in African countries by using industrial cluster principles. Domestic companies could be urged to establish African subsidiaries funded by the donor countries. The aim is to create regional industrial clusters. The local African workforce can then gain competencies in processes and technologies that can be beneficial for later spin-offs. Eventually, African entrepreneurs would be equipped to start companies, and growth would spiral in their area.

The ultimate objective of this presentation is to examine foreign aid programs with an emphasis on Danish foreign aid programs, suggest contemporary policies for foreign aid as they relate to economic and social development in African countries, and propose formation of regional industrial clusters as a marketing management tool to stimulate economic and social growth. The expectations are that this presentation will assist donor organizations and government agencies in justifying donations for economic and social development.

Environmental Forces and Macro Marketing Management in African Economies

Only recently, increasing globalization from industrialization meant opportunities for some countries and threats to others. Many countries introduced trade barriers to protect their markets; African countries were no exception. Trade barriers hampered the industrialization of Africa and its participation in the global division of labor. African markets were not developed, and their governments and institutions were weak, so they lost in the race for global competitiveness. However, Europeans built an infrastructure to better export African resources, which is a positive for future African development. Other advances for Africa have been the Internet and mobile telephone technology. All in all, the digital age has given Africa new opportunities to be well informed about the world through radio and television and to exploit these opportunities.[4]

It is expected that the population of Africa will increase from the present 1.2 billion people to 2.4 billion people in the next 35 years. The main reason is Africa's current lack of economic and social development, which could motivate families to have fewer children. This is due to factors such as industrialization, increased educational levels for both men and women, and family planning programs. Family planning programs are developed only to a limited extent because of weak state formation and ideological resistance. The life expectancy is now 58 years for men and 60 for women, mainly due to Western medicine. In 35 years, every fifth inhabitant on Earth will be African.

Nigeria will be especially populous, with an estimated 250 million inhabitants in 2050—the populations of England, France, Germany, and Italy combined—a rise in population for Nigeria from 40 million people in 1950. The strong growth in the population in Africa and the Middle East contributes to continued poverty and unemployment, which can lead to migration. Religious and political division also contributes. What is epoch-making, however, is the strong growth in communication and transport, which enables people to be aware of better standards of living in other countries and the ease of traveling to them.

Nielson points out that 49 of the least developed countries in Africa have had duty-free and quota-free access to the European Union (EU) market for all categories of goods except weapons since 2001. He finds that liberalization of the local African markets is not part of the problem but rather part of the solution.

Individually, the economies are too small and too undiversified to be the basis of sustainable growth. He finds increased trade between neighbors in Africa's regions a necessary part of partnerships, for example in the East African Partnership.[5]

The 16 sub-Saharan countries are expected to grow at a rate of more than 6.0% according to the International Monetary Fund (IMF), and this growth is expected to come from all sectors of the economy. The growth is expected to come from different exporters and in different commodities, unlike in the past, when single exporters or single commodities accounted for most of the income accumulation of the high-level political and economic elite. There has also been a complete mind shift in how governments operate and how willing they are to welcome investors.[6]

Many African countries are small economies. Somalia, for example, has the same state budget as a middle-sized municipality in Denmark of about 20,000 inhabitants. In a discussion paper, McCormick researched eight clusters in Kenya and other African countries, but she characterized only two of them as clusters with internal structure and wider market access. The rest of the clusters were microenterprises selling in localized markets.[7]

In Kenya, the primary sectors (agriculture, fishery, and plants) are important but not always high tech. There is demand for cooling technology and solar energy. It could be the start of a cluster. A big wind park was under construction between 2015 and 2017 by the Danish wind turbine maker Vestas at Lake Turkana in Kenya. It was designed to add 15% to Kenya's electricity capacity. To build the wind park in a remote Kenyan windy area, the consortium had to build more than 250 km of roads for the wind farm. It is the largest single private sector investment in Kenya's history.[8]

Another recent success story is a railway built by the Chinese linking Addis Ababa, the capital of Ethiopia, with the port of Djibouti on the Indian Ocean. It is a railway of 470 miles and cost 3.4 billion US dollars to build. It is a huge investment for landlocked Ethiopia. A journey that formerly required 1,500 trucks daily can now be made by the railroad, and the travel time has been reduced from 2 days to 12 hours. Travelers can now see greenhouses growing flowers for export and factories with Turkish, Indian, and Chinese ownership along the trail. Foreign investment in Ethiopia has grown from 108 million US dollars in 2009 to an estimated 2 billion US dollars in 2016.[9]

Other Chinese investments in Africa include steel production in Nigeria, Kohl's yoga pants, Levi's jeans, Reebok athletic wear production in Lesotho, and drug production in Ethiopia. In fact, private Chinese companies now make more than 150 investments in Africa, up from only 2 in 2000. These companies primarily employ local workers. There is a supply-side effect from the rising wages in China with wage increases of 12% annually since 2001 resulting in productivity-adjusted manufacturing wages nearly tripled from 2004 to 2014. The wage increases will push Chinese workers out of low-skilled manufacturing jobs, which can be taken over by other developing countries of which Africa is a good candidate. The

Danish Foreign Aid Perspectives on African Economies

Danish developmental aid was originally part of the common work within the Foreign Ministry, but in the late 1960s, developmental aid became more professionalized with specialists. Danish foreign aid, since its inception in 1953, has been split one-half for unilateral aid and one-half for bilateral aid. For Danish companies, unilateral aid was advantageous. There were, however, disadvantages for Africa, according to this conclusion in 1989 of 17 evaluations of Danish unilateral aid: The technology delivered was too advanced, too expensive, too capital intensive rather than work intensive, and the target groups poorly defined. For this reason, receiving countries preferred investments in physical infrastructure in general to investments into directly productive sectors. Today, only about a quarter of Danish foreign aid is granted as bilateral aid. It is perceived that unilateral aid is often more efficient. Institutions such as the United Nations are often more professional than national foreign aid organizations. There are also cost savings from not using resources for project selection, implementation, and control and by funding unilateral organizations before national ones.[11]

The evaluation of DANIDA's *B2B Program* lists some experiences from the DANIDA *B2B Program* 2006–2011—there is a risk that the objective to establish partnership programs overrules the main objective of poverty reduction; the program has had too little focus on the broader effects of company funding, such as removing bottlenecks, market information, logistics, and technology.[12] Bigger focus on corporate social responsibility (CSR) should be taken; the projects within the agricultural sector has had the biggest development effects; the recommended structure of the partnerships has been the joint venture form, but this should be broadened out to other forms of partnerships; small and medium-sized enterprises can be as effective as larger, more robust companies; matchmaking seems to be the most efficient way to fund partnerships—better than project support; there are success stories in both attractive investment countries and less attractive ones; the *B2B Program* did not contain mechanisms for broadening knowledge, technology, and experiences between companies; equality measures for women were too little used in the program; the evaluation of the effects of the *B2B Program* was not efficient mainly because of an overload of reporting for the companies involved. For future programs, it is recommended to make the reporting simpler and more outcome focused. Cooperation with the IFU is recommended.

The Danish government decided in 2014 to suspend the two facilities, DANIDA Business Partnerships and Business Project Development, to get them in line with EU regulations.[13] IFU has increasingly been involved in investments in the Danish government's African focus countries, and this has meant that a natural network has been established by the small and medium-sized enterprises involved.

78 Jens Graff

The Danish government thinks that earlier there was a disharmony between the demand of the African consumer and the supply from Danish marketers. Danish goods and services were typically much too expensive for African circumstances, and considerable adaptation of products and services should take place.[14]

African Economic and Social Perspectives

African Economic Outlook for 2015 published jointly by the African Development Bank Group, Organisation for Economic Co-operation and Development (OECD) Development Centre, and United Nations Development Programme (UNDP) in its special issue titled 'Regional Development and Spatial Inclusion,' focused on several topics including alternative strategic options for Africa's transformation. It balances strengths and opportunities facing many African countries balanced with economic and social opportunities and threats. The general impressions are that African countries have potential economic and social opportunities but are confronted by weak institutions. Strong institutions and governments are needed to provide the education and skills the growing population needs to function in world markets. It also focused on regional development and spatial inclusion and concludes that multi-sectoral, place-based, and participatory development strategies can contribute to unlocking the potential of Africa's diverse regions.

Urbanization improves the conditions for Africa's economic development through four main channels: (1) increased agricultural productivity and rural development, (2) industrialization, (3) services-led growth, and (4) more foreign direct investment (FDI) in African cities. Urbanization is changing the labor and food markets as it creates upward demand, for food production in Africa, increases efficiency in post-farm segments, and transforms the rural on-farm and non-farm economy.[15]

In the Executive Summary of Challenges of African Growth, the authors draw six key lessons to inform the growth strategies in sub-Saharan Africa: (1) African countries' growth experience is extremely varied and episodic; (2) although lower levels of investment are important for explaining Africa's slower growth, it is the slower productivity growth that more sharply distinguishes African growth performance from that of the rest of the world; (3) consistent with much of the cross-country growth analysis, evidence from the literature reviewed earlier suggests that policy and governance matter a great deal for growth; (4) overcoming disadvantages arising from geographic isolation and fragmentation, as well as natural resource dependence, will be necessary if Africa is to close the growth gap with other regions; (5) growth of trading partners' economies has a very powerful influence; and (6) the analysis points to a very large role played by the delayed demographic transition in Africa in explaining its relatively slower growth performance.[16]

The authors point at four pillars that are critical to but not comprehensive for investments to accelerate growth: (1) improving the investment climate, (2) infrastructure, (3) innovation, and (4) institutional capacity. They claim, for example, that African countries can make a huge leap forward over antiquated technology by exploiting the newest information, communication, and technological advantages as late starters. Each African country faces challenges and opportunities, which is why the recommended strategies must be adapted to the specific country context.[17]

The 2013 Chinese initiative One Belt One Road will provide a great boost to the world economy, including the African economy. Adjusted for inflation, it is at least 12 times the size of the Marshall Plan, the history-changing U.S. program that helped rebuild Western Europe from rubble after World War II.[18] The projects are organized in the recently formed Asian Infrastructure Investment Bank (AIIB), China's answer to the World Bank; its activities are expected to reach 100 billion US dollars annually over the next decade. China has earmarked as much as 3 trillion US dollars equivalent for it. An example of the investment is General Electric's sale of 60 sets of wind turbines to a Chinese partner for a project in Kenya.

The General Agreement on Tariffs and Trade (GATT) and its follower since 1995 World Trade Organization (WTO) have been very beneficial for global trade by reducing tariffs and non-tariff barriers, but in vital agrarian areas, African producers have been exempted from participating in global trade, for example, in cotton and sugar. On the positive side has been the Lomé Convention, an agreement which gave the poorest African countries tariff-free access to world markets.

For decades, Africa has received funds from international organizations including the United Nations, the World Bank, and national foreign developmental aid organizations. The outcome measured in economic wealth has been meager. Why is this so? Why aren't many more investors interested in investing in Africa? The climate is favorable for many crops, and the continent is rich in raw materials. It has a young population, so why isn't Africa rather than China producing the world's consumer goods? The answer is complex. There is no single cause. Explanations include bad politicians, corruption, violence, lack of institutions, and minimal public or private motivation. Whatever the reasons are, probably a combination of management and foreign government funds would drive economic development in the right direction.

Riskær thinks that Africa has started growth based on African investments during the last 10 years. The help has come from rapidly developing countries such as China, India, Korea, and Brazil. Also, Russia and the oil-rich Middle East countries are increasingly present in Africa. He believes that part of this success is the unconventional way these countries have funded Africa. Their interests primarily have been Africa's resources. These countries and their businesses created a dynamism that is quite valuable for the African economy. He believes that the combination of developmental aid and targeted promotion of private investments could be decisive in ensuring fast economic and social development in Africa. He argues, however, that Western donors' demand of fully developed democracy in the receiving countries as a precondition of funding is neither realistic nor

80 Jens Graff

defensible. He thinks that the economic development in China and Korea has shown that the reverse sequence is more natural and sustainable.[19]

Developing countries new to giving developmental aid rather than receiving it are often better attuned to what developing countries need and how the aid should be managed. Korea is an example of a donor new to the world market that has been renowned for its assertive way of helping. Gården thinks that Danish farmers can be as successful in China as they are in Central and Eastern Europe where they have built up big pig farms and subsequent agricultural exports. The same could be done in Africa with building up a whole agrarian society with pig and milk cattle farms, slaughterhouses, and agricultural companies.[20]

The establishment of industrial clusters in Africa would accelerate economic development in the regions in which they are established and broaden the development to the whole country. People moving into the middle class and above traditionally demand influence on political decisions that will provide a basis for democratic development in the country.

A charter city is a local area selected by the host country to be managed by outside government bodies or large companies. The idea of charter cities could potentially create growth in industrial clusters. Charter cities represent large-scale investment, which only very large companies or foreign government bodies can manage and control. It would be interesting if, for example, DANIDA allocated most or all of its developmental aid to charter cities. Imagine also if the United Nations distributed its development funds to be managed by appointed countries in the developed world. Germany would, for example, oversee Ghana and be part of a steering group for Ghana that included Ghanaian officials and managed development projects in Ghana. After, say, 5 years, the baton would go to another country, perhaps Australia, to continue in the steering group for Ghana.

The railway from Addis Ababa to Djibouti recently built by the Chinese has already caused numerous companies to establish themselves along the railroad. Infrastructure is, indeed, a generator of growth. In this example, the railway also brought electricity and communication with it thus further opening the area for the enterprise.

Brautigam concluded, 'Although there had been numerous attempts to invest big in Africa, the majority of projects had either failed or simply had not been implemented.'[21] China would not feed Africa and would not exploit African resources simply because it would be too expensive to take these resources home to China—mainly due to infrastructure reasons. Infrastructure comes first; production later. Maybe the Chinese investment in the Addis Ababa-Djibouti railroad is a successful forerunner for this? Maybe the Chinese Belt and Road initiative will take off rapidly to the benefit of Africa?

Formation of Regional Industrial Clusters

Porter introduced the traditional cluster theory to explain, from a historical perspective, how different industrial environments influenced the competitiveness of industries in the United States.[22] The author summarized his findings in a model consisting of six factors: (1) factor conditions (the cost and quality of inputs), (2) demand conditions (the sophistication of local customers), (3) the context for firm strategy and rivalry (the nature and intensity of local competition), (4) related and supporting industries (the local extent and sophistication of suppliers and related industries), (5) government (government can influence each of the previous four determinants of competitiveness), and (6) chance (occurrences outside of a firm's control). These factors interact in creating a stimulating and dynamic business environment. Porter called a cluster the manifestation of the diamond at work. The discussion of growth through clustering will be made in this framework.

Factor Conditions

In *African Economic Outlook 2015*, the outlook for industrialization is good, as the people pyramid is young and almost 30 million additional jobs must be created in Africa. The outlook pointed to several factors as threats to a progressive industrialization process: the lack of skills and education in a still more technologically demanding world.[23]

Using Africa's natural resources is obvious. Africa has around 24% or 6 million hectares of the world's arable land and an abundance of the sun for solar cell energy; these both mean that it has the conditions for green growth. It has the people, land, and conditions for green energy, so its future should be bright.

In the first decade of the 2000s, African exports to Europe doubled, exports to emerging economies quadrupled, and exports to China alone increased by a factor of 12. Commodity demand was high, and prices soared.[24]

Demand Conditions

According to AfDB 2011, Africa's combined consumer spending was 680 billion US dollars in 2008 and is projected to 2.2 trillion US dollars in 2030 (*AEO 2015* p. xvii). Consumers' desire to consume is evident all over the world, especially because the influence of television and the Internet has heightened the awareness of consumer products and upscale lifestyles. Consumers are quick to demand better and more diverse quality products the moment their incomes justify it.

African Economic Outlook 2016 regards urbanization as a megatrend to strongly transform African societies and thinks this development can turn African cities and towns into engines of growth and sustainable development for the continent. *AEO 2016* expects new opportunities for improving economic and social development for the continent.[25]

Firm Strategy and Rivalry

African Economic Outlook 2015 estimates that African economies will continue to struggle in the world market regarding costs, quality of goods and services, and production potential. Although African companies increasingly participate in global value chains, the impact on business development and job creation in proper companies has been limited. This is probably caused by relatively low education and skill levels of African workers compared with world suppliers combined with increasing automation of world production.[26]

Related and Supporting Industries

The extent and sophistication of suppliers and related industries is low especially in geographically remote areas of Africa. This makes it difficult for industrial clusters to emerge. Urbanization in Africa has, so far, occurred without industrialization. The migration from agriculture to cities has not resulted in higher economies of agglomeration and knowledge spillovers in city economies. Farmland has not profited either, as an increased openness to cheap food imports has hampered the farmlands' ability to supply their products to cities.[27]

Government

AEO 2015 reports that many countries that recorded growth below 2.0% during the period 1986–1999 suffered from civil wars, military coups, or social unrest, whereas in the period 2001–2014, violent conflict receded overall and political stability improved, although some countries still experienced political unrest.[28]

Some countries have promoted structural transformations from traditional toward more productive activities, for example, the resource-poor countries of Ethiopia and Rwanda, which have attained high annual growth rates of 8.0% or above.[29]

Chance

Companies can be established by chance in the sense that an entrepreneur starts something successfully and progress from where he lives. Successful Danish companies such as Danfoss and Grundfos are examples of this. They were both established in remote areas of Denmark and grew to major international successes with their headquarters still in the region of their establishment. African entrepreneurship can happen everywhere in Africa and be the basis for successful companies, as *AEO 2015* also concluded. The *AEO 2015* focuses on regional development and spatial inclusion. It concludes that multi-sectoral, place-based, and participatory development strategies can contribute to unlocking the potential of Africa's diverse regions.[30]

Companies in a cluster's geographical area cooperate and use each other for selfish reasons, but at the same time, benefit the whole (like Adam Smith's invisible hand). A successful producer needs tooling, components, and services, which innovative people start to produce nearby to be close to the successful producer.

As a result, supplier and buyer cross-fertilize each other, and a positive spiral evolves. Knowledge, relationships, and motivation are key ingredients in cluster formation. Eventually, the cluster reaches critical mass, productivity rises, and its competitiveness improves.

In an African context, Porter's opinion on the prosperity of any state or nation is that it is productivity that matters—not exports or natural resources. He thinks that the microeconomic foundations for competition will ultimately determine productivity and competitiveness. Natural resources, however, tend to stimulate formation of geographically remote industrial clusters (GRICs), especially if these resources can be used in industrial processes, for example, lumber, pulp, wine, or ethanol production. Regional universities represent unique core knowledge to support the formation of GRICs. The abundance of labor in rural areas represents new approaches to GRIC development. Also, Internet penetration in rural areas makes the GRICs less remote for international marketers in a communication sense.[31]

The history of business shows that companies working together in networks or clusters and cooperating with universities have better growth opportunities than other companies. It happens through the transference of new knowledge, methods, and ideas. In particular, companies that are already internationalized can contribute through their international network. Steno defines five basic categories of clusters or networks: (1) matchmaking and knowledge sharing, for example, through workshops and professional networks, (2) concrete cooperation projects, for example, innovation projects with knowledge institutions, (3) competence development, for example, courses and discussions, (4) communications, for example, conferences and seminars, and (5) internationalization, for example, cooperation with foreign clusters and knowledge institutions.[32]

The Internet, breakthroughs in container transport, and globalization have made most markets accessible. Today, the qualified demand that makes it easier for clusters to develop is not located in any one place but can arise anywhere on the globe. It is, therefore, important for local companies to look internationally for cooperation partners.

These findings are consistent with a Norwegian study of small and medium-sized companies. Researchers interviewed a sample with 1,604 small and medium-sized enterprises in Norway's five biggest cities. They found that the interaction of firms within regional clusters or with other national partners had a negligible effect on innovation, whereas interaction with international partners tends to move innovation and production of more radical innovations. They also found that open-minded managers had a greater diversity of international partners and relied more on international pipelines had a propensity to produce more radical innovations.[33]

Closing Comments

The following reservations of the DANIDA evaluations on their earlier subsidy programs are repeated here: small and medium-sized enterprises can be as good as larger more robust companies; matchmaking seems to be the most efficient way to fund partnerships—better than project support; the *B2B Program* did not contain mechanisms for broadening knowledge, technology, and experiences between companies; and cooperation with the IFU is recommended.

The following activities can be recommended to address these concerns for small and medium-sized enterprise growth in Africa:

Network Building

DANIDA could support network building between African prospects and institutions and Danish companies and institutions by making meetings free of charge. The Danish company Nordecon organizes network meetings (Africa Innovation Network) for those interested in Africa that seem to be valuable for participants. Similarly, the Confederation of Danish Industries (DI) is organizing seminars on Africa. Both Nordecon and DI demand membership or non-membership payment for participation, which is an obstacle, especially for small and medium-sized enterprises.

Knowledge Dissemination

Knowledge and experiences of Danish collaboration in Africa can be disseminated by, for example, white papers from DANIDA (or some other organization) to interested prospects in Denmark and Africa. This could be done in a weekly newsletter format.

Collaboration With the Investment Fund for Developing Countries (IFU)

A major part of DANIDA's yearly funding should be channeled through IFU. IFU is known to be an effective executive arm of Danish funding. They operate on the basis of business feasibility studies and invest as an intermediate partner.

Appoint Growth Ambassadors for Africa

DANIDA should appoint growth ambassadors for ferreting out opportunities in the African market that Danish companies/institutions could use.

Allocate Business School PhD Scholarships for African Students for Doing Research Projects for Africa

This could be in the range of five scholarships per year. The studies should take place jointly in Africa and in Denmark. Their home university/business school should be in Africa to strengthen their African ties.

Establish Special Africa Classes for Business

College studies at the business academy and bachelor level study lines, such as business, technology, innovation, and IT. Similarly, classes should be provided at the business school level for Masters of Science and MBA. They could be organized on a dual degree basis (joint degree from African university and Danish business school). All students would be contractually obliged to return to Africa after completion of their studies in Denmark. The hallmark of business academy courses is their close connection to companies as their theses are prepared for specific companies and their market issues. All these should be prepared for African market issues.

Innovation Lofts

Ten seats should be sponsored at innovation lofts in Denmark for prospective African entrepreneurs with business ideas. IFU could do the screening process.

To facilitate economic growth in Africa on a more aggregate level, the following activities are recommended:

Strengthen Education Inside Africa

For primary school pupils, government budgets should be increased and private education providers should be encouraged to participate. They are not always welcomed by governments and teachers' unions, but 'rather than crack down on low-cost private schools, governments should welcome them.[34]

A business college education should be widely supported from the lowest to the highest level. The system should be designed with a progression in the curricula and built-in merit transfer to the next level of education. Vocational business training should be favored as well.

Investors should support programs delivered as distance learning programs with centrally designed courses fit for specific curricula for individuals or course providers to use. Lecturers could then focus more on blended learning and tutoring.

Enhance a Mind-Set of National Pride

U.S. President John F. Kennedy urged citizens to ask not what the country could do for them, but what they could do for their country. It is currently easier for young people to emigrate rather than stay in their country and help develop it. That outgoing traffic is neither sustainable nor fair. Societies such as China, Vietnam, and Korea have developed gradually by their workforce and have done it surprisingly well in only a few decades.

86 Jens Graff

Invest in Solar Panels

It seems that solar panels can be a cost-efficient way to distribute electricity to people. Electricity can be collected centrally in solar panel parks and then distributed by the grid or collection can be decentralized by solar panels for individual consumer families. American investor Warren Buffett is a proponent of solar and wind power at utility scale produced at large plants connected to the power grid, whereas Tesla founder and solar investor Elon Musk favors a 'distributed network' model in which homeowners and companies generate their own energy.[35]

Table 3.1 shows how all the recommended activities address the factors of the Porter Diamond. The activities are all intended to strengthen motivation, skill, and competencies for participating in business life in Africa.

For the diamond to work, it requires management. Here IFU can come in, with its strong management experience in developing countries. Networking will increase the knowledge of growth ambassadors and business college students. These students can then write theses about African companies or Danish companies interested in Africa. It will further increase awareness, which will create

TABLE 3.1 The Recommended Activities Would Strengthen the Porter Diamond

Porter's Diamond Activities	Factor Conditions	Demand Conditions	Firm Strategy, Structure, and Rivalry	Related and Supporting Industries	Government	Chance
Network building	*	*	*	*	**	*
Knowledge dissemination	*	*	*	*	*	*
IFU participation	*	*	***	*	***	*
Growth ambassadors	*	*	*	*	***	*
PhD scholarships	*	*	*	*	***	*
Business college scholarships	*	*	**	*	***	*
Innovation lofts	*	*	**	**	***	*
Strengthen education inside Africa	***	***	**	**	***	*
Enhance mind-set of national pride	***	***	*	*	**	*
Invest in solar panels	***	***	**	**	***	*
Charter cities	***	***	***	***	***	***

Legend: *: supports minor/long term; **: supports medium; ***: supports strongly
Source: Author, 2017

knowledge, interest, and finally actions to generate business activities in Africa. The latest decades have produced high growth rates for many African economies. The 'how to approach Africa' question is still a factor to overcome, but companies' successes in Africa will soon create enthusiasm and lead to a positive spiral for new African ventures.

Africa is rich in natural resources and young people. Africa needs education, infrastructure, and management in order to use these production factors together. Consequently, this is where the focus should be and developmental aid focused. Africa can get into the same development cycle as did Japan, South East Asia, and China, where local entrepreneurs partnered with investors from developed countries and created new businesses. They created a trade cycle situation, where local entrepreneurs evolved into effective producers, which could compete with imports and finally be competitive on the global market. The still-rising production costs in China will free low-skilled production in China, which African entrepreneurs can pick up.

Foreign governments could fund successful domestic companies for establishing productive subsidiaries in selected African countries. They should produce under foreign government economic guarantees. The aim is to get the ball rolling. If the invited companies are supplementing themselves after cluster thinking, these greenfield operations could be hubs of growth with long-range importance for African workers. They will achieve competencies and get know-how for use in innovative new businesses. Newly developed countries such as South Korea and China are especially relevant in this development, as they have remembrance and recent experiences from their home countries. They often accept less than perfect solutions to problems and bootstrap the development.

Danish funding through DANIDA should be reorganized along the lines described here, that is, in a more direct and hands-on way and primarily directed toward companies and businesses in general. Business relations and the business they can generate are forerunners of economic development. Here, the focus should be in the first fragile decades of development. Ethnocentric values of donor countries should be dampened. Projects in Africa should be kept simple with not too advanced technology and with simple administrative processes. The focus should be on human resource development. The development can evolve in a bootstrapping manner, where companies and organizations learn on the go.

The most advanced investment should be in charter cities. Imagine if growth in these cities could take the shape of Hong Kong or Singapore. Singapore was founded in 1965, and after only a few decades, it had developed to an astonishing level and is today in the top 10 of economies per capita.

Whether the recommendations in this chapter are politically feasible is unknown. Danish funding of developing countries has traditionally focused on ethical and human rights issues and basic preconditions for human life and only in recent decades on mutual business activities between donor and receiver. Further research could reveal if business activities pay off better in a developmental

88 Jens Graff

sense. The recommended activities should be evaluated after 1 year, 5 years, and 10 years. Motivational, interest, and performance factors should be evaluated.

Rosenberg interviewed policy makers and had dialogues with executives responsible for African strategy and operations in sub-Saharan Africa—the 48 African countries below the Sahara Desert. She found seven prevalent myths that skew companies' perception of doing business there:

Myth #1: There is no competitive urgency to build a presence in sub-Saharan Africa.

Myth #2: Sub-Saharan Africa's growth is all about natural resources and consumer spending.

Myth #3: Fast economic growth means quick returns.

Myth #4: Sub-Saharan Africa is too volatile and unpredictable.

Myth #5: Sub-Saharan African markets can be prioritized merely by using data.

Myth #6: Relying solely on distributors is a sustainable Africa strategy.

Myth #7: South Africa is the natural hub from which to manage a sub-Saharan Africa business.

Rosenberg concludes,

> Companies should accelerate their expansion into Sub-Saharan Africa as the region continues to grow, becomes increasingly competitive, and is unlikely to be derailed despite sporadic volatility. To succeed in the continent, executives must develop long-term plans while remaining prepared to weather short-term disruptions.[36]

Refuting these seven myths would be wonderful separate research topics for future studies.

Notes

1 Gunnar Myrdal, "Relief Instead of Development Aid," *Intereconomics* 16 (1981): 86–89.
2 Sven Riskær, *Afrikas Vej Fra Bistand Til Velstand?* (Copenhagen: Handelshøjskolens Forlag, 2011).
3 George Tesar and Jan Bodin, *Marketing Management in Geographically Remote Industrial Clusters* (Singapore: World Scientific, 2013).
4 Klaus Winkel, *Hvorfor Er Det Så Svært For Afrika?* (Odense: Geografforlaget, 2007).
5 P. Nielson, "Afrika Er Ikke En Viljeløs Kliet," *Berlingske Debat*, January 26, 2015.
6 David Malingha Doya and Mike Cohen, "New Hope in Africa," *Bloomberg Business*, November 6, 2014, 50.
7 Dorothy McCormick, "Enterprise Clusters in Africa: On the Way to Industrialisation?" Discussion Paper, Institute of Development Studies, University of Nairobi, 1998.
8 Vestas Wind Systems A/S, Company material, 2016.
9 Paul Schemm, "New Chinese-Built Railroad Opens in Ethiopia," *Washington Post*, October 5, 2016, accessed July 13, 2017, http://wapo.st/2dsjY42.

Stimulation of Entrepreneurship **89**

10 Irene Yuan Sun, "The World's Next Great Manufacturing Center," *Harvard Business Review* 95 (2017): 122–129.
11 Klaus Winkel, *Udvikling—Om Danmarks Bistand* (Frederiksberg: Frydenlund, 2014).
12 DANIDA, "Evaluering af DANIDAS Business-to-Business Program 2006–2011" Evaluering Resumé 2014.5, accessed July 13, 2017, http://um.dk/en/~/media/UM/Danish-site/Documents/Danida/Resultater/Eval/201405resume.pdf.
13 Ibid.
14 Riskær.
15 African Economic Outlook 2016, *Special Theme: Sustainable Cities and Structural Transformation* (Paris: OECD Publishing).
16 Benno Ndulu et al., *Challenges of African Growth Opportunities, Constraints and Strategic Directions* (Washington, 2007), accessed July 13, 2017, http://siteresources.worldbank.org/AFRICAEXT/Resources/AFR_Growth_Advance_Edition.pdf
17 Ibid.
18 Scott Cendrowski, "China Spreads the Wealth Around," *Fortune*, December 15, 2016.
19 Riskær.
20 Hugo Gården, "Vi Har Brug For Chinese Dynamite," *Berlingske Politiko*, December 13, 2014.
21 Deborah Brautigam, *Will Africa Feed China?* (Oxford: Oxford University Press, 2015).
22 Michael E. Porter, *The Competitive Advantage of Nations* (New York: Free Press, 1990).
23 *African Economic Outlook 2015*, "Regional Development and Spatial Inclusion" (Paris: OECD Publishing).
24 Ibid., p. x.
25 *African Economic Outlook 2016*.
26 *African Economic Outlook 2015*, p. xi.
27 *African Economic Outlook 2015*, pp. xvi–xvii.
28 *African Economic Outlook 2015*, p. x.
29 Ibid., p. x.
30 Ibid., p. xvii.
31 Tesar and Bodin.
32 Carsten Steno, "Virksomheder Kommer I Front Via Netværk," *Berlingske Business*, January 14, 2015.
33 Rune Dahl Fitjar and Andrés Rodríguez-Pose, "Interaction and Innovation Across Different Sectors: Findings from Norwegian City-Regions," *Regional Studies* 49 (2015): 818–833. doi:10.1080/00343404.2015.1016415.
34 "Emerging Markets Should Welcome Low-Cost Private Schools." *The Economist*, January 28, 2017, p. 13.
35 Stephen Gandel and Katie Fehrenbacher, "Warren Buffett's All-In Clean-Energy Bet," *Fortune*, December 15, 2016.
36 Anna Rosenberg, "7 Myths About Doing Business in Sub-Saharan Africa," *Harvard Business Review* (July 3, 2015), accessed July 13, 2017, https://hbr.org/2015/07/7-myths-about-doing-business-in-sub-saharan-africa.

Bibliography

African Economic Outlook. *Regional Development and Spatial Inclusion*. Paris: OECD Publishing, 2015.
African Economic Outlook. *Special Theme: Sustainable Cities and Structural Transformation*. Paris: OECD Publishing, 2016.
Brautigam, Deborah. *Will Africa Feed China?* Oxford: Oxford University Press, 2015.
Cendrowski, Scott. "China Spreads the Wealth Around." *Fortune*, December 15, 2016.

DANIDA. "Evaluering af DANIDA Business-to-Business Program 2006–2011." Evaluering Resumé 2014.5. Accessed July 13, 2017. http://um.dk/en/~/media/UM/Danish-site/Documents/Danida/Resultater/Eval/201405resume.pdf.

Doya, David Malingha, and Mike Cohen. "New Hope in Africa." *Bloomberg Business*, November 6, 2014, 50.

"Emerging Markets Should Welcome Low-Cost Private Schools." *The Economist*, January 28, 2017, p. 13.

Fitjar, Rune Dahl, and Andrés Rodríguez-Pose. "Interaction and Innovation Across Different Sectors: Findings from Norwegian City-Regions." *Regional Studies* 49 (2015): 818–833. doi:10.1080/00343404.2015.1016415.

Gandel, Stephen, and Katie Fehrenbacher. "Warren Buffett's All-In Clean-Energy Bet." *Fortune*, December 15, 2016.

Gården, Hugo. "Vi Har Brug For Chinese Dynamite." *Berlingske Politiko*, December 13, 2014.

McCormick, Dorothy. "Enterprise Clusters in Africa: On the Way to Industrialisation?" Discussion Paper. Institute of Development Studies, University of Nairobi, 1998.

Myrdal, Gunnar. "Relief Instead of Development Aid." *Intereconomics* 16 (1981): 86–89.

Ndulu, Benno et al. *Challenges of African Growth Opportunities, Constraints and Strategic Directions.* Washington: World Bank, 2007. Accessed July 13, 2017. http://siteresources. worldbank.org/AFRICAEXT/Resources/AFR_Growth_Advance_Edition.pdf.

Nielson, P. "Afrika Er Ikke En Viljeløs Kliet." *Berlingske Debat*, January 26, 2015.

Porter, Michael E. *The Competitive Advantage of Nations.* New York: Free Press, 1990.

Riskær, Sven. *Afrikas Vej Fra Bistand Til Velstand?* Copenhagen: Handelshøjskolens Forlag, 2011.

Rosenberg, Anna. "7 Myths About Doing Business in Sub-Saharan Africa." *Harvard Business Review*, July 3, 2015. Accessed July 13, 2017. https://hbr.org/2015/07/7-myths-about-doing-business-in-sub-saharan-africa.

Schemm, Paul. "New Chinese-Built Railroad Opens in Ethiopia." *Washington Post*, October 5, 2016. Accessed July 13, 2017, http://wapo.st/2dsjY42.

Steno, Carsten. "Virksomheder Kommer I Front Via Netværk." *Berlingske Business*, January 14, 2015.

Sun, Irene Yuan. "The World's Next Great Manufacturing Center." *Harvard Business Review* 95 (2017): 122–129.

Tesar, George, and Jan Bodin. *Marketing Management in Geographically Remote Industrial Clusters.* Singapore: World Scientific, 2013.

Vestas Wind Systems A/S. Company material. 2016.

Winkel, Klaus. *Hvorfor Er Det Så Svært For Afrika?* Odense: Geografforlaget, 2007.

Winkel, Klaus. *Udvikling—Om Danmarks Bistand* Frederiksberg: Frydenlund, 2014.

4

SOCIAL MARKETING AND HEALTH CARE

George Tesar

Wireless communication services and the Internet are changing social structures, stimulating evolution of the middle class, and generally reorganizing the way many African societies operate. These changes are reflected in how individuals communicate with other individuals, how they interact with social institutions, and how they communicate over social media. Wireless communication services and the Internet offer opportunities for individuals to communicate with others over long distances to express concerns and articulate social needs in a new way, and often directly to social institutions, which they could not reach in the past. Individuals can communicate directly with government officials, local administrators, and service providers such as hospitals, educational institutions, and local schools. The modern form of communication is a two-way process, frequently based on willingness, trust, and openness, especially in societies where communication technology precedes cultural and social changes.

Mobile telephones and related communication devices along with the Internet offer unprecedented opportunities for entrepreneurs who communicating with customers, clients, suppliers, social institutions, and public entities. Entrepreneurs have the ability to identify innovative opportunities, initiate start-up operations, and build small enterprises. Entrepreneurs can communicate over vast distances and gather information from sources worldwide. They can develop innovative products, offer unique services, and assist with social initiatives. In emerging economies, there are typically two types of entrepreneurs; both types provide platforms for market and social development. The first type starts enterprises for profit, whereas the second type forms not-for-profit initiatives. Wireless communication accelerates development of opportunities fundamentally necessary for economic and social growth for both types of entrepreneurs.

Modern communication capabilities provide flexibility for entrepreneurial start-ups in finding the information they need to manage and operate their ventures and reach their markets. For social entrepreneurs, wireless communication and the Internet are channels for social interactions, especially in rural areas where physical infrastructures are minimal but wireless transmissions are possible. Social entrepreneurs may provide services even across borders because their intangibility is without the traditional bureaucratic difficulties such as tariffs, custom taxes, other challenging deterrents to trade (see Example 1 at the end of this chapter).

An increasing number of entrepreneurs in several African countries are developing and managing of new social initiatives. Many of these initiatives are in health care, delivery of medical services, distribution of pharmaceutical products and services, and in other socially focused initiatives. In urban and rural areas across Africa, social entrepreneurs take on environmental challenges that were not possible before wireless communication options or the Internet was available. Recent economic and social developments suggest that the new generation of social entrepreneurs formed around the new communication options and the Internet have a better chance of succeeding than many large-scale initiatives introduced by governmental agencies or international non-governmental organizations have had in the past.

Social entrepreneurs who operate in the broad social space and cut across public and private markets frequently share initiatives with citizens and let them participate in innovative ventures. Social entrepreneurs provide services designed to improve discussions among citizens, institutions, and social agencies. Such initiatives are formulated to improve understanding of how society benefits and builds consensus to increase social welfare, especially in rural communities. Most social entrepreneurs recognize that even the most problematic societal objectives can be solved in the context of social marketing. In many situations, they were educated or trained abroad and bring new approaches to their home communities. Social marketing is becoming one of the new approaches.

Social marketing is a managerial tool that is relevant in both private and public entrepreneurial initiatives. It provides a managerial framework for analysis and decision making. Social marketing can be used to build consensus. It is a relatively new concept useful in many fast-growing African economies and represents a new evolution in building small entrepreneurial initiatives that bring community and individual efforts together for purposes of building social consensus, improving social services, and stabilizing social development and socio-economic growth. More specifically, social marketing provides a new means of communication and information dissemination to the public necessary to understand and share socially beneficial entrepreneurial initiatives.

One industry within the rapidly evolving entrepreneurial climate in several African countries based on the notion, concepts, and applications of social marketing in creation, delivery, and support of information is the health care industry, mostly due to improved communication systems and the Internet.

The objective of this presentation is to provide information and to explain social marketing and to relate social marketing to the health care industry. The health care industry and health care–related issues are emerging throughout Africa on the platform of telecommunication and Internet-based resources and rapidly reaching an emerging middle class in several African countries, such as Ghana, Tanzania, and Zambia, which have an ongoing discussion of growing a middle class (see Example 2 at the end of this chapter).

Implications of Social Marketing

Since its formulation in the mid-1960s, social marketing has evolved into a useful set of tools suitable for resolving issues, facing challenges, and solving problems in broad areas of societal concerns. Although social marketing is an extension of traditional marketing, its methodologies, concepts, theories, and applications are beneficial not only for understanding and managing markets but also for meeting societal needs.

Recent socially relevant environmental developments, broad communication capabilities, and the Internet are leading to adjustments and modifications in social behavior and, at different stages of life, have compelled individuals to change their personal behavior. Many individual changes in social behavior have been generated by environmental pressures resulting from changes in economic conditions, technological innovations, spontaneously surfacing and changing social forces, or rapidly changing lifestyles. Broad communication capabilities cut across national borders and bring individuals, groups, or communities closer together. The Internet allows individuals, wherever they are, to explore international lifestyles and provides the ability to purchase products or services previously not available to them. These developments produce social consumption discontinuities, resulting in alternative choices for individuals, and sometimes lead to social discontent in individuals' lives.

Depending on individuals' inherent propensity to cope with social discontent, instability, and discontinuity, and depending on the strength of these forces, some individuals are able to optimize their decisions within the context of bounded rationality. However, individuals whose abilities to cope with a variety of social pressures are limited tend to approach their decision making irrationally. This irrationality in personal decision making tends to transform itself into social and personal behavioral deviance.

A few examples follow. New social trends or legislation prohibiting certain behaviors such as smoking in public, drinking alcoholic beverages in public places, or sleeping overnight in city parks frequently leads to irrational behavior when attempts to comply or not to comply with imposed social norms conflict with an individual's own habitual behavior. Individuals faced with changing social norms frequently exhibit elevated stress levels and more pronounced aggression levels.

Rapid introduction of new technology potentially produces similar behavioral adjustments. New displays on mobile (cellular) telephones using unfamiliar icons to represent applications that have little meaning for older populations segments require additional instructions from and reliance on public or private support groups. Older telephones that were easy to read and use are no longer widely available even in secondary resale markets. Older population segments require younger tutors or mentors if they are to use more modern telephones. Without private or public support for older populations, their inability to understand more advanced telephone technology may result in increased anxiety and removal from mainstream society.

Increases in the cost of gasoline may lead to major shifts in consumption patterns in many economically challenged countries. In markets that depend on private rather than public local transportation, individuals are willing to adjust or even completely rearrange their consumption and reset their priorities so they can remain independently mobile. They are willing to give up some non-essential goods and services to afford a scooter, motorbike, or a small automobile.

Finally, accelerating changes in lifestyles, such as societal concerns over physical well-being that become evident through public pressure for periodic exercise and dietary adjustments, may lead to extreme behavioral measures or total rejection of social values by individuals who cannot deal with such societal concerns. Such is the case of ill-advised diets that lead to obesity.

One of the key factors in the manifestation of collective societal behavior is the general concern over health care combined with associated personal consumption issues. Today, concerns over improvements in quality health care and the general well-being of all individuals are clearly broad societal concerns in many rapidly growing African countries. These societies are evaluating and assessing these concerns and are attempting to reduce or eliminate public pressure on individuals and thereby improve the quality of life, extend the life expectancies of their citizens, and reduce the number of difficult consumption decisions confronting individuals daily. Many of these initiatives are still in their infancy.

Societal concerns are being identified and studied by university, non-governmental organizations, or other domestic or foreign specialists from a number of scientific disciplines. According to many of these specialists, most societal concerns can be successfully identified, described, and explained to societal constituencies. The problem is to identify and select the appropriate and necessary mechanisms needed to respond to these concerns. An additional problem is how to deliver the solutions to the targeted groups, communities, or constituencies in need of these solutions. Past attempts to deliver such solutions have utilized available knowledge from the behavioral and social sciences. These methods are no longer sufficient in today's multimedia communication channels.

As the behavioral and social sciences have gained more knowledge and realized their potential, new mechanisms and conceptual tools are introduced to transfer knowledge into practice more effectively. Such is the case of marketing. As a social discipline, marketing developed from the behavioral and social sciences. Psychology, sociology, economics, and anthropology, among other sciences, provided a solid conceptual and theoretical base for marketing. Today, marketing is considered an applied discipline capable of communicating and delivering solutions to problems specific to groups, communities, constituencies, and even individuals on various consumption levels.

Marketing

Marketing has evolved over the years into a managerial philosophy of doing business. The philosophy is grounded in a foundation of constructs, concepts, theories, and practices that together form the marketing discipline. Marketing as a managerial discipline has several fields of applications ranging from profit to non-profit applications on one hand and domestic to international marketing on another. Marketing's strategic and operational philosophy is reflected in such professional fields as health care, arts, and social marketing, among others. Because marketing is still in an advanced evolutionary stage, its definition is periodically updated.

In 2007, the American Marketing Association, a principal academic and professional association representing marketing practice in the United States, announced a new definition of marketing: 'Marketing is the activity, set of institutions, and processes for creating, communicating, delivering, and exchanging offerings that have value for customers, clients, partners, and society at large.'[1] This definition encompasses products and services intended for profit and non-profit marketing and is able to create value for groups such communities and constituencies, among others.

Marketing, as practiced, includes several areas of specializations and applications ranging from consumer to business-to-business marketing in the commercial sector. However, marketing also has the potential of focusing on other activities such as global marketing, marketing of services, non-profit marketing, and social marketing, among others.

From a managerial perspective, marketing is a state of mind, with a philosophy of focusing on the requirements of the ultimate consumer or user. It implies an element of entrepreneurship in the identification of opportunities and initiatives. Marketing as a strategic and operational philosophy is responsible for assessing opportunities, planning and programming the development of optimal opportunities, building organizational mechanisms to introduce optimal opportunities to markets, and fostering leadership for organizational mechanisms, and it has the aptitude to objectively control marketing activities.

Traditional marketing has been questioned from two perspectives over the years: the first is its profit motive orientation, which has implications for marketing's abilities to function in the non-profit sector, and the second is its ethical stance in competitively dynamic markets.

The profit motive orientation has been discussed extensively by sociologists, economists, and other scholars as well as practicing managers. The general perception of the profit motive in marketing today, both in marketing research studies and practice, is that profit is a reward for satisfying the ultimate consumer. This perception suggests that consumers have choices and can decide which product or service they prefer to purchase.

Marketing has been viewed more positively because of recognition of marketing in general and the thriving expansion of marketing into the non-profit sector, primarily due to its strategic and operational philosophy. The notion that the ultimate individual benefiting from marketing products or services may be satisfied without generating a profit has been accepted as a viable notion.

The question of the ethical stance of marketing in general is an ongoing process. Eventual resolution of this question is more systemic and philosophically related directly to the overall practice of marketing by a variety of corporations, institutions, and organizations. The question of ethical behavior within the practice of marketing may never be resolved.

Greater acceptance of marketing as a social discipline has expanded and increased the amount of knowledge and its discipline-based philosophy. Applications of marketing techniques, within the context of its philosophy, have also increased. Marketing specialists suggest that marketing techniques can be successfully used in areas outside of traditional marketing. This expansion into other areas of marketing started early in the development of traditional marketing. One such area suitable for the application of marketing techniques, within the context of its philosophy, is social marketing.

Social Marketing

The primary focus of social marketing is to create social value. The contemporary definition of social marketing is: 'Social marketing is the use of marketing principles and techniques to influence a target audience to voluntary accept, reject, modify, or abandon a behavior for the benefit of individuals, groups, or society as a whole.'[2]

The notion of influencing a target audience to voluntarily accept, reject, modify, or abandon a behavior is the key factor on which social marketing has been built. The concern over profit motivation is not part of the social marketing philosophy. Some elements of ethical behavior might depend on the type of behavior that is sought in the context of a specific social marketing effort.

Demand for social marketing action, or more specifically, societal action, is typically generated by an individual with entrepreneurial propensities and abilities, an interested group of individuals, or other societal forces that may be initiated by public opinion, social needs, societal events, collective discussions, or even legislative means. In all cases, as compared with traditional marketing, social marketing focuses on intangible ideas rather than tangible commodities. The demand for societal intangibles may be homogeneous for some ideas and highly heterogeneous for others.

If the demand is heterogeneous, it may be necessary to build a strong consensus among targeted individuals, groups, or societies. Consequently, the social marketing specialist may have to develop strategies that include multiple layers of action ranging from defining the idea, identifying the target audience for the idea, building demand consensus, communicating the idea to the targeted audience, delivering the idea as a solution to a societal problem, and following up on its implementation. The creation of a multifaceted strategy that can address all the necessary factors in a social marketing program is the primary key to its success.

Another key factor in social marketing is its ability to apply marketing research techniques to identify the necessary data and information regarding the perceptions, preferences, and attitudes of various constituencies toward the societal issue in question. Marketing strategies, particularly social marketing strategies, need to be formulated on the basis of facts. In most cases, this requires that marketing research is based on both qualitative and quantitative studies that reflect perceptions, preferences, and attitudes of large samples of participants with diverse opinions about the same idea. This may be difficult in some African societies based on highly structured hieratical units such as extended families (see Example 3 at the end of this chapter).

Social marketing, more than traditional marketing, not only relies extensively on conventional survey approaches to marketing research but also uses observation and participatory research techniques. Observation-type research employs a trained observer, skilled at collecting data and information, to determine the relevancy of the societal issues in the frame of the targeted audience. The participatory research approach requires that a skilled researcher becomes an integral part of the targeted audience and seeks insight into the issue over time.

Conventional marketing research studies are difficult to implement in African societies not only because of the complex and sometimes indirect communication process between researchers and their targets, but also because of structural obstacles such as issues with conventional mail, availability of telephone directories and access to telephone numbers, or more recently, the ability to respond to Internet-based surveys. Social entrepreneurs have a better chance of generating necessary information from observatory or participatory research approaches than from a traditional marketing research approach.

Formulating solutions in social marketing programs frequently requires multidisciplinary approaches. If there are many viable solutions to societal problems, it might be necessary to map out the potential solution with respect to the overall well-being of the entire society. This cannot be accomplished only by social marketers. Social marketers need to work closely with other specialists who are also connected with societal issues. Social marketing can provide a strategic and operational philosophy, a framework for solving problems, information gathering techniques, and strategy formation approaches, but it cannot provide knowledge that is discipline specific and relevant to the societal issues associated with collective behavior (see Example 4 at the end of this chapter).

Social Marketing and Health Care

Social marketing's ability to cooperate with other social or scientific disciplines is particularly critical in the health care industry. Shortages of social workers and issues between doctors and medical personnel and their patients are problematic. Lack of understanding of medical terminology by patients is also a major problem. Application of social marketing to health care issues requires fundamental understanding of the critical issues and finding solutions for them. Social marketing does not have core knowledge of the health care industry but can facilitate critical peripheral issues such as improving communications between doctors or medical specialists and their patients, eliminating medical biases and beliefs among populations, and improving acceptance of health care or medical initiatives.

Social marketing can offer the health care industry several specific tools in addition to marketing philosophy and techniques. The most important are (1) idea definition, conceptualization, and development; (2) effective knowledge of the communication process between the provider of an idea and the intended recipient; (3) a sound understanding of a delivery system of ideas on an individual or collective basis; and (4) a social value creation system.

The social value creation system is probably social marketing's most significant contribution. Since social marketing frequently considers profit as a reward, or in some cases, simply revenue to cover necessary expenses, social value is the most important success factor in social marketing. More specifically, the (1) actors, (2) participants, (3) institutions, (4) organizations, and (5) corporations combined develop social value. This notion also suggests that many of the activities within social marketing are performed on a non-profit basis consistent with the key notion of social marketing—to create social value. For example, community cooperatives, medical facilities managed by voluntary organization such as non-governmental organizations, and entities staffed by professional medical volunteers create social value without seeking financial rewards.

Recent developments in communication technology combined with Internet capabilities offer entrepreneurial initiatives in creating social value by delivering better health to individuals in rural areas. Doctors in distant hospitals, frequently outside of specific countries, can provide medical diagnoses to patients in remote geographic areas and even communicate with local medical assistance in person via the Internet, or in most cases, via wireless telephone communication. The new telecommunication technology combined with resources worldwide contribute to local social value.

Social Marketing Applications in Health Care

Initially, application of social marketing in the health care industry, depending on the systemic environmental condition, can focus on specific societal needs. These societal needs can be classified according to the apparent knowledge gaps related to social marketing capabilities. In other words, social marketing can assist in solving some gaps, but not all.

Specialized decision-making approaches, modeling techniques, or examination of vast medical databases suitable for decision making in the health care industry are some of the gaps that social marketing can help close. A decision-making process typically begins with systematic and objective definition of the concerns that target audiences may have. Concerns tend to be generally pervasive in target audiences and may be heterogeneously distributed within the target audience. These concerns can be identified, defined, and specified using marketing research so they can be converted into social issues.

Conversion of concerns into social issues is a systematic process that requires agreement on the importance and relevancy of each concern to the targeted audience. If the targeted audience does not agree on the importance of a concern, the concern cannot be converted into a relevant social issue. If there is agreement that a given concern is a relevant social issue, the issue then needs to be examined in the context of what implementation challenges the issue presents for relevant individuals in the targeted audience. All known and identifiable challenges need to be identified, evaluated, and assessed in terms of what problems need to be solved to address the original concern, resolve the relevant issue, overcome the challenges, identify the core problem, and offer a realistic solution for the problem.

Social marketing provides a systematic problem-solving process for the health care industry—a five stage model that is capable of (1) identifying concerns, (2) formulating them into issues, (3) identifying challenges, (4) specifying the core problems, and (5) providing solutions.

The second important contribution that social marketing makes to the health care industry is the ability to open an effective communication process between and among all the actors within the health care system. Social marketing techniques can be deployed to formulate relevant optimal messages needed within an entire health care system. Message formulation not only relies on marketing research but also utilizes techniques from advertising, promotion, public relations, and personal sales to deliver the right message to the right audiences. In addition, the communication processes can be developed to function both on the impersonal level as general messages for the target audience or they can be developed to function on a highly personal level such as between physician and patient, for example.

Definition of the standards of performance is another area in health care that can benefit from the techniques found in social marketing. Performance effectiveness of a marketing strategy can be objectively measured, as can advancements or increases in penetration of a social cause or the ability of the targeted audience to accept a solution to a core problem. Clear performance standards can be set for specific tasks and operations that can be objectively measured using social marketing criteria.

A final example of how social marketing philosophy and techniques are applicable to the entire health care systems is education. Through an effective communication process and appropriate verbal and written messages, actors in the health care industry can learn how to communicate with participants; for example, health care providers with patients. Above all, the educational process inherent in social marketing can be used to increase the awareness of various levels of health care and thereby improve the overall efficiency and effectiveness of the entire health care system.

Social Marketing and Health Care Integration

There is systemic demand for social marketing specialists in the health care industry throughout African countries, particularly in rural areas of Tanzania, Kenya, and Nigeria. Social marketing specialists need training; they need to understand qualitative and quantitative marketing research techniques to communicate within a health care system given its level of sophistication and diversity of issues and problems. Potentially, there might be a need for two types of social marketing specialists. The first type are specialists with strong marketing and marketing research skills who can communicate across disciplines and have fundamental understanding of the health care industry. The second type might be specialists trained as scientists with suitable research skills within the health care industry. Both types of specialists need to have a deep understanding of health care issues, especially in rural areas that may be culturally diverse such as in many parts of Africa.

There also is a role for consultants in the social marketing field—consultants who can implement research findings, build organizations, develop leadership potential, and develop control systems for clients in the health care industry. The approach of a social marketing consultant is more that of a marketing manager able to make appropriate decisions concerning the previous issues.

Recently, entrepreneurs using social marketing techniques and approaches have important roles in the health care industry in rural parts of Africa. Many social entrepreneurs active in the health care industry in African rural communities are individuals who can identify available resources locally or abroad and develop delivery health care services through non-traditional channels such as the Internet. They open walk-in facilities for patients who directly or indirectly describe their problems to health care specialists located in distant medical facilities. Medical personnel in these distant facilities then provide the diagnosis and recommend possible care. Although some of these facilities generate profits, most are intended to be non-profit community-based services (see Example 5 at the end of this chapter).

Summary

There is a need to effectively utilize social marketing as a conduit in order to improve health care delivery and facilitate better communication between medical personnel and patients throughout Africa. There are several ways to utilize social marketing. Social entrepreneurs can use techniques of social marketing to identify the main gaps in health care delivery and use the latest wireless communication systems including the Internet to close them. Social entrepreneurs can use wireless communication and the Internet to search across borders to identify local shortcomings and solve them by providing innovative solutions.

Social entrepreneurs found in a number of African countries are typically those who were educated abroad and returned to apply the knowledge they gained. They built personnel networks abroad and gained valuable perspectives on solving fundamental problems with innovative solutions. Social entrepreneurs may use obsolete technology from abroad to solve problems in home markets in some cases. They have the ability to combine solutions to local problems with old or new technology available elsewhere.

Notes

1 Marketing definitions, American Marketing Association, www.ama.org/resources/Pages/Marketing-Dictionary.aspx (January 9, 2018).
2 Kotler, Philip, Ned Roberto, and Nancy R. Lee, *Social Marketing: Improving the Quality of Life* (Thousand Oaks, CA: Sage, 2002).

Bibliography

This bibliography was developed to allow interested researchers to fully appreciate the scope and the depth of social marketing and its relationship to the health care industry. It consists of leading articles focusing on evolutionary changes in traditional marketing, developments and issues in the formative years of social marketing, and implications for the health care industry. The bibliography is intended as a source of further research on the subjects discussed earlier.

Most of the items in the bibliography are available in databases such as AIB/INFORM Global, Academic Search Premier, Business Full Text, ERIC, Health Sciences Collection, Humanities Full Text, MedLine [EBSCO host], and Science Citation Index Expanded. Reprints and newer editions of the books listed in this bibliography are available in book stores throughout Europe and North America and on the Internet.

Aaker, David A. *Strategic Market Management*, 7th ed. New York: John Wiley & Sons, Inc., 2005.
Ackoff, Russell L. *The Design of Social Research*. Chicago: The University of Chicago Press, 1953, classic.
Andreasen, Alan R. "Marketing Social Marketing in the Social Change Marketplace." *Journal of Public Policy & Marketing* 21, no. 1 (Spring 2002): 3–13.
Babbie, Earl R. *The Practice of Social Research*, 2nd ed. Belmont, CA: Wadsworth Publishing Company, Inc., 1979 [1973].
Binney, Wayne, John Hall, and Peter Oppenheim. "The Nature and Influence of Motivation Within the MOA Framework: Implications for Social Marketing." *International Journal of Nonprofit and Voluntary Sector Marketing* 11, no. 4 (November 2006): 289–301.

Bloom, Paul, and William D. Novelli. "Problems and Challenges in Social Marketing." *Journal of Marketing* 45, no. 2 (1981): 70–88.

Brenkert, George G. "Ethical Challenges of Social Marketing." *Journal of Public Policy & Marketing* 21, no. 1 (Spring 2002): 14–25.

Buchanan, James M., and Gordon Tullock. *The Calculus of Consent: Logical Foundation of Constitutional Democracy*. Ann Arbor: The University of Michigan Press, 1962, classic.

Crane, Andrew. "Societal Marketing and Morality." *European Journal of Marketing* 36, nos. 5 and 6 (2002): 548–569.

Hanan, Mack, James Cribbin, and Herman Heiser, *Consultive Selling*. New York: Amacom, 1973.

Hunt, Shelby D. *Marketing Theory: The Philosophy of Marketing Science*. Homewood, Illinois: Richard D. Irwin, Inc., 1983.

Hunt, Shelby D. "The Nature and Scope of Marketing." *Journal of Marketing* 40 (July 1976): 17–28.

Kerlinger, Fred N. *Foundations of Behavioral Research*, 2nd ed. New York: Holt, Rinehart and Winston, Inc., 1973 [1964], first and second editions are classics.

Kotler, Philip. "A Generic Concept of Marketing." *Journal of Marketing* 36 (April 1972): 46–54.

Kotler, Philip. *Marketing for Nonprofit Organizations*, 2nd ed. Englewood Cliffs, NJ: Prentice-Hall, Inc., 1982 [1975].

Kotler, Philip, and Nancy R. Lee. "Best of Breed: When It Comes to Gaining a Market Edge While Supporting a Social Cause, 'Corporate Social Marketing' Leads the Pack." *Stanford Social Innovation Review* 1, no. 4 (Spring 2004): 14–23.

Kotler, Philip, and Nancy R. Lee, "Marketing in the Public Sector: The Final Frontier." *Public Manager* 36 (Spring 2007): 12–17.

Kotler, Philip, and Gerald Zaltman. "Social Marketing: An Approach to Planned Social Change." *Journal of Marketing* 35 (July 1971): 3–12.

Kroger, Fred. "Towards a Healthy Public." *The American Behavioral Scientist* 38, no. 2 (November 1994): 215–223.

Lauterbach, Albert. *Psychological Challenges to Modernization*. Amsterdam: Elsevier Scientific Publishing Company, 1974.

Lazer, William. "Marketing's Changing Social Relationships." *Marketing Management* 5, no. 1 (Spring 1996): 52–57.

Lazer, William, and Eugene J. Kelley. *Social Marketing: Perspectives and Viewpoints*. Homewood, IL: Richard D. Irwin, Inc., 1973.

Levitt, Theodore. *Innovation in Marketing: New Perspectives for Profit and Growth*. New York: McGraw-Hill Book Company, 1962, classic.

Lovelock, Christopher H. *Services Marketing*. Englewood Cliffs, NJ: Prentice-Hall, Inc., 1984, classic.

Marshall, Kimball P., and Ulysses J. Brown III. "Target Marketing in a Social Marketing Context: Gender Differences in Importance Ratings of Promoted Intrinsic and Extrinsic Restricted Exchange Benefits of Military Enlistment." *International Journal of Nonprofit and Voluntary Sector Marketing* 9, no. 1 (February 2004): 69–85.

Padanyi, Paulette, and Brenda Gainer. "Market Orientation in the Nonprofit Sector: Taking Multiple Constituencies Into Consideration." *Journal of Marketing Theory and Practice* 12, no. 2 (Spring 2004): 43–58.

Peattie, Sue, and Ken Peattie. "Ready to Fly Solo? Reducing Social Marketing's Dependence on Commercial Marketing Theory." *Marketing Theory* 3, no. 3 (2003): 365–385.

Rogers, Everett M. "The Field of Health Communication Today." *The American Behavioral Scientist* 38, no. 2 (November 1994): 208–214.

Rogers, Everett M. "New Product Adoption and Diffusion." *Journal of Consumer Research* 2, no. 4 (March 1976): 290–301.

Rogers, Everett M., and F. Floyd Shoemaker. *Communication of Innovations: A Cross-Cultural Approach* (Revised Edition of Diffusion of Innovation) New York: The Free Press, 1971.

Tesar, George, and Jan Bodin. *Marketing Management in Geographically Remote Industrial Clusters: Implications for Business-to-Customer Marketing.* Singapore: World Scientific Publishing Co. Pte. Limited, 2013.

Tesar, George, and John Kuada, ed. *Marketing Management and Strategy: An African Casebook.* New York: Routledge, 2013.

Vasquez, Rodolfo, Luis Ignacio Alvarez, and Maria Leticia Santos. "Market Orientation and Social Services in Private Non-Profit Organizations." *European Journal of Marketing* 36, nos. 9 and 10 (2002): 1022–1046.

Examples

EXAMPLE 1

A young entrepreneur who recently received a doctoral degree in management education from a European university returned to Tanzania intending to start a primary school. Most of his students would come from the region where they could attend daily from their homes. After checking the basic requirements, receiving permits, and certifying his qualifications to administer a primary school, he received permission from the regional authorities to proceed if he has the necessary funds to build a suitable building and operate it for the first 4 years.

In order to secure the funding, the social entrepreneur called on his European colleagues and friends to raise the necessary capital. The capital was raised by placing a webpage on the Internet in several languages, and most of the funds received as donations were from his supporting colleagues and friends. The rest of the needed funds were obtained from individual donors who learned about the initiative from the webpage.

EXAMPLE 2

Social entrepreneurs are becoming more involved with delivery of health care to individuals in remote regions of Ghana and Tanzania and perhaps in other countries. Most of the new social entrepreneurs returned from studies abroad and have limited medical education or training, but by cooperating with local individuals skilled in care of individuals or older experienced individuals, they organized local computer-based medical information (kiosk) stations. These stations are connected with voluntary medical organizations, hospitals, or even individual doctors abroad who have received grants from various international organizations to improve the medical conditions of patients in African countries.

104 George Tesar

Local individuals with undetermined symptoms may visit the station (kiosk) to explain the symptoms to the responsible individual who sends the information to the contacts abroad for analysis and suggested treatment potentially available locally. The individual seeking the analysis knows almost instantaneously what the symptoms mean and how the problem could be treated. If the treatment is not available locally, a search for treatment is conducted in the region.

EXAMPLE 3

A local community in a remote region of Zambia has a major problem developing on its main commercial street. Merchants expand their space to display and sell their merchandise, and street vendors offer a variety of products directly to stopped cars or passengers on buses going by. Shoppers frequently cannot walk the street because there are no designated walking areas. The local administrators are not interested in solving the increasingly complex social problem.

Social marketing is an ideal tool for solving similar problems. There is a need for individuals who will motivate other interested individuals to identify the various constituencies directly involved—merchants, street vendors, shoppers, individual walkers—who are interested in solving the problem. The problem needs to be defined to include the interests of all relevant constituents. Solutions to the problem must be proposed. Each solution may offer a partial, but not necessarily complete, solution to each constituency. A compromise may need to be reached by consensus. Under ideal and agreeable conditions, once the consensus for the selected solution is discussed with administrators, the solution can be implemented collectively.

EXAMPLE 4

There are several social marketing methodologies for problem solving. One suited to stimulate collective action and resolve social issues of groups or individuals consists of these steps: (1) define a problem, situation, issue, or other social phenomenon perceived by a group or an individual; (2) obtain commitment by an individual or a group to lead the effort for resolving the defined social phenomenon; (3) identify the lasting benefits and reinforcements potentially derived from the initiated social action; (4) identify any social costs, social benefits, or individual or group annoyances that may result from implementing the social action; (5) analyze the trade-offs of costs, benefits, or annoyances from social action for other members of society; (6) identify dormant demand among other social groups for intended social action; and (7) specify and reach a market segment whose cohorts initiated the social action and are key to acceptance of the selected social action.

Several members of a small geographical community are concerned about the lack of available water in case a fire would start due to changing weather conditions. A member of the community who recently returned from an extended trip abroad volunteered to consider the issue. Other community members agreed that they need to protect their properties in case of fire and agreed to find a commonly acceptable solution. Community elders agreed to petition the regional administration for a grant to build a container for holding enough water in case of fire. A grant was awarded with the stipulation that the container would hold water for use only in case of fire—no other use of the water was allowed. The grant also stipulated that all community members were to benefit equally.

EXAMPLE 5

Social marketing and health care are closely related. Members of some remote communities are reluctant to travel long distances for medical help. In Tanzania and Ghana, for example, national health authorities introduced mobile health care delivery systems similar to medical and dental health care delivery systems in Switzerland. Doctors and nurses periodically visit remote communities in mobile clinics and laboratories to service patients. Several private services mostly supported by non-governmental organizations recently were established in sub-Saharan Africa. For reasons that are being studied, their success has been limited.

5

BUSINESS TO BUSINESS MARKETING IMPLICATIONS FOR SMALLER ENTERPRISES IN AFRICA

George Tesar

The rapid growth of smaller enterprises in several African countries is due to two major initiatives: (1) the availability of better wireless communication including the Internet, and (2) the rapid growth of entrepreneurs. The availability of better wireless communication is a worldwide phenomenon. Depending on how it is used, wireless communication and the Internet create many opportunities for entrepreneurs to start new initiatives because they can obtain information from outside their normal sphere of operation and use the information to gain competitive advantages in their local markets. Typically, there are two types of entrepreneurs operating in African countries where stable economic and social conditions provide a solid foundation for private or public ventures. The first type are entrepreneurs who understand local conditions and are able to identify specific niches to exploit. They combine local knowledge with information gained from foreign sources. They build products or offer services because they identify gaps between what is known or available locally and what is not. The second type of entrepreneur represents individuals who were most likely educated or trained abroad and return home to use the knowledge gained abroad to start new initiatives and offer products or services not previously available. The former entrepreneurs are frequently known as conventional entrepreneurs and the latter are labeled as leading-edge entrepreneurs.

Local conventional entrepreneurs recognize opportunities open to them via the Internet or over increasingly more available mobile communication services. Local entrepreneurs can market their products and services over the Internet, where potential customers or clients can purchase either without major difficulties. The products typically offered by these entrepreneurs are either custom-made products, sometimes specifically crafted for the customers, or low production consumer products such as dry vegetables, fruits, or herbs, among other agricultural products. Some products in demand in local markets are replacement parts for low technology items such as bicycles, agricultural equipment, and even automotive replacement parts. Some local conventional entrepreneurs start small enterprises and build furniture, sew clothes, and even build electronic equipment. The services they offer are relatively limited to repairs, maintenance, and occasional customized service for larger enterprises such as technical support or equipment maintenance services.

The leading-edge entrepreneurs represent a new cadre of entrepreneurs who are most often educated abroad and return to start a private or public initiative. The leading-edge entrepreneurs almost exclusively depend on a combination of local and cross-border markets. These are major innovators who, with the help of the wireless communication infrastructure and especially the Internet, bring ideas for innovative products and services into the economic and social environments that are transformed by them. Many innovations brought by these entrepreneurs either merge technologies from other environments and introduce innovations that improve consumers' lives in the process. For example, they may use portable solar panels to generate electricity for computers where electricity is not commercially available. Or they may design energy sufficient and efficient homes with solar powered heating and cooling systems, water purification and recycling capacity, and air circulating systems.

Leading-edge entrepreneurs introduce socially significant innovations including services not previously available. These include developing emergency medical services where patients describe their symptoms to a medical technician and the technician sends the information via the computer to a major hospital, sometimes located abroad, where medical specialists analyze them and send recommendations back to the local technician. Another example is the introduction of delivery services in urban and rural areas. Groceries, medications, or other products are delivered directly to clients using bicycles, scooters, or other appropriate modes of transport.

Both conventional and leading-edge entrepreneurs need supplies to perform their activities or they supply other enterprises with products or services. In either case, they do not function in a commercial vacuum. They rely on suppliers for their needs as others rely on their offerings. These transactions, regardless of the entrepreneurial activities, represent business to business transactions without which commercial activities cannot exist. Business to business marketing was previously known as industrial marketing; lately, it represents a function within supply chains or even value chains. Both types of entrepreneurs need to understand the importance of business to business marketing and how it functions within the commercial levels on which it is practiced. They must realize that business to business marketing is essential to their existence.

Business to Business Framework

In its fundamental form, business to business marketing consists of all marketing activities within an entire supply chain that extends from the natural or synthetic sources of raw materials to the manufacturers of consumer products or services and beyond to the ultimate consumers or users. A supply chain consists of transactions and relationships between and among various links in that supply chain. It links sources of raw materials to producers of component parts, accessories, supplies, professional services, capital equipment, and industrial installations needed to produce, distribute, and consume products and services.

From a broader social perspective, business to business marketing involves all activities that are needed to deliver products and services to customers, consumers, or users. In order to accomplish these objectives, business to business marketing involves the utilization of natural resources, dissemination of new technologies, development of new products and services, and delivery of products into appropriate markets. In an increasingly more complex market system and even more competitive external business environment, business to business marketing is based on a set of relationships between suppliers and manufacturers on every level of the supply chain.

The relationships that exist between suppliers and customers create bonds, trust, and cooperative arrangements out of necessity. Such relationships also stimulate competitive pressures, lead to codevelopment and engineering of components, subassemblies, and even development of new technological innovations. In many cases, such relationships also lead to mutual ownership of technologies at various levels of the supply chain or throughout the entire supply chain which often creates fluctuations in competitiveness among suppliers. Depending on the size of the suppliers and their market strength, the benefits of supply chain membership may be highly desirable or detrimental to individual members of the supply chain.

Specialized components are developed on the basis of new technology or on concentrated research and development efforts in many complex domestic, international, and global supply chains, such as in the automotive industry, the medical equipment and instrumentation industry, or the electronics industry. Such components are intended to reduce competition and create better market positions for members of the supply chain. For example, recent alternative propulsion systems such as hybrid, electric battery, or hydrogen technologies are all results of cooperative efforts between major automobile manufacturers and their suppliers. It would be difficult for individual automobile manufacturers to introduce such technologies to the market without close cooperation with suppliers within the supply chain.

Similar relationships between manufacturers and suppliers exist in the medical equipment and instrumentation market. Major manufacturers of medical equipment need component parts based on the latest available technology in order to compete. Many smaller suppliers must innovate and be technologically timely to be competitive. Their technological agility frequently provides the competitive advantage for major manufacturers of medical equipment and instrumentation. The entire field is based on an ability to analyze, identify, and measure signals, values, and phenomena for which specialized software is required. Manufacturers that need such software frequently look to small specialized software developers with the technological know-how to develop such software to their specifications or to develop unique software applications.

Contemporary manufacturers of electronics also cooperate very closely in the context of the supply chain and business to business marketing. Solid state electronics, the core elements of many products today, are custom developed and integrated into products produced by their suppliers. Many electronics suppliers serve several major clients, their subsidiaries, and even their competitors by providing custom designed internal components of televisions sets, automobiles, washing machines, and other intermediate products such as measuring equipment, medical instruments, and operating room medical devices. Computers come in many different shapes, sizes, speeds, and configurations and are invariably engineered to a customer's specifications.

These types of cooperation and relationships require a great deal of communication up and down the supply chain in addition to trust and mutual respect. These arrangements frequently result in anticompetitive situations and other practices that might seriously restrict free market operations.

It is important to examine markets for business to business products and services in order to fully understand the entire concept of business to business marketing. Globally, there are three ultimate markets: (1) business markets consisting of large global enterprises; (2) institutional markets that include education, health care providers, and other non-governmental institutions; and (3) governmental markets that are made up of national, regional, state, or local governments. Each market has its own unique consumption requirements and institutional buying characteristics. Business markets purchase and market differently from institutional markets or government markets. Nevertheless, the relationships between suppliers and customers or clients tend to follow prescribed customary and orderly conventions and practices.

All the conventions and practices of applied business to business marketing are implemented by marketing managers. Marketing managers are on various managerial levels depending on how an entity is organized and how it implements the marketing function. Some enterprises tend to be highly structured around the marketing function, with a top enterprise manager responsible for marketing; other enterprises have diffused the marketing function throughout and managers on every level in the enterprise assume responsibility for marketing. In general, however, top enterprise executives tend to be responsible for strategic aspects of marketing with line managers or team managers responsible for operational aspects of marketing.

The creative and competitive efforts of managers need to be interpreted from several perspectives. Enterprise level marketing managers are responsible for market assessment. They look for opportunities and need to systematically assess these opportunities in the context of their marketing and technological capability and resource availability. They further need to prioritize opportunities that seem realistic given available resources. Opportunities selected for implementation then need organizational structures and entrepreneurial leadership dedicated to them. Line or team marketing managers then become responsible for the development, implementation, and performance of each opportunity.

Enterprise scientists, scientists working in public and private laboratories, and academic researchers all contribute to the technological innovativeness and competitiveness of enterprises. New product ideas are generated from scientific findings, discoveries, and inventions transferred into the marketplace through the complex process of technology transfers, generation of new product ideas and concepts, and even new products. Enterprises, governmental agencies, and institutions are frequent participants in this scientific technology transfer process.

Technology in business to business markets can be introduced in two different ways. First, a significant market need for new technology can be identified through systematic marketing research studies and new products are developed to meet the need—this approach is typically called technological market pull. Second, a new technology is identified for which a clear market need does not exist, but a broad market may benefit from the new technology. In this case, a market study is initiated to identify alternatives as to how to introduce the technology in the market. Such studies are commonly conducted via demonstration projects where the technology is slowly introduced or demonstrated for potential users— this approach is called technology push.

Some examples of the two processes follow. Technology pull marketing is a viable approach for sequential or nominal innovations, usually in consumer marketing. For example, sequential versions of computers, home appliances, and other consumer products respond to changing consumer demand. Manufacturers in business to business markets respond to consumer demand by integrating incremental innovations from their suppliers into new generations of products. In technology push marketing, manufacturers introduce dramatically new technological innovations by devising new versions of products encompassing complete innovations that might be based on scientific findings, discoveries, or inventions. These products based on new technology may revolutionize product use, introduce additional functions, or drastically redesign the product. One example is the difference between the old clamshell design to a camera-equipped iPhone. This involves developing totally new component parts for technologically new products using updated production methods and technical support services for business to business markets. Consequently, business to business marketing is responsible for most of marketing efforts and the majority of commercial activities in a given economy. Marketing managers in business to business marketing serve as market arbitrators between suppliers and customers. Scientists, innovators, and entrepreneurs serve business to business marketing as generators of technological innovations.

Scope of Business to Business Activities

Business to business marketing plays an important role on both macroeconomic and microeconomic levels. On the macroeconomic level, it motivates development of new technology, stimulates economic activities within the market, contributes to changing lifestyles of both consumers and citizens of each country, and positively and negatively influences the social climate of each country. More specifically, business to business marketing influences the formation of ethical, political, and legal postures in each economic system. On the microeconomic level, business to business marketing activities provide an impetus for manufactures to market products with optimal technology most suitable for local market conditions.

In its applied form and overall scope of its operations, business to business marketing makes significant contributions to innovation in the market, is instrumental in transferring technology from research laboratories to the market, and uses specific methodologies in formulating new product ideas. The contribution of innovations, technology transfer processes, and formulation of new product ideas can be described as intangible or soft contributions of the entire business to business marketing process. Since marketing managers simply do not have the necessary financial resources to develop every marketing opportunity that presents itself, some ideas, applications, and solutions can be marketed to other enterprises. This secondary market for so-called soft know-how also contributes to the overall economy.

In most instances, the internal business to business marketing process within an enterprise begins with the development of a tangible technology for development of a specific product for a clearly identified target market. New product development cannot be undertaken without substantial marketing research studies designed to define the core market, the target market in which there is a need for a product to be developed, and specification of the characteristics of key customers in business to business marketing or consumers in consumer marketing.

Marketing research in consumer markets provides valuable information for business to business marketers. Information from these sources must be systematically compared with planned functional, physical, and psychological attributes of the proposed product. Even though business to business marketers supply only a part, component, or an accessory for a new product, they need to understand the impact of the item on the ultimate consumer of the product.

A product concept is the outcome of a marketing research process combined with the core knowledge of an enterprise. The entire new product development process begins when a product concept is turned over to the new product development group. Although there are a number of approaches to new product development, the typical new product development process begins with simultaneous development and creation of three sets of product attributes—functional, physical, and psychological—and the engineering of the actual physical form of the product. The new product development process starts with the formulation and refinement of the product concept and ends with completion of the final product. The entire process is considered to be the tangible, or hard, part of technology transfer.

It is important to note that services are developed with a similar process and differ based on their degree of tangibility only. Some products are considered incidental in offering professional and consumer services.

112   George Tesar

Intermediate steps in the new product development process include physical development of a product, prototype building, prototype testing, selection of the optimal prototype, preparation of the optimal prototype for the market, and market readiness of the new product. These stages are frequently conducted sequentially, but in some instances, and with appropriate modifications, can be performed simultaneously. Sometimes unique new product development teams are created for the various functions, while at other times, an enterprise appoints and manages a dedicated staff of new product development specialists.

The development of a reliable supply chain also begins almost simultaneously from the start of the new product development process. The new product development process in most global and large enterprises is supplemented with input and technical information from potential suppliers. Some enterprises conduct Internet auctions and direct bidding exercises to learn what new technology is available in the supply chain for improving the value of a new product under development.

Consequently, the development of a new product for some enterprises is preceded by a solicitation process designed to evaluate new technologies available in the potential supply chain. The automobile, medical equipment and instruments, and electronics industries have functioned this way since the introduction of the Internet. An interesting question in many research studies is whether the supply chain influences the functional, physical, and psychological attributes of many new products.

Another aspect of business to business marketing starts when a new product is introduced in the market or taken over by a client, user, or customer. Market introduction of new products, processes, or services becomes highly coordinated efforts by marketing managers responsible for marketing strategies. Marketing strategies require coordination of sales efforts with technical support services and post-service technical follow-ups. These efforts must be integrated, synchronized, and implemented at the same time. Products, processes, and even services cannot just be sold—they must be delivered, installed, and made operational to the satisfaction of clients, user, and customers. Business to business products, processes, and services are considered productive assets by participants in value chains today and must be used effectively and efficiently.

An additional facet of the business to business marketing effort is employed to ensure effectiveness and efficiency. Special groups of marketing managers responsible for management of existing products in the market are responsible for the ongoing performance of their products. These managers monitor the performance of each product in the market and identify each change in the market life of each product. The concept of a product life cycle is a common managerial tool. The assumption is that, on the basis of past information, every product follows a predictable path that consists of several stages in the life of the market and the product—introduction, growth, maturity, decline, and removal. The sales volume and profitability of each product are determined for each product life cycle and used to make strategic decisions about a product's performance. The introduction of competitors' products can also be tracked in the product life cycle model.

Replacing technologically obsolete products with technologically new products also becomes an important domain of business to business marketing. A product needs to be replaced as it approaches the end of its market or technological life. The key question becomes, at what exact point in its life cycle should the product be replaced and what product characteristics should the replacement product have? Should the replacement product be a modified product or a new product based on new technology? Newly developed products incorporating the latest technology are generally preferred in a highly competitive global marketplace.

Assessment of market performance of products, processes, and services is another performance issue that faces business to business marketing managers. Marketing managers use standard criteria such as sales volume, profitability, market share, product quality assessments, market image, and market perception of the enterprise image to assess market and competitive performance. However, many marketing managers consider these to be traditional performance indicators. They need new measures of performance that simulate or even predict performance.

Some global market participants have developed computer-based simulation software programs, competitive games, and even war games to predict performance of their entire array of marketing strategies and specific products from three important perspectives—market, competition, and technology. High technology approaches are used to monitor various aspects of product performance. Large players in the market have the resources, know-how, and computer specialists to internally design, develop, and utilize such high technology means of product and market assessment. Smaller enterprises lack the necessary resources to use similar managerial know-how.

Control is one of the most important aspects of the entire process of assessing and monitoring the performance of business to business products in the market. Every marketing strategy needs independent and unbiased evaluation of each product in the market. Some evaluation is done internally by keeping records of past performance and following standard internal auditing or accounting practices. But there is a need for more objective measures from a strategic perspective. Independent assessments need to be made periodically by financial as well as marketing specialists not directly connected in any way with the performance of any of the products being marketed or managed.

There is also a need for special types of assessments designed to determine the impact each individual product, process, or service has on society and the environment given the recent emphasis on social corporate responsibility and environmental issues. Concerns about the carbon footprint of any business to business activity are subject to public exposure and need to be considered by top enterprise executives. These types of assessments typically need to be performed by qualified outside professional agencies.

114 George Tesar

Business to business marketing activities today can be divided into internal and external marketing activities. Today, any given enterprise may not survive as an autonomous self-sufficient entity. The age of large trusts and giant manufacturing complexes is over. Today's enterprises rely on their suppliers to deliver what they need, but also to combine their efforts and focus on new product development, manufacturing processes to produce finished products, and necessary professional services to support the product in the market. They also rely on independent external professional agencies to track their performance without damaging the fragile life space around them.

Enterprises today are still internally capable of creating technologically innovative products and profitably offer them on the market. Business to business marketing managers on all enterprise levels need to manage the core values of their enterprises more effectively and need to be more creative in the market. Their core values and increased market creativity make them more competitive. Relying extensively on suppliers for new technology, innovative products, or even entrepreneurship within an enterprise is not an effective way to manage marketing activities in the local or global marketplace.

Concerns in African Business to Business Marketing

There are three concerns in business to business marketing that challenge top management of many local, national, or global enterprises today: (1) management of green environment issues, (2) management of renewable resources, and (3) innovative organizational structures. These concerns are driven by outside forces in the environment in which enterprises function. Societies demand products that do not damage the natural environment around them.

Perhaps the most important concern in business to business marketing today is green management of environmental issues. It requires top management of many business to business enterprises to seriously consider what consumptions options they offer for the end consumer or user. Business to business marketing managers need to be more innovative and entrepreneurial since consumers demand greener products and services that help increase their standard of living and improve their life span. At the same time, business to business marketing managers must better understand consumption behavior associated with these demands. There is a significant need among the business to business marketing managers for more information about the concept of what the public calls green management and about consumption patterns and behavior underlying this concept.[1]

Managing renewable resources is another concern for business to business marketing managers. Markets demand that materials, component parts, equipment, and other intermediate and final products are manufactured from renewable materials. Two fundamental types of materials are recycled and naturally grown. The key issue of this concern is the need to understand what technologies are available to optimize the mix of materials needed for production of end products. In other words, what percentage of products need to be manufactured from materials that cannot be recycled or naturally grown? This issue requires a great deal of scientific and marketing research.

In order to provide at least partial responses to the marketplace, especially end consumers and users, it is necessary to introduce new perspectives to the entire process of how utilization of resources is organized in society. Innovative organizational and institutional structures are needed to introduce new perspectives; consumers' and users' standards of living and life spans will be increased through such structures.

Recent examples of the three main concerns are (1) development of environmentally clean sources of electrical energy—wind and solar; (2) electric powered systems for transportation, water pumping and purification, clean cooking and heating devices, among others; (3) private and public construction using recycled existing structures or building materials such as refurbished industrial warehouses, public facilities, or private housing constructed from recycled material.[2]

Research Topics

The previous concerns confront business to business marketing managers in African countries, especially Kenya, Nigeria, and Uganda. Research is required to understand the links between long-term strategies and everyday operations. For example, business to business enterprises need to change their focus and include recycled materials as part of their total offerings to builders of private homes. Developers of housing projects need to consider existing structures as possibilities for communal housing. Research studies are needed to examine how these issues contribute to the consumption options of end consumers or users and how they can improve their standards of living and ultimately their longevity.

The previous concerns are fundamentally connected as far as business to business marketing management is concerned. There appears to be a clear relationship between resource activities of business to business marketing and market management activities. Business to business managers need to better employ resources today to produce the desirable impact on distinct markets in various African countries. Additional research is needed to increase understanding of these concerns.

Notes

1 In this context, green products are products that do not damage the natural environment, are consumer or user friendly, and leave a minimal—if any—carbon footprint. End consumers or users consider green products to be essential for energy conservation, healthier lifestyles, increased standards of living, and individual longevity.
2 According to many environmental groups in Europe, North America, and Australia, wind-generated electrical power is environmentally clean; however, there are critics of wind-generated electric power. Some interest groups are concerned about the visual pollution of landscapes combined with noise pollution.

116 George Tesar

Bibliography

This bibliography was developed to allow interested researchers to fully appreciate the scope and depth business to business marketing and business to business marketing management in contemporary settings. The bibliography is intended as a source of further research on the entire subject outlined earlier.

Most of the items in the bibliography are available in databases such as AIB/INFORM Global, Academic Search, Business Full Text, or ERIC. Some are also available on the Internet via Google Scholar or several other search programs. Most of the books are available in major public or university libraries. Reprints and newer editions of the books listed are also available on the Internet.

Barabba, Vincent P. *Meeting of the Minds: Creating the Market-Based Enterprise*. Boston, MA: Harvard Business School Press, 1995.

Frambach, Ruud T. "An Integrated Model of Organizational Adoption and Diffusion of Innovation." *European Journal of Marketing* 27, no. 2 (1993): 22–41.

Gullestrup, Hans. *Cultural Analysis—Towards Cross-Cultural Understanding*. Copenhagen: Copenhagen Business School Press, 2006.

Harwood, Tracy. "Business Negotiations in the Context of Strategic Relationship Development." *Marketing Intelligence & Planning* 20, no. 6 (2002): 336–348.

Hutt, Michael D., and Thomas W. Speh. *Business Marketing Management: B2B*, 9th ed. Mason, OH: Thomson South-Western, 2007.

Jolly, Dominique R., and François Thérin. "New Venture Technology Sourcing: Exploring the Effect of Absorptive Capacity, Learning Attitude, and Past Performance." *Innovation: Management, Policy, & Practice* 9 (2007): 235–248.

Kuada, John, ed. *Global Mindsets: Exploration and Perspectives*. New York: Routledge, 2016.

Levitt, Theodore. *The Marketing Imagination*. New York: The Free Press, 1983.

Lyne, M. Bruce. "Research Institutes Have Become Industry Partners." *Research-Technology Management* (July–August 2007): 42–48.

Meyer, Marc H. et al. "Corporate Venturing: An Expanded Role for R&D." *Research-Technology Management* (January–February, 2008): 34–42.

Schnaars, Steven P. *Marketing Strategy: A Customer-Driven Approach*. New York: The Free Press, 1991.

Tesar, George. "An Examination of Planning Strategies Among Small and Medium-Sized Firms." *Research at the Marketing/Entrepreneurship Interface*, 173–179. Ed. Gerald E. Hills. Marietta, GA: United States Association for Small Business and Entrepreneurship.

Tesar, George, and Jan Bodin. *Marketing Management in Geographically Remote Industrial Clusters: Implications for Business to Consumer Marketing*. Singapore: World Scientific Publishing, Co., Ptc., Ltd., 2013.

Tesar, George, and John Kuada, eds. *Marketing Management and Strategy: An African Casebook*. London, UK: Routledge, 2013.

Tesar, George et al. *Smaller Manufacturing Enterprises in an International Context: A Longitudinal Exploration*. London, UK: Imperial College Press, 2010.

Woodside, Arch G. "Middle-Range Theory Construction of the Dynamics of Organizational Marketing-Buying Behavior." *The Journal of Business & Industrial Marketing* 18, nos. 4–5 (2003): 309–335.

PART II
Micro Marketing
Section A: Finance

6

ICT-FACILITATED FINANCIAL SERVICE DELIVERIES IN AFRICA

John Kuada

Introduction

The turn of this century has witnessed a steady economic growth in several sub-Saharan African (SSA) countries. Real GDP in the subcontinent as a whole rose by an average of 4.9% a year from 2000 through to 2008, and between 5% and 6% from 2009 to 2013.[1] This growth was more than twice its pace in the 1980s and 1990s. Thus, the subcontinent is now among the world's most rapidly growing economic regions. Some scholars have, however, warned that previous periods of rapid growth across Africa have often been followed by phases of economic decline which have erased many of the gains that countries have achieved in per capita income.[2] In fact, economic activities in the region have markedly weakened in recent years, decelerating from 4.6% in 2014 to 3.4% in 2015.

The decrease has partly been attributed to weak financial sector performance, including tightening borrowing conditions. Economists argue that where financial systems operate effectively, they contribute to growth by mobilizing savings and channeling them to investors that have identified productive investment opportunities.[3] This is currently not the case in most SSA countries. Africa's financial sector has generally been described as underdeveloped, risk averse, highly concentrated in urban areas, and offering only a limited range of financial services, compared with other developing regions of the world.[4] Most banks on the subcontinent are still characterized by low loan-to-deposit ratios, and lending is mainly of a short-term nature.[5] Furthermore, the banking sector has hitherto been unwilling or unable to tap into the large 'under/unbanked' segments of populations across the subcontinent, thereby keeping large segments of the economy non-monetized. Available evidence shows that only 34% of adults in SSA countries had bank accounts in 2014.[6] Financial inclusiveness, therefore, remains one of the key challenges in stimulating growth in Africa. Without inclusive financial systems, poor individuals and small enterprises need to rely on their personal wealth or internal resources to invest in their education, become entrepreneurs, or take advantage of promising growth opportunities.[7]

Previous research has indicated that banks have traditionally been reluctant in extending their services to low-income and rural populations in developing countries, largely because their returns on investments do not justify opening branches in these areas. But the increasing adoption of modern information and communication technology (ICT) in the financial sector and its widespread usage in SSA countries (especially mobile communication systems) have created hope among scholars and policy makers that the innovation will create new powerful channels for providing financial services to the rural populations.[8] A common example cited in the policy literature is the rapid evolution of the M-Pesa system in Kenya. M-Pesa is a SMS-based money transfer system that allows individuals to deposit, send, and withdraw money using their cell phone. It has grown rapidly since its inception, reaching approximately 38% of Kenya's adult population in 2015. It is, therefore, widely viewed as a success story to be emulated across Africa.

In spite of these promising developments, academic interest in ICT-facilitated financial sector development in Africa has been limited. The available literature in the field is limited to policy documents, consultancy reports, and advocacy briefings from non-governmental organizations with interest in poverty alleviation in rural communities. The aim of this chapter is, therefore, to provide an overview of the debate and to encourage academic research into the challenges and opportunities of leveraging mobile technology to extend financial services to large segments of unbanked poor people in the rural communities in sub-Saharan Africa. It seeks to do so by pulling together the available literature and engaging it with theoretical discourses that focus on the role of the financial sector in the growth and development processes in SSA countries.

In terms of structure, the chapter continues with a review of the theoretical foundations of the current financial inclusion debate, which draws largely on neoclassical and socio-institutional perspectives on economic growth and poverty alleviation. It then discusses emerging perspectives on ICT's contribution to financial sector development in developing countries in general and in SSA countries in particular. This is followed by the presentation of the M-Pesa case, showing how this mobile phone transfer system has found and filled a niche in the market. The chapter then discusses the lessons to be learned from the M-Pesa case as well as implications for policy, strategy, and future research.

Theoretical Foundations of the Financial Inclusion Debate

A key debate within the financial access literature in developing countries concerns how accessibility impacts growth in incomes of individuals and families as well as economic growth of their nations. The theoretical foundation of the debate can be traced to neoclassical economic thinking. The general understanding produced in this strand of literature is that wealth accumulation can be maximized by putting idle resources to work, achieving allocative efficiency, and producing continuous dynamic changes in key economic sectors in terms of their relative contributions to growth.[9] High-growth economies have been found to be those in which the share of manufacturing increases gradually and makes the highest contribution to growth.[10] This requires increased productivity in the agricultural sector (and the subsequent transfer of resources into manufacturing) as well as taking advantage of gains from trade.

Proponents of this thinking argue that the financial sector has an important role to play in stimulating dynamic economic activities and inter-sector linkages necessary for sustainable economic growth. The dominant understanding is that the structure and performance of financial systems in a country influence not only the efficiency of resource allocation throughout the economy but also the comparative economic opportunities of individuals from relatively rich or poor households. Beck, Demirgüç-Kunt, and Honohan argue that since stronger financial systems can promote new-firm entry, enterprise growth, innovation, equilibrium size, and risk reduction, then they will almost inevitably improve aggregate economic performance.[11]

Neoclassical economists also argue that richer segments of a population tend to have a higher marginal propensity to save than the poorer segments. Since there is a need to finance large, indivisible investment projects in the process of economic growth, wealth concentration is an inevitable requirement for growth. In other words, societies must accept a trade-off between growth and social justice. More generally, Kuznets reasoned that this trade-off meant that inequality would increase in the early stages of development until the benefits of growth spread throughout the economy.[12]

These earlier perspectives on economic growth and wealth distribution have been criticized for being rigidly economistic in their assumptions. That is, they see economic actors as responding in a rational, predictable way to incentives and constraints. They also assume that economic changes can be engineered through a deliberate transformation of the framework of rules and institutions.[13] Critics say reality always proves to be a lot messier than what theories predict. For example, the lives of poor people are a lot more complex than economic models assume, and poor people can make substantial contributions to economic growth through consumption and small enterprise development if economic policies are inclusive.[14] Thus, an understanding of this complexity in ways that help build diverse socio-economic systems capable of serving the varied needs of ordinary people is a key to economic development and poverty alleviation. That is, researchers and policy makers must put the needs of persons living in poverty at the center of economic growth discourses in order to provide realistic developmental guidelines. This perspective has encouraged the extension of development economics

122 John Kuada

studies to embrace institutional and sociological theories. The emerging emphasis in this strand of research is that financial inclusion must not only play an integral role in reducing rural poverty by facilitating saving and borrowing but also empower the poor to actively participate in the economic life of their societies to insure themselves against a number of vulnerabilities in their lives.

Placing the poor at the center of the debate implies taking a critical look at factors that produce financial exclusion. This requires answering the following set of questions: To what extent is access to finance a constraint to growth? What are the channels through which improved access affects growth and poverty? What aspects of financial sector development matter for broadening access to different types of financial services? What techniques are most effective in ensuring sustainable provision of credit and other financial services on a small scale?

Scholars of economic sociology focus research attention on the ways in which inequality can adversely affect growth prospects through limiting human capital accumulation and occupational choices. They argue that financial sector reforms that promote broader access to financial services are needed to redress the inequities engendered by financial market imperfections. It is in light of these observations that the current debate on the role of ICT in general (and mobile phones, in particular) in the development of pro-growth and pro-poor financial system are being anchored.

The emerging evidence suggests that the introduction of mobile phone technology into the financial sector in Africa has allowed millions of Africans to effectively transfer money across wide distances. As Jack and Suri have observed, phone companies have long allowed individuals to purchase prepaid cell phone credit that can be used for voice or SMS communication, so-called air-time, a means of credit that can be sent to other users.[15] It was, therefore, natural for the phone companies to add new business lines to their operations in countries where conditions have made them possible.

ICT's Contribution to Financial Sector Development

In spite of ICT's apparently significant impact on the financial sectors in an increasing number of SSA countries, there are only a few influential published academic studies that have given adequate attention to the phenomenon. These studies reveal two streams of research and perspective. The first focuses attention on the delivery mechanisms available—that is, the supply side.[16] The second stream focuses attention on identifying factors that either encourage or prevent usage of financial services in a given service provision context.[17] The supply-side discussions are predicated on the understanding that there is no shortage of funds within the global economy, but it is the ability to move money from the sender to the receiver (the so-called velocity of money) that is the stumbling block. The limited outreach of formal financial services has created an opportunity for informal systems such as rotating savings and credit associations (ROSCAs) to flourish. People living in rural communities have relied on these informal services to cover financial commitments such as paying school fees for their children and paying hospital bills as well as funeral or other occasional expenses.[18] The arrangement works in such a manner that members are both savers and borrowers. That is, each member contributes the same amount at each meeting, and one member takes the whole sum once. As a result, each member is able to access a relatively larger sum of money during the life of the ROSCA and use it for whatever purpose she or he wishes. The transactions are trust based; no records are kept, and no money is retained inside the group. This method of saving and borrowing has also been variously described as peer-to-peer banking or peer-to-peer lending and serves as an alternative to saving at home, with the risk of family and relatives demanding access to the savings.

The ICT-enabled financial service innovation has, to a significant extent, bridged the financial service access gap in many rural communities in Africa. It allows users to deposit and transfer funds as well as purchase a range of goods and services using their mobile phone. It has been observed that there are opportunities for scaling up the financial services currently provided through the mobile phone networks and further extend outreach in several countries. But the chances of a mobile money scheme taking root depend on a range of factors, including the strength of the mobile operator within a country, the speed of innovation adoption, and the institutional mechanisms that facilitate the process to ensure product offerings and service quality.

The second stream of research provides insight into the socio-culturally entrenched financial practices and norms that may influence the adoption of the mobile financial service innovation. The studies, therefore, lean on classical innovation adoption theories to understand the processes and constraints to inclusive financial mechanisms. Some of these studies have relied on the Technology Acceptance Model to explain and predict the adoption of the mobile technology services in the rural communities.[19] This theory introduces two factors that determine users' acceptance or rejection of information technology, namely perceived usefulness (PU) and perceived ease of use (PEOU). PU is usually defined as the degree to which a person perceives that adopting the system will improve his or her need fulfillment, whereas PEOU is defined as the degree to which an individual believes that adopting the technology will be relatively easy—that is, effortless. Some studies have combined this theory with such other theories as Innovation Decision Process Theory (DPT) and Perceived Attributes Theory (PAT) to explain the innovation adoption process. With regard to the innovation decision process, the argument is that knowledge about the technology and persuasion strategies is important to ensure adoption. Furthermore, individuals who are risk takers are more likely to adopt the technology at a faster rate than risk-averse individuals. The perceived attributes theorists introduce constructs such as trialability (the extent to which the innovation can be tried out), observability (the extent to which the results can be observed), and complexity (the innovation is not overly complex to learn or use) into their explanatory models.[20]

The available empirical evidence from mobile money transfers suggests that the difficulties of adoption anticipated in these theories have not occurred in

124 John Kuada

practice. The adoption of mobile phones in Africa has occurred at perhaps the fastest rate and deepest level of any consumer-level technology in history. The critical mass of adopters needed to convince the majority of the technology's efficacy was quickly reached in countries that have launched the innovations. In addition to this, the high frequency of usage has ensured successful diffusion efforts. Therefore, some researchers now predict that even the poorest countries are very likely to create a universal ICT access infrastructure in the short term to be able to provide a platform for a wide range of new services.

The general knowledge from the operations of mobile phone–enabled financial services in Africa is that they have introduced a large measure of convenience into domestic remittance transactions, allowing people living in rural communities to get fairly regular incomes, particularly from relatives living in the urban centers. This has enabled them to fulfill their financial obligations. Mobile money also has a cost advantage that reinforces its growing popularity in SSA countries. A study by McKay and Pickens found that, on average, branchless banking (including mobile money) was 19% cheaper than alternative services.[21]

But hitherto the services have been used less extensively to finance investments in small rural farming and non-farming businesses. Thus, the expectations that mobile money can become a general platform that transforms entire economies in the developing world has not as yet been fulfilled. Some academic observers and policy analysts still believe that the technology will eventually be adopted across commerce, health care, agriculture, and other sectors.

The M-Pesa Case

The M-Pesa system in Kenya has been hailed as one of the most successful financial service innovations in SSA countries, with profound implications for rural communities and a harbinger of microfinance revolution in Africa. According to Mas and Radcliffe, there were 16,900 retail stores at which M-Pesa users could cash-in and cash-out in 2010, and nearly half of these stores were located outside urban centers.[22] They also noted that person-to-person (P2P) money transfers in Kenya in 2010 were about US $320 million per month. On an annual basis, this amounted to approximately 10% of Kenya's gross domestic product. Thus, M-Pesa has become a relatively cheap and convenient means through which family members and friends exchange financial assistance in the form of remittances, especially in remote areas of Kenya, where there is limited or no access to formal financial institutions. This section of the chapter provides an overview of the M-Pesa story.

The Beginning

In 2006, only 19% of Kenya's population of 35 million had bank accounts—an indication of the low penetration of conventional banking channels.[23] However, there was an enormous need for money transfers from people living in the towns and cities to their family members in the rural areas. The most common channel for sending money was via informal bus and matatu (shared taxi) drivers. M-Pesa emerged to facilitate the transfer process. It all started in March 2007 when Safaricom, the leading cell phone company in Kenya, in collaboration with Vodafone and the Department for International Development (DFID) of the United Kingdom, started the electronic payment system that was made accessible through mobile phones. The 'M' of M-Pesa stands for 'mobile' and 'Pesa stands for 'money' in Swahili. Thus, the name gave it a clear local identity and image.

The original core offering was person-to-person (P2P) payments. The product concept itself is very simple: An M-Pesa customer can use his or her mobile phone to transfer money directly to another mobile phone user. The advantage is that the process is convenient, quick, and safe. Neither the customer nor the recipient of the money needs to have bank accounts. The customer must simply register with Safaricom for an M-Pesa account. (Customer registration and deposits are free.) The customer then pays cash to a Safaricom dealer, who converts it into e-money. There are simple instructions to guide the customer and recipient in how to use their phones to effect and receive the transferred amount. Security is ensured through the use of PIN-codes. All transactions are authorized and recorded in real time using secure SMS and are capped at US $500. Customers pay a flat fee of around US 40 cents for person-to-person (P2P) transfers and bill payments, and US 33 cents for withdrawals (for transactions less than US $33).

To offer M-Pesa services, dealers (agents) pre-deposit a sum of money (called the 'float') in a bank account, from which the electronic value is used to guarantee all customer deposits and withdrawals. The use of a float meant that there would be no credit risk taken by Safaricom or the dealer. M-Pesa dealers hold e-float balances on their own cell-phones, purchased from Safaricom, and maintain cash on their premises. Dealers must, therefore, net e-float needs to be able to smoothly serve their customers.[24]

The growth history of M-Pesa has been phenomenal. It has quickly become the most successful mobile phone–based financial service in the developing world. In May 2008, 14 months after the launch, its users numbered 2.7 million and were served by almost 3,000 dealers. By the beginning of 2010, 9 million M-Pesa accounts had been registered, indicating that nearly 40% of the Kenyan adult population (about that time) had become users and 12,000 dealers were serving them. The number of customers increased to 25 million by the end of March 2016. There were also operations in other African countries including Lesotho, Mozambique, Tanzania, and Ghana. A survey of over 3,000 M-Pesa customers commissioned by the Central Bank of Kenya in 2008 showed that over 80% of the Kenyan customers were happy with the services offered.[25] Most used M-Pesa for domestic remittances—sending about US$25 per transaction, twice a month.

Lessons From the M-Pesa Case

The question is often asked why many other countries and financial institutions have not adopted M-Pesa or other similar mobile financial innovations in Africa

126 John Kuada

since every service offered in a traditional bank setting can be implemented on a mobile banking platform. The empirical evidence from some previous adoption attempts suggests that it may not be possible to replicate the Kenyan story. Vodafone (the owner of Safaricom) itself has not been able to fully replicate its service in other African countries in which it operates. Following Mas and Radcliffe, M-Pesa's market success can be interpreted as the interplay of three sets of factors: (1) preexisting country conditions that made Kenya a conducive environment for a successful mobile money deployment, (2) a clever service design that facilitated rapid adoption and early capturing of network effects, and (3) a business execution strategy that helped M-Pesa rapidly reach a critical mass of customers.[26] These three conditions may not be present at the same time in many countries.

It has been suggested that the latent demand for domestic remittances is related to urbanization ratios. More propitious markets will be those where the process of rural-urban migration produces large migration flows without depleting the rural populations. There is also the cultural factor; societies in which family members are required to support their relatives will see a greater degree of money transfer than societies that do not impose such obligations on family members. The nature of the regulatory environment also has an impact on the degree and speed of adoption of mobile money transfer technologies. In the case of M-Pesa, it has been observed that the Central Bank of Kenya did not place any regulatory restrictions on Safaricom's pilot launching of M-Pesa. This lenient regulatory environment contributed to M-Pesa's success. Other regulatory institutions in Africa appear more apprehensive about similar innovations.

Furthermore, the ability of M-Pesa stores to convert cash to e-value for customers depends on how easily they can rebalance their liquidity portfolios. This will be more difficult to achieve if bank branch penetration is very low, as this will force the dealers to develop alternative cash transport mechanisms. In other words, a dealer network will need to rely on a minimal banking retail infrastructure.

Even if replication of M-Pesa–type systems may not be immediately possible in other countries, there are lessons that can be learned. Some marketing analysts have pointed at Safaricom's use of customer feedback in its product iteration; its smart marketing strategies, including its use of dealers as customer contact points to facilitate less costly spread of the services, are among the best practices that can be emulated.

Some Future Research Directions

Exploring Successful Business Models in Financial Inclusion

The previous discussions indicate that mobile banking has, so far, been successful in facilitating money transfers in a number of SSA countries. But is has not succeeded in achieving comprehensive financial inclusion. For financial inclusion to make real impact on economic growth process, it must offer other services as well. Services such as savings, borrowing, and insurance are not included in the current product portfolio. There is also the need to target small farming and non-farming activities in the rural economies with financial products that address the peculiar needs of these small business owners. The question is whether mobile banking can cover these other services in the future or SSA countries must concurrently encourage the development of other inclusive financial arrangements. If this is the case, what types of arrangements must be encouraged, and under what conditions will they prove successful? These are issues requiring additional research attention.

Marketing Mobile Financial Services

As noted earlier, the chances of a mobile money scheme taking root in an economy depend partly on the strength of the mobile operator within a given country. In this regard, the quality of marketing strategies has been listed as a key determinant. Strategies that are able to secure a large customer base and facilitate the cross-selling of mobile money services and ensure strong brand recognition and trust among potential customers are all important. Making informed strategic marketing decisions always requires comprehensive knowledge about the target customers, and the financial sector is no exception. Research knowledge is, therefore, needed to guide these strategic decisions.

Furthermore, it is erroneous to assume that rural customers who are the targets of inclusive financial services constitute a homogenous group. There is a dearth of research knowledge that can provide reliable profiles of these target customers. Future research should help uncover the demographic characteristics of the rural communities in the various SSA countries, and their financial service needs require detailed investigations. Such studies are necessary to guide prospective service providers in refining their services and/or in developing new products in response to the target customers' needs and preferences.

Cross-Border Transfers

In addition to domestic remittances, studies have shown that inflow of remittances from Africans living outside their home countries have been on a significant rise since the beginning of the 21st century. Conservative estimates put their annual remittances at $40 billion in the destination countries in Europe and North America.[27] Nearly nothing is known about cross-border transfers within Africa itself. The prospect of cross-border mobile remittance transfers is, therefore, significant and deserves attention. Cross-border mobile payments in general hold much promise in promoting financial integration within regional clusters, adding a new dimension to the benefits of financial inclusion and economic growth. They, therefore, deserve research attention.

Following Beck et al., the lack of systematic information on access is one of the reasons why there has been limited empirical research on cross-border mobile financial service deliveries.[28] Building data sets that benchmark countries annually

128 John Kuada

would help focus policy makers' attention on cross-border remittances and allow them to track and evaluate reform efforts to broaden access.

Designing Suitable Regulatory Mechanisms

The growth of mobile financial services has also raised some fundamental policy questions for regulators. There is the challenge for African governments to craft policies and regulations that can keep pace with emerging banking and payment technologies—including regulatory mechanisms that mitigate criminal exploitations of the technologies without constraining the flexibility and dynamism that may result from their usage. Lessons so far suggest that building an adaptive regulatory framework will facilitate outreach extension in individual countries and across countries. Without clear regulatory frameworks, reputable providers are likely to be unwilling to commit the resources to launch and sustain the ICT-driven financial systems.[29] Furthermore, because the mobile money industry exists at the intersection of finance and telecommunication, it has a diverse set of stakeholders, with players from different fields competing with each other. This poses additional regulatory challenges that require academic attention.

Conclusions

The discussions in this chapter suggest that the adoption of financial service by mobile phone providers have contributed greatly to addressing some of the financial needs of the unbanked segments of the populations in SSA countries. However, expanding access to affordable financial services will remain an important challenge in most of these countries in the coming decades, since the magnitude of the challenges faced by the financial sectors varies across the subcontinent. For example, there are critical differences between the financial systems in low- and middle-income SSA countries. Research knowledge is required to provide insight into the scope and limits of ICT as an inclusive financial service delivery mechanism. Furthermore, as Dzodonu reminds us, ICTs cannot be a panacea for all socio-economic development problems of a given nation since development is dependent on many factors.[30] Factors such as political stability, macroeconomic governance, transparency and accountability of national and local administrations, physical infrastructure, and basic literacy should also be addressed in an explicit manner—and ICT should not be seen as a substitute.

Notes

1 African Economic Outlook, Basic Statistics, accessed November 12, 2016, www.african economicoutlook.org/en/statistics.
2 Stephen Broadberry and Leigh Gardner, *Africa's Growth Prospects in a European Mirror: A Historical Perspective* (London School of Economics and Political Science Department of Economic History Working Papers No. 202, April 2014), 2.

3 Thorsten Beck, Asli Demirgüç-Kunt, and Patrick Honohan, "Access to Financial Services: Measurement, Impact, and Policies," *The World Bank Research Observer* 24, no. 1 (February 2009): 120.

4 John Kuada, "Financial Market Performance and Growth in Africa," *African Journal of Economic and Management Studies* 7 (2016): 3.

5 Thorsten Beck et al., *Financing Africa Through the Crisis and Beyond* (Washington, DC: The World Bank, 2011): 10.

6 European Investment Bank, *Digital Financial Services in Africa: Beyond the Kenyan Success Story*, 6, accessed November 22, 2016, www.eib.org/attachments/country/study_digital_financial_services_in_africa_en.pdf.

7 Beck et al., 121.

8 Ignacio Mas and Daniel Radcliffe, "Mobile Payments Go Viral: M-PESA in Kenya, in *Yes Africa Can: Success Stories from a Dynamic Continent* (Washington, DC: The World Bank, 2010), 5, accessed November 21, 2016, www.microfinancegateway.org/sites/default/files/mfg-en-case-study-mobile-payments-go-viral-m-pesa-in-kenya-mar-2010.pdf.

9 Hollis Chenery, S. Sherman Robinson, and Moshe Syrquin, *Industrialization and Growth: A Comparative Study* (New York: Oxford University Press, 1986): 42.

10 Hollis Chenery and Lance Taylor, "Development Patterns Among Countries and Over Time," *Review of Economic and Statistics* 51 (November 1968): 391–416.

11 Beck et al., 121.

12 Simon Kuznets, *Modern Economic Growth* (New Haven, CT: Yale University Press, 1966): 50.

13 Kurt Weyland, "The Political Economy of Market Reform and A Revival of Structuralism," *Latin American Research Review* 42 (2007): 235.

14 John Kuada, *Private Enterprise-Led Economic Development in Sub-Saharan Africa: The Human Side of Growth* (London: Palgrave Macmillan, 2015): 20.

15 William Jack and Tavneet Suri, *The Economics of M-PESA*, accessed November 4, 2016, www.mit.edu/~tavneet/M-PESA.pdf.

16 Richard Duncombe and Richard Boateng, "Mobile Phones and Financial Services in Developing Countries: A Review of Concepts, Methods, Issues, Evidence and Future Research Directions," *Third World Quarterly* 30 (2009): 1237.

17 Richard Duncombe, "An Evidence-Based Framework for Assessing the Potential of Mobile Finance in Sub-Saharan Africa," *Journal of Modern African Studies* 50 (2012): 369.

18 Peter Kimuyu, "Rotating Saving and Credit Associations in Rural East Africa," *World Development* 27 (1999): 1299.

19 Fred D. Davis, Richard Bagozzi, and Paul Warshaw, "User Acceptance of Computer Technology: A Comparison of Two Theoretical Models," *Management Science* 35 (1989): 982–1003.

20 Mas and Radcliffe, 6.

21 Claudia McKay and Mark Pickens, "Branchless Banking 2010: Who's Served? At What Price? What's Next?" Focus Note 66, Consultative Group to Assist the Poor (Washington, DC, 2010), accessed November 21, 2016, www.cgap.org/publications/branchless-banking-2010-who%E2%80%99s-served-what-price-what%E2%80%99s-next.

22 Mas and Radcliffe, 7.

23 Alliance for Financial Inclusion, Enabling Mobile Money Transfer: The Central Bank of Kenya's Treatment of M-Pesa, accessed November 4, 2016, 4, www.afi-global.org/sites/default/files/publications/afi_casestudy_mpesa_en.pdf.

24 See Jack and Suri, 2010.

25 Alliance for Financial Inclusion, 6.

26 Mas and Radcliffe, 8.

27 Adams B. Bodomo, "African Diaspora Remittances Are Better Than Foreign Aid Funds," accessed June 3, 2016, www.modernghana.com/news/449528/1/african-diaspora-remittances-are-better-than-forei.html.

130 John Kuada

28 Beck et al., 122.
29 David Porteous, "Competition and Interest Rates in Microfinance," CGAP Focus Note 33 (2006), www.cgap.org/docs/FocusNote_33.pdf.
30 Clement Dzodonu, "An Analysis of the Role of ICTs To Achieving the MDGs," 15, accessed November 21, 2016, http://unpan1.un.org/intradoc/groups/public/docu ments/un-dpadm/unpan039075.pdf.

Bibliography

African Economic Outlook. *Basic Statistics*. Accessed November 12, 2016. www.african economicoutlook.org/en/statistics.

Alliance for Financial Inclusion. *Enabling Mobile Money Transfer: The Central Bank of Kenya's Treatment of M-Pesa*, 1–17. Accessed November 4, 2016. www.afi-global.org/sites/default/files/publications/afi_casestudy_mpesa_en.pdf.

Beck, Thorsten, Asli Demirgüç-Kunt, and Patrick Honohan. "Access to Financial Services: Measurement, Impact, and Policies." *The World Bank Research Observer* 24, no. 1 (February 2009): 119–145.

Beck, Thorsten et al. *Financing Africa Through the Crisis and Beyond*. Washington, DC: The World Bank, 2011.

Bodomo, Adams B. "African Diaspora Remittances Are Better Than Foreign Aid Funds." Accessed June 3, 2016. www.modernghana.com/news/449528/1/african-diaspora-remittances-are-better-than-forei.html.

Broadberry, Stephen, and Leigh Gardner. *Africa's Growth Prospects in a European Mirror: A Historical Perspective*. London School of Economics and Political Science, Department of Economic History. Working Papers No. 202, April 2014, 2.

Chenery, Hollis, S. Sherman Robinson, and Moshe Syrquin. *Industrialization and Growth: A Comparative Study*. New York: Oxford University Press, 1986, 42.

Chenery, Hollis, and Lance Taylor. "Development Patterns Among Countries and Over Time." *Review of Economic and Statistics* 51 (November 1968): 391–416.

Davis, Fred D., Richard Bagozzi, and Paul Warshaw. "User Acceptance of Computer Technology: A Comparison of Two Theoretical Models." *Management Science* 35 (1989): 982–1003.

Duncombe, Richard. "An Evidence-Based Framework for Assessing the Potential of Mobile Finance in Sub-Saharan Africa." *Journal of Modern African Studies* 50 (2012): 369–395.

Duncombe, Richard, and Richard Boateng. "Mobile Phones and Financial Services in Developing Countries: A Review of Concepts, Methods, Issues, Evidence and Future Research Directions." *Third World Quarterly* 30 (2009): 1237–1258.

Dzodonu, Clement. "An Analysis of the Role of ICTs to Achieving the MDGs." Accessed November 21, 2016. http://unpan1.un.org/intradoc/groups/public/documents/un-dpadm/unpan039075.pdf.

European Investment Bank. *Digital Financial Services in Africa: Beyond the Kenyan Success Story*, 6. Accessed November 22, 2016. www.eib.org/attachments/country/study_digital_financial_services_in_africa_en.pdf.

Jack, William, and Tavneet Suri. *The Economics of M-PESA*. Accessed November 4, 2016. www.mit.edu/~tavneet/M-Pesa.pdf.

Kimuyu, Peter. "Rotating Saving and Credit Associations in Rural East Africa." *World Development* 27 (1999): 1299–1308.

Kuada, John. "Financial Market Performance and Growth in Africa." *African Journal of Economic and Management Studies* 7 (2016): 3–6.

Kuada, John. *Private Enterprise-Led Economic Development in Sub-Saharan Africa: The Human Side of Growth*. London: Palgrave Macmillan, 2015, 20.

Kuznets, Simon. *Modern Economic Growth*. New Haven, CT: Yale University Press, 1966, 1–80.

Mas, Ignacio, and Daniel Radcliffe. "Mobile Payments Go Viral: M-PESA in Kenya." In *Yes Africa Can: Success Stories from a Dynamic Continent*. Washington, DC: World Bank, 2010, 5. Accessed November 21, 2016. www.microfinancegateway.org/sites/default/files/mfg-en-case-study-mobile-payments-go-viral-m-pesa-in-kenya-mar-2010.pdf.

McKay, Claudia, and Mark Pickens. "Branchless Banking 2010: Who's Served? At What Price? What's Next?" *Focus*. Note 66, Consultative Group to Assist the Poor. Washington, DC. 2010. Accessed November 21, 2016. www.cgap.org/publications/branchless-banking-2010-who%E2%80%99s-served-what-price-what%E2%80%99s-next.

Porteous, David. "Competition and Interest Rates in Microfinance." *CGAP Focus*. Note, 2006, 33. www.cgap.org/docs/FocusNote_33.pdf.

Weyland, Kurt. "The Political Economy of Market Reform and a Revival of Structuralism." *Latin American Research Review* 42 (2007): 235–242.

7

MOBILE TRANSACTIONS

A Powerful Channel to Drive Financial Inclusion. Evidence From Kenya: M-Pesa Model

Mario Testa and Marco Pellicano

> "(...) the *poor households we met actively*
> *employ financial tools not* despite *being poor,*
> *but* because *they are poor".*
> —Collins D. et al. "Portfolios of the Poor: How the World's Poor Live on $2 a
> Day," 2009, p. 30

Introduction

In a few short years, the proliferation of mobile phone networks has transformed economic and social life in sub-Saharan Africa (SSA). It has also allowed Africans to skip the landline stage of development and jump right to the digital age. At present, cell phones are pervasive in this region. Since 2002, cell phone ownership has exploded; indeed, in that year only 9% of Kenyans said they owned a mobile phone, whereas today, there are 83%, with a more than tenfold increase. Similar growth in mobile penetration is seen in all African countries where survey data are available.[1]

In several African countries, mobile connectivity has extended beyond the reach of the electricity grid. There are currently 34 million people in Kenya who lack formal access to energy and over 19 million off-grid mobile Subscriber Identification Module (SIM) connections.[2] Put simply, many Kenyans have a phone before they have a place to charge it. The mobile industry is unique in the size and reach of its power infrastructure, penetration rates and brand power, providing an opportunity for unprecedented scale in impacting lives.

Mobile connections are expected to keep rising in the next years, with mobile service available in 40% of the country, covering over 95% of the population. Nevertheless, the large majority of the population (approximately 76%) lives in rural areas, where grid power distribution and reliability remains poor.[3]

At the same time, one of the many effects of globalization on lesser-developed countries (LDCs) has been the rise of cash payments in traditionally barter economies. With more than 70% of the world's poor living in rural areas, accessibility to cash and the financial institutions that manage currency can be challenging. However, recent innovations have emerged in areas where the formal banking sector has failed to provide access to financial services at affordable prices to low-income, rural populations and other vulnerable groups. One of these new technologies arose in the years following the boom in mobile phone infrastructure: mobile money transfers. In developing countries, e-money demonstrated it can reach millions of unbanked individuals, providing a significant step toward financial inclusion.[4]

Launched in Kenya in 2007, M-Pesa is one of the world's first mobile money services. It is a money transfer system operated by Safaricom, Kenya's largest cellular phone provider. M-Pesa allows users to exchange cash for e-float on their phones, to send e-float to other cellular phone users, and to exchange e-float back into cash. The growth of mobile telephones in Africa is a tectonic and unexpected change in communications technology, and this has been the background of the development of M-Pesa.[5] Within 8 months of its inception, in March 2007, over 1.1 million Kenyans had registered to use M-Pesa, and over US$87 million had been transferred over the system.[6]

Nowadays, Kenya leads the world in developing mobile money payment systems and in widespread usage, despite Kenya's extreme poverty, ranking 187 in per capita GDP. Of the country's 47 million people, about seven out of ten adults have financial accounts. In addition to mobile money, financial services are available through a diverse group of providers, including banks, non-bank financial institutions, and informal financial groups.[7]

A well-functioning financial system is an essential precondition for the economic and social development of every community, especially enhancing the prospects of the poor through a better access to the financial services and financial inclusion.

Financial Inclusion in Kenya

In 2008, Kenya had a stable, growing banking sector that appeared to have avoided most of the problems arising from the global financial crisis. However, despite the strong growth of leading local retail banks, like Equity Bank, in the preceding 5 years, only 19% of Kenya's population of 35 million in 2006 had bank accounts. In Kenya, as in many developing economies, banking was still generally considered to be the business of the rich, who could afford the regular and expensive fees, or those less well-off but who lived in urban centers with more accessible bank branches.[8]

With around 70% of the population still living in rural communities, there was limited access not only to basic infrastructure, but also even to affordable financial services, such as payment facilities or savings. Actually, there existed little incentive for banks to serve the unbanked, mainly due the significant costs of establishing a branch network and the tight margins associated with banking the poor. This was indicative by the low penetration of conventional banking channels. At the time of the first M-Pesa application, there were only 1.5 bank branches per 100,000 people and only one automated teller machine (ATM) per 100,000 people.[9]

But for every Kenyan who had access to a bank account, at least two others had access to a mobile phone. Mobile phone penetration in 2006 was nearly 30% and growing much faster than bank account penetration.

The Financial Access Survey carried out in 2006 first highlighted to the Central Bank of Kenya (CBK) the very low reach of the traditional banking sector, with more than a third excluded from all financial services, and another third dependent only on informal services. Over time, the concept of financial inclusion, as well as its definitions and measurements, have evolved from classifying individuals and enterprises according to a dichotomous division as either included or not, to viewing financial inclusion as multidimensional. With the aim of defining a more complete concept of inclusion, the Financial Inclusion Data Working Group of the Alliance for Financial Inclusion (AFI FIDWG) agreed on three main dimensions of financial inclusion that provide the underpinning for data collection: access, usage, and quality.[10]

The 2016 FinAccess household survey[11] reports track financial inclusion according to different measures and identifies some barriers and drivers of inclusivity. These measures include level of formality (access strand), choice of institution (e.g., bank, informal group, SACCOs)[12] and functionality (e.g., savings, credit, and insurance).[13] The access strand classifies users according to their most formal service provider used as defined in Table 7.1. For example, if users have any financial service/product from any formal category, they are placed in the formally included category, even though they may additionally use an informal service. If users have an informal group only, they are placed in the informally included category.

The number of Kenyans formally included by the financial system has grown by 50% in the last 10 years. Over three-quarters (75.3%) of Kenyans are now formally included, up from 66.9% in 2013.[14] Financial exclusion, which is now down to 17.4%, has more than halved since 2006.[15] (Figure 7.1).

The use of most types of financial services, especially banks and informal groups, increased between 2006 and 2016. The exception is SACCOs, which experienced a dip in usage but are becoming popular again (Figure 7.2).

The growth of mobile financial services[16] has slowed since 2009. Meanwhile, with 18% of the population using new mobile banking services such as M-Shwari

TABLE 7.1 Classification of the Access Strand

Classification	Definition
Formal (prudential)	Financial services used through prudentially regulated service providers and are supervised by independent statutory agencies (CBK, CMA, IRA, RBA, and SASRA).
Formal (non-prudential)	Financial services through service providers that are subject to non-prudential oversight by government departments/ministries with focused legislations or statutory agencies.
Formal (registered)	Financial services through providers that are legally registered and/or operate through direct government interventions.
Informal	Financial services through forms not subject to regulation but have a relatively well-defined organizational structure.
Excluded	Individuals who report using financial services only through family, friends, or neighbors, or who keep in secret places.

Source: "2016 FinAccess Household Survey," FinAccess, February 2016, http://fsdkenya.org/wp-content/uploads/2016/02/The-2016-FinAccess-household-survey-report1.pdf.

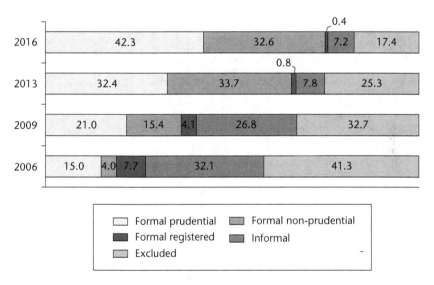

FIGURE 7.1 Access Strand Over the Years 2006–2016

Source: "2016 FinAccess Household Survey," FinAccess, February 2016, http://fsdkenya.org/wp-content/uploads/2016/02/The-2016-FinAccess-household-survey-report1.pdf.

and KCB M-Pesa, the proportion of bank account users has now risen to 38%, a 10% increase since 2013.

There is clear evidence that mobile money contributes to financial inclusion, providing financial services to the disadvantaged groups.

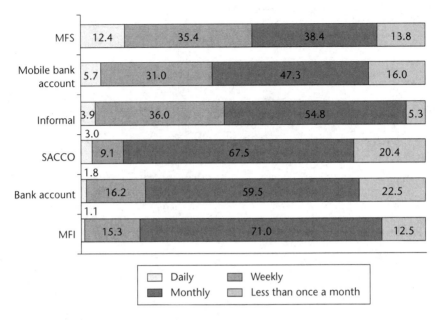

FIGURE 7.2 Frequency of Use of Financial Service

Source: "2016 FinAccess Household Survey," FinAccess, February 2016, http://fsdkenya.org/wp-content/uploads/2016/02/The-2016-FinAccess-household-survey-report1.pdf.

The Kenyan ICT Landscape and a Brief Description of Safaricom

Information and communication technologies (ICTs) have the potential to transform business and government in Africa, driving entrepreneurship, innovation, and economic growth. As several reports have highlighted, the ICT sector has proven to be a strong driver of GDP growth in nations across the world; from developing countries to developed nations, the ICT sector has contributed to the success of these national economies.[17] The ICT sector is socially and economically relevant especially to Africa in that it has been the major economic driver in sub-Saharan Africa over the past decade. Although mobile and Internet penetration remains comparatively low in Africa, never before in the history of the continent has the population been as connected as it is today.[18] The regional breakdown between these indicators also shows a substantial digital divide, with Africa achieving lower ICT density levels than other regions. This is illustrated by the data for mobile phone and broadband subscriptions in Figure 7.3 and for Internet users in Figure 7.4.

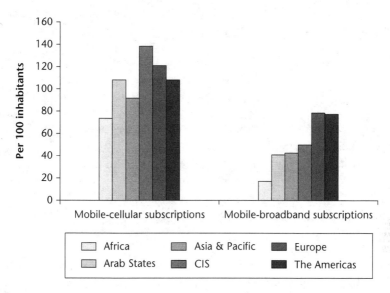

FIGURE 7.3 Percentage of ICT Access by Region, 2015

Source: "Measuring the Information Society Report," International Telecommunication Union, Geneva: International Telecommunication Union, 2015, www.itu.int/en/ITU-D/Statistics/Documents/publications/misr2015/MISR2015-w5.pdf

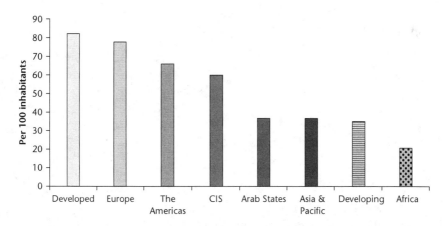

FIGURE 7.4 Percentage of Individuals Using the Internet by Development Status and Region, 2015

Source: "Measuring the Information Society Report," International Telecommunication Union, Geneva: International Telecommunication Union, 2015, www.itu.int/en/ITU-D/Statistics/Documents/publications/misr2015/MISR2015-w5.pdf

Kenya has made great strides in ICT development in the past few years and is now considered to be a leader within Africa. The government's focus on developing an ICT-enabled country has contributed to development of a robust ICT landscape.

In Kenya, Safaricom Limited (Safaricom) is the leading mobile network operator and dominates the market, with more than 65% of market share. It has over 25 million customers and annual revenues in excess of KSh 195 billion.[19]

Safaricom is an integrated communications company, providing voice, data, and financial (mobile money) products and services to consumers, businesses, and public sector clients. It was formed in 1997 as a fully owned subsidiary of Telkom Kenya. In May 2000, Vodafone Group Plc of the United Kingdom acquired a 40% stake and management responsibility for the company. It operates solely in Kenya, and its headquarters are located at Safaricom House in Nairobi. Its operations consist of Safaricom House 1, 2, and 3, the Safaricom Care Centre, the Jambo Contact Centre, 44 retail stores and a network of 3,800 2G-enabled base stations, of which 2,517 are 3G and 463 are 4G enabled. Its shareholding structure is composed of the Government of Kenya (35%), Vodafone Group Plc (40%), and free float (25%). It is listed on the Nairobi Stock Exchange, trading in the telecommunications and technology segment.

The company's business model explains how it operates and how it executes strategy and achieves its vision of transforming lives. The several services include mobile and fixed voice, messaging, data, Internet, and M-Pesa platform. In a Sustainability Report they affirm:

> We aspire to use our products and services to transform lives and contribute to sustainable living throughout Kenya. Based on this fundamental aspiration, our vision sets out how we use our ability to deliver connectivity and innovative services to improve the quality of life and livelihoods of the people we reach. Central to achieving this vision is our commitment to managing our operations responsibly and ethically.[20]

The Safaricom true value bridge shows that the total value we created for Kenyan society in FY16 was KSh 414 billion, around 10.86 times greater than the financial profit the company made.[21] Figure 7.5 shows some interesting financial data of Safaricom in the period 2013–2016.

Communications technology is an essential part of most people's lives and is transforming the world in which we live. The strategic vision of Safaricom is summarized as follows: "we can continue to grow our business and enhance our brand by developing innovative, commercially viable solutions that both support sustainable development and improve the quality of life of Kenyans. Our M-PESA mobile money transfer product, for instance, has become a platform for a range of services that are improving livelihoods."[22]

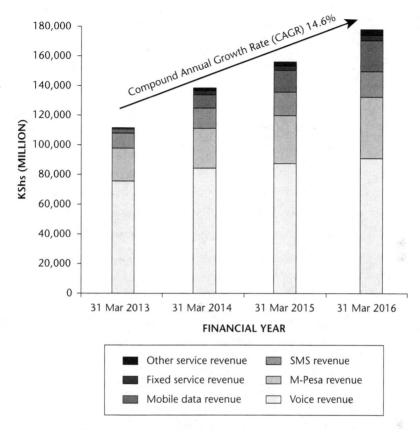

FIGURE 7.5 Safaricom Financial Performance

Source: "Sustainability Report: Widening Our Vision, Sharpening Our Focus," Safaricom, 2016, www.safaricom.co.ke.

M-Pesa Model: Presentation of the Case

M-Pesa is an m-banking application that facilitates branchless banking via the mobile phone. The name comes from the Swahili '*pesa*' meaning 'money,' and the original idea began as a development aid project to enable microfinance repayments. It targets the unbanked, prepaid segment of the population and was officially introduced onto the Kenyan market in March of 2007 by Safaricom. It was funded by Department for International Development (DFID), the part of the UK government that provides aid to developing countries, in conjunction with Vodafone, the UK telecommunications company.[23] The original concept behind M-Pesa was a project in neighboring Mozambique via the operator M-Cel. Researchers funded by DFID had noted that people in countries like Uganda, Botswana, and Ghana were spontaneously using mobile phone airtime credits as a way of transferring money to relatives. Their research in 2002 led to the first credit-transfer scheme offered by M-Cel in 2004. Gamos (the research consultants) then proposed using a similar scheme to help repayment of microfinance loans in Kenya and, with DFID support, began working with Vodafone in 2005. The software supporting M-Pesa began as a student development project and was then taken up by the technology consultants Sagentia; this underpinned the launch of M-Pesa in 2007.[24]

Although M-Pesa does not pay interest on deposits and does not make loans, it can usefully be thought of as a bank that provides transaction services and that has operated, until recently, in parallel with the formal banking system.[25]

To access the service, customers must first register at an authorized M-Pesa retail outlet. They are then assigned an individual electronic money account linked to their phone number and accessible through an application stored on the SIM cards of their mobile phones. The application has two main functions. First, it allows customers to deposit cash to and withdraw cash from their accounts by exchanging cash for electronic value at a network of retail stores. Second, it allows users to transfer funds to others, to pay bills, and to purchase mobile airtime credit. Retail stores are paid a fee by Safaricom each time they exchange cash for M-Pesa credit on behalf of customers. All M-Pesa transactions are authorized and recorded in real time using secure Short Messaging Service (SMS) and are capped at US$500.[26] Figure 7.6 synthesizes the M-Pesa model and its applications.

Many people work in cities but send money back to relatives in their home villages and M-Pesa allows them to do this safely without the risks of robbery or

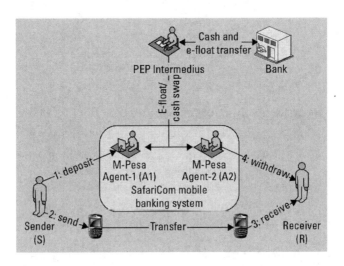

FIGURE 7.6 Working Model of M-Pesa

Source: Nir Kshetri, and Sharad Acharya, "Mobile Payments in Emerging Markets," *IT Professional* 14, IEEE, July–August (2012): 9–13.

the inconvenience of having to make the journey.[27] In Kenya, Tanzania, Uganda, and Madagascar, there are now more mobile money accounts than bank accounts; in sub-Saharan Africa overall, more people have mobile money accounts than Facebook accounts.[28]

M-Pesa continues to grow and evolve from a simple mobile money transfer service into a robust payment platform and a driver of financial inclusion. Revenue from the service grew by 27.2% from KSh 32.63 million in FY15 to KSh 41.50 during the year. Likewise, the number of users (active in the last 30 days) leapt by 19.8%, from 13.86 million to 16.6 million in March 2016.

One pleasing aspect of this growth is that our M-Shwari banking service, which makes it possible for ordinary Kenyans to save, earn interest, and borrow money using their mobile phones and the M-Pesa service, has grown from 3 million to 3.9 million active users and has facilitated KSh 8.1 billion in deposits and KSh 7.4 billion in loans at 2.0% interest. Safaricom also has 100,744 M-Pesa agents, whose number grows continuously, who support and administer transactions for customers.

Its business and social performance is of great interest to its large local customer and shareholder base, the government, and international portfolio investors, whereas the phenomenal success of M-Pesa in Kenya attracts the interest of the technology and development community worldwide.

As Ignacio Mas and Dan Radcliffe underline effectively, Safaricom recognized that it would be difficult to scale M-Pesa incrementally, because it had to overcome some significant obstacles common to any new electronic payment system: adverse network effects, the chicken-and-egg trap, and trust.[29]

As regarding the first obstacle, adverse network effects, the value to the customer of a payment system depends on the number of people connected to and actively using it as in the typical network effect. When a network effect is present, the value of a product or service is dependent on the number of users, because the more people are on the network, the more useful it becomes. Network effects can facilitate a scheme gain momentum once it reaches a critical mass of customers; they also make it difficult to attract early adopters of the new technology.

To grow, M-Pesa had to catch the attention of customers and, at the same time, stores. It is difficult to attract customers if there are few stores to serve them, and simultaneously it can be hard to convince stores to sell the service when there are few customers to be had (thus, the chicken-and-egg trap). This consideration explains why M-Pesa adopted an aggressive acquisition policy for both customers and stores.

With regard to the trust, a company will be winning in attracting customers only when they will have confidence in the reliability of the new system. In Kenyan M-Pesa, customers had to be reassured about a payment system operated by a mobile operator, without a bank retail outlet to satisfy financial needs, and using mobile phones to access account information and implement transactions.

Initially, the problems previously described have represented a considerable barrier to growth, especially for many other mobile money deployments that remained subscale. Nevertheless, M-Pesa overcame this hurdle through quite vigorous actions on two different strategies: (1) considerable up-front investments in well-built service brand for M-Pesa, and (2) successfully leveraged own extensive network of airtime resellers in order to build a trustworthy and steady retail network able to satisfy customers' liquidity needs.[30]

Conclusion in Light of Blue Ocean Strategy

Blue Ocean Strategy, created by W. Chan Kim and Renée Mauborgne of the INSEAD Blue Ocean Strategy Institute, underlines the difference between companies that traditionally work in 'red ocean' conditions, where businesses ruthlessly fight against each other for a share of the marketplace and those that have found a way to work in a marketplace that is free of competitors.[31]

The authors describe Blue Ocean Strategy as creating an industry that is not in existence today, and they note that there are two ways to create a blue ocean: (1) creating a completely new industry that was not in existence, or (2) creating a new market from an existing market. The latter is what Safaricom did with M-Pesa, creating a leap in value for the company, its buyers, and its employees while unlocking new demand and making the competition irrelevant, which allows the firm to break the value/cost trade-off.

The pervasiveness of the mobile phone in developing countries has recently caused two effects. First, it has instigated the development of applications designed to alleviate poverty. According to the international development community, the aim of these initiatives is to empower poor constituents by providing them access to formal financial services. Second, the innovation enabling the creation of blue oceans. As the authors argued, the innovation often could not be a new technology, but a new business model or a new approach to capturing a different market with a different combination of existing products and services.

By adopting a cross-sector approach, Safaricom bypassed two overcrowded industries, banking and ICT, developing an untapped market space where no other competitors existed. In African markets, less than 30% of the population has a bank account and even less has a credit card. Cash purchases are the norm. The amount of cash in someone's pocket at any one time can vary massively, and this is what drives purchase decisions. Safaricom in Kenya pushed for a mobile-driven model, cashless future, contributing to begin a new era of financial services.[32]

In order to identify the uncontested market space and increase both its profit and value for customers, Safaricom followed the six principles (four Formulation Principles and two Executive Principles) of Blue Ocean Strategy. The four Formulation Principles are (1) reconstruct market boundaries; (2) focus on the big picture, not the numbers; (3) reach beyond existing demand; and (4) get the strategic sequence right. The two Executive Principles are (1) overcome key organizational hurdles, and (2) build execution into strategy.

Nevertheless, it seems useful to highlight that Safaricom has put in place an additional principle giving a supplementary value for its customers concerning a number of ethical consequences. The significant rise of mobile money use is showing important implications for the private sector, offering several business opportunities and improving sustainable development projects for Kenyan economy. Indeed, there is often a close relationship between appropriate technology and traditional habit, as the M-Pesa example shows. The innovative use of mobile phone technology to drive financial inclusion in Kenya has been generally acclaimed around the world, but much more remains to be done because lack of good financial options is certainly one of the reasons why poor people are trapped in poverty. To really convert the financial lives of underserved people, mobile money must become a central monetization mechanism, universally available across a greater range of digital transactions. By making mobile money more vital to the financial lives of users, greater financial inclusion, economic growth, and sustainable social development can be achieved.

Notes

1 "Cell Phones in Africa: Communication Lifeline," *Global Attitudes & Trends*, Pew Research Center April 2015, www.pewglobal.org/2015/04/15/cell-phones-in-africa-communication-lifeline/.
2 "Safaricom-Kenya-Feasibility Study," *GSMA*, 2012. www.gsma.com/mobilefordevelop ment/wp-content/uploads/2013/02/Safaricom-Feasibility-Study.pdf.
3 Ibid.
4 Deborah Carey, "Mobile Money and Macroeconomic Development: Case Study on M-PESA," *The World Mind: A Magazine for International and Public Affairs*, Spring 2016, accessed January 13, 2018, https://edspace.american.edu/theworldmind/wp-content/uploads/sites/723/2016/12/The-World-Mind-Vol.-1-No.-2.pdf.
5 Allan Mugambi, Christopher Niunge, and Samuel C. Yang, "Mobile-Money Benefits and Usage: The Case of M-PESA," *IT Pro* 16 (May–June 2014). http://doi.ieeecom putersociety.org/10.1109/MITP.2014.38.
6 Isaac Mbiti and David N. Weil, "Mobile Banking: The Impact of M-PESA in Kenya," National Bureau of Economic Research, Cambridge, Massachusetts, Working Paper WP 17129 (June 2011), doi:10.3386/w17129.
7 "Kenya," *Financial Inclusion Insights*, accessed November 20, 2016, http://finclusion. org/country/africa/kenya.html.
8 "Enabling Mobile Money Transfer: The Central Bank of Kenya's Treatment of M-Pesa," Alliance for Financial Inclusion (AFI), accessed November 20, 2016, www.afi-global. org/sites/default/files/publications/afi_casestudy_mpesa_en.pdf
9 Ibid.
10 Thouraya Triki and Issa Faye, "Financial Inclusion in Africa," African Development Bank, 2013, www.afdb.org/fileadmin/uploads/afdb/Documents/Project-and-Opera tions/Financial_Inclusion_in_Africa.pdf.
11 The 2016 FinAccess household survey is the fourth in the series of surveys that measure the drivers and usage of financial services in Kenya. The baseline survey was released in 2006. These results provide the first ever 10-year perspective on the financial inclusion landscape.
12 Savings and Credit Cooperative Societies (SACCOs) is a special type of cooperative offering financial services, with major focus on mobilization of funds and provision of affordable credit, to its members who are both the owners and users.

144 Mario Testa and Marco Pellicano

13 "2016 FinAccess Household Survey," Central Bank of Kenya, Kenya National Bureau of Statistics and FSD Kenya, February 2016, http://fsdkenya.org/wp-content/uploads/2016/02/The-2016-FinAccess-household-survey-report1.pdf.
14 Ibid.
15 According to the 2016 data, women still have significantly reduced access to formal services such as banks: 34.6% of women use banks, compared with 50.3% of men. The north of Kenya has poorer than average access, North-eastern province where over half (52.2%) are excluded, meaning they have no access to formal financial services whatsoever.
16 Mobile financial service providers include Airtel Money, M-Pesa, MobiKash, Orange Money, and Tangaza Pesa.
17 Javier Ewing et al., "ICT Competitiveness in Africa," in *eTransform Africa: The Transformational Use of ICTs in Africa*, eds. Enock Yonazi et al. (Washington: World Bank, 2012), http://siteresources.worldbank.org/EXTINFORMATIONANDCOMMUNICATIONANDTECHNOLOGIES/Resources/282822-1346223280837/MainReport.pdf.
18 Ibid.
19 "Sustainability Report: Widening Our Vision, Sharpening Our Focus," Safaricom, 2016, www.safaricom.co.ke.
20 "Sustainability Report: Transforming Lives," Safaricom, 2015, 15, www.safaricom.co.ke.
21 "Sustainability Report: Widening Our Vision, Sharpening Our Focus," Safaricom, 2016, www.safaricom.co.ke.
22 Ibid.
23 Olga Morawczynski and Gianluca Miscione, "Examining Trust in Mobile Banking Transactions: The Case of M-PESA in Kenya," *International Federation for Information Processing* (IFIP) 282 (2008), doi:10.1007/978-0-387-84822-8_19; and Chrisanthi Avgerou, Matthew L. Smith, and Peter van den Besselaar, *Social Dimensions of Information and Communication Technology Policy* (Boston: Springer, 2008), 287–298.
24 "M-PESA Case Study," accessed November 20, 2016, http://johnbessant.net/resources/case-studies/m-pesa-case-study/.
25 William Jack and Tavneet Suri, "Mobile Money: The Economics of M-PESA," National Bureau of Economic Research, Cambridge, Massachusetts Working Paper 16721, 2011, doi:10.3386/w16721.
26 Ignacio Mas and Dan Radcliffe, "Mobile Payments Go Viral: M-PESA in Kenya," *Financial Services for the Poor*, Bill and Melinda Gates Foundation, March 10, 2010, http://siteresources.worldbank.org/AFRICAEXT/Resources/258643-1271798012256/M-PESA_Kenya.pdf.
27 "M-PESA Case Study," accessed November 20, 2016, http://johnbessant.net/resources/case-studies/m-pesa-case-study/.
28 Mugambi et al., "Mobile-Money Benefits and Usage: The Case of M-PESA," 2014.
29 Mas and Radcliffe, "Mobile Payments Go Viral: M-PESA in Kenya," 2010.
30 Ibid.
31 W. Chan Kim and Renee Mauborgne, *Blue Ocean Strategy* (Boston, MA: Harvard Business School Press, 2015).
32 Mobile money case study, "How M-PESA Is Driving Africa's Cashless Future," Digital Marketing Industry Case Study Library, www.digitaltrainingacademy.com/casestudies/2015/01/mobile_money_case_study_how_mpesa_is_driving_africas_cashless_future.php.

Bibliography

Alliance for Financial Inclusion. "Enabling Mobile Money Transfer: The Central Bank of Kenya's Treatment of M-Pesa." Accessed November 20, 2016. www.afiglobal.org/sites/default/files/publications/afi_casestudy_mpesa_en.pdf.

Avgerou, Chrisanthi, Matthew L. Smith, and Peter van den Besselaar. *Social Dimensions of Information and Communication Technology Policy*. Boston, MA: Springer, 2008.

Carey, Deborah. "Mobile Money and Macroeconomic Development: Case Study on M-PESA." *The World Mind: A Magazine for International and Public Affairs*, Spring 2016. Accessed January 13, 2018. https://edspace.american.edu/theworldmind/wp-content/uploads/sites/723/2016/12/The-World-Mind-Vol.-1-No.-2.pdf.

"Cell Phones in Africa: Communication Lifeline." *Global Attitudes & Trends*. Pew Research Center (April 2015). www.pewglobal.org/2015/04/15/cell-phones-in-africa-communication-lifeline/.

Ewing, Javier et al. "ICT Competitiveness in Africa." In *eTransform Africa: The Transformational Use of ICTs in Africa*. Eds. Enock Yonazi et al. Washington: World Bank, 2012. http://siteresources.worldbank.org/EXTINFORMATIONANDCOMMUNICATIONANDTECHNOLOGIES/Resources/282822-1346223280837/MainReport.pdf.

FinAccess. "2016 FinAccess Household Survey." February 2016. http://fsdkenya.org/wp-content/uploads/2016/02/The-2016-FinAccess-household-survey-report1.pdf.

Financial Inclusion Insights. "Kenya." Accessed November 20, 2016. http://finclusion.org/country/africa/kenya.html.

GSMA. "Safaricom-Kenya-Feasibility Study." 2012. www.gsma.com/mobilefordevelopment/wp-content/uploads/2013/02/Safaricom-Feasibility-Study.pdf.

Jack, William, and Tavneet Suri. "Mobile Money: The Economics of M-PESA." Working Paper 16721. Cambridge, MA: National Bureau of Economic Research, 2011. doi:10.3386/w16721.

Kim, W. Chan, and Renee Mauborgne. *Blue Ocean Strategy*. Boston, MA: Harvard Business School Press, 2015.

Mas, Ignacio, and Dan Radcliffe. "Mobile Payments Go Viral: M-PESA in Kenya." *Financial Services for the Poor*. Bill and Melinda Gates Foundation. March 10, 2010. http://siteresources.worldbank.org/AFRICAEXT/Resources/258643-1271798012256/M-PESA_Kenya.pdf.

Mbiti, Isaac, and David N. Weil. "Mobile Banking: The Impact of M-PESA in Kenya.". Working Paper 17129. Boston, MA: National Bureau of Economic Research, June 2011. doi:10.3386/w17129.

Morawczynski, Olga, and Gianluca Miscione. "Examining Trust in Mobile Banking Transactions: The Case of M-PESA in Kenya." *International Federation for Information Processing (IFIP)* 282 (2008). doi:10.1007/978-0-387-84822-8_19.

M-PESA Case Study. Accessed November 20, 2016. http://johnbessant.net/resources/case-studies/m-pesa-case-study/.

Mugambi, Allan, Christopher Niunge, and Samuel C. Yang. "Mobile-Money Benefits and Usage: The Case of M-PESA." *IT Pro* 16 (May–June 2014). http://doi.ieeecomputersociety.org/10.1109/MITP.2014.38.

"Sustainability Report: Transforming Lives." Safaricom, 2015. www.safaricom.co.ke.

"Sustainability Report: Widening Our Vision, Sharpening Our Focus." Safaricom, 2016. www.safaricom.co.ke.

Triki, Thouraya, and Issa Faye. "Financial Inclusion in Africa." *African Development Bank*, 2013. www.afdb.org/fileadmin/uploads/afdb/Documents/Project-and-Operations/Financial_Inclusion_in_Africa.pdf.

8

THE MOBILE MONEY REVOLUTION

Jan-Erik Jaensson

Introduction

Innovations are enhancing product and service development, but most of the development is incremental. We rather seldom notice 'new to the world' innovations that change the behavior of an industry and the consumers. Innovations also need a portion of entrepreneurial activities and risk taking. The Internet and smartphones are typical innovations that have changed the behavior of consumers and industries a lot. These innovations are the foundations of many new products and services using the technology to solve problems and make life easier for consumers and companies. However, they could also be a challenge to the established industrial structure since the investments and entrance barriers mostly are low. Many products and services are based on the mentioned technology, but few are considered to be game changers in a market.

Traditionally, most innovations are made in the Western world, and we tend to think that other parts of the world (e.g., developing countries) have low capacity to develop products and services that could be successes and attract millions of customers. However, some innovations from Africa have been great successes built on mobile phone technology and the Internet. Innovations in East Africa in new mobile phone technology have been expanding for the last decade. One of the most successful ones is the development of mobile money created in Kenya in 2007, which also led to social and cultural development. The Kenyan company Safaricom[1] developed a platform for sending money through the mobile devices called M-Pesa[2] ('M' is for 'mobile' and 'Pesa' means 'money' in Swahili), and it is now an international success, improving market conditions in many developing countries:

> Paying for a taxi ride using your mobile phone is easier in Nairobi than it is in New York, thanks to Kenya's world-leading mobile-money system, M-PESA.[3]

History and Technology

The development of mobile money actually came from research about emerging behaviors associated with mobile phone use in Africa. The market research concluded that the ownership of mobile phones was low, but Africans had accepted telephones into their communication behaviors. The research also showed the potential for expansion of the use of mobile telephones since was already visible.[4]

An innovative behavior among mobile phone users was obvious because people were using airtime as a virtual currency. For example, people purchased a voucher in one city, then texted the code to their relatives in the rural areas or another city. The relatives then could choose to put the code on their phone and get airtime to call with, or sell the airtime to friends or merchants as equivalent to cash. This innovative use of airtime as cash implicated a demand for financial services, as, for example, the transfer of money within the country.[5]

From the beginning, the aim was to introduce a microfinancing system based on mobile phone technology. Since the telecommunication companies had a large number of resellers of airtime (prepaid vouchers) around the country, it would create an easy access to withdraw and repay the money in a loan agreement. The cost of handling these microloans would be reduced drastically compared with the cost of handling cash, and the interest rates could be competitive. Safaricom started their pilot project in Kenya in 2005, and in 2007, they launched their new mobile phone-based payment and money transfer service: M-Pesa. The international telecommunication company Vodacom bought 35% of Safaricom in May 2017 and uses their platform. The service[6] enables its users to:

- Deposit and withdraw money
- Transfer money to other users and non-users
- Pay bills
- Purchase airtime
- Transfer money between the mobile accounts and, in some markets like Kenya and Tanzania, a bank account.

It has grown rapidly in Kenya, and M-Pesa was used by 70% of households in 2014, and about US $20 billion was transferred through their system. This is equivalent to over 40% of the Kenyan GDP. In Tanzania, there are more mobile accounts than formal bank accounts.[7,8]

The adoption of this new service has been impressive. Already after 1 year, it had 2 million users, and after another 6 months, they had 4 million users. On March 31, 2016, it had 25 and one-third million users in the world, of which 6 million are outside Kenya.[9] The figure is very high, since about 33 million Kenyans own a mobile phone.[10]

Governments have also begun to make it possible to pay tax, apply for a driver's license, and so forth. The availability of mobile money payments reduces their cost of administration significantly.

Conditions for Development

Three factors were the pillars for the success of the mobile money transfer system (including bank services): innovation, inaction, and monopoly. At the beginning of this millennium, the number of mobile phones started to grow rapidly in the African continent. The most common way of paying for airtime was through prepaid vouchers, where you put a voucher number into your mobile operator's account through the phone.

The innovation originated from the customers' innovative behavior, which was later developed to a flexible financial service from the telecommunication company Vodafone. The behavior was monitored, and from that behavior, the development of a value-added service started.

One precondition to the rapid growth was the inaction of regulators in Kenya. M-Pesa was not regarded as a bank and could in that way grow without restrictions and regulations from the bank sector. The regulators were taken by surprise. However, the banks tried later to enforce the same regulations on the mobile money as for the banks, without any success.

Vodafone had about 69% of the market and had a monopoly situation. The M-Pesa system was from the beginning locked into the system of Vodafone, and customers could transfer money only between their customers' accounts. They opened up the system as their telecommunication competitors Tigo, Airtel, and so forth also launched their mobile money systems. Now customers could send money between the operators and also to mobile accounts in other countries as well as pay for a vast number of products and services.

Vodafone has expanded the M-Pesa concept to Tanzania, South Africa, Afghanistan, India, Romania, Albania, Mozambique, Lesotho, Egypt, Ghana, and Democratic Republic of Congo.[11] All of these countries' launches had not been a success. Markets with well-developed money markets as, for example, South Africa, did not adopt the mobile payment system at the expected pace. There they were forced into the same regulatory system as for the banks, and credit cards are a well-functioning system for business owners and customers'.

Access for Poor/Rural People

About 80% of the population in Kenya lives in rural areas without access to grid electricity. However, most of the families and small business owners have a mobile phone (often charged with small solar powered units). The only way of sending money to relatives before was to give an envelope to a bus driver heading for the rural area, without knowing if someone would steal the envelope before it reached the receiver.

This new service made it much easier for relatives earning money in the cities to support their families in rural areas. The SME also got a value-added function in their daily life since many payments are made through the mobile phone, which is safer than with money.

Added Value/Usage

Vodafone launched a marketing campaign after starting the M-Pesa service named 'send money home with M-Pesa,' which made people sign up for M-Pesa accounts. Now, customers of all mobile money suppliers could use it also to pay (depending on the country) for goods and services, tax, taxi, water, power, charity, air ticket, school fees, and food at restaurants.

Another benefit is the original objective to get access to financial services (microfinance). It also increases safety and security to do transactions with electronic money rather than cash.

One clear effect is the boost of rural business. Before, traders had to travel many hours from the rural areas to deposit the earnings from their sales into a bank account. Now, they get it in the mobile account. The sales also increased for many traders since they could do business the whole time instead of spending time traveling to the bank.

It has also helped the traditionally disadvantaged group of women to possess their own money account without a signature from their husband (if they should open a bank account). Through this service development, women became empowered to handle their own income, to do business and keep the money in their possession instead of handing it over to the husband, who sometimes spent the money himself.

The Business Model

The business model (Figure 8.1) includes the banking system and distribution channels. Through the established distribution channel of vouchers, the expansion

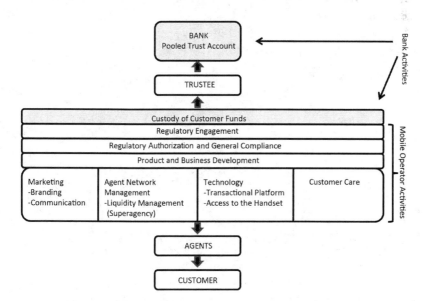

FIGURE 8.1 The Business Model[12]

of the M-Pesa services grew rapidly. The regulatory environment was friendly, and the number of existing customers with mobile phones was large. The aforementioned factors were the pillars for the innovation to take place and to be implemented and used by the customers through marketing.

Innovation in Services

Innovation refers to the creation or significantly improved products, marketing, processes and/or organization that add value to consumers and society. Investments in innovation are considered to be the best way of creating a competitive advantage for a company and to contribute to the economy of a country.

Innovations in services are considered to be an important component of customer satisfaction.[13,14] Some researchers argue that close interaction with customers is beneficial for service providers with respect to developing and introducing innovations because customers are a source of knowledge and ideas for innovation and may act as partners in the innovation development process.[15] However, with this customer perspective, the innovations tend to be incremental only and not radical innovations.[16,17,18]

Radical innovations are rare in the services industry, but they exist, as shown earlier with the mobile money innovation. Radical innovations often form a new business logic and create new opportunities for firms to create a competitive advantage as well as open up possibilities for the customers to get value-added services. Factors enhancing radical innovations in services are, for example, technology, added value to core products, privatization, and security issues.

There are some theories describing innovation and the innovation process. In this, the focus is on three of them, two from the strategic management literature and one from the service marketing literature: entrepreneurial orientation and market orientation. Both are supposed to enhance innovation and service-dominant logic (S-D logic), which looks upon innovations of services as something different from innovations of products. For entrepreneurial orientation, it is mostly an internal process to create substantial/radical innovations in products/services and/or new markets. For market orientation, it is a process where the customer is in focus for innovations. S-D logic deals with value creation together with the customers.

Entrepreneurial Orientation and Market Orientation

Innovations in the service industry are mostly characterized as incremental innovations rather than radical innovations. Here, we could compare with the two theoretical areas of market orientation (MO) and entrepreneurial orientation (EO). Market orientation is considered to be the implementation of the marketing concept that focuses on needs and wants of target markets and on delivering value better than competitors.[19,20] Entrepreneurial orientation is the development of the theories about the entrepreneurs but aggregated to the firm level.[21,22,23,24]

EO consists of five dimensions: innovativeness, proactiveness, risk taking, competitive aggressiveness, and autonomy.[25,26] MO consists of different dimensions depending on the origin and stream of development. For this chapter, the seminal article by Narver and Slater[27] will be used and then the core dimensions are customer orientation, competitor orientation, and inter-functional coordination.

EO could be classified as an inside-out process where the firm leads the customers, contrary to MO, which can be classified as an outside-in process where the customers lead the firm in market and product development. However, there are some important differences between the concepts, which could be addressed to the service industry in the following areas: customer needs, innovation, and risk taking.

To start, the customers' needs are addressed in different ways. For MO, it is all about matching customers' expressed needs and nothing else. EO, on the contrary, concentrates on customers' future needs through new product/service development and new markets.[28,29,30]

The innovation aspect also differs, and MO is more about incremental innovation and exploitation of innovations, whereas EO is about exploration innovation process with radical innovations and a high degree of innovativeness often introducing breakthrough products or identifying unattended market segments.[31,32,33]

The risk-taking aspect of a business is discouraged in the MO concept but encouraged in the EO concept. This is linked to the innovation area where EO innovations are on a higher risk level but could give the firm a more substantial return on investment.[34]

The conclusion of this discussion is that for developing successful radical innovations, also in the service industry, we need a shift from focusing mostly on the MO concept to also use the EO concept. However, in the mobile money example, both concepts were used.

EO could be defined in different ways as in, for example, what Lumpkin and Dess call[35] 'the process, practices, and decision-making activities that lead to new entry.' More recent definitions are from Avlonitis and Salavou, who state[36] 'EO constitutes an organizational phenomenon that reflects a managerial capability by which firms embark on proactive and aggressive initiatives to alter the competitive scene to their advantage,' and Wiklund and Shepherd:[37] 'a firm's strategic orientation, including entrepreneurial decision making and practices.'

It is clear from most definitions that EO is considered to be a company strategy where decision making is strongly emphasized and development of the company's position in the market is focused. EO leads the customers, and new technology could be used to develop products or services consumers didn't know they needed (e.g., smartphones and mobile money). EO concentrates on customers' future needs through new product/service development and new markets.[38,39,40]

EO is the radical innovation process with a high degree of innovativeness often resulting in breakthrough products or identifying unattended market segments.[41,42,43] The risk-taking aspect of the business is encouraged in the EO

152 Jan-Erik Jaensson

concept and innovations are on a higher risk level, but they could give the firm a more substantial return on investment and sustainable competitive advantage.[44]

The conclusion of this discussion is that there is a need for more EO in the service industry, which could lead to a higher degree of innovativeness and more radical/breakthrough service offerings. However, we could note that the development of mobile money together with the customers is a very clear example of a breakthrough innovation that has made a great change for many people in Africa, both in the business world and from private users (including the empowerment of women).

Service-Dominant Logic

For decades, innovations were done in the perspective of Goods-Dominant Logic (G-D logic), where the focus was on tangible resources. The value was created in the exchange of these tangible resources, and the customer was outside the process. The theories of New Product Development (NPD) were developed from this logic, and innovations were made in the product, processes, and organization.[45]

A definition of innovation from the G-D logic is as follows: 'Innovation processes involve opportunities for new or improved products, processes, or services, based either on an advance in technical practice ("know-how"), or change in market demand, or a combination of the two'.[46]

Services have for a long time been considered as having a low grade of innovations and more like copying existing ideas (adopters of existing technologies), but in fact, services have specific innovation potential.[47] In the G-D logic, firms are oriented toward new products focusing on R&D, but in the Service-Dominant Logic (S-D logic), firms are oriented more toward organizational change, including use of technology, staff training, and cooperation with customers.

Services-based innovations have, therefore, concentrated on knowledge-intensive businesses, where innovation tends to be an open process developed in close cooperation with clients.[48] Because of this view, it is difficult to follow the S-D logic with product, process, and organization where customers and staff training are left out.

It all started at the beginning of the 21st century, when attempts to conceptualize and develop a new logic for services innovations took place.[49,50] The new logic is the S-D logic, which recognizes knowledge management in combination with firm resources in theory and practice.[51] Resources like knowledge, skills, and competences are central for a firm's capability to compete in a market.[52]

Some core issues in the S-D logic are *Value generation*: This is a process that includes several actors, such as service provider and customer, which ultimately leads to value for the customer. *Value-in-use*: This is the value for customers encapsulated in the resources offered by a service firm. *Value creation*: Value creation is the customers' process to obtain value from the usage of resources. Value creation is the customers' creation of value-in-use. *Co-creation*: Co-creation is the process of creating something together in a process of direct interactions between two or more actors, merging into one collaborative process.[53] The value generation, value-in-use, and value creation for both Safaricom and the customers was clearly added with this new way of using the mobile phone, and the adoption process of the new service was impressive.

Value co-creation together with the customers is especially emphasized in the S-D logic, and the S-D logic acts as a complement to the former G-D logic. This means that the S-D logic is not considered to replace the old thinking, but rather to complement it.[54,55,56]

The implication of this mobile money story is that marketing managers should be aware of the importance of the combination of market orientation and entrepreneurial orientation for successful innovation processes. Furthermore, the innovation should be conducted in a service-dominant logic, where the value is in focus both for the service provider and the customer. For radical innovations, the management of entrepreneurial orientation is essential, since the literature shows that it is from an inside-out perspective (EO) the radical innovations are created.

Summary and Conclusion

This story was about the development of a new service that was adopted rapidly and added significant value to mobile phones. With this new service, the phone was also a financial device that made life easier for many people and made many SMEs increase sales, especially in the rural areas. It also empowered women, since with this service they could manage their own money.

The mobile money is clearly a 'new to the world' innovation and, as such, a radical innovation. The use of the new technology came from the customers' innovative behavior, and the development was done from an S-D logic perspective. With this new way of handling money, the mobile phone was adding an important value for the customers in a sort of value co-creation. This was a clear value-in-use offer from the service provider, and the adoption of the new service was very fast, showing that the innovation was adding a high value for the customers.

The development was done by a combination of market orientation and entrepreneurial orientation in the best of processes. It was market orientation because the idea came from a market research where they discovered an innovative customer behavior. It was entrepreneurial orientation because they were proactive, innovative, and aggressive in the market to be a market leader. It started with an outside-in process that later became an inside-out process where new services were developed from the insights of the consumer behavior. This confirms that the two concepts could work together, which has been an academic debate for some time.[57,58]

Notes

1 Safaricom, Ltd, "Celebrating 10 Years of Changing Lives," Safaricom Company website, accessed September 7, 2016, www.safaricom.co.ke/mpesa_timeline/timeline.html.
2 "M-Pesa,"Wikipedia, last modified August 23, 2017, accessed August 24, 2017, https://en.wikipedia.org/wiki/M-Pesa.
3 "Why Does Kenya Lead the World in Mobile Money?" *The Economist* (blog), May 27, 2013, accessed July 12, 2016, https://www.economist.com/blogs/economist-explains/2013/05/economist-explains-18
4 Simon Batchelor, "Changing the Financial Landscape of Africa: An Unusual Story of Evidence Informed Innovation, Intentional Policy Influence and Private Sector Engagement," *IDS (Institute of Development Studies) Bulletin* 43, no. 5 (Hoboken, NJ: Blackwell Publishing, 2012).
5 Ibid.
6 Vodacom (webpage), accessed August 22, 2017, www.vodacom.com/
7 Eugene Ngumi and Frank Nyambweke, "Mobile Money in Kenya Part 1: The Story of Success—Innovation, Inaction, and Monopoly," *africapractice* (blog), 2015, accessed July 12, 2016, www.africapractice.com/blog-posts.
8 Eugene Ngumi and Frank Nyambweke "Mobile Money in Kenya Part 2: The Story of Success—Innovation, Inaction, and Monopoly," *africapractice* (blog), 2015, accessed July 12, 2016, www.africapractice.com/blog-posts.
9 "Vodafone M-Pesa Reaches 25 Million Customers Milestone," Vodafone (press release), April 25, 2016, accessed October 20, 2016, www.vodafone.com/content/index/media/vodafone-group-releases/2016/mpesa-25million.html#
10 Brian Muthiora, "Enabling Mobile Money Policies in Kenya: Fostering a Digital Financial Revolution." *GSMA* (2015), accessed October 20, 2016, www.itu.int/en/ITUT/focusgroups/dfs/Documents/2015_MMU_Enabling-MobileMoney-Policies-in-Kenya.pdf
11 Vodacom (webpage), accessed August 22, 2017, www.vodacom.com/
12 Lesley S. Marincola, "How Mobile Money Is Transforming Africa," *Huffington Post* (blog), March 24, 2015, accessed July 12, 2016, www.huffingtonpost.com/lesleysilverthornmarincola/how-mobile-money-is-trans_b_6524836.html.
13 Jay Kandampully, "Innovation as the Core Competency of a Service Organisation: The Role of Technology, Knowledge and Networks," *European Journal of Innovation Management* 5, no. 1 (2002): 18–26.
14 Jon Sundbo, "Management of Innovation in Services," *Service Industries Journal* 17, no. 3 (1997): 432–455.
15 Silvia Bellingkrodt and Carl M. Wallenburg, "The Role of Customer Relations for Innovativeness and Customer Satisfaction," *The International Journal of Logistics Management* 26, no. 2 (2015): 254–274.
16 Kwaku Atuahene-Gima and Anthony Ko, "An Empirical Investigation of the Effect of Market Orientation and Entrepreneurship Orientation Alignment on Product Innovation," *Organization Science* 12, no. 1 (2001): 54–74.
17 William E. Baker and James M. Sinkula, "Learning Orientation, Market Orientation, and Innovation: Integrating and Extending Models of Organizational Performance," *Journal of Market-Focused Management* 4 (1999): 295–308.
18 Henri Hakala, "Strategic Orientations in Management Literature: Three Approaches to Understanding the Interaction Between Market, Technology, Entrepreneurial and Learning Orientations," *International Journal of Management Reviews* 13 (2011): 199–217.
19 Ajay K. Kohli and Bernard J. Jaworski, "Market Orientation: The Construct, Research Propositions, & Managerial Implications," *Journal of Marketing* 54 (1990): 1–18.
20 John C. Narver and Stanley F. Slater, "The Effect of a Market Orientation on Business Profitability," *Journal of Marketing* October (1990): 20–35.

21 Jeffrey G. Covin and Dennis P. Slevin, "Strategic Management of Small Firms in Hostile and Benign Environments," *Strategic Management Journal* 10, no. 1 (1989): 75–87.

22 Jeffrey G. Covin and Dennis P. Slevin, "A Conceptual Model of Entrepreneurship as Firm Behavior," *Entrepreneurship Theory and Practice* 16, no. 1 (1991): 7–25.

23 G.T. Lumpkin and Gregory G. Dess, "Clarifying the Entrepreneurial Orientation Construct and Linking It to Performance," *Academy of Management Review* 21, no. 1 (1996): 135–172.

24 Danny Miller, "The Correlates of Entrepreneurship in Three Types of Firms," *Management Science* 29 (1983): 770–791.

25 Lumpkin and Dess, "Clarifying the Entrepreneurial . . ."

26 Miller, "The Correlates of Entrepreneurship . . ."

27 Narver and Slater, "The Effect of a Market Orientation . . ."

28 Atuahene-Gima and Ko, "An Empirical Investigation . . ."

29 Baker and Sinkula, "Learning Orientation . . ."

30 Stanley F. Slater and John C. Narver, "Market Orientation and the Learning Organization," *Journal of Marketing* 59 (1995): 63–74.

31 Atuahene-Gima and Ko, "An Empirical Investigation . . ."

32 Baker and Sinkula, "Learning Orientation . . ."

33 Hakala, "Strategic Orientations . . ."

34 Slater and Narver, "Market Orientation . . ."

35 Lumpkin and Dess, "Clarifying the Entrepreneurial. . . ," 136.

36 George J. Avlonitis and Helen E. Salavou, "Entrepreneurial Orientation of SMEs, Product Innovativeness, and Performance," *Journal of Business Research* 60 (2007): 567.

37 Johan Wiklund and Dean Shepherd, "Entrepreneurial Orientation and Small Business Performance: A Configurational Approach," *Journal of Business Venturing* 20, no. 1 (2005): 74.

38 Atuahene-Gima and Ko, "An Empirical Investigation . . ."

39 Baker and Sinkula, "Learning Orientation . . ."

40 Slater and Narver, "Market Orientation . . ."

41 Atuahene-Gima and Ko, "An Empirical Investigation . . ."

42 Baker and Sinkula, "Learning Orientation . . ."

43 Hakala, "Strategic Orientations . . ."

44 Slater and Narver, "Market Orientation . . ."

45 Christina Mele, Maria Colurcio, and Tiziana Russo-Spena, "Research Traditions of Innovation," *Managing Service Quality* 24, no. 6 (2014): 612–642.

46 Keith Pavitt, "Innovation Process," in *The Oxford Handbook of Innovation*, eds. J. Fagerberg, D.C. Mowery, and R.R. Nelson (Oxford, UK: Oxford University Press, 2004), 87.

47 Annica Schilling and Andreas Werr, "Managing and Organizing for Innovation in Service Firms: A Literature Review with Annotated Bibliography," Stockholm School of Economics, Stockholm, Vinnova Report No. VR 2009:06, accessed October 18, 2016, www.vinnova.se/upload/EPiStorePDF/vr-09-06.pdf.

48 Pim den Hertog, "Knowledge-Intensive Business Services as Co-Producers of Innovation," *International Journal of Innovation Management* 4, no. 4 (2000): 491–528.

49 Christian Grönroos, "Service Logic Revisited: Who Creates Value? And Who Co-Creates?" *European Business Review* 20, no. 4 (2008): 298–314.

50 Mele et al., "Research Traditions . . ."

51 Evert Gummesson, Robert F. Lusch, and Stephen L. Vargo, "Transitioning From Service Management to Service-Dominant Logic: Observations and Recommendations," *International Journal of Quality and Service Sciences* 2, no. 1 (2010): 8–22.

52 Stephen L. Vargo and Robert F. Lusch, "Evolving to a New Dominant Logic for Marketing," *Journal of Marketing* 68, no 1. (2004): 1–17.

156   Jan-Erik Jaensson

53 Christian Grönroos and Johanna Gummerus, "The Service Revolution and Its Marketing Implications: Service Logic vs Service-Dominant Logic," *Managing Service Quality* 24, no. 3 (2014): 206–229.
54 Ibid.
55 Gummesson, Lusch, and Vargo, "Transitioning . . ."
56 Lusch, Robert F. and Stephen L. Vargo, "Service-Dominant Logic: A Necessary Step," *European Journal of Marketing* 45 no. 7/8 (2011): 1298–1309.
57 Atuahene-Gima and Ko, "An Empirical Investigation . . ."
58 Hakala, "Strategic Orientations . . ."

Bibliography

Atuahene-Gima, Kwaku, and Anthony Ko. "An Empirical Investigation of the Effect of Market Orientation and Entrepreneurship Orientation Alignment on Product Innovation." *Organization Science* 12, no. 1 (2001): 54–74.

Avlonitis, George J., and Helen E. Salavou. "Entrepreneurial Orientation of SMEs, Product Innovativeness, and Performance." *Journal of Business Research* 60 (2007): 556–575.

Baker, William E., and James M. Sinkula. "Learning Orientation, Market Orientation, and Innovation: Integrating and Extending Models of Organizational Performance." *Journal of Market-Focused Management* 4 (1999): 295–308.

Batchelor, Simon. "Changing the Financial Landscape of Africa: An Unusual Story of Evidence Informed Innovation, Intentional Policy Influence and Private Sector Engagement." *IDS (Institute of Development Studies) Bulletin* 43, no. 5. Hoboken, NJ: Blackwell Publishing, 2012.

Bellingkrodt, Silvia, and Carl M. Wallenburg. "The Role of Customer Relations for Innovativeness and Customer Satisfaction." *The International Journal of Logistics Management* 26, no. 2 (2015): 254–274.

Covin, Jeffrey G., and Dennis P. Slevin. "A Conceptual Model of Entrepreneurship as Firm Behavior." *Entrepreneurship Theory and Practice* 16, no. 1 (1991): 7–25.

Covin, Jeffrey G., and Dennis P. Slevin. "Strategic Management of Small Firms in Hostile and Benign Environments." *Strategic Management Journal* 10, no. 1 (1989): 75–87.

den Hertog, Pim. "Knowledge-Intensive Business Services as Co-Producers of Innovation." *International Journal of Innovation Management* 4, no. 4 (2000): 491–528.

Grönroos, Christian. "Service Logic Revisited: Who Creates Value? And Who Co-Creates?" *European Business Review* 20, no. 4 (2008): 298–314.

Grönroos, Christian, and Johanna Gummerus. "The Service Revolution and Its Marketing Implications: Service Logic vs. Service-Dominant Logic." *Managing Service Quality* 24, no. 3 (2014): 206–229.

Gummesson, Evert, Robert F. Lusch, and Stephen L. Vargo. "Transitioning From Service Management to Service-Dominant Logic: Observations and Recommendations." *International Journal of Quality and Service Sciences* 2, no. 1 (2010): 8–22.

Hakala, Henri. "Strategic Orientations in Management Literature: Three Approaches to Understanding the Interaction Between Market, Technology, Entrepreneurial and Learning Orientations." *International Journal of Management Reviews* 13 (2011): 199–217.

Kandampully, Jay. "Innovation as the Core Competency of a Service Organisation: The Role of Technology, Knowledge and Networks." *European Journal of Innovation Management* 5, no. 1 (2002): 18–26.

Kohli, Ajay K., and Bernard J. Jaworski. "Market Orientation: The Construct, Research Propositions, & Managerial Implications." *Journal of Marketing* 54 (1990): 1–18.

Lumpkin, G.T., and Gregory G. Dess. "Clarifying the Entrepreneurial Orientation Construct and Linking It to Performance." *Academy of Management Review* 21, no. 1 (1996): 135–172.

Lusch, Robert F., and Stephen L. Vargo. "Service-Dominant Logic: A Necessary Step." *European Journal of Marketing* 45, no. 7/8 (2011): 1298–1309.

Marincola, Lesley S. "How Mobile Money Is Transforming Africa." *Huffington Post* (blog), March 24, 2015. Accessed July 12, 2016. www.huffingtonpost.com/lesley-silverthorn marincola/how-mobile-money-is-trans_b_6524836.html.

Mele, Christina, Maria Colurcio, and Tiziana Russo-Spena. "Research Traditions of Innovation." *Managing Service Quality* 24, no. 6 (2014): 612–642.

Miller, Danny. "The Correlates of Entrepreneurship in Three Types of Firms." *Management Science* 29 (1983): 770–791.

"M-Pesa." Wikipedia. Last modified August 23, 2017. Accessed August 24, 2017. https://en.wikipedia.org/wiki/M-Pesa.

Muthiora, Brian. "Enabling Mobile Money Policies in Kenya: Fostering a Digital Financial Revolution." *GSMA*, January 2015. Accessed October 20, 2016. www.itu.int/en/ITU-T/focusgroups/dfs/Documents/2015_MMU_Enabling-Mobile-Money-Policies-in-Kenya.pdf.

Narver, John C., and Stanley F. Slater. "The Effect of a Market Orientation on Business Profitability." *Journal of Marketing* October (1990): 20–35.

Ngumi, Eugene, and Frank Nyambweke. "Mobile Money in Kenya Part 1: The Story of Success—Innovation, Inaction, and Monopoly." *africapractice* (blog), 2015. Accessed July 12, 2016. www.africapractice.com/blog-posts.

Ngumi, Eugene, and Frank Nyambweke. "Mobile Money in Kenya Part 2: The Story of Success—Innovation, Inaction, and Monopoly." *africapractice* (blog), 2015. Accessed July 12, 2016. www.africapractice.com/blog-posts.

Pavitt, Keith. "Innovation Process." In *The Oxford Handbook of Innovation*, 86–114. Eds. Jan Fagerberg, David C. Mowery and Richard R. Nelson. Oxford, UK: Oxford University Press, 2004.

Safaricom, Ltd. "Celebrating 10 Years of Changing Lives." Safaricom Company website. Accessed September 7, 2016. www.safaricom.co.ke/mpesa_timeline/timeline.html.

Schilling, Annica, and Andreas Werr. "Managing and Organizing for Innovation in Service Firms: A Literature Review with Annotated Bibliography." *Vinnova Report* (2009), No. VR 2009:06. Stockholm: Stockholm School of Economics. Accessed October 18, 2016. www.vinnova.se/upload/EPiStorePDF/vr-09-06.pdf.

Slater, Stanley F., and John C. Narver. "Market Orientation and the Learning Organization." *Journal of Marketing* 59 (1995): 63–74.

Standage, Tom. "Why Does Kenya Lead the World in Mobile Money?" *The Economist* (blog). May 27, 2013. Accessed July 2016. www.economist.com/blogs/economist-explains/2013/05/economist-explains-18.

Sundbo, Jon. "Management of Innovation in Services." *Service Industries Journal* 17, no. 3 (1997): 432–455.

Vargo, Stephen L., and Robert F. Lusch. "Evolving to a New Dominant Logic for Marketing." *Journal of Marketing* 68, no 1. (2004): 1–17.

Vodacom Group Limited. Vodacom company website. Accessed August 22, 2017. www.vodacom.com/.

Vodafone Group Plc. "Vodafone M-Pesa Reaches 25 Million Customers Milestone." *Vodafone Group Plc.* press release, April 25, 2016. Vodafone website. Accessed October 20, 2016. www.vodafone.com/content/index/media/vodafone-group-releases/2016/mpesa-25million.html#.

Wiklund, Johan, and Dean Shepherd. "Entrepreneurial Orientation and Small Business Performance: A Configurational Approach." *Journal of Business Venturing* 20, no. 1 (2005): 71–91.

9

FINANCING BEHAVIOR OF ENTREPRENEURIAL VENTURES IN TANZANIA

Tumsifu Elly

Financing Business Venture: The Theoretical Background

Choices made in financing small business have a sheer impact on firm performance. As such, the growth, development, and success of a particular business venture is determined essentially by the choices and availability of finance. Considering small businesses that represent entrepreneurs' enterprising tendency, financing is a way of fulfilling owners' vision and dreams. Obviously, without adequate financing, entrepreneurs' ability to achieve growth is much compromised. Small ventures require sufficient and appropriate funding in setting up and broadening their business operations as well as launching new products and developing its human resources, among others.[1] Additionally, access to finance is seen as a means through which a firm could acquire productive assets required for increased productivity and reduced unit cost of production, which are important in attaining the economies of scale.

Contrariwise, poor access to finance constraints the establishment and growth of small businesses in developing countries. Getting access to finances in this context is utterly challenging given the dysfunctional financial markets and social and institutional context embedding entrepreneurship.[2] When considering financing, literature has espoused on the bottlenecks, availability, and access to and use of both external and internal sources of financial capital by small firms. Thus, mostly at their onset, small ventures rely on informal sources of funds, which include entrepreneurs' own funds. Raison d'être is lack of information about the sources of finance, deterring lending by banks and other financial institutions, poor records, and unavailability of collateral, among others. Due to these hitches, most of the small firms resort to the informal and internal means in financing the businesses.

Little attention has, however, been given on the social and behavioral aspects that determine both the choice of the sources of financing and the availability and use of such resources. It is important to reckon that ventures do not exist in a socio-economic vacuum but in a well-established, time-and-space, and time-and-place specific context. As such, the context influences both the availability and options taken by entrepreneurs in financing their venture. Thus, the social relations, rules, regulations, and economic and political environment influence entrepreneurs' access to resources—in particular, finances.[3]

The sources of finance are mainly grouped into three categories. The formal financing sources, which are the financial institutions that are regulated, hence offer loans that are highly structured and nearly inaccessible by small firms. The semi-formal sources represent sources from institutions falling between the formal and informal ones. These are the financial institutions that do not necessarily follow regulations, as in the case of the commercial regulated banks and other formal financial institutions. They rather have other goals for financing small business, which include, but are not limited to, social aspirations. The last one presents the informal sources, which include a broad range of sources such as family members, acquaintances, friends, owners' personal savings, and retained earnings as well as bootstrapping options. Others are venture capital, trade credit, and angel financiers. However, access to and use of these sources remains entrepreneurs' own choice. Nonetheless, the choices are contingent to the prevailing environment and other external factors. The reminder of this chapter considers financing options available for small firms as being formal or informal and that the informal ones are those that an entrepreneur could access without having to fulfill stringent requirements such as providing for collateral or security and, as such, those that are not regulated. Thus, this category is being termed as 'equity financing,' whereas the formal external sources, particularly those that are obtained from regulated commercial banks and financial institutions, represent debt financing.

Financing options accessible to entrepreneurs vary throughout the different stages of a business's life cycle. This means different options unveil at varying stages of a business's life cycle.[4] On their onset, for instance, most small ventures lack business history and records and are characterized by information opacity as well as high risk of failure. Such characteristics could make small businesses better candidates for equity financing.[5] Under normal circumstances, as ventures grow along their business life cycles, the capital structure is expected to change. This is due to availability of records and history of the business, among others, that facilitate access to the external formal sources of finance *ceteris Paribas*.

Throughout the subsequent growth stages, and as the entrepreneurial ventures mature, they begin to create track records together with the ability to provide collateral. Thus, firms tend to improve their creditworthiness and attract investors' willingness to supplement money into the business. As a result, firms start replacing the internal and informal financing sources with formal external financing. Small firms' financial requirements are aligned with their growth and

Entrepreneurial Ventures in Tanzania **161**

development. In this case, four stages of firm development are matched with the expected sources of finance. At start-up stage, small firms tend to operate using entrepreneurs' own sources, retained earnings, or informal finances from family and other friends. The second stage of growth constitutes firms in their development phase, which continues to rely on entrepreneurs' sources while progressively becoming credit worthy. The established firms in the third stage have potential to attract sophisticated debts and other formal external financing. Fourth, the mature business firms are able to access a wide array of debt and formal external finances without much barrier to entry. While this is rather a typical financing trajectory, norms, behavior, and customs which are the social aspects could drift the trajectory. To the contrary, therefore, the growth pattern might not amply explain the choice and preference made by entrepreneurs mainly on external sources of finance in real terms.[6]

Looking at financing preferences, the packing order theorists explain the capital structure of the firm as following a certain order. The highest preference being the use of internal over external sources. Reasons being high preference on internal sources are that firms don't experience the flotation costs as well as extra disclosure of proprietary financial information. On the other hand, if a firm is to opt for external sources, then the preferred sources would begin as in the following sequence: debt, preferred stock, common stock, and convertible securities. This sequence provides a great motivation for managers, since they can take control of the firm. Basically, there are two assumptions prevailing in this theory. First, the asymmetric information, whereby the firms' owner knows more about the business growth and investment opportunities than the externals. The use of internal source of finance prevents the owners from making disclosures to the public with regard to firm's potential investment opportunities. Second, firms will always act in the best interest of the shareholders. Emerging firms are more likely to adopt a pecking order model of financing by preferring more internal sources of finance than external sources like debts. Though with maturity, firms might follow a reverse of the pecking order model of financing.

In a nutshell, for most start-up firms, equity seems to be the most common option. The most cited and obvious advantage of equity is the potential to improve the emerging firm's creditability through demonstrating the sophisticated financial management that the firm attains over time. Unlike equity financing, when opting for debts, owners will have to borrow money in order to finance their business, and this normally is attached with strict conditions in addition to having to pay the interest rates as well as the principal amount within a specified period of time. Others have observed that financing decisions among small firms do relate to the use of either equity, debt, or both sources of finance as compared with the large firms. This chapter presents the choices made to finance small ventures in conjunction with reasons for anomalous financing behavior native to entrepreneurs' culture, norms, and customs; the social-cultural milieu; and the government policies and directives.

The Glitches

Explaining why some small venture borrow and others decide to finance their business alone is still debatable.[7] While this debate continues, we present facts showing that culture, norms, customs, and some context-specific behavior could explain the behavior. Additionally, the whole aspect of financing might be influenced by prevailing policies and directives given by the government. A point of departure is the fact that with growth of a small firm, it is expected that there will be changes in financing options from equity to debts *ceteris Paribas*. Otherwise, the anomalous financing behavior could be explained by other factors.

Small Businesses Financing Behavior in Tanzania

We use information from a set of data collected mainly through in-depth interviews of 177 different business cases in Tanzania (see Figure 9.1). The data were collected from Kinondoni district in Dar es Salaam region. Respondents were chosen conveniently and purposefully on the basis of their availability and willingness to participate in the study and in meeting the set criteria, which was the year of establishment. In this case, firms that had business experience of fewer than 5 years were not picked. Thus, findings are not for generalization, but rather are

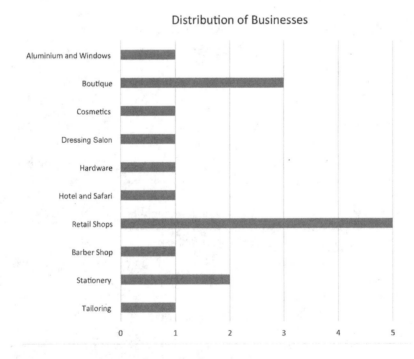

FIGURE 9.1 Distribution of Cases by Business Type

indicative of the most likely prevailing financing behavior among entrepreneurs in the context being referred. Thematic analysis was used to analyze qualitative data on specific objectives.[8]

The data provided are from 17 cases from Dar es Salaam. The business was established in years between 1998 and 2010. Entrepreneurs were engaged in tailoring, stationery, barber shops, retailing, hotels and safari, hardware, dressing salon, cosmetics, boutique, and aluminium and windows. The choice of the cases considered their year of establishment to reflect the growth and potential requirements for financing the businesses.

Financing Behavior Among Business Cases

The following radar scheme (see Figure 9.2) shows the behavior of the entrepreneurs in financing their ventures throughout the business life cycle. At the beginning of the business endeavors, entrepreneurs used equity as the source of their start-up capital. However, along the course (keeping the business afloat), 17 entrepreneurs out of 11 continued with equity as the major source, whereas 6 out

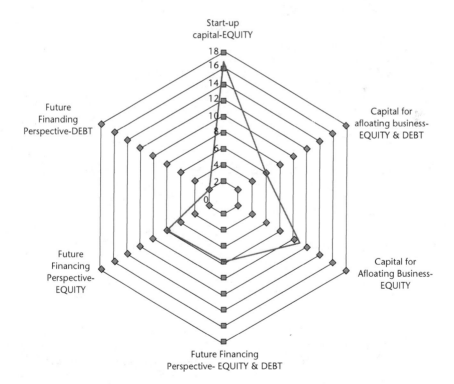

FIGURE 9.2 Financing Options by Cases

of 17 cases opted for both equity and debt financing. Interestingly, entrepreneurs from the 17 cases had mixed perspectives for their future financing options. Of all cases, 8 would opt for both equity and debt financing, whereas the same number of cases would consider only equity as the source of finance. Only one case considers opting for debt financing in the future.

Decipherment of the Social-Cultural Milieu About Business Financing

Small businesses used equity financing as the sole means in financing their business activities (Figure 9.2). Though this observation is in line with the extant literature, reasons as to why owners opted for the internal sources are less expounded. It is not uncommon to find an unremitting list related to lack of history, collateral, business experience, and networks being cited against choices for informal sources of finance. Much as these reasons are obvious in business footings, some social and cultural behavior that accentuate the choices made are opaque in the literature. Interviews with entrepreneurs in question indicate that there are reasons beyond the requirements from the financial institutions that could explain why they behave and take such financing decisions. Responses are summarized in Scenario 1. The summarized themes reveal the choices made by entrepreneurs in some cultural setting are far beyond conjectures in the pecking order theory and the stages of financing and development. Despite a vast theoretical and empirical test, factors influencing the choice of particular financing option have remained elusive.[9] We take the position that entrepreneurs' context has a great influence in determining the option for financing the business activities.

The External Environment (Government, Social-Cultural Milieu): Scenario 1

The responses from entrepreneurs about the influence of social-cultural settings and government policies and directives on the choices of the mode of financing businesses:

> . . . *Our community perceives a venture with a loan as belonging to the bank or moneylender* . . .
> . . . *If I borrow the money, it is like working for the bank or the lender* . . .
> . . . *It is disgusting to have had failed to service a loan. I wouldn't prefer a loan as my first option* . . .

> . . . *One is insecure when borrowing and investing under changing business environment . . .*
>
> . . . *Think of someone borrowing to invest in Dar es Salaam and become a supplier. If one was targeting the major government offices as potential customers, then a move to Dodoma will affect the ability to service the loan . . .*
>
> . . . *Borrowing might be a risk undertaking, suppose one borrowed and invested in selling alcohol in sachets. Government ban of alcohol in sachets would be a big loss to such businesses but more so if one borrowed the money . . .*
>
> . . . *I know a person who borrowed and constructed a mega accommodation and hotel facility. In the verge of finishing the construction, the government barred all its activities from being conducted in private facilities. As a result, we see some hotels turning to hostels in a way downgrading . . . the ability to pay off the loan has been immensely affected . . . not far from bankruptcy . . . since these changes were so abrupt, happening unprepared . . .*

Mostly entrepreneurs didn't consider taking a loan or even asking for one when setting up the business, partly because of the social reasons and erratic government orders and policies. Some entrepreneurs are reluctant to borrow due to the mischief borne from the general society and the perceptions from the community at large. For instance, establishment associated with a loan on its inception is seen as belonging to the moneylender rather than the owner. Such social-cultural and political-institutions have been reported as being the key drivers of the entrepreneurs' attitudes and motives and eventually the resources that can be mobilized.

Furthermore, these cultural milieu and state interventions legitimize or disapprove and/or promote or stifle entrepreneurial activities. Entrepreneurial behavior is influenced by the cultural context, thus making entrepreneurship a problematic phenomenon embedded in societies and culture and moderated by the laws and state policies. Thus, apart from the known traditional challenges that an entrepreneur faces when seeking the formal sources of finance, it is obvious that some won't even attempt, given the societal myths about borrowing as well as the prevailing institutional barriers encompassing rules and regulations. Then, considering the context in question, the perceptions of how society looks at a borrower lend themselves in and as ill-social virtue or anti-prosocial values toward debt financing, which are thwarting the borrowing behavior of the small enterprises. This context presents a more complex mixture of the social-cultural issues and erratic state policies and orders that contribute to explaining why entrepreneurs will have a remote chance of considering debt financing. Looking at it differently, moneylenders and entrepreneurs might take some of the government policies and intentions loosely, given delays in enforcing policies and directives of the former. Thus, the moneylender and entrepreneurs ignore or take advantage of poor enforcement, which is seen as a business opportunity. When policies and directives are enacted, entrepreneurs remain the weak link and encounter financial risks from such changes.

Likewise, the community of business owners is becoming doubtful about intermittent policies and directives that have been and could be introduced by the government in the future. There is a rampant concern about the unstable business environment, which brings about uncertainty that could obscure repayment of loans. One borrowing and investing in an ephemeral business opportunity that could fade away due to changes in policy, considers loan repayment difficult. Cited cases where there have been drastic changes in demand for hotel and accommodation facilities, the decision to move the capital to Dodoma, and banning alcohol in sachets portray unstable business environments and hence prohibit and/or slow the propensity toward borrowing. Said otherwise, entrepreneurs who borrow shall have a long-term commitment with the lender and that they are vulnerable to sudden changes in government policy. The argument is clear, at least about different time scales: the long-term credit requiring a borrower to service the loan versus the shorter time scale of political convenience, which threatens to undermine the efforts taken by entrepreneurs at the stroke of a pen. Such that perhaps predictable business environment would stimulate smallholders' investment and elude cynical behavior specifically that of avoiding borrowing from among entrepreneurs. This could eventually lead some owners withholding their capital, whether informal or formal, for a while to allow for a stable business environment.

The preceding discussion about the influence of the state policies and directives could be looked at from a different angle. That is, entrepreneurs operate chiefly pursuing the available business opportunities. Business opportunities are intertwined in and with a particular microenvironment. This environment is mainly governed by the government and other economic forces. Else the business environment is defined by, among others, its social settings intertwined with the state provisions that provide for certain business opportunities. If at all the opportunity structures are erratic and ill defined, entrepreneurs evade them, whereas the opposite is true should there be a favorable business environment. Hitherto, defining entrepreneurs' financing behavior as a constituent of the social settings, the state policies and directives, and the well-known traditional requirements from lenders or financial institutions.

Apart from the social context, other reasons that promote equity in the context being referred as gathered from the entrepreneurs are summarized in Scenario-2.'

Equity Financing: Scenario 2

> Other reasons that made entrepreneurs opt for equity financing:
>
> ... Equity provides freedom in business management, since there is no doubt about loan repayment risk ...
>
> ... Equity allows for ample time to learn and understand the business environment through longitudinal business evaluation and assessment. Thereafter, it is possible to make a well-informed decision about other means of financing ...
>
> ... Equity gives room to develop financial discipline and management before engaging in other sources of finance ...
>
> ... Equity offers minimum cash outflow in the form of interest as compared with debt financing ...
>
> ... Equity is not subjected to bureaucratic procedures and, therefore, provides a smooth environment for starting business ...
>
> ... With equity, one has less stress, hence paving a way for learning and mustering the business ...
>
> ... If you experience challenges (with equity financing) and fail you still have a chance to borrow. Debt is a fall-back option ...
>
> ... One fears the risks of losing all he had accumulated before starting an enterprise in cases of failure to repay the loan ...
>
> ... Debt financing may be a way to bankruptcy and total exit from business ...

Even when the social-cultural myths are held, the constant majority of entrepreneurs still considered equity over debt financing.[10] Reasons given were freedom to manage business and run it from owners' perspective, providing enough time for an entrepreneur to understand how to run and manage the business, and gaining control over the business environment while maintaining minimum cash outflow as it would have been with debt through interest rate. Additionally, equity is seem as being free from possible loss of owners' other properties in form of collateral and as providing a space for a fall-back position when an entrepreneur could consider debt as an alternative. Such that an entrepreneur remains with an option to borrow than it would have been with debt financing. Thus, it is thought that an entrepreneur gets enough space to exercise own entrepreneurial capabilities when there is no external agent that enforces some procedures and reporting standards on the borrower. Additionally, equity is preferred, as most entrepreneurs think that it is safe since there is room for studying and gaining understanding of the business and management requirement as well as the cash flow.

The finding, though, provides for some room to look at the entrepreneurs' reasoning, like saying equity provides space for learning and gaining business experience. This premise suggests that there is a need for a provision to and for understanding the business operations and financial management as well as business environment. Whether this kind of learning is a function of the span of the time a person operates a particular business without external pressure from debtor remains a grand question. The downside of relying on equity is its potential failure in promoting and facilitating opportunity-driven entrepreneurship, which might require sufficient financial resources to implement novel business ideas. Critical shortage of resources renders entrepreneurs unable to implement the opportunity-driven entrepreneurship, and as a result, the majority end up with small-scale business undertakings aimed at survival and livelihood provision.[11]

Scenario 3 looks at reasons given by entrepreneurs with respect to combining both equity and debt.

Combining Equity and Debt Financing: Scenario 3

Some entrepreneurs coalesce or thought of combining equity and debt financing at least in keeping their business afloat for some reasons as summarized as follows:

Themes generated from the interviews with entrepreneurs on why they opt for a combination of debt and equity financing.

. . . With debt and equity, one has an assurance of getting lump sum amount of money to invest, unlike equity alone, which may take long time to accumulate . . .

. . . Taking both options—equity and debt—helps rescue a business from the risks of bankruptcy. This is because the pinch of debt is shared with available equity . . .

. . . When financing the business with a loan, you are not skipping your meal or children requirements for the purpose of rescuing your business. This means financial positions remains the same or is upgraded . . .

Combining the sources of finance as reported by the entrepreneurs provides for a big chunk of money at once that could be challenging to raise through equity in the short term. Else it is a way of avoiding bankruptcy, meaning that entrepreneurs borrow when the businesses are shaky and not otherwise. But also, borrowing comes as a way of ensuring that the owners retain cash that would otherwise be subject to equity for family or own use. Even though the reasons provided might not hold water when faced with stiff competition, entrepreneurs' attempts to obtain and the willingness for the two options could provide room for enhancement. Given time-space, time-place and variations in the purpose and objective of a firm, different types of finance across firm's life cycle are inevitable. Financing options, being internal, external, informal or formal, in whatsoever form such as short-term or long-term credit are important and often complement and/or substitute of one another. Hence, equity or debt serves different purposes in time-and-space and depending on prevailing opportunities and constraints. Entrepreneurs should be able to choose the right combination or a perfect substitute that will lead to growth of the firm given prevailing condition.

From entrepreneurs' perspectives, it is important to understand what motivates them to seek outside financing and how they proceed to repay loans, as shown in Scenario 4.

Domain for Entrepreneurs' Debt Financing: Scenario 4

Themes generated from the interviews with entrepreneurs about reasons for taking a loan and time they consider taking loan are as follows:

> . . . I take a loan to stabilize my business . . .
> . . . Taking a loan helps me release funds for other use, building a house or covering school fees . . .
> . . . If your business is not doing well, taking a loan can help reinstate it . . .
> . . . A loan is a way of recovering my initial investment . . .
> . . . I borrow when there is an opportunity to borrow or availability of moneylender . . .
> . . . I borrowed to increase my resources and the size of business capital . . .
> . . . I didn't thought of taking a loan when my business was performing well . . .
> . . . I did not consider a loan when there was an increase in demand of the products from customers . . .

The reasons and time at which entrepreneurs considered borrowing present a complex explanation of the debt financing in the context. First, the fact that entrepreneurs considered borrowing to stabilize their businesses or just borrowing when the business is facing challenges such as poor performance indicates a low level of business acumen among actors. If at all the causes of poor performance are not related to lack of funds or at least finance is not one of the factors, acquiring external funds cannot be a ransom. Poor performance could be related to other factors such as poor management and lack of a sound business model, among others. Neither financing a poorly managed business or a deprived business model can reinstate the business. Second, if borrowing happens with the emergency of the moneylender, literally speaking there is no plan on how to use the funds for the sake of the business in question. Third, apparently, most entrepreneurs won't consider taking a loan as an opportunity for business growth in terms of being able to fulfill increased demand from customers or as an opportunity to further enhance the firm's performance. Fourth, some entrepreneurs consider borrowing in order to release some funds to use for other purpose than the items of and in the business plan. This kind of financing could be dangerous, because the other uses of the fund might not benefit an enterprise and could be a liability in real terms.

Deductions on Financing Behavior and Its Consequences

Our findings show that the following:

- Entrepreneurs' source of finance in this context, is mediated by the business environment comprising the social-cultural milieu and the state policies and directives as well as the entrepreneurs' subsequent behavior and attitudes.
- Essentially, entrepreneurs' choice is equity financing all along the business life cycle, with some preferring a combination of both equity and debt financing for keeping afloat their businesses.
- Equity financing was preferred over debt financing due to the need for freedom in managing the business away from lenders' follow-ups and constraints, avoiding the risk of high interest rates and lack of prerequisites such as collateral and or securities.
- Apart from all other reasons, entrepreneurs are embedded in a defined context that shapes their collective behavior, beliefs, and actions or financing options. Thus, the social-cultural milieu and the state policies and directives have had obscuring and risky proxies that make borrowing an unsafe attempt.
- The absence of preference toward debt financing is engrained in attitudes and norms related to the poor perceptions on borrowing and financing businesses from formal external sources of finance.
- The unpredictable state policies and directives leaven entrepreneurs in an indeterminate state toward debt financing.
- Therefore, the social-cultural milieu and the government policies and directives have led us to the possibilities that financing behavior and choices made by entrepreneurs are not only a result of the stringent conditions and requirements from the moneylenders and financial institutions, but also other factors that account for such anomalous behavior.
- Even when debt financing is an option, entrepreneurs have had weak reasons for taking a loan or borrowing. Some borrow to rescue failing businesses,

whereas others borrow merely for complement equity, such that appropriate reasons that could mean adding to the capacity of the firm to pursue growth and development are missing.

That said, the majority of the entrepreneurs in question have had a plethora of illusive and behavioral hindrances toward business financing. Such that malpractices related to choices made between equity and debt financing, the mismatch in timing and business circumstances that are appropriate to go for either of the financing options are a commonplace in this context. Besides, these malpractices and mismatches are either a function or are intertwined in and with social values that look down on borrowers in a way of despising achievements borne from debt financing and hence suppressing the borrowing behavior. It is likely that majority of the owners won't even think of borrowing to meet a surge in demand of the products or services, neither could they borrow for tax advantages, among others. Yet some entrepreneurs consider borrowing in the circumstances of poor performance. Will financing be a panacea for an ill-performing business? This and the aforementioned derelictions call for a tailored financial literacy on equity and debt financing on one hand and appropriate business climate as defined by stable government policies and predictable directives on the other. Improving both the formal and informal institutions is probably the best way of relaxing the financing constraints small businesses face or else financial and regularity deficiencies might hamper the growth of entrepreneurship and enterprising tendencies. Otherwise, with the status quo remaining unabated, entrepreneurship is reduced to small-scale activities meant to cater for livelihoods and not opportunity-driven and growth-oriented entrepreneurial activities.

Notes

1 Marta Lindvert, Darush Yazdanfar, and Håkan Boter, "Perceptions of Financial Sources Among Women Entrepreneurs in Tanzania," *African Journal of Economic and Management Studies* 6 no. 2 (2015): 197–218. doi.org/10.1108/AJEMS-10-2013-0090.

2 Thorsten Beck and Asli Demirguc-Kunt, "Small and Medium-Size Enterprises: Access to Finance as a Growth Constraint," *Journal of Banking and Finance* 30 (2006): 2931–2943. doi.org/10.1016/j.jbankfin.2006.05.009.

3 Robert Kloosterman, "Matching Opportunities With Resources: A Framework for Analysing (Migrant) Entrepreneurship From a Mixed Embeddedness Perspective," *Entrepreneurship & Regional Development* 22 no.1 (2010): 25–45. https://doi:org/10.1080/08985620903220488

4 Allen N. Berger and Gregory F. Udellc, "Economics of Small Business Finance: The Roles of Private Equity and Debt Markets in the Financial Growth Cycle." *Journal of Banking and Finance* 22 nos. 6–8 (1998): 613–673. doi.org/10.1016/S0378-4266(98)00038-00037.

5 Nancy Huyghebaert and Linda M. Van de Gucht, "The Determinants of Financial Structure: New Insights From Business Start-Ups," *European Financial Management* 13 no. 1 (2007): 101–133. doi:10.2139/ssrn.296841.

6 David A. Walker, "Financing the Small Firm," *Small Business Economics* 1, no. 4 (1989): 285–296. doi.org/10.1007/BF00393807.

172 Tumsifu Elly

7 Abdulaziz M. Abdulsaleh and Andrew Worthington, "Small and Medium-Sized Enterprises Financing: A Review of Literature," *International Journal of Business and Management* 8 no. 14 (2013): 36–54. doi:10.5539/ijbm. v8n14p36.
8 Virginia Braun and Victoria Clarke, "Using Thematic Analysis in Psychology," *Qualitative Research in Psychology* 3 no. 2 (2006): 77–101. doi/abs/10.1191/1478088706qp063oa.
9 Frank Murray and Vidhan K. Goyal, "Capital Structure Decisions: Which Factors Are Reliably Important?" *Financial Management* 38, no. 1 (Spring, 2009): 1–37. doi:10.1111/j.1755–1053X.2009. 01026.x.
10 Joakim Winborg and Hans Landstrom, "Financial Bootstrapping in Small Business: Examining Small Business Resource Acquisition Behavior," *Journal of Business Venturing* 16, (2000): 235–254. doi.org/10.1016/S0883-9026(99)00055-5.
11 Ernest Mwasalwiba, Heidi Dahles, and Ingrid Wakkee, "Graduate Entrepreneurship in Tanzania: Contextual Enablers and Hindrances," *European Journal of Scientific Research* 76 (2012): 386–402. http://hdl.handle.net/10072/52887.

Bibliography

Abdulsaleh, Abdulaziz M., and Andrew Worthington, "Small and Medium-Sized Enterprises Financing: A Review of Literature." *International Journal of Business and Management* 8, no. 14 (2013): 36–54. doi:10.5539/ijbm.v8n14p36.
Beck, Thorsten, and Asli Demirguc-Kunt. "Small and Medium-Size Enterprises: Access to Finance as a Growth Constraint." *Journal of Banking and Finance* 30 (2006): 2931–2943. doi:org/10.1016/j.jbankfin.2006.05.009.
Berger, Allen N., and Gregory F. Udellc. "Economics of Small Business Finance: The Roles of Private Equity and Debt Markets in the Financial Growth Cycle." *Journal of Banking and Finance* 22, nos. 6–8 (1998): 613–673. doi:org/10.1016/S0378-4266(98)00038-7.
Braun, Virginia, and Victoria Clarke. "Using Thematic Analysis in Psychology." *Qualitative Research in Psychology* 3, no. 2 (2006): 77–101. doi:abs/10.1191/1478088706qp063oa.
Huyghebaert, Nancy, and Linda M. Van de Gucht. "The Determinants of Financial Structure: New Insights From Business Start-Ups." *European Financial Management* 13, no. 1 (2007): 101–133. doi:10.2139/ssrn.296841.
Kloosterman, Robert. "Matching Opportunities with Resources: A Framework for Analysing (Migrant) Entrepreneurship From a Mixed Embeddedness Perspective." *Entrepreneurship & Regional Development* 22, no. 1 (2010): 25–45. doi:abs/10.1080/08985620903220488.
Lindvert, Marta, Darush Yazdanfar, and Håkan Boter. "Perceptions of Financial Sources Among Women Entrepreneurs in Tanzania." *African Journal of Economic and Management Studies* 6, no. 2 (2015): 197–218. doi:org/10.1108/AJEMS-10-2013-0090.
Murray, Frank, and Vidhan K. Goyal. "Capital Structure Decisions: Which Factors Are Reliably Important?" *Financial Management* 38, no. 1 (Spring, 2009): 1–37. doi:10.1111/j.1755–1053X.2009. 01026.x.
Mwasalwiba, Ernest, Heidi Dahles, and Ingrid Wakkee. "Graduate Entrepreneurship in Tanzania: Contextual Enablers and Hindrances." *European Journal of Scientific Research* 76 (2012): 386–402. http://hdl.handle.net/10072/52887.
Walker, David A. "Financing the Small Firm." *Small Business Economics* 1, no. 4 (1989): 285–296. doi:org/10.1007/BF00393807.
Winborg, Joakim, and Hans Landstrom. "Financial Bootstrapping in Small Business: Examining Small Business Resource Acquisition Behavior." *Journal of Business Venturing* 16 (2000): 235–254. doi:org/10.1016/S0883-9026(99)00055-5.

Section B: Consumption

10

ADVANCING WATER PURIFICATION TECHNOLOGY AND DELIVERY IN AFRICA

Steven W. Anderson

Introduction

The lack of clean and fresh water is a problem that permeates much of the world. When a lens is applied to Africa, we find that approximately one-third of the population has no access to clean water and nearly two-thirds have no access to clean sanitation. This has led to a widespread proliferation of diseases including malaria, typhoid, dysentery, and many others. In addition to the microbial pollutants that can lead to these aforementioned diseases, chemical contaminants, including those gleaned from bedrock, pose an adverse effect on health, agriculture, and industry. Aside from this severe impact on health and well-being, the lack of suitable water has ramifications on productivity and economic growth.[1] Approximately 75% of Africa's drinking water arises from groundwater. In the Royal Society of Chemistry report on Africa's water quality,[2] it was stated the population growth in sub-Saharan Africa is averaging 2.5% per year, but the lack of safe water and sanitation mitigates economic growth at twice that rate.

The market potential for companies that can deliver proper water solutions is significant. In Kenya alone in 2015, 16 million of 40.6 million people (39%) did not have access to safe water.[3] Households in urban areas lacking access to piped water spend from 3% to 11% of their income on water. In addition, sustainable business models where the ongoing cost of management and maintenance can be derived from the revenue of water sales are necessary. Women and children spend more than 200 million hours each day collecting water from distant and often-polluted sources, taking time from more productive activities. The World Health Organization (WHO) estimates that for every US$1 invested in clean water technology there will be returns of US$3 to US$4, depending on the region and technology.[4] The UN Development Program estimates that every US dollar invested

176 Steven W. Anderson

in access to safe water will yield an eightfold return in terms of improved living conditions and productivity in the communities. Hence, better and more affordable solutions are needed.

Introducing new water technology in economically and socially challenged nations, which suffer a diversity of socio-economical-political-traditional constraints, presents unique challenges. In considering solutions to water delivery and purification, marketing managers must weigh and understand the scientific implications inherent in providing more effective, lower-cost methods to deliver, disinfect, and decontaminate waters from source to point-of-use. Proper science that incorporates the scientific method must necessarily be part of the decision-making process and utilized to defend the ultimate course of action. Ideally, the goals should be attained without further stressing the environment or endangering human health by the treatment itself. Furthermore, systems need to be robust for often-harsh environmental conditions, resistant to tampering, and easy to use. A broader approach incorporating sustainable energy sources while implementing educational and capacity building strategies is of equal importance.

This chapter will begin with a brief examination of representative technical solutions that target water availability, access, purity, and delivery. Specific smaller-scale solutions to be covered will include LifeStraw, The Straw, the Drinkable Book, and the Nanofilter. These will be evaluated in terms of their scientific viability, public interest, entrepreneurship, and perturbations to the existing infrastructure, marketing, implementation, and cultural impact. A more detailed examination will be afforded to Grundfos LIFELINK, a nearly comprehensive M2M (machine-to-machine) solution. Attention will be given to all phases of the development of LIFELINK and the impact it has had in Kenya, where it was first launched, followed by a look at expanded efforts. Finally, other water sanitation programs' (WSPs) leveraging M2M connectivity will be examined.

Small-Scale Technical Solutions for Water Purity

LifeStraw and The Straw

LifeStraw started in 1994 when The Carter Center[5] approached LifeStraw's parent Swiss company, Vestergaard Frandsen (VF), to develop a filter that could remove Guinea worm larvae contaminant from water.[6] VF designed a cloth filter that later evolved into a more effective pipe form in 1999 that is reportedly usable in any water source.[7,8] LifeStraw consists of a plastic tube 10 inches long and 1 inch in diameter that hangs around the neck of a person by a strap. The tube is equipped with membranes, iodine crystals, and activated carbon. The two-stage membrane filtration system, which includes a halogenated resin, reduces harmful particles from 125–15 microns. The hollow membrane fibers, which contain pores less than 0.2 microns in diameter, act as a microfiltration device. Any dirt, bacteria, or parasites are trapped in the fibers while the clean water passes through. Iodine will kill bacteria in water by disrupting the ionic balance within the pathogenic cells.[9] It replaces the chemicals necessary for the bacteria or virus to thrive with iodide ions. Activated carbon removes some organic chemicals and the bitter iodine taste through adsorption. Test results have shown the filter will kill nearly 100% of bacteria and 99% of the introduced viruses. Not included are cryptosporidium and giardia. The device does not remove heavy metals such as lead, iron, or arsenic. However, there is a version that can filter arsenic. With average use, the filter will last 1 year. It clogs internally when spent.

The LifeStraw Family, introduced in 2008, is a point-of-use microbial water treatment system intended for routine use in low-income households. Using only the force of gravity, this unit can purify up to 18,000 liters of water, enough to supply a family of five with clean drinking water that meets US Environmental Protection Agency (EPA) standards for 3 years before the filters need to be replaced.

While the first iteration of LifeStraw used iodine to kill bacteria, the 2012 version contains no chemicals. Instead, the product incorporates microfiber mechanical filtration. After drinking, one simply blows air out of the straw to expel dirty water and flush the filter membranes.[8]

The Straw, a device analogous to LifeStraw, was developed in 2007 at the impetus of Ken Surritte.[10] From an experience while working in Kenya, he observed that children were getting sick from a drilled water well at a school. Several inspections of the well revealed that the source of the problem was a stagnant pond. The Straw was Surritte's answer to on-the-spot water purification for the children. In 2009, the non-profit WATERisLIFE was created. Its mission is dedicated to providing an accessible clean water solution to the poorest and neediest nations, with an emphasis on children. Like the LifeStraw, The Straw employs a three-stage filtration system.[11,12] As of this writing (2017), WATERisLIFE had distributed approximately 70,000 straws in 33 countries.[13,14]

Hunter and colleagues reported[15] in 2009 results of field testing the LifeStraw in El-Masraf camp within Gezira State, Sudan. Surveys were taken before and after the provision of LifeStraws for diarrheal rates of 647 participants. At the outset, 16.8% of people reported becoming sick over a two-week period. After filter usage, the percentage dropped to 15.3%. The smaller-than-anticipated reduction (1.5%) is overshadowed by many other sanitation-related health concerns in poor countries. For example, if residents do not thoroughly wash their hands, they can still become ill. Aware of these issues, VF has taken steps to ensure that LifeStraws are usually distributed with inclusive education programs.[16,17] They have several studies in progress they hope will more accurately capture the health impact instant access to clean water can provide. The Sudan study also revealed, remarkably, that 87% of participants said they always used the filters.

LifeStraw is not without its detractors. Nathalie Rothschild[18] questions whether this may be 'the most degrading gadget ever invented.' She finds the idea of impoverished people sucking dirty water through straws demeaning. While

178 Steven W. Anderson

acknowledging that the LifeStraw is an ingenious device for use under extenuating circumstances, she takes the CEO, Vestergaard Frandsen, to task for not 'doing business with doing good,' as he described himself to CNBC. She feels the company should at least acknowledge that a device like LifeStraw—no matter how clever the design—is neither a long-term nor ideal solution.

VF believed that the LifeStraw Family could make an immediate and profound difference for households in developing countries. The challenge was in making it affordable. Given that philanthropic donors for point-of-use water programs tend to make short-term investments, VF sought an alternative solution that could make their donation program sustainable. VF launched an integrated campaign in 2008 aimed at preventing the spread of malaria, diarrheal disease, and HIV in Western Kenya. Participants were offered free HIV counseling and testing services as well as a preventative CarePack including condoms, an insecticide-treated bed net, and a household water filter. In partnership with the Kenyan Ministry of Health, this campaign included 6 weeks of radio ads and road show presentations, collateral distribution, and public health education in order to inform, prepare, and mobilize the community.

Alison Hill, VF's Managing Director, Climate, stated

> In order to reach the poorest and most vulnerable households and achieve an equitable distribution, we felt the best option was to provide the LifeStraw at no cost to households.[19] This meant we needed to seek financing that could cover the cost of the LifeStraw and the ongoing operations of the program.

To accomplish this, carbon financing was linked to providing safe water at the household level. Carbon finance allows developing country projects that reduce carbon emissions to earn carbon credits on the basis of the volume of emissions they prevent. When a project creating the credits provides a direct benefit to and promotes sustainable development in the community where it is based, it can achieve the Swiss-based Gold Standard designation. LifeStraw Family water filters could be installed in homes without access to municipal water sources. In exchange, VF would earn carbon credits on the basis of the premise that the filters made it unnecessary for recipients to boil their water for safety, thereby preventing current and future carbon emissions. Ultimately, this means less firewood is burned as fuel. VF claims carbon credits for the greenhouse gas emissions saved, which can then be sold for revenue to cover program costs. Over a 6-week period in spring 2011, approximately 877,500 LifeStraw Family units were distributed to roughly 90% of all households in Kenya's Western Province. The Gold Standard Foundation and international auditors verified a 91% usage rate (defined as filtering at least once every 2 weeks) at the program's first audit. Even more importantly from a public health perspective, they found that 83% of families were filtering their water at least twice a week, which VF defined as 'regular usage.' At this adoption rate, LifeStraw Carbon for Water generated 1.3 million credits in its first 6 months, nearly twice the amount originally anticipated. VF is monitoring to see how effectively the program meets the needs of the community and if it can sustainably be taken to scale over time. This is one of the largest water treatment programs realized without public sector funding, and it is the first ever to be supported by carbon financing.

Crucially, carbon credits can be obtained only once it is shown that the filters are being used regularly. An Oxford-based organization, ClimateCare, designed the certification methodology that ensures the program delivers real and long-lasting sustainable development benefits. This results-driven system incentivizes important investments in health education and robust monitoring systems. It is anticipated that the use of LifeStraw, coupled with the provision of health and hygiene education, will significantly reduce the risk of contamination and illness. Dr. John Haskew, an Academic Clinic Fellow at Oxford University's Department for Public Health, is leading the health impact evaluation that utilizes cutting-edge mobile phone technology and electronic medical records.[20] Populations most vulnerable to waterborne diseases are the focus of the health impact studies. The Oxford-led team is evaluating the impact of the program on diarrhea and dehydration among children under 5 years old. They will also assess whether the use of LifeStraw can diminish rates of diarrhea and infection among people with HIV and even delay the development of the HIV disease itself.

The Drinkable Book

Recognizing that silver is a potent microbial agent, Dr. Theresa Dankovich, from Carnegie Mellon University and in partnership with WATERisLIFE and a start-up company she founded (in 2014), pAge Drinking Paper, developed[21,22] a book whose tear-out pages purify water. This stemmed, in part, from her doctoral research at McGill University. The book's pages are coated with silver nanoparticles that can trap a reported 99.99% of the bacteria found in cholera, $E.\ coli$, and typhoid.[21] Silver and silver-based compounds are highly antimicrobial to several species of bacteria, including $E.\ coli$. Silver nanoparticles target the outer membrane of bacteria, effecting structural changes that lead to degradation and the eventual death of a microbe. Further field testing campaigns with WATERisLIFE in northern Ghana and Bangladesh suggested that the silver-doped paper can remove up to 99.9% of the $E.\ coli$ bacteria present in a sample.[21] Dankovich et al.[23] recently conducted more extensive testing of paper filters containing silver or copper nanoparticles with water sourced from contaminated streams in Limpopo, South Africa. The water quality of the filtered effluent was evaluated with respect to the colony counts of total coliform and $E.\ coli$ bacteria, turbidity, and either silver or copper ions. Both silver- and copper-treated papers showed complete inactivation of the coliform bacteria. With surface water with higher coliform bacteria levels, both the silver and copper papers showed similar results with a slightly higher bacteria reduction for the silver papers than for the copper papers. *E. coli* results followed similar trends. These results demonstrate good potential for the use of paper embedded with silver and/or copper nanoparticles as effective point-of-use water purifiers.

Each page, resembling a thick coffee filter, can purify up to 100 liters of drinking water, whereas an entire book can supply 4 years' worth of water for a single person. Information about cleaning water and using the filter is printed on the pages in non-toxic ink. The book is a teaching tool as well. It is cited as the first-ever manual that will provide safe water, sanitation, and hygiene education.

As of 2016, a new company, Folia Water[24,25,26] was founded by Dr. Dankovich and Dr. Jonathan Levine. The triple bottom line of the company encompasses a social mission entailing people, planet, and profit. Folia partners with BoP Hub, a Singapore-based accelerator platform. The latest iteration of Folia Filters, as they are now called, fit a regular plastic funnel or a keystone funnel. Filters are sold in packs of 50. The standard keystone funnel is designed to fit between two 2-liter soda bottles or on top of any jerry can. For developing countries, a Safe Water Book is distributed that includes 26 filters, a funnel, operating instructions, and information on water hygiene. The filters are biodegradable, non-toxic, and recyclable. They are lethal for bacteria and some types of viruses. The paper pore size screens out protozoans and dirt particles, and it can absorb some metals (although not completely). However, the paper does not remove pesticides. Each filter will generally purify up to 100 liters of water. In late 2016, Dr. Dankovich stated,[27] 'We're still in the development phase of the project, and don't have a very large impact (yet!).' However, as of January 2017, 20,000 filters had been distributed among the following countries: Morocco, Liberia, Ghana, Cameroon, Ethiopia, Uganda, Tanzania, Zambia, and Malawi. Currently, Folia Water is scaling up paper production, manufacturing operations, and exploring new product features.

The Nanofilter

In work that spanned from 2010 to 2015,[28,29,30,31] Dr. Askwar Hilonga, a lecturer at the Nelson Mandela African Institution of Science and Technology (NM-AIST; Arusha, Tanzania), developed a low-cost customizable filtration system that can be calibrated to target and eliminate contaminants specific to a particular geographic region. Growing up in a very remote village in Tanzania, he was an eyewitness to the suffering caused by waterborne diseases. Having obtained his PhD in South Korea and published widely on nanomaterials, he asked himself what it all meant.

Dr. Hilonga decided to apply his knowledge to solve this problem in his community by establishing a start-up company, Gongali Model Company Limited. After early difficulty seeking start-up capital to test his business idea, a door opened when he received a $7,000 seed-capital intervention by NM-AIST. Professor Chad Jafvert of Purdue University and students in his Global Engineering course also donated filter components for 100 slow sand filters to be integrated with disinfection filters that enabled a prototype to be developed. Dr. Hilonga entered and won the first Africa Prize in 2015 for Engineering Innovation from the United Kingdom's Royal Academy of Engineering. The cash award of GBP25,000 (TZS79 million; US$38,348) seeks to encourage talented engineers in sub-Saharan Africa to find solutions to local challenges and develop them into businesses. With this financial support and special training provided through the award, Gongali Model Company Limited was able to introduce 100 filters to the market. Global Sustainable Partnership (GSP), a U.S. charity, also donated 100 filters the company gave to schools in rural Karatu District. This allowed the company to subsidize the cost of the filters to households at a 'promotion price.'

Dr. Hilonga's patented filtration system combines a slow sand filter with a combination of nanomaterials made from sodium silicate and silver to eliminate toxic heavy metals, fluoride, or other chemical contaminants such as pesticides.[28,29,30,31] Water first passes through the sand and then through the nanomaterials. Whereas other water filters, such as the LifeStraw, offer a 'one-size-fits-all' solution, the Nanofilter can be calibrated for specific needs. Slow sand filters have been used in water purification for over 100 years.[32,33]

Sand is effective in removing bacteria and 99.999% of microorganisms from water. The first method of filtration for slow sand water filters is a simple mechanical filtration. A particle of fine sand is roughly 60 micrometers, and the distance between grains of very fine sand is even smaller. Bacteria are often slightly larger than the spaces between sand and soil particles. As water is passed through the slow sand filter, some of the bacteria will be trapped within the spaces between the sand, and water will continue to pass through. Trapped bacteria will then contribute to a biofilm (hypogeal) layer, the schmutzedecke (German for 'dirt cover'). This contains microorganisms that remove more than 90% of bacteria and 100% of parasites.

Nanofiltration[34] is a membrane filtration-based method that uses nanometer-sized cylindrical through-pores that pass through a polymer (e.g., polyethylene terephthalate) or metal (e.g., aluminum) thin membrane at 90°. Nanofiltration membranes have pore sizes from 1 to 10 nanometers. Pore dimensions are controlled by pH, temperature, and time during development with pore densities ranging from 1 to 106 pores per cm^2. Hence, harmful materials can be filtered out by size exclusion.

Distribution and sales of the nanofilters has been in Tanzania.[29] The filters have been presently rented to 23 entrepreneurs who filter the water and sell it to their community at a reasonable price. The nanofilter will produce 60 liters per day of safe drinking water with nanomaterials generally needing replacement when up to 800 liters of water have been filtered. Gongali Model Company Limited initially had five employees, including Dr. Hilonga. In addition to the Nanofilter, the company provides water quality profiling and testing. Earlier this year, the company began exploring a proposed change of business model from local entrepreneurs running water stations to company-run water stations.

182 Steven W. Anderson

Marketing activities have included full product showcasing (e.g., at religious meetings, farmers' exhibitions, school graduations, hospital staff meetings), lobbying government goodwill, stabilizing the existing water stations to attract new ones, opening water stations in government offices with high population and movements, bottle labels, and online marketing (company website, Facebook, Twitter, YouTube).

In fall 2016, it was reported that 187 water stations were established, with 156 active—serving about 8,000 people daily. Nanofilter provided direct employment to 23 people (Gongali staff) and 187 local entrepreneurs. As of February 2017, there were 92 active water stations and 5 run by Gongali Model Company Limited. The total impact on jobs created is 250, with overall beneficiaries estimated to be 12,000 people every day. In February 2017, the company also announced expansion to Kenya using a GBP 20,000 grant from The Royal Academy of Engineering, United Kingdom (through partnership with three institutions: Plymouth from United Kingdom, Oshwal College, and Masinde Muliro University from Kenya).

All-Encompassing Solutions Employing M2M Connectivity

Grundfos LIFELINK (East Africa) and Sarvajal (India) are the two major ventures that have developed business models based on the use of M2M (machine to machine) connectivity for their purified water delivery. 'M2M is a broad label that can be used to describe any technology that enables networked devices to exchange information and perform actions without the manual assistance of humans.'[35] It is a vital component of warehouse management, remote control, robotics, traffic control, logistic services, supply chain management, fleet management, and telemedicine. M2M systems include sensors, radio frequency identification (RFID), a Wi-Fi link, and autonomic computing software programmed to help a networked device interpret data and make decisions.

Grundfos LIFELINK

Background

Grundfos, headquartered in Bjerringbro, Denmark, is a world-leading pump supplier controlling roughly half of the world market for circulation pumps. Grundfos LIFELINK was developed as a subsidiary in Kenya in 2007,[36] in collaboration with the Investment Fund for Developing Countries (IFU), a financial institution established by the Danish Government in 1967 as a self-governing fund. An initial goal of LIFELINK was to develop solutions to improve living conditions for people in developing countries, primarily covering rural and peri-urban areas in Africa, Asia, and Latin America. As of 2011, the target was to enable access to safe drinking water for 1.5 million people by 2015. Four pillars providing the foundation for sustainability of LIFELINK are (1) technical, (2) financial, (3) environmental, and (4) social.

As mentioned in the beginning of this chapter, there is clearly a business market for large-scale water solutions. Sustainability rates for 7,000 large-scale water projects evaluated in Ethiopia revealed that 30%–40% of these were non-functional.[37] This lack of sustainability can be attributed primarily to lack of resources, capabilities, and spare parts for service and maintenance. Other factors such as vandalism and piracy can also come into play.

The Katitika Project[38,39,40]

Grundfos was familiar with Kenya through previous business interactions. The main targeted areas in Kenya were rural communities in the arid and semi-arid parts where surface water is scarce and in peri-urban areas where the public infrastructure cannot meet the demand for basic services such as water and electricity. These are base of the pyramid markets (BoP) markets composed of customers surviving on less than the equivalent of US$2 a day for living expenses.[41] Grundfos had to consider a number of challenges to mount water delivery in a developing country. While the technical problems were within their realm, the non-commercial aspects represented uncharted territory. Kenya offered a good venue to stress-test their business model in an exacting market.

Operations were initially set up in Katitika in 2008 and further expanded to 16 villages by 2013. This was the first business initiative where Grundfos was involved in the entire process of site identification, social mobilization, technical implementation, community development training, and after-sales service.

In order to obtain rights to local water boreholes, it was necessary for Grundfos to convince local non-governmental organizations (NGOs). These groups had a strong bias to existing operations and suggested villages that were unsuitable for development of a water kiosk. As a result, Grundfos determined it was necessary to control all activities and enroll people in their own design rather than connecting to existing systems. Accordingly, the NGOs were replaced with a Grundfos community consultant. In addition, an anthropologist was hired to gauge community interest in negotiating agreements with LIFELINK.

Fortunately, a borehole, accompanied by a hand pump, had been sunk in Katitika by JIKA, the Czech sanitary ceramics manufacturer. The first LIFELINK unit was installed there in March 2009. In 2010, Katitika had a population of 1,800 in 300 households. The households served by this unit were in the four villages of Mangina, Katitika, Itulu, and Mwanni. Approximately 76% of the residents had mobile phones.

Details of the LIFELINK System[38,40,42]

The LIFELINK is an example of a turnkey water solution. It is built, supplied, and installed complete and ready to operate by Grundfos. The three fundamental components are a submersible solar-driven pump, a GPS-based monitoring system, and fees based on digital payments of water credits. Water is pumped to

184 Steven W. Anderson

an elevated storage tank (typically 10,000-liter capacity) and fed, by gravity, to a small, secure concrete housing structure. The early design of the system also consisted of a water kiosk, a server, and communication unit. Grundfos guarantees they will fix or replace any parts of the system that may break down. A summary of the LIFELINK components is given in Table 10.1.

TABLE 10.1 Components of the LIFELINK System

Component	Principal Features
AQtap water dispenser	• Robust/tamper resistant • Uses groundwater or surface water • Connects to public water network for single kiosk or grid of grouped kiosks • Simple, intuitive, and accessible user interface • Payment with water (smart) card or water key • Valve and flow restrictor adjusts to high or low pressures • Fully functional without Internet connection • Data transmitted daily, in case of alarm, or other warnings
AQpure	• Modular automated ultrafiltration of bacteria, viruses, and particles from raw source water • Filters selected ranging for treating orange water (most polluted; rivers and lakes in tropical season) to blue water (least polluted; groundwater, rain water, or public water) • Modules selected on the basis of further specific needs such as chlorination (kill certain bacteria and other microbes), activated carbon (removal of chlorine, dissolved organics, pesticides, taste, and odor), and UV disinfection (inactivation of bacteria and viruses)
Water Management System	• Operates in cloud, tracking all water data and credit transactions at Grundfos headquarters in Denmark. • Dashboard displays overview of AQtap dispensers with record of alarms/warnings, unit performance, water tracking, and water and credit transactions • Reports display time tracking of credits and water consumption as well as consumption patterns according to consumer type • Notification function allows the system to be configured to broadcast alarms and warnings via email or text messages
Remote management	• Status of the entire system viewable on map or aerial photo • Secure data channel with encryption • Alarms triggered and viewed online when satellite connection lost, modem or power line communication modem fails, or when water reservoir is empty
SQflex energy control unit	• Solar panels or wind turbines (as an option) that adapt to the characteristic regional weather profile • Generator or backup battery provided • Dry-running protection provided that shuts down pump if water shortage detected; pump restarts automatically when water returns to well

Source: www.grundfos.com/market-areas/water/lifelink/Products.html

Advancing Water Purification Technology **185**

A supplier for a water purification system was initially located in Denmark. However, Grundfos encountered problems with the supplied unit. Testing in Denmark revealed that it did not work as advertised, requiring more maintenance and daily filter cleanings and gave reduced water output. Given the more severe operating conditions in rural Kenya, Grundfos repositioned to develop their own purification unit. To reduce costs, the system was initially developed for groundwater use and would later be adapted for surface water applications.

Evolution of the Business Model[38,40]

The initial business model for LIFELINK was based on a commercial model where communities or entrepreneurs would obtain a loan to cover the up-front cost of the system. They would then repay the loan on an ongoing basis through water consumption. At the outset, Grundfos had intended to link with a local partner that would facilitate all contacts with local, regional, and global (sponsors) constituents. Grundfos would deliver the technical 'hardware' for the water station. NGO sponsors such as the World Bank and Bill and Melinda Gates Foundation were envisioned.

Nonetheless, on the basis of experience gained from the first four projects implemented in 2009, it became clear this was not a viable way forward in Kenya. The population density, water consumption and price level were incapable of generating sufficient revenue to pay back the loan. The business model was changed to a 'donation model,' where an external donor from the public sector, development organizations, private foundations, or corporate social responsibility programs funded the up-front cost. Ongoing water consumption in the community finances the service and maintenance, thus ensuring a reliable and sustainable water supply. Grundfos anticipates that a semi-commercial and commercial business model based on a loan for the up-front investment will become relevant when expanding to urban areas with higher population density and in Asian countries where the population density and water pricing are ramped up. The system includes a contract where a local team takes charge of service and maintenance activities.

Business models for the operation have steadily evolved with time, ranging from commercial funding and semi-commercial funding, to donations. In the process, the role of LIFELINK evolved from a market actor to a market architect and developer. By moving in this direction, it was incumbent upon Grundfos to document the sustainability of LIFELINK to raise the capital for additional water kiosks in approaching local and international NGOs.

Sustainable business models seek to follow the triple bottom line approach that balances economic prosperity, environmental quality and social equity for all parties involved in the exchange of services.[43] The three principal sustainability factors are financial, managerial, and technical.

At the onset, Grundfos realized that the commercial model would never be primary. Instead of establishing a kiosk in a village and requiring users to pay for current

186 Steven W. Anderson

water consumption, the focus was redirected to how the kiosk could generate local growth once it was established. As a consequence, LIFELINK could be a community development platform that might attract other organizations and NGOs.

The LIFELINK brand is applied only for the total solution, whereas Grundfos LIFELINK is fully in charge as an implementing partner and service provider. In instances where components of the system are sold on a separate basis, the business model is based on the Grundfos brand only.

Developing a Payment Method[38,40]

Various options were weighed on how money transfer to water sale would be accomplished. Initially scratch cards with water credits were proposed. However, this presented problems of managing distribution and recognition. By chance, a temporary research associate for the project had experience with Safaricom, a local Kenyan company associated with Vodaphone, which operates M-Pesa, the prolific mobile banking system. Hence, a logical conduit for water payment was foreseen.

The payment system is a partnership between Safaricom and Grundfos LIFE-LINK. Employing an interface using M-Pesa, users with mobile phones transfer credit to a water key that is used to draw water from a tapping station. Payment is transferred within a closed circuit to a service account, where it finances the ongoing service contract with Grundfos LIFELINK. The local water committee, in accordance with public tariffs for the municipal water supply, determines water pricing.

Grundfos decided to enter into a partnership with Safaricom and, with recognition of the commercial potential, asked to be part of the development team. Engineers at Grundfos developed their own work utility for managing the system that included a keyfob (memory card with credits). A radio-frequency identification tag (RFID) was employed for the exchange of digital information for users who did not possess mobile phones. Grundfos engineers also designed an Internet link to the water station, allowing users and the company to monitor water usage and payments in real time. The avoidance of the exchange of hard cash reduced the risk of corruption and mismanagement. Users receive a smart card embedded with a microchip. The user deposits money from an M-Pesa account into a Grundfos M-Pesa business account. Money is then loaded to the smart card.

Through M-Pesa, the beneficiaries contribute to a community trust that pays for the water pump. Money also goes toward maintenance of the pump. Revenue above and beyond remains in a bank account managed by a local water committee. The community acquires the pumping system on credit. The business model enables communities to acquire pumps while paying for the investment gradually through utility fees. Some projects have been funded through agencies such as the Red Cross. The model includes a local service organization responsible for regular system maintenance and service calls courtesy of the Safaricom infrastructure.

Grundfos issues four types of water cards for the LIFELINK that afford different levels of accessibility.[42] In order of decreasing accessibility these are (1) the AdminCard (issued to water service providers), (2) the VendorCard (issued to water vendors), and (3) the WaterCard (issued to water consumers). A fourth, separate ServiceCard is issued to service technicians.

Partnerships

Grundfos LIFELINK partners with UNICEF, the World Food Program, the Red Cross, the Government of Kenya, the Danish International Development Agency (DANIDA), Nordic Climate Facility, World Vision, private foundations, and corporate social responsibility programs. While the partnership models vary, the common goal is to achieve 10–15 years of sustainability by using the Grundfos LIFELINK system as opposed to more traditional and less sustainable options.

Community Impact

As Grundfos LIFELINK is a business with a social purpose, it has a high priority to measure the social dynamics and the social impact of its system in communities. Key indicators, including time spent and distance covered to retrieve water and average daily water consumption and average daily water consumption pre- and post-installation of LIFELINK, are monitored. Grundfos hired social research consultants to carry out a thorough socio-economic impact assessment.

The World Business Council for Sustainable Development Case Study[36] of 2011 cites that community members and health facilities reported that the occurrence of waterborne diseases among children was reduced by at least 50%. It was also noted that, after installation of the LIFELINK system, more men were likely to procure water. This was attributed to their affinity for high tech. With a reliable year-round water supply, a surge of kitchen gardens was observed. Another benefit has been the growth of entrepreneurs engaged in small business water distribution to area households, providing another source of income that has simultaneously increased the reach of safe water.

In a survey of 96 people impacted by the Katitika Water project, Mbatha[39] found that community water projects have demonstrably improved lives of people, especially women and children, who are primarily expected to obtain and transport water. Her findings indicated that most people were comfortable with the new technology and innovation. Time and energy could now be redirected toward other activities.

Nonetheless, LIFELINK remains a complementary source to river water. Even though the latter is contaminated with human and animal feces, soil, and flies, it is still preferred in hard times. Education is necessary. A report from Katitika for 2009–2010 revealed that 60% of the residents used LIFELINK as the main source of water. The reduction of time expended in water collection led to fewer adult sick days and greater attention to sick children. Indirectly, a growth in local income levels was observed. There are clear benefits from the decreased time in collecting water, fewer adult sick days, and attention to sick children. Andersen[40]

188 Steven W. Anderson

reported that there were zero children sick for 15 days in 2010 versus 12 in 2009. The number of children sick 1–3 days went from 23 to 42 from 2009 to 2010. The data demonstrates not only a reduction in the number of illnesses but also a shift to shorter-term incidents. Mbatha's summary[39] survey found that the majority of residents (equal to or exceeding 88%) believe that management services, technology and innovation, financial status of the community, and maintenance all influence the sustainability of the water system.

The Community Consultant conducts a program of community training in health and development. Some partners share in this enterprise. For example, in conjunction with the Kenyan Red Cross, projects include a 'business in a box' kit consisting of small greenhouses with drip irrigation systems. Community members are also trained how to select and grow the best crops.

Nairobi Case Study[44]

A LIFELINK installation in Nairobi, Kenya, is also impacting the lives of people. It has allowed a viable setup for operating public water kiosks in Mathare, an informal settlement in Nairobi. Prior to this, black market cartels controlled the water supply. Vendors tampered with water lines, filled water tanks, and would sell water of questionable quality in the slum areas at inflated prices. Nairobi Water monitors each tapping point through a cloud-connected system. With a small subsidy, the price can be kept low and fixed. Small business owners have benefited from a ready supply of clean and inexpensive water. Mary Mbetee operates a vegetable stand on one of Mathare's dusty streets. She had to walk several blocks to secure overpriced water to wash the produce. After the LIFELINK installation, she reported,

> It has increased my profit. Instead of spending ten shillings, you spend fifty cents. It is very good. This is what makes my profit grow, and this water has been helpful. And I don't get any stress even if I use a lot of it. It is still cheap.

Phillip Gichuki, Managing Director of Nairobi Water, reports that the data collection, allowing assessment of family water consumption, is a real boon for planning purposes. In addition to the data collection, the AQtap systems have proven to have a 1-year payback time and are generating a profit for Nairobi Water.

Challenges

Most difficulties range from technical maintenance of systems management, cost recovery, planning, transparency of decision making, and communication between community committees and community beneficiaries. Social capital is also a requirement. Mbatha emphasizes[39] that Water Boards need members with managerial skills and reasonable levels of education. In Katitika, the greatest challenge has been maintenance and funds for repair. In 2011, there was no project training offered to repair the kiosk. Despite this, 83% of customers viewed the maintenance response by LIFELINK to be prompt. If local personnel were trained to respond, repairs would certainly be faster and cheaper. Each community in Kenya contributes 30% of the total project cost. The business-like approach afforded by LIFELINK to the Community Water Project instilled a sense of ownership to the members such that they would guard it all costs. Conflict resolution was the most challenging aspect to the water committee. Breakdown of communication between the company and local project members is always a concern.

Financial Sustainability

As of 2009, there were five water kiosks in operation in Kenya. This expanded to 16 sites in the summer of 2011. Grundfos had projected having 70 sites in operation in Kenya by 2013. As of this writing (summer 2017), there are 40 LIFELINK projects in Kenya providing water for nearly 100,000 people in rural and peri-urban communities.

An additional four kiosks are in operation in Uganda. Grundfos signed an agreement in July 2016 with World Vision International to reach 2 million people over the next 5 years by providing 1,000 LIFELINK systems in nine African countries. Andersen[40] has reported profit/loss estimates for the Katitika operation from 2011 to 2013 that are shown in Figure 10.1. Sales showed a 145%

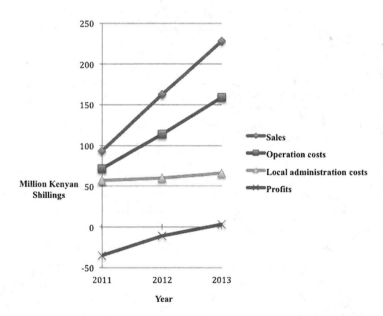

FIGURE 10.1 Profit/Loss Estimate for Grundfos LIFELINK in Katitika, Kenya

Source: Adapted from Andersen[40]

190 Steven W. Anderson

increase while operation costs escalated 124%. Local administration and depreciation showed a modest 16% increase while profits jumped up 109% and became positive in 2013.

Maintenance has been an important cost driver. The establishment of more sites will result in shorter servicing distances.

The goal is to provide a minimum of 10 years' worth of operational sustainability for all 40 water projects. Operating a larger portfolio instead of focusing on each individual project attains overall financial and technical sustainability. Higher-yielding water projects in urban areas contribute to the ongoing operation and service of smaller water projects in rural areas, thus creating a new business model.

Uganda and Malawi Projects[45,46,47,48]

LIFELINK has three projects that are operating in Uganda and Malawi in conjunction with Water Missions International (WMI) under its TradeWater (TW) private delivery service. The TW projects are located in Kikondo, Kimmi Island (Uganda), and Matanda (Malawi). WMI is a U.S.-based non-profit Christian engineering ministry[49] that provides sustainable water solutions to people in developing countries and disaster areas. Source water for the Uganda project is drawn from Lake Victoria, Africa's largest lake, with a solar pumping system, treated with filtration and chlorine disinfection. Kikondo, with a population of over 33 million, is situated on the northern shore of Lake Victoria. A solar pumping system, transmission pipes, Living Water Treatment System (LWTS) and a 10,000-liter storage tank were installed. A small building in the center of town was also purchased for use as the focal point for TW business operations.

Since early 2012, WMI has pioneered the TW model with seven projects in Uganda and additional projects in Haiti and Malawi. The Matanda project also uses a solar pump on a deep borehole with chlorine disinfection. The technical solution utilizes WMI's LWTS and the Grundfos LIFELINK water solution with solar driven pumps, a water dispenser, and the water management system. This is used in settings where community-based management is not feasible. Water is dispensed and revenue collected through water dispensers located in the center of the community or connected in a mini-grid of several water points from the same water source, bringing the water closer to each household.

Typical community-owned water systems are put together by an organization that donates the equipment and provides engineering, design, construction, and training to local personnel. After 12–18 months of start-up and testing, the donor organization withdraws and the community takes ownership and maintenance responsibilities. In a departure from this approach, as part of the TWI business model, WMI—in close collaboration with the communities—constructs and assumes the role of a long-term, committed non-profit water service operator and maintains responsibility for all financial management and administration. This includes the engineering, equipment, water source development, enclosures, tank support towers, solar pumping system, proprietary filtration/disinfection, storage taps, and the distribution tap or network. All up-front capital is covered through a combination of individual and corporate donors. 'The projects are set up as little businesses and run on the non-profit model,' relates George Green III, founder and CEO of WMI. 'This [LIFELINK] adds the ability to monitor all aspects of the project and access information in real time.'[48]

Established members of the community are employed as Water Agents to operate the water system. To supplement sales, Kikondo's local water agent also offers battery and phone charging off the solar system as well as bathing shelters. Proceeds go back into the system, per the non-profit model. WMI staff will train the Water Agents to provide administrative oversight, customer service, and maintenance support. A water business can be sold to a local individual or institution if it is established and breaks even.

LIFELINK units are installed at each site with payment via a 'water key.' Keys are purchased by users and loaded with credit either via mobile money transfer or directly from a 'credit key' held by the Water Agent. The Malawi and Uganda programs both lack mobile banking services, on-the-ground LIFELINK technical support, and necessary water treatment. Local staff from TWI assumes responsibility for operations, money handling, and maintenance. Many households jointly purchase keys. In addition, there are institutional users such as schools, health clinics, and so forth. Inserting the water key into the LIFELINK unit dispenses water with a collection fee deducted from the key as water is withdrawn. All data points are time stamped and labeled with unique water key identification numbers. Data are regularly transmitted to the Grundfos Water Management System. The Water Agent's 'credit key' can be viewed and extended remotely. Continuous LIFELINK data permit Water Agents to make informed decisions regarding water pricing and promotional activities.

Living Water Treatment System (LWTS)[48,50]

Dr. George Greene III, founder and CEO of WMI, and a team of engineers developed this purification system, relying on filtration and disinfection, in 1998. It is likened to a miniature water treatment plant capable of purifying more than 10 gallons per minute or 10,000 gallons of water per day. This translates to roughly enough water for 5,000 people. It is rugged, simple to operate, easily transported, and claimed to be operational for up to 20 years. No electricity is required for operation other than if a pump is needed. Fifteen hundred LWTS units have been deployed around the globe. Water can be readily purified from raw sources including rivers, lakes, springs, ponds, or wells.

Four-stage treatment removes 99.9% of particles less than 3 microns, affords consistently clear water, and provides chlorine disinfection. The system has a venturi based potassium alum[51] ($KAl(SO_4)_2 \cdot 12H_2O$) addition system. The alum reacts

192 Steven W. Anderson

with calcium carbonate, present in water from dissolved carbon dioxide, to form aluminum hydroxide $(Al(OH)_3)$ as an insoluble precipitate. Very small particles in water commonly possess a negative surface charge and can exist as colloids in water. A colloid is a mixture in which one substance of microscopically dispersed insoluble particles is suspended throughout another substance. Since like charges repel, these colloids will not adhere to each other if brought into contact. The aluminum hydroxide (the coagulant) collides with and causes the colloids to coagulate or clump together into 'flocs,' which then float to the top of the liquid, settle to the bottom of the liquid, or can be more easily filtered from the liquid, prior to further filtration and disinfection of the water.[52]

In the next step, water is directed through a primary water filter that removes large particles. It is then sent through a secondary filter that removes smaller particles. An in-line chlorinator follows that is used to disinfect the water. This employs stabilized tablet chlorine and has a test kit for monitoring. Stabilized chlorine is chlorine bound to cyanuric acid.[53,54] Cyanuric acid (Figure 10.2) stabilizes chlorine by binding to free chlorine and releasing it slowly, extending the time needed to deplete each dose of sanitizer.

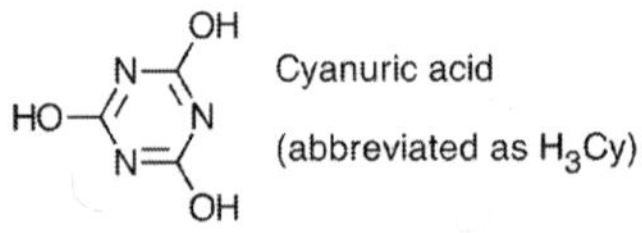

Cyanuric acid

(abbreviated as H_3Cy)

FIGURE 10.2 Cyanuric Acid (Abbreviated as H_3Cy)

Cyanuric acid in its enol form is a weak tribasic acid.[55,56] It ionizes progressively from H_3Cy to H_2Cy^-, HCy^{2-}, and Cy^{3-}. Protons (H^+) are successively replaced by unipositive chlorine (Cl^+) so that $CyCl_3$ is formed. The relevant equilibrium is given by:

$HClCy^- + H_2O <<<---> H_2Cy^- + HOCl$. When cyanuric acid is present, most of the chlorine is bound to it with the chemical equilibrium shown previously shifted predominantly to the left. It is hypochlorous acid (HOCl) that is the active form of chlorine (Cl^+) that disinfects, kills algae, and oxidizes waste in water.

Although not mentioned in the company literature, one of the filters, presumably after the chlorinator, must be an activated carbon filter. These are generally responsible for removing larger particles like sediment and silt. They work by attracting and absorbing these particles. This reduces the amount of chlorine and other contaminants that can give the water an odor and make it unpleasant to drink.[57] The system is incorporated with backwash valves that allow one to clean the filter.

Impact[45,46,47,48]

TW projects are providing reliable water supply access to 44,000 people in rural and peri-urban areas. Although they still feel there is significant work to do to engage the remaining households that are not using safe water, it is considered a success that more than 50% of the market was reached within 3 months. Household surveys from Kikondo have indicated that people are still using lake water to wash clothes, wash dishes, bathe, and cook. Plans are to continue promoting healthy WASH (water, sanitation, and hygiene) practices in the community in order to increase the level of household consumption of safe water.

Financial Sustainability[45]

As of 2013, all three of these TW projects continued operation with a financial deficit where total expenses were more than double the total income. Operating expenses include staff commission, salaries, administrative, chemicals, and transportation. Total expenses account for capital maintenance, major maintenance, and depreciation costs. In each case, the percentage of households collecting water from the TW Business Center has been decreasing with time. Customers who were retained were increasingly satisfied with the level service. As was observed for operations in Katitika, the local water committees face a myriad of technical and financial challenges that go beyond post-construction support.

Armstrong et al.[45] examined GPS labeling of residences associated with water keys in Kikondo, Uganda. From this data, the distances from residences to the TW Business Center could be determined. Household penetration is, therefore, based on the correlation between active users and the total number of households within each radius. Survey trends indicated that households continuing to collect water from TW either increased their consumption or continued to collect at a high volume. For all three projects, users sharing water keys or reselling water from TW increased their consumption over time. Low-volume customers eventually terminated their contracts. As water consumption has remained below the 3% threshold that the United Nations Development Program has set as indicating economic hardship, there appears to be room to increase water consumption or the price without limiting financial accessibility. A 10-month study of Kikondo data also reveals a negative correlation between the distance traveled to the water point and household penetration.

It is mentioned that increasing the parameters of the population size, water price, additional revenue streams, and scale of operation will further strengthen the financial viability and scalability of the TW model. In order to retain financial stability, the operating costs must be reduced or the revenue needs to be increased. Household penetration might be increased with targeted marketing or promotion initiatives.

Marketing[48]

In addition to the marketing initiatives mentioned before, penetration might be increased with the addition of more water distribution points. WMI has partnered

194 Steven W. Anderson

with local health promotion clubs to develop ongoing marketing strategies. Some options considered include pairing promotional offers with creative pricing structures, working with Grundfos to lower the cost of additional LIFELINK units, providing local vendors with incentives to deliver water to areas where on-premises delivery of water would be in high demand, and targeting low-penetration areas.

Reflections on LIFELINK

Andersen[38,40] and Mbtaha[39] have identified several important steps that Grundfos could address in improving current and future LIFELINK installations. Any issues with LIFELINK and interactions with localities should be addressed. LIFELINK was initially complicated to users but has improved with each iteration. Alternative water-buying rights that circumvent the M-Pesa system need to be explored, particularly for users without mobile phones. The service contract needs to be refined. A shift to reliance on local partners for the setup would reinforce ownership and self-esteem. Development of a training program, for one or more members of the water committee, would accrue similar benefits and reduce reliance on external repair crews. This is critically important should the company close. Committee members elected to the community water board need to be equipped with relevant management skills to ensure projects run smoothly. Relocating the water tank to a lower platform (powered pressure) instead of a high tower (gravity pressure) would be an improvement in terms of operation, structural stability, and security. There is a need for flexibility and adjustment in both product offering and business models. Efficient and effective action from stakeholders is necessary to address water issues. Business on the ground in developing countries requires native capability, more social skills in the teams, and a willingness to go above and beyond. Innovative technology and advocacy among established players in the field necessitates a change in the existing mind-set and practice. Good partnerships, including cross-sector partnerships, are valuable and require understanding and learning from both sides. As a public service to other private companies and NGOs, Grundfos has been making user and production data from its projects publicly available to assist in learning about operation costs in BoP markets.

LIFELINK has demonstrated that it is possible to provide a sustainable, self-financing, and transparent model for management and maintenance of water projects, even in remote rural areas. As Andersen points out[40], LIFELINK's strong emphasis on control and exclusion of locally operating NGOs may be seen as controversial, yet this is a principal reason for their success. While the LIFELINK organization in Kenya was costly at first, it was viewed as a critical pilot project for further testing and expansion of ideas. High-tech innovative solutions can and should be applied to improve living conditions of the poor and create sustainable development.

The Future

LIFELINK is ready to expand and scale up across Africa and Asia. Countries that are targeted next include Uganda, Malawi, and Tanzania, followed by other countries in Africa.[42] From 2012 on operations will also start in Asia, beginning with Indonesia, India, and Thailand.

As a side note, the Indian company Piramal Sarvajal,[58,59] founded in 2008, builds water systems that are, in some aspects, similarly configured to LIFELINK. They recruit local entrepreneurs to sell water to their communities using a combination of embedded solutions and mobile payments.

Targeted Solutions Employing M2M Connectivity

In rural sub-Saharan Africa, hand pumps are non-functional from 10% to 67% of the time, and many are never repaired.[60,61] In addition, flawed methodology for evaluating hand pump operation after implementation by non-profits, private companies, and water drillers contributes to the reduction of true water access.

The Oxford Water Network

Based at Oxford University, this research center conducts projects on GSM-enabled rural hand pumps and mobile water payments.[62] In 2013, they trial tested mobile enabled technologies on 66 'smart handpumps.'[63] Hand pumps equipped with cellular network enabled sensors that were repaired in the trial resulted in a decrease in pump downtime from an average of 27 to 2.6 days. Communities that participated also increased their willingness to pay for pump services by over threefold.

SWEETLab

The Sustainable Water, Energy and Environmental Technologies Laboratory (SWEETLab) at Portland State University develops and implements cellular- and satellite-based 'Internet of Things' (IoT) sensor technologies designed to improve the collection of, and action on, data in global health programs.[64] In regard to water delivery and purification, they deploy and study water pumps, household water filters, and sanitation systems. Projects are located in India, Nepal, Indonesia, the Philippines, Rwanda, Kenya, Uganda, Ethiopia, Haiti, and other countries.

In one project in Rwanda,[65] SWEETLab designed sensors that are connected to cell phone networks to automatically report the functionality of hand water pumps. With support from the UK Department for International Development and the GSM Association, and in partnership with Living Water International and the Rwanda Ministry of Natural Resources, this approach was trial tested. In 2014 and 2015, over 181 sensors were installed in clustered or grouped rural settlements

196 Steven W. Anderson

in the Central, Western, and Southern provinces of Rwanda to enable a longitudinal cohort study. Three 'arms' (parallel studies) were conducted. A comparison was made with the current model of operation and maintenance (nominal; call as needed) against a 'best practice' circuit-rider model (where technicians make periodic visits to pumps) that included a feature for communities to report pump outages, against an 'ambulance service' model where sensors directly notified technicians that maintenance is required. Sensors were installed in all three studies, but only in the 'ambulance service' did the technicians see what the sensors were reporting.

The sensor[66] housed a control board, a cellular radio chip, SIM card holder, an accelerometer, and a differential water transducer (to assess water pressure). A fully integrated cellular connectivity system that reported data over cellular networks to an online platform was also included. The sensor was installed within the overflow basin of the pump, attached to the external pump wall by a high strength magnet. All sensors were barcoded for tracking.

The study revealed that a sensor-based service model for hand pumps in rural Rwanda was associated with substantial reductions in the repair interval when compared with both the nominal service model and a 'best practice' circuit-rider approach. Results are summarized in Table 10.2.

Only pumps in the ambulance service model demonstrated a statistically significant improvement in functional time relative to the other two models. An improvement of 25% on the failure rate (over half of the water pumps in some countries) will make the sensors pay for themselves. The authors suggest that the sensor concept, as described, could be incorporated with a pay-for-performance model to incentivize the quality of operation and maintenance to communities.

MoMo

Tim Burke, material sciences doctoral candidate at Stanford, developed the MoMo, a sensor that identifies where hand pumps are broken and alerts repair teams to fix them.[67] MoMo measures whether they are functional, the number of users, and the water per hour. Data from MoMos can also help communities

TABLE 10.2 Sensor Hand Pump Study Summary

Study	% of Implementer's Functional Pumps	Mean Reported Days of Pump Non-Functionality
Baseline	56	214
Nominal	68	152
Circuit rider	57	73
Ambulance service	91	21

Source: Adapted from Thomas et al. 2013.

monitor the effects of infrastructure projects and inform future investments. The MoMo is being distributed through WellDone,[68] an organization that builds technology tools that empower resource-constrained communities with the data they need to provide support to make their infrastructure more reliable and robust. WellDone's Smarter Villages software aggregates data from remote MoMos. The Strato management portal enables device management and data analytics. It alerts local repair teams by SMS when a well in their area breaks down, and it illustrates trends in water use to identify which communities might need more water infrastructure. Automatic alerts to problems with water infrastructure allows fewer water maintenance personnel to care for more water points than a system with manual check-ins. In the summer of 2016, the WellDone team traveled to Tanzania and formed a partnership with WaterAid Tanzania in order to test the impact of their technology. To fund this pilot project, WellDone launched a campaign on IndieGoGo.[69] This pilot project was to finance the production of 300 MoMo devices along with testing, deployment, and monitoring. At last report, only 32% of the necessary capital of US$50,000 had been raised as a flexible goal. When one does a mouseover on the 'flexible goal,' a message appears that 'the campaign has ended and will receive all funds raised.' At this time, no further information is available on the progress.

Conclusions

The scarcity of potable water in Africa and many regions of the world continues to escalate with advancing years. The cross section of solutions discussed in this chapter addressing incremental or comprehensive coverage offer hope. Clearly, there is a need for shared cooperation, clear communication, and mutual trust between service providers and the consumers. Approaches that are least invasive to the existing infrastructure and culture are more readily adopted. While security of installations may still be compromised, innovations in engineering and technology can offset those concerns.

The impressive growth of cellular network coverage, 60% across sub-Saharan Africa as of 2015, will continue to grow.[70] This region had 420 million unique mobile subscribers at the end of 2016 and is projected to reach a half billion by 2020. The increasing affordability of smartphones and a budding recycled smartphone market will also propagate the trend. Mobile will continue to be the preferred platform for creating, distributing, and consuming digital content and services, including those that help address various social challenges.

There should be no doubt that science and technology must play a vital role in devising the solutions that will be necessary to overcome the daunting problems arising from water delivery and purification.[71] Consequently, it is of paramount importance for marketing managers to incorporate proper science in conjunction with their business decisions and integrate these into social, economic, political, environmental, and traditional spheres. Failure to do so could lead to a world

198 Steven W. Anderson

overwhelmed by vexing water issues even though the scientific information needed to solve those problems might be in existence or within reach.

Notes

1 Esther Nakkazi, "Most of Africa's Water Sources Are Polluted With Toxic Matter-Report," *The EastAfrican* (May 3, 2010), accessed July 7, 2017, www.theeastafrican. co.ke/news/2558-910540-sstv98z/index.html.
2 Royal Society of Chemistry, "Africa's Water Quality: A Chemical Science Perspective, a Report by The Pan African Chemistry Network," London: Royal Society of Chemistry, March 2010, accessed March 15, 2017, www.rsc.org/globalassets/04-campaigning-outreach/tackling-the-worlds-challenges/water/rsc-pacn-water-report.pdf.
3 The World Bank, "Sub-Saharan Africa World Development Indicators," The World Bank company website, accessed July 10, 2017, http://data.worldbank.org/region/sub-saharan-africa.
4 World Health Organization, "Water," World Health Organization website, accessed July 17, 2017, http://who.int/topics/water/en/.
5 The Carter Center, accessed August 1, 2017, www.cartercenter.org/.
6 Larry Greenemeier, "Water Filtration System in a Straw," *Scientific American*, February 25, 2008, accessed March 1, 2017, www.scientificamerican.com/article/water-filtration-system/.
7 Medical Continuing Education, "Water is Life—LifeStraw Provides Safe, Affordable, Filtered Water for Survival," *MCE Blog*, August 24, 2013, accessed July 10, 2017, www.mceconferences.com/blog/water-is-life-lifestraw-provides-safe-affordable-filtered-water-for-survival/.
8 Martha Barksdale and Kate Kershner, "How LifeStraw Works," *How Stuff Works: Science*, July 13, 2009, accessed June 2, 2017, http://science.howstuffworks.com/environmental/green-tech/remediation/lifestraw1.htm.
9 Theresa Crouse, "How to Purify Water With Iodine for Survival," *Survivopedia*, May 26, 2014, accessed June 8, 2017, www.survivopedia.com/how-to-purify-water-with-iodine/.
10 Not Impossible, LLC, "Water: Not Impossible—Ken Surritte Stirs Up the Remarkable With WaterIsLife.Com (Pt 1)," Not Impossible, LLC website (blog), November 26, 2014, accessed June 14, 2017, www.notimpossible.com/blog/2014/11/26/water-not-impossible-ken-surritte-stirs-up-the-remarkable-with-waterislifecom-pt-1.
11 Isaac Saul, "The Unexpected Mid-Shower Epiphany That Led to WATERisLIFE's Founding," a plus, 22 March 2017, accessed 13 July 2017, http://aplus.com/a/water-is-life-world-water-crisis?no_monetization=true.
12 WATERisLIFE, "The Straw," WATERisLIFE company website, accessed July 10, 2017, http://waterislife.com/clean-water/the-straw.
13 Tel Technology Exchange Lab, "WATERisLIFE Straw," Tel Technology Exchange Lab website, accessed March 10, 2017, www.techxlab.org/solutions/waterislife-straw.
14 WATERisLIFE, "Global," WATERisLIFE company website, accessed July 10, 2017, http://waterislife.com/transformation/global.
15 Salwa Elsanousi et al., "A Study of the Use and Impacts of LifeStraw in a Settlement Camp in Southern Gezira, Sudan," *Journal of Water and Health* 7, no. 3 (2009): 478–483, accessed June 26, 2017, doi:10.2166/wh.2009.050, www.semanticscholar.org/paper/A-study-of-the-use-and-impacts-of-LifeStraw-in-a-s-Elsanousi-Abdelrahman/a31b832903b7b34607dc7623df2e0e80a3a5cbd2.
16 Peter Murray, "LifeStraw Brings Clean Water to Almost One Million in Kenya (video)," Singularity Hub, November 9, 2011, accessed July 13, 2017, https://singularityhub.com/2011/11/09/lifestraw-brings-clean-water-to-almost-one-million-in-kenya-video/.

17 Stefano Zenios, Stacey McCutcheon, and Lyn Denend, "LifeStraw Carbon for Water: Sustainable Funding for a Public Health Intervention," Stanford Graduate School of Business, Global Health Innovation Insight Series (October 2012): 1–7, accessed July 12, 2017, www.gsb.stanford.edu/faculty-research/publications/lifestraw-carbon-water-sustainable-funding-public-health-intervention.

18 Nathalie Rothschild, "This Invention Really Does Suck," *Spiked*, July 23, 2009, accessed May 28, 2017, www.spiked-online.com/newsite/article/7182#.WW0PyoqQyV4.

19 Clar Ni Chonghaile, "Straw Poll Finds in Favour of Western Kenya's Water and Carbon Solution," *The Guardian*, November 29, 2012, accessed July 17, 2017, www.theguardian.com/global-development/2012/nov/29/straw-western-kenya-water-carbon.

20 University of Oxford, "Award-Winning Programme Uses Carbon Credits to Deliver Safe Water in Kenya," *Water* (newsletter), University of Oxford website (November 20, 2012), accessed July 12, 2017, www.water.ox.ac.uk/lifestraw-carbon-for-water/

21 Matthew Gunther, "'Drinkable Book' Quenches Thirst for Water Purification Solution," *Chemistry World*, August 17, 2015, accessed July 8, 2017, www.chemistryworld.com/news/drinkable-book-quenches-thirst-for-water-purification-solution/8861.article.

22 crunchbase, "pAge Drinking Paper," crunchbase website, accessed March 15, 2017, www.crunchbase.com/organization/page-drinking-paper#/entity

23 Theresa A. Dankovich et al., "Inactivation of Bacteria From Contaminated Streams in Limpopo, South Africa by Silver- or Copper-Nanoparticle Paper Filters," *Environmental Science: Water Research & Technology* (Camb) 1 (2016): 85–96, accessed July 15, 2017, www.ncbi.nlm.nih.gov/pmc/articles/PMC4807622/. doi:10.1039/c5ew00188a.

24 ThinkTech Hawaii, "Drinking Water for the Developing World—The Power of Paper—Folia Water Filters," interview of Dr. Theresa Dankovich by Dr. Ethan Allen, ThinkTech Hawaii, published on January 6, 2017, accessed June 2, 2017, www.youtube.com/watch?v=VXfZlThPEg0.

25 Emily Durham, "Filter Aims to Clean World's Drinking Water," *Carnegie Mellon Today*, October 7, 2016, accessed May 23, 2017, http://cmtoday.cmu.edu/engineering_innovation/filter-aims-to-clean-world-s-drinking-water/

26 Folia Water, Inc., Folia Water, Inc. company website, accessed August 10, 2017, www.foliawater.com/.

27 Theresa Dankovich, email message to the author, October 17, 2016.

28 Catherine Jewell, "Tanzanian Entrepreneur Develops Innovative Water Filter," *WIPO Magazine*, August 2015, accessed July 14, 2017, www.wipo.int/wipo_magazine/en/2015/04/article_0005.html.

29 Gongali Model Company, Gongali Model Company website, accessed July 14, 2017. http://gongalimodel.com/Water-Nanofilter.html.

30 Sibusiso Tshabalala, "Photos: This Tanzanian Engineer Built a Customized Water Filter Using Nanotechnology," *Quartz Africa*, June 11, 2015, accessed June 25, 2017, https://qz.com/424422/photos-this-tanzanian-engineer-built-a-customized-water-filter-using-nanotechnology/.

31 Editor, "Askwar Hilonga," Industry.sa, August 5, 2015, accessed July 14, 2017, www.industrysa.co.za/askwar-hilonga/.

32 Roger S. Wotton, "Water Purification Using Sand," *Hydrobiologia* 469, no. 1–3 (February 2002):193–201. doi:10.1023/A:1015503005899.

33 Luiza C. Campos et al., "Biomass Development in Slow Sand Filters," *Water Research* 36, no. 18 (November 2002): 4543–4551. https://doi.org/10.1016/S0043-1354(02)00167-7.

34 Wikipedia, "Nanofiltration," Wikipedia website, last edited July 6, 2017, accessed July 10, 2017, https://en.wikipedia.org/wiki/Nanofiltration.

35 Margaret Rouse, TechTarget Network, "IoT Agenda, Machine-to-Machine (M2M)," last updated June 2010, accessed August 15, 2017, http://internetofthingsagenda.techtarget.com/definition/machine-to-machine-M2M.

36 World Business Council for Sustainable Development, "Grundfos LIFELINK—Sustainable & Transparent Drinking Water Solutions for the Developing World," World Business Council for Sustainable Development Case Study (December 13, 2011), accessed March 14, 2017, http://wbcsdpublications.org/grundfos-lifelink-sustainable-transparent-drinking-water-solutions-for-the-developing-world-2/.

37 United Nations, "Water in a Changing World," United Nations World Water Development Report WWDR3 (March 16, 2009), accessed August 2, 2017, http://unesdoc.unesco.org/images/0018/001819/181993e.pdf.

38 Poul Houman Andersen, "Imagining and Realizing Network-Based Business Models for BoP Markets: The Case of Grundfos LIFELINK," *Industrial Marketing and Purchasing Group* (2011): 1–32. Accessed March 21, 2017. www.impgroup.org/uploads/papers/7623.pdf.

39 Jane Kasiva Mbatha, "Factors Influencing the Sustainability of Community Water Projects Run by Grundfos LIFELINK-Kenya: A Case of Katitika Water Project, Eastern Province-Kenya" (MA thesis, University of Nairobi, Kenya, 2011), accessed June 8, 2017, http://erepository.uonbi.ac.ke/bitstream/handle/11295/4971/JANE_KASIVA_MBATHA_M.A_PPM_2011.pdf.

40 Poul Houman Andersen, "Grundfos LIFELINK: Solving the Base of the Pyramid Tangle?," *Emerald Emerging Markets Case Studies* 3, no. 1 (2013): 1–21, accessed March 15, 2017, http://dx.doi.org/10.1108/EEMCS-10-2012-0187.

41 Jamie L. Anderson, Costas Markides, and Martin Kupp, "The Last Frontier: Market Creation in Conflict Zones, Deep Rural Areas and Urban Slums," *California Management Review* 52, no. 4 (2010): 6–28.

42 Grundfos, "Developing World Water Solutions: Grundfos Lifelink Water Solutions," Grundfos company website, accessed July 1, 2017, www.grundfos.com/market-areas/water/lifelink.html.

43 Andrew W. Savitz with Karl Weber, *The Triple Bottom Line* (New York: Jossey-Bass, 2006).

44 Grundfos, "Water ATMs Offer Low-Priced Water to Nairobi's Poorest Residents," Grundfos company website, accessed June 26, 2017, www.grundfos.com/cases/find-case/water-atms-offer-low-priced-water-to-nairobis-poorest-residents.html.

45 Andrew Armstrong, Caroline Melchers, and Michael Bazira, "Remote Monitoring of Privately-Managed Rural Water Supplies using Grundfos LIFELINK," IRC International Water and Sanitation Centre publication (2013), accessed March 24, 2017, www.ircwash.org/resources/remote-monitoring-privately-managed-rural-water-supplies-using-grundfos-LIFELINK.

46 Andrew Armstrong, "TradeWater Update: Kikondo, Uganda," Water Mission website (blog), May 16, 2012, accessed March 24, 2017, https://watermission.org/tradewater-update-kikondo-uganda/.

47 Grundfos, "Sustainable Private Water Service Delivery—TradeWater by Water Missions International," Grundfos company website, accessed 29 June 2017, www.grundfos.com/cases/find-case/sustainable-private-water-service-delivery-by-Water-Missions-International.html.

48 John Kosowatz, "Bringing Accountability to Rural Water Systems," The American Society of Mechanical Engineers website (August 2012), accessed July 2, 2017, www.asme.org/engineering-topics/articles/global-impact/bringing-accountability-to-rural-water-systems.

49 Water Mission International website, accessed August 1, 2017, https://watermission.org/.

50 Water Mission International, "Our Solutions: Safe Water Solutions: Living Water Treatment System," Water Mission International company website, accessed July 15, 2017, https://watermission.org/our-solutions/how-we-work/safe-water/.

51 Wikipedia, "Alum," Wikipedia, last edited September 8, 2017, accessed September 8, 2017, https://en.wikipedia.org/wiki/Alum.

52 "One Theory of Alum Coagulation—Sweep Floc," accessed July 25, 2017, www.edasolutions.com/old/MathCad/DrGriffin/alum_coagulation.PDF.

53 Trouble Free Pool, "Thread: Chlorine/CYA Relationship," Trouble Free Pool company website (blog), accessed July 3, 2017, www.troublefreepool.com/threads/86185-Cyanuric-Acid-and-Free-Chlorine-Realtionship.

54 Trouble Free Pool, "Thread: Chlorine/CYA relationship," Trouble Free Pool company website (blog), accessed July 3, 2017, www.troublefreepool.com/threads/63526-Chlorine-CYA-relationship.

55 Wikipedia, "Cyanuric Acid," last edited on August 15, 2017, accessed August 20, 2017, https://en.wikipedia.org/wiki/Cyanuric_acid.

56 Joseph E. O'Brien, John C. Morris, and James N. Butler, "Equilibria in Aqueous Solutions of Chlorinated Isocyanurate," in *Chemistry of Water Supply, Treatment and Distribution*, ed. Alan J. Rubin (Ann Arbor, MI: Ann Arbor Science Publishers, 1974), 333–358.

57 Soft Water Filtration, "The Different Types of Water Filters: Activated Carbon Filters," Soft Water Filtration company website, accessed July 5, 2017, www.softwaterfiltration.com/water-filters/.

58 Piramal Sarvajal company website, accessed March 18, 2017, www.sarvajal.com/.

59 Editor, "Social Entrepreneurs in India: Water for All: A Start-up Demonstrates That Water Can Be Both Clean and Cheap," *The Economist* (blog), March 20, 2013, accessed March 18, 2017, www.economist.com/blogs/schumpeter/2013/03/social-entrepreneurs-india

60 Tim Foster, "Predictors of Sustainability for Community-Managed Handpumps in Sub-Saharan Africa: Evidence From Liberia, Sierra Leone, and Uganda," *Environmental Science Technology* 47, no. 21 (2013): 12037–12046.

61 Rural Water Supply Network (RWSN), "Handpump Data 2009: Selected Countries in Sub-Saharan Africa" (RWSN: St. Gallen, Switzerland, 2009), accessed July 5, 2017, www.rural-water-supply.net/en/resources/details/203.

62 University of Oxford. "Water," University of Oxford website, accessed July 27, 2017. www.water.ox.ac.uk/.

63 Johanna Koehler, Patrick Thomson, and Robert Hope, "Pump-Priming Payments for Sustainable Water Services in Rural Africa," *World Development* 74, no. 74 (2015): 397–411.

64 Portland State University, "The SWEETLab: Projects "CellPump—Rwanda," Portland State University website, accessed July 27, 2017, www.pdx.edu/sweetlab/cellpump-rwanda

65 Corey Nagel et al., "Evaluating Cellular Instrumentation on Rural Handpumps to Improve Service Delivery-A Longitudinal Study in Rural Rwanda," *Environmental Science Technology* 49 (2015): 14292–14300.

66 Evan A. Thomas et al., "Remotely Accessible Instrumented Monitoring of Global Development Programs: Technology Development and Validation," *Sustainability* 5 (2013): 3288–3301. doi:10.3390/su5083288.

67 Stanford University, "Stanford Social Enterprise Hub, Feature Project: MoMo," Stanford University website, accessed July 27, 2017, https://sehub.stanford.edu/feature-story-momo.

68 WellDone, WellDone organization website, accessed August 4, 2017, https://welldone.org/.

69 Indiegogo, Inc., "MoMo: Keep the Water Running: Mobile Devices to Ensure Reliable Access to Water in the Developing World," Indiegogo company website, accessed January 14, 2018, www.indiegogo.com/projects/momo-keep-the-water-running#/.

70 Groupe Spéciale Mobile Association (GSMA), "The Mobile Economy Sub-Saharan Africa 2017," GSMA website, accessed August 5, 2017, www.gsma.com/mobileeconomy/sub-saharan-africa-2017/.

71 William A. Jury and Henry Vaux, Jr., "The Role of Science in Solving the World's Emerging Water Problems," *Proceedings of the National Academic of Sciences* 102, no. 44 (November 1, 2005): 15715–15720, accessed August 18, 2017, www.pnas.org/content/102/44/15715.full.

Bibliography

Andersen, Poul Houman. "Grundfos LIFELINK: Solving the Base of the Pyramid Tangle?" *Emerald Emerging Markets Case Studies* 3, no. 1 (2013): 1–21. Accessed March 15, 2017. http://dx.doi.org/10.1108/EEMCS-10-2012-0187.

Andersen, Poul Houman. "Imagining and Realizing Network-Based Business Models for BoP Markets: The Case of Grundfos LIFELINK." *Industrial Marketing and Purchasing Group* (2011): 1–32. Accessed March 21, 2017. www.impgroup.org/uploads/papers/7623.pdf.

Anderson, Jamie, Costas Markides, and Martin Kupp. "The Last Frontier: Market Creation in Conflict Zones, Deep Rural Areas and Urban Slums." *California Management Review* 52, no. 4 (2010): 6–28.

Armstrong, Andrew. "TradeWater Update: Kikondo, Uganda." Water Mission website (blog), May 16, 2012. Accessed March 24, 2017. https://watermission.org/tradewater-update-kikondo-uganda/.

Armstrong, Andrew, Caroline Melchers, and Michael Bazira. "Remote Monitoring of Privately-Managed Rural Water Supplies Using Grundfos LIFELINK." IRC International Water and Sanitation Centre Publication, 2013. Accessed March 24, 2017. www.ircwash.org/resources/remote-monitoring-privately-managed-rural-water-supplies-using-grundfos-LIFELINK.

Barksdale, Martha, and Kate Kershner. "How LifeStraw Works." *How Stuff Works: Science*, July 13, 2009. Accessed June 2, 2017. http://science.howstuffworks.com/environmental/green-tech/remediation/lifestraw1.htm.

Campos, Luiza C. et al. "Biomass Development in Slow Sand Filters." *Water Research* 36, no. 18 (November 2002): 4543–4551. https://doi.org/10.1016/S0043-1354(02)00167-7.

The Carter Center. Accessed August 1, 2017. www.cartercenter.org/.

Chonghaile, Clar Ni. "Straw Poll Finds in Favour of Western Kenya's Water and Carbon Solution." *The Guardian*, November 29, 2012. Accessed July 17, 2017. www.theguardian.com/global-development/2012/nov/29/straw-western-kenya-water-carbon.

Crouse, Theresa. "How to Purify Water With Iodine for Survival." *Survivopedia*, May 26, 2014. Accessed June 8, 2017. www.survivopedia.com/how-to-purify-water-with-iodine/.

crunchbase. "pAge Drinking Paper." crunchbase website. Accessed March 15, 2017. www.crunchbase.com/organization/page-drinking-paper#/entity.Dankovich, Theresa A. Email message to the author. October 17, 2016.

Dankovich, Theresa A. et al. "Inactivation of Bacteria from Contaminated Streams in Limpopo, South Africa by Silver- or Copper-Nanoparticle Paper Filters." *Environ Sci (Camb)* 1 (2016): 85–96. Accessed July 15, 2017. doi:10.1039/c5ew00188a. www.ncbi.nlm.nih.gov/pmc/articles/PMC4807622/

Durham, Emily. "Filter Aims to Clean World's Drinking Water." *Carnegie Mellon Today* October 7, 2016. Accessed May 23, 2017. http://cmtoday.cmu.edu/engineering_innovation/filter-aims-to-clean-world-s-drinking-water/

Editor. "Askwar Hilonga." *Industry.sa*, August 5, 2015. Accessed July 14, 2017. www.industrysa.co.za/askwar-hilonga/.

Editor. "Social Entrepreneurs in India: Water for All: A Start-Up Demonstrates That Water Can Be Both Clean and Cheap." *The Economist* (blog). March 20, 2013. Accessed March 18, 2017. www.economist.com/blogs/schumpeter/2013/03/social-entrepreneurs-india.

Elsanousi, Salwa et al. "A Study of the Use and Impacts of LifeStraw in a Settlement Camp in Southern Gezira, Sudan." *Journal of Water and Health* 7, no. 3 (2009): 478–483. Accessed June 26, 2017. doi:10.2166/wh.2009.050. www.semanticscholar.org/

paper/A-study-of-the-use-and-impacts-of-LifeStraw-in-a-s-Elsanousi-Abdelrahman/a31b832903b7b34607dc7623df2e0e80a3a5cbd2.

Folia Water, Inc. Folia Water, Inc. company website. Accessed August 10, 2017. www.foliawater.com/.

Foster, T. "Predictors of Sustainability for Community-Managed Handpumps in Sub-Saharan Africa: Evidence From Liberia, Sierra Leone, and Uganda." *Environmental Science & Technology* 47, no. 21 (2013): 12037–12046.

Gongali Model Company. Accessed July 14, 2017. http://gongalimodel.com/Water-Nanofilter.html.

Greenemeier, Larry. "Water Filtration System in a Straw." *Scientific American*, February 25, 2008. Accessed March 1, 2017. www.scientificamerican.com/article/water-filtration-system/.

Groupe Spéciale Mobile Association (GSMA). "The Mobile Economy Sub-Saharan Africa 2017." GSMA website. Accessed August 5, 2017. www.gsma.com/mobileeconomy/sub-saharan-africa-2017/.

Grundfos. "Developing World Water Solutions: Grundfos Lifelink Water Solutions." Grundfos Company website. Accessed July 1, 2017. www.grundfos.com/market-areas/water/lifelink.html.

Grundfos. "Sustainable Private Water Service Delivery-TradeWater by Water Missions International." Grundfos Company website. Accessed June 29, 2017. www.grundfos.com/cases/find-case/sustainable-private-water-service-delivery-by-Water-Missions-International.html.

Grundfos. "Water ATMs Offer Low-Priced Water to Nairobi's Poorest Residents." Grundfos Company website. Accessed June 26, 2017. www.grundfos.com/cases/find-case/water-atms-offer-low-priced-water-to-nairobis-poorest-residents.html.

Gunther, Matthew. "'Drinkable Book' Quenches Thirst for Water Purification Solution." *Chemistry World*, August 17, 2015. Accessed July 8, 2017. www.chemistryworld.com/news/drinkable-book-quenches-thirst-for-water-purification-solution/8861.article.

Indiegogo, Inc. "MoMo: Keep the Water Running: Mobile Devices to Ensure Reliable Access to Water in the Developing World." Indiegogo company website. Accessed January 14, 2018. www.indiegogo.com/projects/momo-keep-the-water-running#/.

Jewell, Catherine. "Tanzanian Entrepreneur Develops Innovative Water Filter." *WIPO Magazine*, August 2015. Accessed July 14, 2017. www.wipo.int/wipo_magazine/en/2015/04/article_0005.html.

Jury, William A., and Henry Vaux, Jr. "The Role of Science in Solving the World's Emerging Water Problems." *Proceedings of the National Academic of Sciences* 102, no. 44 (November 1, 2005): 15715–15720. Accessed August 18, 2017. www.pnas.org/content/102/44/15715.full.

Koehler, Johanna, Patrick Thomson, and Robert Hope. "Pump-Priming Payments for Sustainable Water Services in Rural Africa." *World Development* 74, no. 74 (2015): 397–411.

Kosowatz, John. "Bringing Accountability to Rural Water Systems." The American Society of Mechanical Engineers website, August 2012. Accessed July 2, 2017. www.asme.org/engineering-topics/articles/global-impact/bringing-accountability-to-rural-water-systems.

Mbatha, Jane Kasiva. "Factors Influencing the Sustainability of Community Water Projects Run by Grundfos LIFELINK-Kenya: A Case of Katitika Water Project, Eastern Province-Kenya." MA Thesis, University of Nairobi, Kenya, 2011. Accessed June 8, 2017. http://erepository.uonbi.ac.ke/bitstream/handle/11295/4971/JANE_KASIVA_MBATHA_M.A_PPM_2011.pdf.

Medical Continuing Education. "Water Is Life—LifeStraw Provides Safe, Affordable, Filtered Water for Survival." MCE Blog, August 24, 2013. Accessed July 10, 2017. www.mceconferences.com/blog/water-is-life-lifestraw-provides-safe-affordable-filtered-water-for-survival/.

Murray, Peter. "LifeStraw Brings Clean Water to Almost One Million in Kenya (video)." *Singularity Hub*, November 9, 2011. Accessed July 13, 2017. https://singularityhub.com/2011/11/09/lifestraw-brings-clean-water-to-almost-one-million-in-kenya-video/.

Nagel, Corey et al. "Evaluating Cellular Instrumentation on Rural Handpumps to Improve Service Delivery: A Longitudinal Study in Rural Rwanda." *Environmental Science & Technology* 49 (2015): 14292–14300.

Nakkazi, Esther. "Most of Africa's Water Sources Are Polluted With Toxic Matter-Report." *The EastAfrican*, May 3, 2010. Accessed July 7, 2017. www.theeastafrican.co.ke/news/2558-910540-sstv98z/index.html.

Not Impossible, LLC. "Water: Not Impossible—Ken Surritte Stirs Up the Remarkable With WaterIsLife.Com (Pt 1)." Not Impossible, LLC website (blog), November 26, 2014. Accessed June 14, 2017. www.notimpossible.com/blog/2014/11/26/water-not-impossible-ken-surritte-stirs-up-the-remarkable-with-waterislifecom-pt-1.

O'Brien, Joseph E., John C. Morris, and James N. Butler. "Equilibria in Aqueous Solutions of Chlorinated Isocyanurate." In *Chemistry of Water Supply, Treatment and Distribution*, 333–358. Ed. Alan J. Rubin. Ann Arbor, MI: Ann Arbor Science Publishers, 1974.

"One Theory of Alum Coagulation—Sweep Floc." Accessed July 25, 2017. www.edasolutions.com/old/MathCad/DrGriffin/alum_coagulation.PDF.

Piramal Sarvajal company website, accessed March 18, 2017. www.sarvajal.com/.

Portland State University. "The SWEETLab: Projects—CellPump—Rwanda." Portland State University website. Accessed July 27, 2017. www.pdx.edu/sweetlab/cellpump-rwanda.

Rothschild, Nathalie. "This Invention Really Does Suck." *Spiked*, July 23, 2009. Accessed May 28, 2017. www.spiked-online.com/newsite/article/7182#.WW0PyoqQyV4.

Rouse, Margaret. TechTarget Network. "IoT Agenda, Machine-to-Machine (M2M)." Last updated June 2010. Accessed August 15, 2017. http://internetofthingsagenda.techtarget.com/definition/machine-to-machine-M2M.

Royal Society of Chemistry. *Africa's Water Quality: A Chemical Science Perspective: A Report by The Pan African Chemistry Network*. London: Royal Society of Chemistry, March 2010. Accessed March 15, 2017. www.rsc.org/globalassets/04-campaigning-outreach/tackling-the-worlds-challenges/water/rsc-pacn-water-report.pdf.

Rural Water Supply Network (RWSN). *Handpump Data 2009: Selected Countries in Sub-Saharan Africa*. RWSN: St. Gallen, Switzerland, 2009. Accessed July 5, 2017. www.rural-water-supply.net/en/resources/details/203.

Saul, Isaac. "The Unexpected Mid-Shower Epiphany That Led to WATERisLIFE's Founding." *a plus*, March 22, 2017. Accessed July 13, 2017. http://aplus.com/a/water-is-life-world-water-crisis?no_monetization=true.

Savitz, Andrew with Karl Weber. *The Triple Bottom Line*. New York: Jossey-Bass, 2006.

Soft Water Filtration. "The Different Types of Water Filters: Activated Carbon Filters." Soft Water Filtration company website. Accessed July 5, 2017. www.softwaterfiltration.com/water-filters/.

Stanford University. "Stanford Social Enterprise Hub, Feature Project: MoMo." Stanford University website. Accessed July 27, 2017. https://sehub.stanford.edu/feature-story-momo.

Tel Technology Exchange Lab. "WATERisLIFE Straw." Tel Technology Exchange Lab website. Accessed March 10, 2017. www.techxlab.org/solutions/waterislife-straw.

ThinkTech Hawaii. "Drinking Water for the Developing World—the Power of Paper—Folia Water Filters." Interview of Dr. Theresa Dankovich by Dr. Ethan Allen. ThinkTech Hawaii. Published on January 6, 2017. Accessed June 2, 2017. www.youtube.com/watch?v=VXfZlThPEg0.

Thomas, Evan A. et al. "Remotely Accessible Instrumented Monitoring of Global Development Programs: Technology Development and Validation." *Sustainability* 5 (2013): 3288–3301. doi:10.3390/su5083288.

Trouble Free Pool. "Thread: Chlorine/CYA Relationship." Trouble Free Pool company website (blog). Accessed July 3, 2017. www.troublefreepool.com/threads/63526-Chlorine-CYA-relationship.

Trouble Free Pool. "Thread: Chlorine/CYA Relationship." Trouble Free Pool company website (blog). Accessed July 3, 2017. www.troublefreepool.com/threads/86185-Cyanuric-Acid-and-Free-Chlorine-Realtionship.

Tshabalala, Sibusiso. "Photos: This Tanzanian Engineer Built a Customized Water Filter Using Nanotechnology." *Quartz Africa*. Accessed June 25, 2017. https://qz.com/424422/photos-this-tanzanian-engineer-built-a-customized-water-filter-using-nanotechnology/.

United Nations. "Water in a Changing World." United Nations World Water Development Report WWDR3 (March 16, 2009). Accessed August 2, 2017. http://unesdoc.unesco.org/images/0018/001819/181993e.pdf.

University of Oxford. "Award-Winning Programme Uses Carbon Credits to Deliver Safe Water in Kenya." Water (newsletter), University of Oxford website (November 20, 2012). Accessed July 17, 2017. www.water.ox.ac.uk/lifestraw-carbon-for-water/.

University of Oxford. "Water." University of Oxford website. Accessed July 27, 2017. www.water.ox.ac.uk/.

WATERisLIFE. "Global." WATERIsLIFE company website. Accessed July 10, 2017. http://waterislife.com/transformation/global.

WATERisLIFE. "The Straw." WATERIsLIFE company website. Accessed July 10, 2017. http://waterislife.com/clean-water/the-straw.

Water Mission International website. Accessed August 1, 2017. https://watermission.org/.

Water Mission International. "Our Solutions: Safe Water Solutions: Living Water Treatment System." Water Mission International company website. Accessed July 15, 2017. https://watermission.org/our-solutions/how-we-work/safe-water/.

WellDone. WellDone organization website. Accessed August 4, 2017. https://welldone.org/.

Wikipedia. "Alum." Wikipedia website. Last edited September 8, 2017. Accessed September 8, 2017. https://en.wikipedia.org/wiki/Alum.

Wikipedia. "Cyanuric Acid." Last edited August 15, 2017. Accessed August 20, 2017. https://en.wikipedia.org/wiki/Cyanuric_acid.

Wikipedia. "Nanofiltration." Wikipedia website. Last edited July 6, 2017. Accessed July 10, 2017. https://en.wikipedia.org/wiki/Nanofiltration.

The World Bank. "Sub-Saharan Africa World Development Indicators." The World Bank company website. Accessed July 10, 2017. http://data.worldbank.org/region/sub-saharan-africa.

World Business Council for Sustainable Development. "Grundfos LIFELINK—Sustainable & Transparent Drinking Water Solutions for the Developing World." World Business Council for Sustainable Development Case Study, December 13, 2011. Accessed March 14, 2017.

http://wbcsdpublications.org/grundfos-lifelink-sustainable-transparent-drinking-water-solutions-for-the-developing-world-2/.

World Health Organization. "Water." World Health Organization website. Accessed July 17, 2017. http://who.int/topics/water/en/.

Wotton, Roger S. "Water Purification Using Sand." *Hydrobiologia* 469, nos. 1–3 (February 2002): 193–201. doi:10.1023/A:1015503005899.

Zenios, Stefano, Stacey McCutcheon, and Lyn Denend. "LIFESTRAW CARBON FOR WATER: Sustainable Funding for a Public Health Intervention." Stanford Graduate School of Business, Global Health Innovation Insight Series (October 2012): 1–7. Accessed July 12, 2017. www.gsb.stanford.edu/faculty-research/publications/lifestraw-carbon-water-sustainable-funding-public-health-intervention.

11

UNDERSTANDING CONSUMER BUYING BEHAVIOR IN AFRICA

John Kuada and Andreea I. Bujac

Introduction

Recent economic reports have shown that a growing share of the global consumer class now lives in developing countries, with growth in these economies now accounting for over 70% of global growth.[1,2] For this reason, more than 20,000 multinational corporations (MNCs) are now operating in these economies and expect to find an increasing proportion of their future growth there. One of the high growth regions of the developing world is sub-Saharan Africa (SSA), being the home to six of the world's ten fastest-growing economies between 2001 and 2015.[3] The continent's growth reached 4.8% in 2013 and is expected to be about 5% in 2017.[4] The region's collective GDP was estimated to be \US$2.5 trillion in 2016. Demographic studies also indicate that Africa's population will grow to 2 billion people and account for 20% of the world's population by 2050.[5] Consumer spending on the continent is also expected to increase to nearly US$1 trillion by 2020.[6] In addition, the African population is relatively young—about 60% are under 25 years old. This guarantees a sustainable consumer base for a wide variety of goods and services, granting that these young people are fully integrated into the growing economies.

However, operations in these markets have been difficult for the MNCs and even the large or major international retailers have been surprised at the challenges that the new markets pose. Some of them entered the African market in the belief that they could conveniently apply marketing strategies that have proved successful in the Western economies and tended to wonder if local adaptations of their strategies were actually worth the incremental costs.[7] Not surprisingly, many of them have realized that their planned strategies did not adequately address the marketing challenges they faced and had to fold out their operations.[8]

208 John Kuada and Andreea I. Bujac

Despite the growing practitioner awareness that the African consumer market poses several unexpected challenges, especially to businesses that are new to the market environment, there has been limited academic interest in the field, and consumer buying processes and priorities on the continent remain poorly understood.[9] Thus, there is a yawning gap between what practitioners would like to know about African consumers and the level of knowledge in the field. In order to help address the knowledge gap, this chapter reports findings from a systematic literature search of nearly all the influential academic publications on African consumers during the past four decades. Our aim is to provide a synthesis of the currently available knowledge in the field and to identify issues requiring immediate research attention.

The chapter continues after this brief introduction by presenting an overview of the extant literature, highlighting the major themes that have attracted the attention of researchers. It then discusses some of the major questions that appear to have been ignored by scholars, explaining why knowledge on these issues can improve economic growth and expand the market base for goods and services produced within and outside the economies.

Two Decades of African Consumer Studies

Selection Process and Criteria

The studies reviewed in this chapter cover the period between 1996 and 2016. This time frame coincides with the period of market-oriented policy reforms in African economies in response to serious economic crisis that plagued nearly all the countries in many years. The policy goal of these reforms was to free market forces and roll back state involvement in economic activities in order to energize the economies. Our interest is to investigate the extent to which the ensuing two decades of trade liberalization initiatives have encouraged academic research into marketing, in general and consumer behavior. We have adopted a systematic approach to the literature search, since such an approach is generally assessed to provide rigorous, transparent, and replicable results. We have been inspired by Petticrew and Roberts's seven-stage process of systematic literature review: (1) defining the review objectives, (2) determining the types of studies to be included, (3) undertaking comprehensive literature search, (4) screening the literature on the basis of the agreed inclusion criteria, (5) critically appraising the identified papers, (6) performing synthesis of the papers, and (7) disseminating the findings.[10]

Our main source was ABI/Inform, which then included/at the time included 28 databases. The initial search produced 359 articles (from 104 journals), covering subject areas such as marketing, economics, econometrics, management, strategy, operations and technology, international business, and public sector management. We then reclassified the articles in terms of their quality rankings, using the Association of Business Schools (ABS) journal list as criterion.[11] In addition to the ABS graded journals, we also included a number of influential articles through the backward snowballing technique, by identifying key articles and authors referenced in a number of selected papers. We then read through the abstracts of the 359 articles in order to exclude those that we assessed not to be relevant to this investigation. In total, 41 articles were found to be of interest and accepted as part of the review and discussions.

A quick overview of the years of publication of the articles indicates that academic interest in consumer behavior research in Africa increased significantly after 2007 (see Figure 11.1), with an average of three papers being published in reputed international journals per year, and six papers per year in other journals.

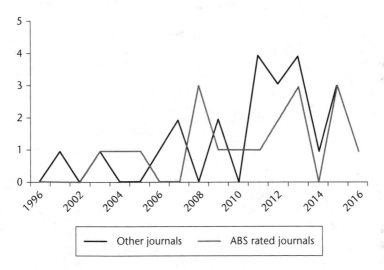

FIGURE 11.1 Number of Articles Published Between 1996 and 2016

Main Themes

Studies during the period can be grouped into four main themes: (1) consumer attitudes, purchase decisions, and willingness to pay; (2) consumer satisfaction and service quality perceptions; (3) consumer ethnocentrism and country-of-origin effects on consumption; and (4) marketing strategy requirements.[12]

Consumer Attitudes, Purchase Decisions, and Willingness to Pay

The marketing literature sees consumers' attitude as a summary construct of their beliefs, feelings and behavioral intentions toward a product or service over time. Since these predispositions serve as a filter through which consumers scrutinize products and services available to them, marketers are enjoined to leverage their understanding of consumers' attitudes in order to predict their behavior.

Our review shows that studies that have explored consumer attitudes in Africa have mainly been in the financial, educational, and non-profit institutions. For example, Gait and Worthington analyzed the attitudes of Libyan retail customers to Islamic methods of finance;[13] Ogenyi and Owusu-Frimpong studied the consumers' attitudes toward purchase of life insurance in Nigeria;[14] du Plessis and Petzer compared the attitudes of Baby Boomers with those of Generations X and Y toward non-profit organizations.[15] A few other sectors have also received some attention. These studies include Kruger and Mostert, who studied young adults' (ages 18 to 25) attitudes toward the South African cell phone network operators,[16] and Quaye et al., who studied Ghanaian consumers' attitude to local and foreign food items.[17]

In the main, the results of these studies confirm the general understanding in the contemporary marketing literature that attitudes are relatively enduring and influence consumer preferences. Thus, Quaye et al. found that socio-culturally related factors (including traditions and ethnic eating habits) influence Ghanaian consumers' attitudes to certain types of food items.[18] Similarly, Dadzie et al. found that normative social norms, beliefs, and practices influence the long-term savings behavior of rural households in Ghana.[19] Again, both Gait and Worthington's study in Libya, and Ltifi et al.'s study in Tunisia found that religious guidelines and practices (e.g., Sharia law) have strong influence on customers' attitudes to retail banks in the two countries.[20,21] Attitudes may also be formed as the result of positive or negative personal experiences regarding a product or service. For example, Ukpere et al. found that factors such as customers' experience of comfort, on-board services, and crew behavior have strong influence on Nigerian travelers' attitudes toward airlines.[22]

It appears from our review of the empirical investigations that African consumers' purchase decisions are largely guided by prices and perceived quality. For example, Bett et al. studied the Kenyan consumers' responsiveness to an increase in prices of the indigenous chicken products and how much they are willing to pay for them in the market.[23] The results showed that consumers were willing to pay about 25% more for local chicken and eggs than imported ones, due to their perceived superior quality. Similarly, consumers were willing to pay relatively higher prices for better quality condoms in Tanzania.[24] The growing health consciousness among the urban consumers also appears to influence their purchasing decisions regarding food items. For example, Kenyan urban consumers were willing to pay a lot more for new gravity-driven membrane (GDM) drinking water filters introduced to the market because they were perceived to have extra health advantages.[25] Similarly, Yahaya et al. assessed consumer motivation and willingness to pay for 'safer' vegetables from the use of treated (as compared with non-treated) wastewater in urban/peri-urban vegetable production in Ghana. They found that consumers were willing to pay an average amount of $2.40 per month for a technology change that would result in the production of 'safer' vegetables. Furthermore, income and sex turned out to be key demographic factors that influenced consumers' willingness to pay the relatively higher amounts for the 'safer' vegetables—females and consumers in the higher-income bracket were more willing to pay the higher prices.[26]

Some studies have examined the extent to which environmental concerns and green marketing efforts impact consumers' purchase decisions. These studies have all found strong associations between environmentally friendly marketing and consumer preferences. For example, Dubihlela and Ngxukumeshe found a significant association between eco-friendly retail product attributes and South African consumers' repurchase intentions.[27] Furthermore, Thanika et al. found that most consumers in Mauritius showed great interest in the protection of the environment, and this appeared to impact their purchase decisions with regard to green products.[28] Pudaruth et al. also found that factors such as lifestyles, self-image, health, and ethical considerations influenced women's decisions to buy eco-friendly cosmetics and beauty care products in Mauritius.[29]

Consumer Satisfaction and Service Quality Perceptions

Customer satisfaction is generally described in the marketing literature as customers' post-consumption experience (in relation to expectations) and their fulfillment response following the consumption experience. It is frequently argued that when perceived performance exceeds a consumer's prepurchase expectation, a positive disconfirmation results and the consumer could be highly satisfied or even delighted. However, when post-purchase performance falls below prepurchase expectation, a negative disconfirmation occurs and the customer is dissatisfied. In a situation where the product or service performs as expected, a simple confirmation occurs. Customer satisfaction has been found to impact customer loyalty, and this can substantially increase customer retention and reduce marketing costs. It is, therefore, generally considered to be an essential competitive tool and a core requirement for firm profitability and survival.

Most of the studies focusing on this theme in Africa have been conducted within the financial sector, apparently due to the dynamic developments in the sector since the 1990s. For example, Woldie studied customers' assessment of the quality of services offered by Nigerian banks,[30] Bick et al. examined South African customers' perceptions of the value delivered by retail banks,[31] and Narteh and Kuada also studied the determinants of customer satisfaction with retail bank services and the moderating role of demographic variables in predicting customers' satisfaction in Ghana.[32]

The general conclusion from the studies is that bank customers attach significant importance to relational, core, and tangible dimensions of banking services offered by retail banks just as their counterparts in Western societies do.[33,34] The relational factors have, however, emerged as the most significant determinant of customer satisfaction, emphasizing the need for banks to relate well with their customers. The understanding is that factors such as the personal attention that

212 John Kuada and Andreea I. Bujac

a bank gives to its customers, the ability of the bank to determine its customers' needs, and the consistency of the interaction it has with the customers have significant impact on customer satisfaction.[35]

The retail banking sector studies have also shown that convenience is an important service quality criterion among African customers. Thus, Guruswamy as well as Narteh and Kuada found that locations of banks, their opening hours, security of customer information, and customer waiting period are key reasons for choosing a particular retail bank.[36,37] An increasing number of African retail banks are, therefore, implementing extended opening hours on weekdays and in selected branches on Saturdays in order to provide more contact hours for customers.

A number of the studies have also shown correlations between employee satisfaction, service quality, and customer satisfaction. For example, Potluri and Zeleke (2009) found that customer relational competencies of Ethiopian employees impact the satisfaction of the main telephone company in that country. The Ethiopian customers indicated that they were not satisfied with the services provided by the telephone company due to the limited competences of the front desk staff. A similar study was conducted by Sanda and Kuada for retail banks in Ghana.[38] The results showed that factors such as employee job satisfaction and organizational commitment are major determinants of customer satisfaction. The study also found statements such as 'the way the bank's system treats its employees, the way promotions are given out in the bank, the nature of employees' work and the way managers notice employees when they do good jobs' were good indicators of job satisfaction within the banks. Studies by Owusu-Frimpong as well as Narteh and Kuada in Ghana and by Guruswamy in Ethiopia produced similar results.[39,40,41]

The understanding from these studies is that frontline employees' promptness in serving customers is a critical factor in consumers' assessment of service quality. When services fail or errors are made, frontline employees are those who can set things right, using their judgment to determine the best course of action for service recovery. This inspires trust and confidence in the services offered. In this sense, African consumers are not different from their counterparts in the developed parts of the world.[42] However, in many African service companies (e.g., hotels, restaurants, shops), the frontline employees are the least paid and have the lowest job security and very little training. Some companies even prefer to use casual or temporal employees as front desk staff and telephone exchange operators.[43] These working conditions tend to negatively impact their job satisfaction and organizational commitment.[44]

Also, there have been few studies that have focused on unique African issues. For example, Johnson and Grier suggest that cultural compatibility, intergroup anxiety (all-black, all-white, or multicultural), and cross-group contact are factors that impact consumers' evaluations of products and services in South Africa.[45] Their study also confirmed Allport's (1954) contact hypothesis, suggesting that contacts between members of different groups (under certain conditions) can work to reduce prejudice and intergroup conflict. Another South African study assessed whether differences exist among various demographic groups' attitudes, preferences, and assertiveness about the use of Afrikaans in marketing communication.[46] The results of this study suggested that, with the exception of age as a demographic variable, there are significant differences in urban Afrikaans-speaking consumers' attitudes, preferences, and assertiveness regarding Afrikaans marketing communication. Female respondents were found to have a more positive attitude and were more likely to act assertively with respect to mother-tongue marketing communication than their male counterparts.

Consumer Ethnocentrism and Country-of-Origin Effects on Consumption

It is generally agreed among marketing scholars that preconceptions and attitudes toward people of a given country tend to influence consumers' evaluation of products coming from the country. For some products, 'country factor' may have a positive impact on consumer perception when sold abroad; for others, the impact may be negative. Studies of the country factor are generally anchored in two main constructs: (1) the psychosocial construct of ethnocentrism, which describes the belief that consumers in a given country hold about goods and services produced in that country as being superior to those produced in other countries, and (2) the country-of-origin effect describing the positive or negative image of products originating from a given country among the host country consumers. These two constructs have received some attention in the African studies.

With regard to ethnocentrism, John and Brady found Mozambican consumers to be moderately ethnocentric and to have relatively unfavorable attitudes toward South African consumer goods.[47] Saffu and Walker also found Ghanaian consumers to be moderately ethnocentric.[48] However, the Ghanaian consumers are willing to buy Ghanaian-made products only when these products are of comparable quality and price to foreign-made products. Furthermore, a study by Pentz et al. in South Africa revealed a positive relationship between age and consumer ethnocentrism and a negative relationship between income and ethnocentrism.[49] Lysonski and Durvasula also found that the level of global orientation of young urban Nigerians impacts their degree of ethnocentrism and materialism.[50]

Previous studies of country-of-origin effect in some emerging economies suggest that products that are manufactured in advanced Western countries are perceived to be better than those from developing or less developed countries. The results of the African studies appear to be inconsistent with this viewpoint. For example, Saffu and Walker found that Ghanaian consumers are willing to buy products that offer the best value for money regardless of country of origin.[51] Similarly, Ngoma and Ntale found that affordability and perceived brand quality are stronger determinants of Ugandan consumers' choice of pharmaceuticals than country of origin.[52]

Marketing Strategy Requirements

With regard to strategy, the marketing literature has consistently regarded consumers as passive recipients of marketing impulses to which they react through acceptance or rejection of value propositions from producers and retailers. The task of marketing is, therefore, described as one of generating enough interest from consumers and encouraging them to actually pay for the product or service marketers offer. The African studies reviewed aim at examining the extent to which the marketing activities of the firms tend to educate, communicate with, and motivate targeted consumers about specific products and services. In that regard, we consider many of the results to be insightful.

Radder and Huang found that advertising played an important role in the awareness of sportswear clothing brands among South African students.[53] However, the impact of advertising on coffee brand awareness was found to be weak. Similarly, Chimboza and Mutandwa found that advertising had significant impact on the level of brand awareness of dairy brands in Chitungwiza and Harare urban markets in Zimbabwe.[54] Again, Human et al. found that outdoor advertising can be used to build attitudinal brand loyalty among low-income consumers in South Africa.[55] Gbadamosi et al. explored South African children's attitudinal reactions to television advertisements and found that they like television advertising in relation to its entertainment features, especially when the messages feature children characters, cartoons, music, celebrities, and humor.[56] The impact of relationship-marketing strategies on customer loyalty has also been examined by Aminu for Nigerian bank customers and by Narteh et al. for customers of luxury and first-class hotels in Ghana.[57,58] Both studies have shown that relationship-marketing practices have a significant and positive effect on customer loyalty.

There has also been some evidence of African consumers not responding to Western-inspired marketing strategies. For example, Deon found that the use of sales promotions to encourage impulse buying in South Africa have had limited impact, suggesting that the shoppers plan their shopping reasonably well and make use of an informal or formal shopping list for shopping purposes.[59] Lee et al. found that Mozambican youth exhibit tendencies of developing consumer-related skills, knowledge, and attitudes through socialization processes (e.g., mimicking peers) rather than falling prey to marketing stimuli.[60]

Reflections and Directions for Future Research

It is evident from our review that most of the studies have been guided by Western-inspired marketing views and theories. The central objective of the authors has been to determine the extent to which these standard marketing theories and models provide good explanations for consumer behaviors in different African countries and sectors. The accumulated knowledge produced suggests that the models and methods used in the West can effectively be applied in African consumer behavior studies. Thus, marketing strategies used in the West can also been applied in Africa with satisfactory results. In this regard, the studies have been insightful in as much as they have led to confirmation and extension of existing marketing models.

However, our review exposes several issues that the existing studies have left unexplored. For example, we consider it important for researchers to focus attention on how marketing and consumption can facilitate high and sustained growth that can lift the majority of Africans out of poverty, bearing in mind the continued high level of poverty on the continent despite recent years of noticeable economic growth. This requires investigations into mechanisms for consumption-driven growth in different African countries, especially in the rural areas where the incidence of poverty is highest.

Studying Consumption-Driven Growth

Development economists have argued that economic growth may be driven by distinctive local consumption activities—that is, goods and services that are locally produced and locally consumed. There are several reasons for this. First, changes in tastes and preferences and (thus, in consumer spending in favor of goods and services that are locally produced) can stimulate job growth. Second, local consumers can be encouraged to intensify their purchases of new types of goods and services that are more likely to be produced locally—for example, education, health services, and housing. Socialization processes and strategic investments may be necessary to expand such local consumption bases. Third, growth in local consumption sectors may produce multiplier effects because the composition of inputs in such sectors may be more labor intensive and thus create jobs held by people whose propensity to spend locally is high. If we see marketing as a system of integrating wants, needs, and purchasing power of consumers with capacity and resources of production, then marketing research may provide knowledge and inputs into how production and consumption of such local-specific goods and services can be facilitated.

The Role of Marketing in Transforming Rural Consumption Patterns

As noted in our literature review, conventional marketing management is based on an understanding of consumers' expectations, preferences, and behaviors. This knowledge enables companies to adapt their products and services to these expectations and to adopt appropriate marketing strategies that enhance the attractiveness of their products to the target consumers. But what happens when consumers do not really know what types of products and services can raise their quality of life and, therefore, cannot communicate their demands and expectations to companies? Or what happens when consumers' needs really fall outside the production and marketing focus of companies that would like to serve them? These are the challenges that conventional marketing faces in African rural communities. Although shopping malls are sprouting up in the continent's major capitals and the urban population's consumption patterns tend to resemble those of the West, a greater proportion of Africans still live in the rural communities where the products found in the shopping malls are outside their immediate needs and expectations. Hitherto, these consumers have been deemed too poor to be viable customers. Prahalad has a different perspective. He estimates that the poor people of the world have buying power equal to US$8 billion per day.[61] This makes the poor a multitrillion-dollar annual market on a global scale. Kotler and Lee convey the same perception when they argue that the poor constitute an incipient demand waiting to be tapped.[62]

Knowing what rural consumers need requires a different approach to marketing research that gives greater emphasis to the voices of these consumers. This understanding has encouraged the emergence of a new strand of marketing research—that is, transformative consumer research.[63] This approach to consumer research seeks to codevelop a new knowledge base with consumers with the view to changing their behavior and consequently enhancing their well-being through new product/service development and consumption processes. This view of marketing requires that marketers see consumers from a different perspective. In some rural communities, it may make sense to see consumers not as individuals but as groups and to develop marketing packages for households, villages, and communities. In this light, Hart and London advise companies that intend to take advantage of the business opportunities that poverty provides to become 'indigenous' or 'native' to the places in which they operate.[64] Doing so will require deeper insight into the dreams and behaviors of the local people.

Methodological Challenges of Studying Consumption and Growth in Africa

Arguably, increasing consumption is unquestionably a goal of high importance in situations where people have insufficient goods and services. But it is important to bear in mind that poverty is more than just a lack of income. It also connotes lack of respect, self-worth, dignity, inclusion, choice, and security.[65,66] Poverty makes people resign to their living conditions and holds their creativity in check.[67] Thus, poverty sets in motion a negative spiral. This means efforts aimed at alleviating poverty are in themselves growth-propelling, since they unleash hitherto untapped psychological and physical human resources within poor communities and thereby help transform a negative spiral into a positive one.

Seen from this perspective, the direct application of Western marketing and management theories and strategies may not always provide the most relevant insights. A shift in paradigm away from positivist paradigmatic approaches that guide conventional marketing research to transformative consumer research may be necessary. A transformative kind of research adopts interpretive and post-positivist methods that draw on the emotional and socio-psychological knowledge of individuals, households, and communities in order to produce novel and relevant insights into consumer behavior. A paradigmatic triangulation may also be considered a useful approach in such types of research.

Conclusion

Consumer behavior studies hitherto conducted in Africa are based on conventional marketing theories, strategies, and processes. They have produced useful insights into the replicability of these conventional perspectives within the African context. However, the African consumption context gives researchers an opportunity to think deeply about a range of unanswered questions. There is an emerging understanding among scholars that consumer behavior is situational and affected by the specific conditions and circumstances in which it takes place. Thus, the divergent constellations of factors affecting consumers' decisions in different parts of the world mean that it is erroneous to assume that there is only one possible or even one preferred road to consumer knowledge creation. To move consumer research knowledge forward in Africa, it is imperative for future research to provide insights into what African consumers want and why they consider these items as important to them as individuals and as households. Stated differently, our concern as marketing scholars must be to investigate how marketing can help African consumers (as individuals and households) enjoy the basic necessities of life and grow their economies in the process. Such concern provides new directions for future consumer behavior research in Africa.

Notes

1 International Monetary Fund, "World Economic Outlook: Uneven Growth," International Monetary Fund, www.imf.org/external/pubs/ft/weo/2015/01/pdf/text.pdf.
2 International Monetary Fund, "World Economic Outlook: Subdued Demand—Symptoms and Remedies," Washington, DC: International Monetary Fund, www.imf.org/external/pubs/ft/weo/2016/02/
3 John Kuada, ed. *Marketing, Economic Growth, and Competitive Strategies of Firms in Africa*, Vol. 7 (London: Emerald Group Publishing Limited, 2016), 2–8.
4 World Bank, *Global Economic Prospects* (Washington, DC: World Bank, 2015).
5 United Nations (UN) Population Division, *World Urbanization Prospects: The 2011 Revision* (New York: United Nations, Department of Economic and Social Affairs, Population Division, 2012).
6 Damian Hattingh et al., *The Rise of the African Consumer* (London: McKinsey Company, 2012).
7 John Kuada, ed. *Private Enterprise-Led Economic Development in Sub-Saharan Africa: The Human Side of Growth* (Basingstoke: Palgrave Macmillan, 2015).
8 Felix Adamu Nandonde and John Kuada, "Modern Food Retailing Buying Behaviour in Africa: The Case of Tanzania," *British Food Journal* 118, no. 5 (2016): 1163.

9 Cristian Chelariu, Abdoulaye Ouattarra, and Kofi Q. Dadzie, "Market Orientation in Ivory Coast: Measurement Validity and Organizational Antecedents in a Sub- Saharan African Economy," *Journal of Business & Industrial Marketing* 17, no. 6 (2002): 456.

10 Mark Petticrew and Helen Roberts, eds. *Systematic Reviews in the Social Sciences: A Practical Guide, Mark Petticrew* (London: Oxford Blackwell Publishing Ltd, 2006).

11 Association of Business Schools (ABS) Journal List (2015).

12 John Kuada and Andrea Bujac, "Perspectives on Consumer Behavior in Africa—Literature Review and Research Agenda." Working Paper Series No. 60, International Business Center, Aalborg University, 2015, 6. The papers are internally available to faculty (http://www.aau.dk) in the International Business Center.

13 Alsadek Gait and Andrew C. Worthington, "Attitudes of Libyan Retail Consumers Toward Islamic Methods of Finance," *International Journal of Islamic and Middle Eastern Finance and Management* 8, no. 4 (2015): 439.

14 Ejye Omar Ogenyi and Nana Owusu-Frimpong, "Life Insurance in Nigeria an Application of the Theory of Reasoned Action to Consumers' Attitudes and Purchase Intention," *The Service Industries Journal* 27, no. 7 (2007): 963.

15 Laureane du Plessis and Daniël Johannes Petzer, "The Attitudes of Donors Towards Non-Profit Organisations (NPOs) in Gauteng, South Africa: A Generational Perspective," *African Journal of Business Management* 5, no. 30 (2011): 12144.

16 Liezl-Marie Kruger and Pierre G. Mostert, "Young Adults' Relationship Intentions Towards their Cell Phone Network Operators," *South African Journal of Business Management* 43, no. 2 (2012): 41.

17 Wilhemina Quaye et al., "The Extent of Marketability and Consumer Preferences for Traditional Leafy Vegetables—a Case Study at Selected Markets in Ghana," *International Journal of Consumer Studies* 33, no. 3 (2009): 244.

18 Ibid.

19 Kofi Q. Dadzie, Evelyn Winston, and Kofi Afriyie, "The Effects of Normative Social Belief Systems and Customer Satisfaction on Rural Savings Programs in Ghana," *Management Decision* 41, no. 3 (2003): 233.

20 Alsadek Gait and Andrew C. Worthington, "Attitudes of Libyan Retail Consumers Toward Islamic Methods of Finance," *International Journal of Islamic and Middle Eastern Finance and Management* 8, no. 4 (2015): 439–454, https://doi.org/10.1108/IMEFM-04-2013-0056.

21 Moez Ltifi et al., "The Determinants of the Choice of Islamic Banks in Tunisia," *The International Journal of Bank Marketing* 34, no. 5 (2016): 710.

22 Wilfred Ukpere et al., "Determinants of Airline Choice-Making: The Nigerian Perspective," *African Journal of Business Management* 6, no. 15 (2012): 5442.

23 Hillary K. Bett et al., "Estimating Consumer Preferences and Willingness to Pay for the Underutilised Indigenous Chicken Products," *Food Policy* 41 (2013): 218.

24 Robert Brent, "A Cost-Benefit Analysis of a Condom Social Marketing Programme in Tanzania," *Applied Economics* 41, no. 4 (2009): 497.

25 Roy Brouwer et al., "Comparing Willingness to Pay for Improved Drinking-Water Quality Using Stated Preference Methods in Rural and Urban Kenya," *Applied Health Economics and Health Policy* 13, no. 1 (2015): 81.

26 Iddrisu Yahaya, Fred A. Yamoah, and Faizal Adams, "Consumer Motivation and Willingness to Pay for 'Safer' Vegetables in Ghana," *British Food Journal* 117, no. 3 (2015): 1043.

27 Job Dubihlela and Tandiswa Ngxukumeshe, "Eco-Friendly Retail Product Attributes, Customer Attributes and the Repurchase Intentions of South African Consumers," *The International Business & Economics Research Journal* 15, no. 4 (2016): 163.

28 Devi Juwaheer Thanika, Pudaruth Sharmila, and Marie Monique Emmanuelle Noyaux, "Analysing the Impact of Green Marketing Strategies on Consumer Purchasing Patterns in Mauritius," *World Journal of Entrepreneurship, Management and Sustainable Development* 8, no. 1 (2012): 36.

29 Sharmila Pudaruth, Thanika Devi Juwaheer, and Yogini Devi Seewoo, "Gender-Based Differences in Understanding the Purchasing Patterns of Eco-Friendly Cosmetics and

Beauty Care Products in Mauritius: A Study of Female Customers," *Social Responsibility Journal* 11, no. 1 (2015): 179.

30 Atsede Woldie, "Nigerian Banks- Quality of Services," *Journal of African Business* 4, no. 2 (2003): 69.

31 Geoffrey Bick, Beric Brown Andrew, and Russell Abratt, "Customer Perceptions of the Value Delivered by Retail Banks in South Africa," *International Journal of Bank Marketing* 22, no. 5 (2004): 300.

32 Bedman Narteh and John Kuada, "Customer Satisfaction with Retail Banking Services in Ghana," *Thunderbird International Business Review* 56, no. 4 (2014): 353.

33 Nana Owusu-Frimpong, "An Evaluation of Marketing Practices in Banks in Ghana," *Journal of African Business* 2, no. 3 (2001): 75.

34 Bedman Narteh and Nana Owusu-Frimpong, "An Analysis of Students' Knowledge and Choice Criteria in Retail Bank Selection in Sub-Saharan Africa: The Case of Ghana," *International Journal of Bank Marketing* 29, no. 5 (2011): 373.

35 Bedman Narteh and John Kuada, "Customer satisfaction with retail banking services in Ghana," *Thunderbird. International Business Review* 56 no. 4 (2014): 353–371.

36 D. Guruswamy, "Customer Inclinations for the Retail Services by Commercial Banks in Ethiopia," *Anvesha* 6, no. 2 (2013): 11.

37 Narteh and Kuada, "Customer Satisfaction . . .", 353–371.

38 Mohammed-Aminu Sanda and John Kuada, "Influencing Dynamics of Culture and Employee Factors on Retail Banks' Performances in a Developing Country Context," *Management Research Review* 39, no. 5 (2016): 599.

39 Nana Owusu-Frimpong, "An Evaluation of Customers' Perception and Usage of Rural Community Banks (RCBs) in Ghana," *International Journal of Emerging Markets* 3, no. 2 (2008): 181.

40 Narteh and Kuada, "Customer Satisfaction . . .", 353–371.

41 Guruswamy, "Customer Inclinations . . .", 11–16.

42 Valarie A. Zeithaml, Mary Jo Bitner, and Dwayne D. Gremler, *Services Marketing: Integrating Customer Focus Across the Firm*, 5th ed. (Boston: McGraw Hill, 2009).

43 John Kuada and Robert Hinson, *Service Marketing in Ghana: A Customer Relationship Management Approach*, ed. John Kuada, Elektronisk udgave (London: Center for Sustainability and Enterprise Development, 2014).

44 Sanda and Kuada, "Influencing Dynamics of Culture and Employee Factors on Retail Banks' Performances in a Developing Country Context," 599–628.

45 Guillaume D. Johnson and Sonya A. Grier, "Understanding the Influence of Cross-Cultural Consumer-to-Consumer Interaction on Consumer Service Satisfaction," *Journal of Business Research* 66 (2013): 306–313.

46 Jana Slippers, Anské Grobler, and Neels van Heerden, "Urban Afrikaans-Speaking Consumers' Attitudes, Preferences and Assertiveness Regarding Mother-Tongue Marketing Communication," *Management Dynamics* 22, no. 3 (2013): 2.

47 Anna V. John and Malcolm P. Brady, "Consumer Ethnocentrism and Attitudes Toward South African Consumables in Mozambique," *African Journal of Economic and Management Studies* 2, no. 1 (2011): 72.

48 Kojo Saffu and John Walker, "The Country-of- Origin Effect and Consumer Attitudes to "Buy Local" Campaign: The Ghanaian Case," *Journal of African Business* 7, no. 1–2 (2006): 183.

49 Chris Pentz, Nic S. Terblanche, and Christo Boshoff, "Measuring Consumer Ethnocentrism in a Developing Context: An Assessment of the Reliability, Validity and Dimensionality of the CETSCALE," *Journal of Transnational Management* 18, no. 3 (2013): 204.

50 Steven Lysonski and Srinivas Durvasula, "Nigeria in Transition: Acculturation to Global Consumer Culture," *Journal of Consumer Marketing* 30, no. 6 (2013): 493.

51 Saffu and Walker, "The Country-of-Origin Effect . . .", 183–199.

52 Muhammed Ngoma and Peter Ntale, "Perceived Brand Quality in Uganda's Pharmaceutical Industry: The Role of Country of Origin, Marketing Orientation and Brand Affordability," *Advances in Management and Applied Economics* 5, no. 6 (2015): 1.

53 Laetitia Radder and Wei Huang, "High-Involvement and Low-Involvement Products: A Comparison of Brand Awareness Among Students at a South African University," *Journal of Fashion Marketing and Management* 12, no. 2 (2008): 232.

54 Denford Chimboza and Edward Mutandwa, "Measuring the Determinants of Brand Preference in a Dairy Product Market," *African Journal of Business Management* 1, no. 9 (2007).

55 Gert Human et al., "Advertising, Brand Knowledge and Attitudinal Loyalty in Low-Income Markets: Can Advertising Make a Difference at the 'Bottom-of-the-Pyramid'?," *Management Dynamics: Journal of the Southern African Institute for Management Scientists* 20, no. 2 (January 2011): 33–45.

56 Ayatunji Gbadamosi et al., "Children's Attitudinal Reactions to TV Advertisements: The African Experience." *International Journal of Market Research* 54, no. 4 (2012): 543–566.

57 Al-Farouq Stats Aminu, "Empirical Investigation of the Effect of Relationship Marketing on Banks' Customer Loyalty in Nigeria," *Interdisciplinary Journal of Contemporary Research in Business* 4, no. 6 (2012): 1249–1266.

58 Bedman Narteh et al., "Relationship Marketing and Customer Loyalty: Evidence From the Ghanaian Luxury Hotel Industry," *Journal of Hospitality Marketing & Management* 22, no. 4 (2013): 407–436.

59 Tustin Deon, "The Prevalence of Impulsive, Compulsive and Innovative Shopping Behaviour in the Economic Retail Hub of South Africa: A Marketing Segmentation Approach," *African Journal of Business Management* 5, no. 14 (2011): 5424.

60 Richard Lee et al., "The Underlying Social Identities of a Nation's Brand," *International Marketing Review* 27, no. 4 (2010): 450.

61 C. K. Prahalad, *The Fortune at the Bottom of the Pyramid: Eradicating Poverty Through Profits* (Upper Saddle River, NJ: Prentice Hall, 2005).

62 Philip Kotler and Nancy Lee, *Up and Out of Poverty: The Social Marketing Solution* (Upper Saddle River, NJ: Wharton School Publishing, 2009).

63 Søren Askegaard and Linda Scott, Editorial, "Consumer Culture Theory: The Ironies of History," *Marketing Theory* 13, no. 2 (2013): 139–147.

64 Stuart L. Hart and Ted London, "Developing Native Capability," *Stanford Social Innovation Review* 3 (Summer 2005): 28–33.

65 Ibid.

66 Kotler and Lee, *Up and Out of Poverty*.

67 Maria Letelier, Fernando Flores, and Charles Spinosa, "Developing Productive Customers in Emerging Markets," *California Management Review* 45, no. 4 (2003): 77.

Bibliography

Allport, Gordon W. *The Nature of Prejudice*. Cambridge, MA: Perseus Books, 1954.

Aminu, Al-Farouq Stats, "Empirical Investigation of the Effect of Relationship Marketing on Banks' Customer Loyalty in Nigeria." *Interdisciplinary Journal of Contemporary Research in Business* 4, no. 6 (2012): 1249–1266.

Askegaard, Søren, and Linda Scott. Editorial, "Consumer Culture Theory: The Ironies of History." *Marketing Theory* 13, no. 2 (2013): 139–147.

Association of Business Schools (ABS). *Journal List*, 2015.

Bett, Hillary K. et al. "Estimating Consumer Preferences and Willingness to Pay for the Underutilised Indigenous Chicken Products." *Food Policy* 41 (2013): 218–225.

Bick, Geoffrey, Beric Brown Andrew, and Russell Abratt. "Customer Perceptions of the Value Delivered by Retail Banks in South Africa." *International Journal of Bank Marketing* 22, no. 5 (2004): 300–318.

Brent, Robert. "A Cost-Benefit Analysis of a Condom Social Marketing Programme in Tanzania." *Applied Economics* 41, no. 4 (2009): 497–509.

Brouwer, Roy et al. "Comparing Willingness to Pay for Improved Drinking: Water Quality Using Stated Preference Methods in Rural and Urban Kenya." *Applied Health Economics and Health Policy* 13, no. 1 (2015): 81–94.

Chelariu, Cristian, Abdoulaye Ouattarra, and Kofi Q. Dadzie. "Market Orientation in Ivory Coast: Measurement Validity and Organizational Antecedents in a Sub-Saharan African Economy." *Journal of Business & Industrial Marketing* 17, no. 6 (2002): 456–470.

Chimboza, Denford, and Edward Mutandwa. "Measuring the Determinants of Brand Preference in a Dairy Product Market." *African Journal of Business Management* 1, no. 9 (2007).

Dadzie, Kofi Q., Evelyn Winston, and Kofi Afriyie. "The Effects of Normative Social Belief Systems and Customer Satisfaction on Rural Savings Programs in Ghana." *Management Decision* 41, no. 3 (2003): 233–240.

Deon, Tustin. "The Prevalence of Impulsive, Compulsive and Innovative Shopping Behaviour in the Economic Retail Hub of South Africa: A Marketing Segmentation Approach." *African Journal of Business Management* 5, no. 14 (2011): 5424–5434.

Dubihlela, Job, and Tandiswa Ngxukumeshe. "Eco-Friendly Retail Product Attributes, Customer Attributes and the Repurchase Intentions of South African Consumers." *The International Business & Economics Research Journal* (Online) 15, no. 4 (2016): 163.

Fournier, Susan, and David Glen Mick. "Rediscovering Satisfaction." *Journal of Marketing* 63 (October 1999): 5–23.

Gait, Alsadek, and Andrew C. Worthington. "Attitudes of Libyan Retail Consumers Toward Islamic Methods of Finance." *International Journal of Islamic and Middle Eastern Finance and Management* 8, no. 4 (2015): 439–454.

Gbadamosi, Ayantunji et al. "Children's Attitudinal Reactions to TV Advertisements: The African Experience." *International Journal of Market Research* 54, no. 4 (2012): 543–566.

Guruswamy, D. "Customer Inclinations for the Retail Services by Commercial Banks in Ethiopia." *Anvesha* 6, no. 2 (2013): 11–16.

Hart, Stuart L., and Ted London. "Developing Native Capability." *Stanford Social Innovation Review* 3 (Summer 2005): 28–33.

Hattingh, Damian et al. *The Rise of the African Consumer.* London: McKinsey Company, 2012.

Human, Gert et al. "Advertising, Brand Knowledge and Attitudinal Loyalty in Low-Income Markets: Can Advertising Make a Difference at the 'Bottom-of-the-Pyramid'?" *Management Dynamics: Journal of the Southern African Institute for Management Scientists* 20, no. 2 (2011): 33–45.

International Monetary Fund. *World Economic Outlook: Subdued Demand—Symptoms and Remedies.* Washington, DC: International Monetary Fund. www.imf.org/external/pubs/ft/weo/2016/02/.

International Monetary Fund. *World Economic Outlook: Uneven Growth.* Washington, DC: International Monetary Fund. www.imf.org/external/pubs/ft/weo/2015/01/pdf/text.pdf.

John, Anna V., and Malcolm P. Brady. "Consumer Ethnocentrism and Attitudes Toward South African Consumables in Mozambique." *African Journal of Economic and Management Studies* 2, no. 1 (2011): 72–93.

Johnson, Guillaume D., and Sonya A. Grier. "Understanding the Influence of Cross-Cultural Consumer-to-Consumer Interaction on Consumer Service Satisfaction." *Journal of Business Research* 66 (2013): 306–313.

Kotler, Philip, and Nancy Lee. *Up and Out of Poverty: The Social Marketing Solution*. Upper Saddle River, NJ: Wharton School Publishing, 2009.

Kruger, Liezl-Marie, and Pierre G. Mostert. "Young Adults' Relationship Intentions Towards Their Cell Phone Network Operators." *South African Journal of Business Management* 43, no. 2 (2012): 41–49.

Kuada, John. "Marketing, Economic Growth, and Competitive Strategies of Firms in Africa." *African Journal of Economic and Management Studies* 7, no. 1 (2016): 2–8.

Kuada, John. *Private Enterprise-Led Economic Development in Sub-Saharan Africa: The Human Side of Growth*. London: Palgrave Macmillan, 2015.

Kuada, John, and Andreea Bujac. "Perspectives on Consumer Behavior in Africa—Literature Review and Research Agenda." Working Paper Series No. 60, International Business Center, Aalborg University, 2015.

Kuada, John, and Robert Hinson. *Service Marketing in Ghana: A Customer Relationship Management Approach*. London: Adonis and Abbey, 2014.

Lee, Richard et al. "The Underlying Social Identities of a Nation's Brand." *International Marketing Review* 27, no. 4 (2010): 450–465.

Letelier, Maria, Fernando Flores, and Charles Spinosa. "Developing Productive Customers in Emerging Markets." *California Management Review* 45, no. 4 (2003): 77–103.

Ltifi, Moez et al. "The Determinants of the Choice of Islamic Banks in Tunisia." *The International Journal of Bank Marketing* 34, no. 5 (2016): 710–730.

Lysonski, Steven, and Srinivas Durvasula. "Nigeria in Transition: Acculturation to Global Consumer Culture." *Journal of Consumer Marketing* 30, no. 6 (2013): 493–508.

Nandonde, Felix Adamu and John Kuada. "Modern Food Retailing Buying Behaviour in Africa: The Case of Tanzania." *British Food Journal* 118, no. 5 (2016): 1163–1178.

Narteh, Bedman, and John Kuada. "Customer Satisfaction with Retail Banking Services in Ghana." *Thunderbird International Business Review* 56, no. 4 (2014): 353–371.

Narteh, Bedman, and Nana Owusu-Frimpong. "An Analysis of Students' Knowledge and Choice Criteria in Retail Bank Selection in Sub-Saharan Africa: The Case of Ghana." *International Journal of Bank Marketing* 29, no. 5 (2011): 373–397.

Narteh, Bedman et al. "Relationship Marketing and Customer Loyalty: Evidence from the Ghanaian Luxury Hotel Industry." *Journal of Hospitality Marketing & Management* 22, no. 4 (2013): 407–436.

Ngoma, Muhammed, and Peter Ntale. "Perceived Brand Quality in Uganda's Pharmaceutical Industry: The Role of Country of Origin, Marketing Orientation and Brand Affordability." *Advances in Management and Applied Economics* 5, no. 6 (2015): 1–11.

Ogenyi, Ejye Omar, and Nana Owusu-Frimpong. "Life Insurance in Nigeria an Application of the Theory of Reasoned Action to Consumers' Attitudes and Purchase Intention." *The Service Industries Journal* 27, no. 7 (2007): 963–976.

Oliver, Richard L., and Wayne De Sarbo. "Response Determinants in Satisfaction Judgments." *Journal of Consumer Research* 14 (1988): 495–507.

Owusu-Frimpong, Nana. "An Evaluation of Customers' Perception and Usage of Rural Community Banks (RCBs) in Ghana." *International Journal of Emerging Markets* 3, no. 2 (2008): 181–196.

Owusu-Frimpong, Nana. "An Evaluation of Marketing Practices in Banks in Ghana." *Journal of African Business* 2, no. 3 (2001): 75–91.

Pentz, Chris, Nic S. Terblanche, and Christo Boshoff. "Measuring Consumer Ethnocentrism in a Developing Context: An Assessment of the Reliability, Validity and Dimensionality of the CETSCALE." *Journal of Transnational Management* 18, no. 3 (2013): 204–208.

Petticrew, Mark, and Helen Roberts. *Systematic Reviews in the Social Sciences: A Practical Guide*. Ed. Mark Petticrew. London: Oxford Blackwell Publishing Ltd, 2006.

Plessis, Laureane du, and Daniël Johannes Petzer. "The Attitudes of Donors Towards Non-Profit Organisations (NPOs) in Gauteng, South Africa: A Generational Perspective." *African Journal of Business Management* 5, no. 30 (2011): 121–144.

Potluri, Rajasekhara Mouly, and Awgichew Abiye Zeleke, "Evaluation of Customer Handling Competencies of Ethiopian Employees." *African Journal of Business Management* 3, no. 4 (2009): 131–135.

Prahalad, C.K. *The Fortune at the Bottom of the Pyramid: Eradicating Poverty Through Profits*. Upper Saddle River, NJ: Prentice Hall, 2005.

Pudaruth, Sharmila, Thanika Devi Juwaheer, and Yogini Devi Seewoo. "Gender-Based Differences in Understanding the Purchasing Patterns of Eco-Friendly Cosmetics and Beauty Care Products in Mauritius: A Study of Female Customers." *Social Responsibility Journal* 11, no. 1 (2015): 179–198.

Quaye, Wilhemina et al. "The Extent of Marketability and Consumer Preferences for Traditional Leafy Vegetables—a Case Study at Selected Markets in Ghana." *International Journal of Consumer Studies* 33, no. 3 (2009): 244–249.

Radder, Laetitia, and Wei Huang. "High-Involvement and Low-Involvement Products; a Comparison of Brand Awareness Among Students at a South African University." *Journal of Fashion Marketing and Management* 12, no. 2 (2008): 232–243.

Saffu, Kojo, and John Walker. "The Country-of-Origin Effect and Consumer Attitudes to 'Buy Local' Campaign: The Ghanaian Case." *Journal of African Business* 7, nos. 1–2 (2006): 183–199.

Sanda, Mohammed-Aminu, and John Kuada. "Influencing Dynamics of Culture and Employee Factors on Retail Banks' Performances in a Developing Country Context." *Management Research Review* 39, no. 5 (2016): 599–628.

Slippers, Jana, Anské Grobler, and Neels van Heerden. "Urban Afrikaans-Speaking Consumers' Attitudes, Preferences and Assertiveness regarding Mother-Tongue Marketing Communication." *Management Dynamics* 22, no. 3 (2013): 2–12.

Thanika, Devi Juwaheer, Pudaruth Sharmila, and Marie Monique Emmanuelle Noyaux. "Analysing the Impact of Green Marketing Strategies on Consumer Purchasing Patterns in Mauritius." *World Journal of Entrepreneurship, Management and Sustainable Development* 8, no. 1 (2012): 36–59.

Ukpere, Wilfred et al. "Determinants of Airline Choice-Making: The Nigerian Perspective." *African Journal of Business Management* 6, no. 15 (2012): 5442–5455.

United Nations (UN) Population Division. *World Urbanization Prospects: The 2011 Revision*. New York: United Nations, Department of Economic and Social Affairs, Population Division, 2012.

Woldie, Atsede. "Nigerian Banks: Quality of Services." *Journal of African Business* 4, no. 2 (2003): 69–87.

World Bank. *Global Economic Prospects*. Washington, DC: World Bank, 2015.

Yahaya, Iddrisu, Fred A. Yamoah, and Faizal Adams. "Consumer Motivation and Willingness to Pay for 'Safer' Vegetables in Ghana." *British Food Journal* 117, no. 3 (2015): 1043–1065.

Zeithaml, Valarie A., Mary Jo Bitner, and Dwayne D. Gremler. *Services Marketing: Integrating Customer Focus Across the Firm*, 5th ed. Boston, MA: McGraw-Hill, 2009.

12

FACTORS DETERMINING THE RISE OF MODERN FOOD RETAILING IN EAST AFRICA

Evidence From Tanzania

Felix Adamu Nandonde and John Kuada

Introduction

The global economy has witnessed a substantial shift in consumption centers from the developed economies to the emerging market economies. This shift has introduced new dynamics into the international marketing process, with companies having to adjust their strategies to new and hitherto unknown realities. The growing populations in the emerging markets have provided new market opportunities for retail companies facing saturation in their traditional markets. But they also pose new challenges due to their individual peculiarities.

Recent evidence suggests that some African countries have emerged as destinations for market growth, especially for international food retailers. Africa's average annual economic growth between 2000 and 2010 was 5.4 %, adding $78 billion annually to GDP (in 2015 prices). Although growth slowed to 3.3%, annually between 2010 and 2015, it added US$69 billion a year to the continent's GDP.[1] Out of 54 African countries, 24 more than doubled their per capita income over 1990–2010.[2] In 2015, seven of the ten fastest-growing economies in the world were in Africa.

Demographic trends also favor overall market growth. By 2050, Africa's population is expected to reach 2 billion people (accounting for 20% of the world's population), and 1 billion will be under 18 years old. Consumer spending on the continent is expected to increase to nearly US$1 trillion by 2020.[3] It is also estimated that by 2022, more Africans will move out of poverty to become middle-income consumers, granting that economic policies can be crafted to provide the young people with the education and skills they need to contribute effectively to economic growth.

Thus, although short-term risks remain, Africa has strong long-term growth prospects, propelled both by external trends in the global economy and internal

The Rise of Modern Food Retailing **225**

changes in the continent's societies and economies. There is some evidence that these changes are already reshaping the competitive landscape for both domestic and foreign firms operating in the different African countries, and many foreign firms now see Africa as a viable investment destination. But these changes are also challenging previous perspectives on the role of marketing in African economies.

Specific regions of the continent stand out as growth areas worth extra attention. For example, a study showed that the East African Community (EAC) has been among the fastest-growing regions.[4] Per capita income growth in the region reached 3.7% a year between 2005 and 2010, almost quadrupling the rate achieved in the previous 15-year period. Another study noted that at 6.2%, the EAC's (unweighted) average growth rate in 2004 to 2013 was in the top one-fifth of the distribution of 10-year growth rate episodes experienced by all countries worldwide since 1960.[5] Rwanda, Tanzania, and Uganda have had the longest periods of high growth.

Despite these impressive developments, research interest in marketing activities in Africa has been rather low, and strategic marketing processes and priorities remain poorly understood in Africa.[6] The potential role of marketing in Africa's economic growth, therefore, remains largely unexplored. This chapter seeks to contribute to the scanty knowledge in the field by bringing together fragmented theoretical and empirical knowledge about the roles that international retailers are playing in the EAC countries and to report on food retail activities in Tanzania. Specifically, the chapter wants to answer the following research question: What are the key factors determining the rise of modern food retailing in Tanzania?

The remainder of the chapter is structured as follows. First, we present an overview of previous studies into retailing in developing countries in order to provide a theoretical backdrop for the discussions about food retailing in EAC. Subsequently, the development of the food retail sector in Africa will be examined, noting some of the opportunities and challenges identified in previous studies. Finally, the results of our investigations in Tanzania will be presented with a discussion of the implications of that study for an understanding of drivers of growth within the food retail sector in the East African region.

Previous Theoretical Insights Into Retailing in Developing Countries

The internationalization process of firms is usually driven by both internal and external motives. It has been noted that factors such as regulatory constraints, stiff competition, and saturations in domestic markets that result in declining sales, shrinking market shares, and limited growth opportunities tend to push international retailers to seek market opportunities in developing countries. Changes within the business environments in the developing countries also tend to facilitate the internationalization process. As we noted earlier, there is a growing middle class income group in most of these countries, and this has helped expand the market for good quality imported food items. Furthermore, studies have demonstrated how consumers in most of the developing countries are 'leapfrogging' technological trends in the markets—for example, jumping straight from not having any piece of equipment for personal use at all to having smartphones and enjoying their usage in novel ways that have become the envy of consumers in the developed countries. An example is mobile pay systems that have shown a widespread usage in countries such as Kenya, thereby allowing marketers to target the consumers with communication strategies via mobile devices.[7] In terms of food consumption, it has been noted that the growing middle-income urban consumers tend to demand superior quality food items that are sold in clean environments. They have also been found to be more open-minded than other segments of their populations, more spontaneous, and more willing to try new products. All these developments create opportunities for growth for modern retail outlets.

However, there is growing evidence suggesting that retail operations in the emerging markets have not been smooth sailing for international retailers and even the larger retailers have been surprised at the challenges that the new markets pose. In Asia, Africa, and Latin America, retail stores fail and have to exit their operations due to their inability to effectively tackle the diverse range of unfamiliar consumer behaviors and clever local competitive strategies. For example, some studies have shown that local retailers have successfully used their local knowledge and networks to outcompete the international new entrants. Other scholars have drawn attention to factors such as 'emotional proximity' between customers and shop owners or empathy shown by small shop owners to customers as effective marketing strategies.[8]

Most of the previous studies of the internationalization process of retail firms have been anchored on such theories as the 'big middle' theory, the network theory, and institutional theory.[9] Scholars who adopt the 'big middle' theoretical framework in studying the process of retail sector development focus attention on the impact that prices and innovation have on consumers' decision to shop in supermarkets. The concept of '*big middle*' is used in the literature to refer not to a geographical marketplace, but rather to connote a mind space that lies between the competitive arenas such as low price and innovativeness. It defines how retailers seek to position themselves in the minds of consumers. Innovation increases positive shopping experience, convenience, and perceived 'value for money' among consumers. There is evidence from some African countries suggesting that consumers prefer to shop in modern stores because they can move freely in the stores. This is particularly important in Muslim-dominant countries, where women may worry about physical contacts with men.[10] Innovation also improves product quality and draws consumers away from open market shopping to international retail stores, which are generally considered as carrying superior quality products.

Some of the previous studies have used resource based view (RBV) to explain the growth process of international retailers. These studies also focused attention on firms' food innovation characteristics in order to explain their performance. The central argument from these studies is that the development of unique value propositions that meet consumers' needs constitute the key for retailers' success. They also argue that non-price factors such as product quality and shopping environment are among the most important growth factors.

Scholars using the network theory see marketing in terms of coordination of exchange activities involving direct and indirect partners with the view to mobilize and coordinate critical resources through inter-firm relationships. In terms of food marketing, this approach has been used to study the management of relationships between suppliers and retailers.[11] The central argument in studies based on the network approach is that all businesses require network orientation in order to be successful. Having such an orientation encourages companies to identify the roles, strengths, and resource configurations of other actors within the network. In this way, they can position themselves within the network and be able to design strategies that improve their access to resources controlled by other companies. The higher the number of contacts, the more resources they are able to leverage within the networks.

There are other studies that are based on institutional theoretical frameworks. These scholars argue that the retail industry in every country has its own set of institutional norms that have evolved over time through the interactions of different social actors within the setting of the local culture.[12] International retailers have to gain legitimacy and support from the social actors in order to be successful in a host market. Some of the studies suggest that successful retailers in developing countries tend to adopt an 'isomorphic' response to both the objective (task/economic) and symbolic (institutional/social-moral) norms of the countries within which they operate. The adoption of institutionally adaptive orientation in host markets may require building networks of relationships with key stakeholders, including consumers, suppliers, and government agencies. This task requires that international retailers acquire new kinds of competencies that enable them to establish relational bonds that facilitate product and process adjustments, logistical coordination, and overall operational efficiency in addition to legitimacy benefits. Seen from a sociological perspective, a major driver of these relationships is trust. Trust has been shown to increase cooperation, improve flexibility, lower the cost of coordinating activities, and increase the level of knowledge transfer and potential for learning.[13] Where trust exists between people in relations, they are willing to sacrifice their short run individual self-interests for the attainment of joint goals or longer-term objectives.

Development of the Food Retail Sector in Africa

As noted earlier, Africa has seen the arrival of international retailers in its changing business landscape during the past three decades. Their arrival has witnessed a shift from public to private standards, from spot market relations to vertical coordination of the supply chain using contracts and market inter-linkages, and shift from local sourcing to sourcing via national, regional, and global networks. This modernization has been adopted to reduce costs, to differentiate products in the supermarkets from those sold in the traditional marketplaces, and to provide incentives to producers to increase food quality. Due to high expenditure on food by African consumers, these changes in retail development are expected to have substantial impacts on growth of the sector and the economies at large.

However, the operations of these international retailers have not always been easy in their new host countries. For example, after 2 years of operations in Egypt, Sainsbury had to pull out in 2001 due to consumers' boycott.[14] Carrefour also left Algeria in 2009 after 2 years of operation. And South African retailer Metro Cash and Carry failed in Kenya in 2005 and Uganda in 2007. Shoprite (another South African retailer) entered Tanzania in 2001 but had to sell its stores to Nakumatt (a Kenyan retailer) in 2014.[15] Some evidence suggests that consumers are not always satisfied with the prices and quality of local products found in the supermarkets.

Other studies have drawn attention to the huge infrastructural deficits that raise the cost of distribution and constrain the coordination of logistical services within local and regional food value chains.[16] Some estimates have suggested

TABLE 12.1 List of International Retail Companies Operating in East Africa as of the End of 2015

Name of the Firm	Origin	Countries it Operates in	Number of Stores
Tusky's	Kenya	Uganda and Kenya	48
Metro Cash and Carry	South Africa	Uganda and Kenya	Closed in 2007 in Uganda and 2005 in Kenya
Pick N Pay	South Africa	Tanzania	Closed in 2002
Walmart/ MassMart	South Africa/ United States	Uganda and Tanzania	4
Shoprite	South Africa	Tanzania and Uganda	Exited Tanzania 2014 and Uganda in 2015
Woolworths	South Africa	Tanzania and Uganda	4
Nakumatt	Kenya	Tanzania, Kenya, Uganda, and Rwanda	52
Deacons	Kenya	Tanzania, Kenya, Rwanda, and Uganda	34
Uchumi	Kenya	Tanzania, Kenya, and Uganda,	39, exited Uganda and Tanzania in 2015
Carrefour	France	Kenya	1

Source: Felix. A. Nandonde *Integrating Local Food Suppliers in Modern Food Retail in Africa* (2016)

that transport costs for exports from one African country to another are five times higher than tariff costs.[17] The infrastructural challenges are compounded by bureaucratic bottlenecks. One of the most frequently cited indications of anti-business attitudes in Africa is the mounting of roadblocks on the highways that link various trading centers in Africa.

Modern Food Retailing in Tanzania

Turning to Tanzania, international retailers have appeared on the urban food marketing scene since the late 1990s. An A.T. Kearney (a global management consulting firm) report in 2014 suggests that supermarket penetration in Tanzania is growing rapidly. However, 80% of the food items sold from these outlets are imported into the country. It has also been suggested that the operations of these outlets have resulted in some changes in consumer behavior as an increasing number of middle class consumers are shifting their food purchases from traditional markets and small shops to supermarkets. Shoppers' Plaza (a local supermarket) at Msasani was the first supermarket to be established in Tanzania in 1997. This was followed by Imalaseko Supermarket at Pamba House in Dar es Salaam in 1998. In 2001, Pick N Pay, a South African retailer, opened its first store in Tanzania, but folded just a year later. In 2002, another South African retailer, Shoprite Supermarket, opened a store in Dar es Salaam. In 2011, Nakumatt (a Kenyan supermarket) opened a store in Kilimanjaro. Shoprite sold all of its three stores to Nakumatt Supermarket in 2014 and left the country. Local supermarkets such as Panone Supermarket, TSN, Shrijee Supermarket, and Village Supermarket are also operating alongside their international competitors with apparent success. Government officials estimate that the annual growth rate of these supermarkets has ranged between 10% 13% during the past 10 years. An A.T. Kearney report ranks the country fourth among African countries in terms of opportunities for the growth of modern food distribution after Rwanda, Nigeria, and Namibia. Table 12.2 provides an overview of modern retailers (local and foreign) operating in the country as of the end of 2015.

TABLE 12.2 Supermarkets Operating in Tanzania as of the End of 2015

Retailers	Country of Origin	Number of Stores
Uchumi	Kenya	Exited in 2015
Nakumatt	Kenya	4
Pick N Pay	South Africa	Exited in 2002
Shoprite	South Africa	Exited in 2014
Massmart/Walmart	South Africa/United States	1
TSN	Tanzania	7
Imalaseko	Tanzania	4
Woolworths	South Africa	4

Opportunities and Challenges of Modern Food Retailing in Tanzania

This section of the chapter reports the results of interviews conducted with owners/managers of seven supermarkets in order to provide insights into the opportunities and challenges the retailers face in their operations.[18] We included only supermarkets that have been in operation in Tanzania for over 3 years in our sample. The sample consists of Panone Supermarket, Imalaseko Supermarket, Tanzania Standard Supermarket (TSN), Shop-N-Save, Game Supermarket, Uchumi Supermarket, and Nakumatt Holding Supermarkets. (See Table 12.3 for an overview of the companies and the respondents interviewed.)

The data for the study were collected using semi-structured interview guides, and all the interviews were recorded on a voice recorder. The interviews were done in Swahili, and the data were initially transcribed into Swahili and then into English.

Profile of the Case Companies

Panone Supermarket is a family business owned by a Tanzanian, Mr. Patrick Ngiloi Ulomi. The company has 12 stores, with 10 located in the northern region of the country (i.e., Kilimanjaro and Arusha) and the remaining 2 located in the coastal region. The company is a subsidiary of Panone Petroleum, which deals in petroleum products, including gasoline and lubricants. The stores are, therefore, located within the petroleum filling stations.

TABLE 12.3 A List of Supermarkets That Participated in the Investigation

Case Company	Year of Establishment	No. of Outlets	No. of Employees	Respondents
Nakumatt Holding Supermarkets	2011	4	208	Branch Manager
Uchumi Supermarket	2012	6	400	Procurement Officer and Floor Manager
Game Supermarket	2006	1	36	Branch Manager and Fresh Food Manager
Shop-N-Save Supermarket	2000	3	20	Branch Manager
Tanzania Standard Supermarket (TSN)	2004	6	1,000	Procurement Officer and Managing Director
Panone Supermarket	2008	12	30	Deputy Managing Director
Imalaseko Supermarket	1998	4	200	Personal Assistant to Managing Director

Imalaseko Supermarket Investment Limited is also a family business owned by Mr. Jumanne Kibera Kishimba, who has extensive business experience from a number of African countries, including Botswana and Zimbabwe. The company started operations in 1998 at Pamba House, in Dar es Salaam. It now has five outlets, with four in Dar es Salaam and one in Mwanza.

Tanzania Standard Supermarket (TSN) is also a local family business owned by Mr. Farouq Baghoza. It was established as a subsidiary of the TSN group of companies, which includes TSN petroleum, distribution services, and logistics. It started as a distribution company, importing consumer goods from the United Kingdom for the Tanzanian market. Currently, TSN has seven stores; six are in Dar es Salaam and one opened in Mwanza. It is planning to open its eighth store in Dar es Salaam at Kigamboni and Sinza Mori. With the slogan: '*Tanzania sisi ni nyumbani*' (Tanzania is our home), the company plans to open additional stores in towns like Tanga and Morogoro.

Shop-N-Save Supermarket is another family business owned by Mr. Raju. It started operations in 1990 in food confectionary in Dar es Salaam by processing bread. It now has three outlets in Dar es Salaam in the city center. Its main target group is the Tanzanian-Asian population (estimated to be 5% of the Tanzanian population but with comparatively higher purchasing power).

Game Supermarket is a subsidiary of Massmart, a South African retail company that is listed on Johannesburg Stock Exchange. It started operations in Tanzania in 2006 by opening an outlet in Mlimani City shopping mall in Dar es Salaam. Its slogan is '*We won't be beaten on price.*' That is, if a customer bought something from them and found the price to be higher than those of its competitors, the customer may get a refund or a discount of 10% of the competitor's price. Furthermore, customers are allowed to return damaged items within 30 days of the day of purchase.

Uchumi Supermarket is a Kenyan retail store that entered the Tanzanian market in 2012 by opening its first store at Quality Plaza Shopping Mall in Dar es Salaam. By 2015, Uchumi had six stores—five in Dar es Salaam and one in Moshi, and there were plans to open additional outlets in Mwanza, Arusha, Mbeya, and Morogoro. But in 2015, the company folded its operations due to losses for 5 consecutive years. When it closed, the six Uchumi stores in Tanzania had employed 460 people.

Nakumatt is also a family business originating from Nakuru, Kenya. It is owned by Mr. Atul Shah. It started as a retailer of mattresses and expanded into groceries. Nakumatt Holding operates in Kenya, Uganda, Rwanda, and Tanzania with 52 stores in all of those countries. It is considered one of the leading supermarkets in East Africa, estimated to be worth US$400 million. It employs 7,000 people across the East African region, with 38 stores in Kenya, 8 in Uganda, 2 in Rwanda, and 4 in Tanzania. It has four outlets in Tanzania after acquiring all three of Shoprite's stores in 2014. It plans to open additional outlets in Mbeya, Mwanza, and Morogoro.

Determinants of Modern Retail Sector Growth in Tanzania

Table 12.4 shows a comparison of the variables that emerged from our data to account for the growth of the supermarkets in Tanzania. Three major factors have been listed by the respondents as contributing to the growth: (1) changes in consumers' lifestyle, (2) availability of local suppliers, and (3) acceptance of terms of collaboration imposed by the supermarkets.

Changes in Consumers' Lifestyle

All the respondents pointed at the growing urban middle class in Tanzania as a key determinant of the growth of the retail sector. This consumer market segment has a lifestyle that is different from the dominant lifestyle of the ordinary Tanzanian population. Since some of them close from work late and cannot buy fresh food items from the traditional (open) markets, they find it convenient to buy all their food items under one roof in a supermarket. They also consider the stable price policies in the supermarkets as an extra advantage, since this makes it easier for them to make their household budgets. Furthermore, supermarkets allow their customers to return items that have been found to be in some way defective or unsuitable for consumption after purchase. This policy has made these outlets a lot more attractive than the traditional marketplace.

The Availability of Local Suppliers

The availability of local suppliers has been linked partly to problems that supermarkets face with imports. That is, the poor levels of infrastructure combine with the hassles of importation in Tanzania (i.e., the bureaucratic procedures, red tape

TABLE 12.4 Determinant Factors for the Rise of Modern Food Retailing

Attributes	Modern Food Retailers						
	Nakumatt	Uchumi	Game	TSN	Shop-N-Save	Panone	Imalaseko
Innovation	Yes	Yes	Yes	No	No	No	No
Lifestyle	Yes	Yes	Yes	Yes	Yes	Yes	Yes
Suppliers' availability	Yes	Yes	Yes	Yes	Yes	Yes	Yes
Institutions' support	Yes	Yes	Yes	No	No	No	No
Administrative reasons	Yes	Yes	Yes	No	No	No	No
Acceptance of trade credit	Yes	Yes	Yes	Yes	Yes	Yes	Yes

The Rise of Modern Food Retailing **233**

at all levels of administration) to make it preferable for the supermarkets to source as many food items as possible locally. This preference is reinforced by government policies that require supermarkets to buy at least 40% of locally produced food items that they sell from Tanzanian producers. In addition to this, the supermarkets have realized that the availability of supplies from local sources reduces cost associated with importation of food items. Our interview results also show that Tanzanian consumers prefer to buy items such as cooking oil, chicken, and vegetable from local sources. They consider the taste and quality of the local products to be superior to the imported ones.

Acceptance of Trade Credit

Seen from a value chain perspective, the supermarkets function as lead firms, deciding on the inclusion or exclusion of local suppliers within the chain and defining the conditions under which they should supply. One of these conditions is that local suppliers must grant the supermarkets a 90-day credit on all items they supply. The local suppliers must also agree to take back any item that has not been bought in the supermarkets before the expiration date. In effect, the supermarkets have shifted part of the financial burden of distribution to the local suppliers. They have also compelled the local suppliers to invest in product and process upgrading in order to fulfill consumer expectations.

The local suppliers have grudgingly accepted the conditions of the supermarkets because they are ensured reliable outlets for their products, and they trust that the supermarkets will make payments on agreed dates. This is in contrast to local intermediaries that are considered largely unreliable by suppliers. One of the suppliers explains the basis of their decision to sell to the supermarkets in this way:

> Food prices have been high, indeed, and this has been a challenge for us. Our solution was to keep prices low and to focus on value chain optimization. In so doing, we have kept our customers happy and our company growing. It is true that some supermarkets take a long time to pay and that is a major challenge, especially in times where bank lending rates are high. This affects the rate of expansion of our business. But we are happy to play ball.[19]

With respect to suppliers' upgrading activities, our interviews reveal that the poultry farmers have made some of the biggest investments in recent years. For example, the procurement officer of TSN informed us that TSN has undertaken substantial investment to modernize and expand its poultry farm and has introduced its own brand of chicken. He explained their investment decisions as follows:

> Due to the high demand for fresh products, we have established a TSN butcher. It's an in-house butcher that is under our control. And we have started poultry keeping

> *for our stores. Our poultry farm is at Bunju in Dar-es-Salaam. Therefore, our own capacity combined with Interchick and other suppliers are able to satisfy our consumers. Our brand is known as TSN Fresh Chicken. In reality, it is to give mileage to our company, and TSN Fresh Chicken is a good sign towards brand image. Our plan is to have everything with the TSN brand.*

Other East African countries appear to experience similar challenges in the development of the capacity of the local suppliers to support the growth of their retail sectors. This change has encouraged some venture capitalists to support the local food processing industries. For example, information shows that Fanisi Capital in Kenya has invested $50 million in agribusiness value-addition activities in that country and through its subsidiaries the company supplies to a number of supermarkets including Uchumi and Nakumatt. Furthermore, Fanisi Capital bought an undisclosed stake at of Kijenge Animal Product in Arusha, Tanzania.[20] The founding Chairman of Kijenge Animal Product, Mr. Andrew Mollel, was reported to have said the following:

> *Having talked to a number of private equity funds over the years, we felt that Fanisi was the right partner for us. This partnership provides us with growth capital which will enable us to diversify our product offering and further support our customers' needs.*

Some supermarkets have acknowledged the enormity of the financial burden of the local suppliers, resulting in changes in payment policies by some. For example, supermarkets such as Shop-N-Save, Panone, and TSN now operate with flexible modes of payment—that is, they make earlier payments for products supplied to them. TSN also provides some logistic services to selected local suppliers that have difficulties in transporting their products to the supermarket. TSN is able to do this because it is part of the TSN group of companies that includes distribution and logistics.

Some Challenges and Strategies

Issues of training, product quality, innovation, and administrative bottlenecks have been identified by some of the respondents as challenges that the sector continues to grapple with. In this regard, the international retailers (e.g., Game, Uchumi, and Nakumatt) see institutional support as an important factor in addressing some of the challenges. Aspects of institutional support highlighted by the international retailers include training in issues relating to food laws and hygiene, flexibility of the laws and regulations, and cracking down on hawkers. Training services provided by such institutions as Tanzania Food and Drugs Authority (TFDA), Tanzania Bureau of Standards (TBS), and Small Industries Development Organization

(SIDO) enable increasing numbers of local food suppliers to meet the country's set food standards that modern retailers are expected to follow. Furthermore, TFDA and TBS have special schemes to facilitate small-scale enterprises to acquire certificates and training on food standards under support facilities offered by some donor organizations. Through these initiatives, many small businesses get access to TFDA certifications, which enable them to produce and sell their food items to the supermarkets.

The local supermarkets do not consider the institutional services to be as important. This difference is perhaps due to the notion that local retailers seem to understand the country's business environment a lot better than their international counterparts. Also, local retailers tend to rely a lot more on agencies and distributors of the imported food items to supply them with good quality products, whereas the international retailers have direct relationships with suppliers in their home countries or local suppliers in Tanzania. For example, Game Supermarket still imports most of its products directly from South Africa.

Some supermarkets have noted the challenges of customer loyalty as a result of the increasing number modern retail outlets in the country. The international retailers indicated that the marketing innovation strategies they have introduced have enabled them to retain customers from all walks of life. Initially, supermarkets were perceived to be outlets for people with high incomes who were living in the major cities. However, some of the supermarkets introduced loyalty cards whereby consumers can earn points that can be redeemed to purchase some specific items in stores. The earned points were not transferred into cash. The emerging evidence is that consumers from low-income groups make use of their points to purchase basic food items such as sugar and bread. The Nakumatt branch manager who we interviewed explained the importance of the loyalty cards this way:

> Consumers who visit our stores daily are getting a lot of benefits. Because every day they are visiting our stores and every day we have promotion, therefore, they come across those opportunities. For example, now we have one thing known as smart shopping, have you seen that one? Enhee . . . if you have come across with smart shopping, that's good. So for those consumers who are visiting our stores, they are getting some points. Now, there will come a day he or she is broke and can tell us, 'Hello, I need to redeem my points for sugar.' We can redeem them, and he can get sugar.

The importance of the marketing innovations for general consumer patronage of the supermarket is well acknowledged in other countries in East Africa where Nakumatt also operates. The following quotes from some of the popular newspapers provide evidence of this effect in Uganda:

> Capital Shoppers say the customer loyalty program, where clientele are given cards on which they can redeem whenever they shop above a certain amount of money is

a major plus for their customers. Other players in the retail business also have such cards, but the rewards are more competitive.

Other supermarkets such as Uchumi, Shoprite, and Quality also have a similar system, but Capital Shoppers beats them on the rewards. For instance, a customer will get up to 4% discount on every Shs 5,000 spent. Other players in the market are offering discounts of between 1.5%–2%—half of that of Capital Shoppers.

There are some administrative challenges that some of the respondents have drawn attention to. One is the problem of enforcing food quality regulations that sustain the reputation of the sector. For example, the respondent from Uchumi suggested that although the Milk Industry Act of 2004 prohibits selling of raw milk, hawkers are still selling such milk. Furthermore, the modern food retailers and food suppliers are required to have TRA certificates and business licenses in order to sell raw milk. But this provision does not apply to hawkers. As a result, they can sell such items as raw milk at lower prices. Understandably, the supermarkets consider this unfair competition. The respondent, a Nakumatt Supermarket branch manager, explained it as follows:

If you look at Zambia and other countries, small shops in streets have been closed. You cannot see a butcher or a bakery in the streets. This has been done to allow government to collect taxes . . . but the situation in Tanzania is different.

Summary and Concluding Remarks

The discussions in this chapter show that the growth of the food retail sector in EAC, in general, and Tanzania, in particular, can be attributed to both internal and external factors. The internal factors are those related to changes in marketing practices within the food value chain itself. These include the availability of local food suppliers in a given country, innovation and upgrading within the value chain, and suppliers' acceptance of conditions of payment demanded by the supermarkets. Our study confirms arguments made by some earlier scholars that trade credit from suppliers is an important, but often neglected, source of finance for the growth of enterprises in developing economies.

The external factors include the growing middle class in individual East African countries, the changes in their lifestyle and work habits that make it convenient for them to shop at the supermarkets, and institutional support for the supermarkets and the local suppliers. The middle-income consumers are willing to buy their food items under better hygienic conditions, even if this means paying a little extra for the items. The results of our empirical investigations in Tanzania show that there has been a migration of low-income consumers from the traditional marketplaces to the supermarkets, due to loyalty marketing tactics adopted by the supermarkets. This trend has changed the image of the supermarkets, which were previously seen as shops for the affluent segments of the populations.

The Rise of Modern Food Retailing **237**

There is also evidence of supermarket-driven changes within the food retail sector in the East African region. Their emergence has encouraged the diffusion of minimum public quality standards for a wide range of locally produced food items. It has been noted that where public standards are lacking the supermarkets have introduced and enforced their private quality standards. It is not clear if this diffusion has influenced operations in the traditional markets as well. This issue should be a subject for future research.

We have noted that the supermarkets face some serious challenges that have led some to fold just a few years after they had started their operations. We have been unable to provide cogent reasons for these failures. Earlier scholars have also noted that research into the failure of international retailers has received limited attention in the existing literature. For example, relationships between countries and locations (stores) that have exited, and the reasons behind closures or withdrawals, may tell us more about the activity, process, company realities and the preconditions in target markets for the internationalization of the retail sector. We, therefore, suggest that this is a subject that requires more elaborate empirical investigation.

The discussions have also shown that there is the potent danger that the relational practices that the supermarkets adopt in countries such as Tanzania may result in the marginalization of the smaller local suppliers that may not have the investment resources required to upgrade their capacities or to wait for several months to receive payment for goods supplied.

Acknowledgment

This work originated from a PhD thesis submitted at Aalborg University by the first author and in which the second author was a supervisor. The authors would like to thank DANIDA for its support during PhD studies at Aalborg University in Denmark.

Notes

1 World Bank Global Economic Prospects (Washington, DC: World Bank, 2015).
2 African Development Bank, The Bank's Human Capital Strategy for Africa (2014–2018) (OSHD Department, May 2014).
3 Damian Hattingh et al., *The Rise of the African Consumer* (London: McKinsey Company, 2012).
4 Catherine McAuliffe, Sweta C. Saxena, and Masafumi Yabara, "The East African Community: Prospects for Sustained Growth," IMF Working Paper WP/12/272 (2012), accessed June 27, 2016, www.imf.org/external/pubs/ft/wp/2012/wp12272.pdf.
5 Mauro Paolo Gigineishvili and Ke Wang, "How Solid Is Economic Growth in the East African Community?," IMF Working Paper WP/14/150 (2014), accessed May 24, 2016, www.imf.org/external/pubs/ft/wp/2014/wp14150.pdf
6 John Kuada, "Marketing, Economic Growth, and Competitive Strategies of Firms in Africa," *African Journal of Economic and Management Studies* 7 (2016): 2.

7 Marion Mbogo, "The Impact of Mobile Payments on the Success and Growth of Micro-Business: The Case of M-Pesa in Kenya," *Journal of Language, Technology & Entrepreneurship in Africa* 2 (2010): 184.
8 Guillermo D'Andrea, Belen Lopez-Aleman, and Alejandro Stengel, "Why Small Retailers Endure in Latin America," *International Journal of Retail & Distribution Management* 34 (2006): 661.
9 Constanza C. Bianchi and Stephen J. Arnold, "An Institutional Perspective on Retail Internationalization Success: Home Depot in Chile," *The International Review of Retail, Distribution and Consumer Research* 14 (2004): 149.
10 Khairia Sehib, Elizabeth Jackson, and Matthew Gorton, "Gender, Social Acceptability and the Adoption of Supermarkets: Evidence From Libya," *International Journal of Consumer Studies* 37 (2013): 379.
11 Martin K. Hingley, "Power Imbalance in UK Agri-Food Supply Channels: Learning to Live With the Supermarkets?," *Journal of Marketing Management* 21, nos. 1–2 (2005): 64.
12 Ayman El-Amir and Steve Burt, "Sainsbury's in Egypt: The Strange Case of Dr Jekyll and Mr Hyde?" *International Journal of Retail & Distribution Management* 36 (2008): 300.
13 Robert M. Morgan and Shelby D. Hunt, "The Commitment-Trust Theory of Relationship Marketing," *The Journal of Marketing* 20 (July 1994): 25.
14 William A. Orme, "A Grocer Amid Mideast Outrage: Sainsbury Becomes a Target of Rumour of Israel Boycott," *The New York Post*, January 25, 2001, accessed June 14, 2014, www.nytimes.com/2001/01/25/business/grocer-amid-mideast-outrage-sainsbury-becomes-target-rumors-israel-boycott.html?pagewanted=all.
15 For the purpose of this study, Metro Cash and Carry will be considered a South African supermarket because in 1987 European investors withdrew from the firm due to political pressure.
16 Tjalling Dijkstra, Matthew Meulenberg, and Aad Van Tilburg, "Applying Marketing Channel Theory to Food Marketing in Developing Countries: Vertical Disintegration Model for Horticultural Marketing Channels in Kenya," *Agribusiness* 17 (2001): 230.
17 Kofi Q. Dadzie, Evelyn Winston, and Robert Hinson, "Competing With Marketing Channels and Logistics in Africa's Booming Markets: An Investigation of Emerging Supply Chain Management Practices in Ghana," *Journal of Marketing Channels* 22, 2 (2015): 137.
18 The data were collected September 2014 and February 2015 by the first author as part of his PhD dissertation work. For details, see Felix. A. Nandonde *Integrating Local Food Suppliers in Modern Food Retail in Africa* (PhD dissertation, Aalborg University, 2016).
19 "Capital Shoppers' Unstoppable Growth," *New Vision*, June 28, 2014.
20 "Fanisi Invest $6m in Tanzanian Firms," *The East African*, July 10, 2015.

Bibliography

African Development Bank. *The Bank's Human Capital Strategy for Africa: 2014–2018*. Abidjan, Côte d'Ivoire: OSHD Human and Social Development Department, May 2014.
Bianchi, Constanza C., and Stephen J. Arnold. "An Institutional Perspective on Retail Internationalization Success: Home Depot in Chile." *The International Review of Retail, Distribution and Consumer Research* 14 (2004): 149.
Dadzie, Kofi Q., Evelyn Winston, and Robert Hinson. "Competing With Marketing Channels and Logistics in Africa's Booming Markets: An Investigation of Emerging Supply Chain Management Practices in Ghana." *Journal of Marketing Channels* 22, no. 2 (2015): 137–152.
D'Andrea, Guillermo, Belen Lopez-Aleman, and Alejandro Stengel. "Why Small Retailers Endure in Latin America." *International Journal of Retail & Distribution Management* 34 (2006): 661.

Dijkstra, Matthew Meulenberg, and Aad van Tilburg. "Applying Marketing Channel Theory to Food Marketing in Developing Countries: Vertical Disintegration Model for Horticultural Marketing Channels in Kenya." *Agribusiness* 17 (2001): 227–241.

El-Amir, Ayman, and Steve Burt. "Sainsbury's in Egypt: The Strange Case of Dr Jekyll and Mr Hyde?" *International Journal of Retail & Distribution Management* 36 (2008): 300–322.

Gigineishvili, Mauro Paolo, and Ke Wang. *How Solid Is Economic Growth in the East African Community?* IMF Working Paper WP/14/150, 2014. Accessed May 24, 2016. www.imf.org/external/pubs/ft/wp/2014/wp14150.pdf.

Hattingh, Damian et al. *The Rise of the African Consumer.* London: McKinsey Company, 2012.

Hingley, Martin K. "Power Imbalance in UK Agri-Food Supply Channels: Learning to Live With the Supermarkets?" *Journal of Marketing Management* 21, nos. 1–2 (2005): 63–88.

Khairia, Sehib, Elizabeth Jackson, and Matthew Gorton. "Gender, Social Acceptability and the Adoption of Supermarkets: Evidence From Libya." *International Journal of Consumer Studies* 37, no. 4 (2013): 379–386.

Kuada, John. "Marketing, Economic Growth, and Competitive Strategies of Firms in Africa." *African Journal of Economic and Management Studies* 7, no. 1 (2016): 2–8.

Mbogo, Marion. "The Impact of Mobile Payments on the Success and Growth of Micro-Business: The Case of M-Pesa in Kenya." *Journal of Language, Technology & Entrepreneurship in Africa* 2, no. 1 (2010): 182–203.

McAuliffe, Catherine, Sweta C. Saxena, and Masafumi Yabara. "The East African Community: Prospects for Sustained Growth." IMF Working Paper WP/12/272, 2012. Accessed June 27, 2016. www.imf.org/external/pubs/ft/wp/2012/wp12272.pdf.

Morgan, Robert M., and Shelby D. Hunt. "The Commitment-Trust Theory of Relationship Marketing." *The Journal of Marketing* 20 (July 1994): 20–38.

Nandonde, Felix. A. "Integrating Local Food Suppliers in Modern Food Retail in Africa." PhD dissertation, Aalborg University, 2016.

Orme, William A. "A Grocer Amid Mideast Outrage, Sainsbury Becomes a Target of Rumor of Israel Boycott." *The New York Post*, January 25, 2001. Accessed June 14, 2014. www.nytimes.com/2001/01/25/business/grocer-amid-mideast-outrage-sainsbury-becomes-target-rumors-israel-boycott.html?pagewanted=all.

World Bank. *Global Economic Prospects.* Washington, DC: World Bank, 2015.

Section C: Agriculture

13

UNDERSTANDING THE ROLE OF BUSINESS DEVELOPMENT SERVICES IN DEVELOPING AGRIBUSINESS SMEs IN TANZANIA

Lola-Bona Vincent Lema and Daniel Wilson Ndyetabula

Introduction

In today's world, small and medium-sized enterprises (SMEs) find themselves in a constant business environment change.[1] If these changes are ignored, they may become a significant threat, but if anticipated, they may become valuable opportunities.[2] Almost all economies in developing countries are relying on primary export of agricultural products,[3] an activity that is dominantly undertaken by the informal private sector and SMEs. SMEs have proven to be the potential motor for economic growth in both the industrialized world and the developing world because of its great demonstration in dynamism and innovation.[4]

The importance of SMEs to social and economic development in Africa is undeniable.[5] SMEs are acknowledged for their contribution in improving national GDP through employment creation, income generation, foreign exchange earnings, and overall economic development and poverty reduction. For several decades, international aid agencies, donor agencies, and governments have seen the importance of supporting developing economies toward poverty alleviation.[6] Many funding agencies have invested heavily on support to business sector. Without regard to the potential role of SMEs in developing countries, absence of dynamic business sector that is efficiently linked to the dominant SME growth activities in developing countries makes it unlikely that these countries will reach the millennium development goals aiming to alleviate poverty.

In the context of Tanzania, SMEs account for more than 70% of all the registered businesses. According to Chang et al.,[7] Tanzania defines SMEs in terms of number of employees and the investment capital in such a way that small enterprises are those engaging between 5 and 49 employees with a capital investment starting from TShs. 5 million to 200 million, and medium enterprises are those engaging between 50 and 99 employees and have a capital investment from TShs. 200 million to 800 million.[8]

Apparently, SMEs contribute about 40% of Tanzania's GDP. Despite its significance in the contribution to the economy and creation of employment, seemingly SMEs in Tanzania perform poorly in terms of product development, standard, and quality.[9] Thus SMEs in Tanzania remain uncompetitive.[10] Chang et al.[11] indicated further that in recent years, for example, there has been a massive increase of imports to substitute the low-quality SME products from Tanzania. This situation threatens the survival of small-scale producers in Tanzania since the domestic markets are flooded with imports whose qualities are relatively high and less costly as compared to Tanzania's SME products.

In collaboration with several stakeholders, the government of Tanzania has been developing different policies and strategies to support the growth of private sector and SMEs.[12] One such development is the passing of SME policy in 2003, which led to the strengthening of such institutions as Small Industries Development Organization (SIDO) that works directly with SMEs in Tanzania. Institutionally, the government links with such private organizations as Tanzania Private Sector Foundation (TPSF), Private Agricultural Sector Support (PASS), Small and Medium Enterprises Competitiveness Facility (SCF) and many others to support, facilitate, and strengthen, among others, SME activities in Tanzania.[13]

It is important at this point to mention that potential and contribution of SMEs in such developing countries as Tanzania cannot be overemphasized. SMEs dominate the private sector in Tanzania, and they potentially employ large numbers of people in the country, especially in the agribusiness sector.[14] However, the key question that emerges against this background is why are SME activities especially in the agribusiness sector in Tanzania still not competitive, and what does the intervention to support SMEs do? This question seems to be complex due to several contextual backgrounds of Tanzania as a poor country. This study was undertaken to analyze SMEs in the agribusiness sector in Tanzania to enhance an understanding of the role of SME supportive interventions in Tanzania.

Previous studies have shown that sub-Saharan African (SSA) countries need to design policies and strategies that encourage entrepreneurship (private enterprise involvement) in agribusiness, upgrade agricultural technology, encourage innovation, and enhance value-added activities within the sector.[15] Diao and Dorosh[16] analyzed demand constraints on agricultural growth in seven East and Southern African countries using an applied general equilibrium framework.[16] The results showed that the best prospect for agribusiness activities remains in the food sector, where domestic and regional demand represent a large and growing market.

As most African economies are dependent on agriculture, agricultural value-addition activities are in the hands of private sector that is mainly dominated by private SMEs. Food sector activities in these countries are also done mainly by SMEs that are acknowledged for their contribution in improving national GDP through employment creation, income generation, foreign exchange earnings, and overall economic development and poverty reduction. In Tanzania, SMEs employ about 70% of the workforce and contribute to about one-third of GDP.[17] Nevertheless, most SMEs in Tanzania are informal and perform poorly.[18] There has also been a problem with low capital investments, financial constraints, low-quality products, standard issues, poor management skills, and market access.[19]

Dorward et al.[20] summed up all these SME problems into a collective market coordination problem. In this regard, they underscore the importance of market coordination and argue that coordination failure, increased transaction costs, and discouraged market participation are one of the most important factors explaining the poor performance of the African and, for that matter, Tanzanian agribusiness SME activities.

In efforts to intervene and facilitate SMEs to overcome market coordination challenges, several developing countries have developed SME intervention frameworks.[21] In Tanzania, for example, SMEs Competitiveness Facilities (SCF), a DANIDA project under Business Sector Program Support III, in collaboration with the Ministry of Industry and Trade in Tanzania, are established to support SMEs engaging in food processing and marketing by providing business development services (BDS) through the use of matching grant funds. The major purpose is to improve quality of their products, expand to new markets, and increase competitiveness among SMEs domestically and internationally.

Depending on their abilities to tackle the aforementioned problems, SMEs can take advantage of the market. However, there is still little understanding of how to go about it. It also happens that there is lack of research in the Tanzanian context, which covers the gap relating to learning and empowerment for small businesses and development or growth of the business as one of the needs that can improve SMEs' ability to address their most common problems. BDS is also young and still growing. It is a recent practice that donors accepted as a guiding thrust to small enterprise development.[22] It appears, therefore, that an understanding of SME support activities/intervention in developing countries is imperative to add to the knowledge of SME development in developing countries. It is the interest of this study to develop such understanding.

The overall objective of this study is to develop an understanding of how intervention through business development support services affects the performance of SMEs engaging in agri-food processing and marketing. To achieve the overarching objective, this study addresses the following research questions: How does intervention through business development support and affect the performance of SMEs engaging in agro-food processing and marketing? What types of BDS are provided to agro-food processing SMEs in Tanzania through the SCF intervention framework? What kind of model do BDS providers use to deliver services? How do agro-food SMEs perceive the received BDS in terms of improving their business? To what extent are SMEs' plans implemented, and how flexible are they in relation to the dynamic business environment? How do BDS providers bring in the concept of learning in small firms' businesses environment?

The knowledge gained from this study will contribute to the understanding of the role of BDS intervention in supporting agribusiness SMEs in Tanzania. This foundation is considered important to the policy makers, agribusiness SMEs, and other stakeholders such that it is made core to this study. Policy makers may integrate the understanding of the role of BDS intervention into different policy implicative strategies to further support and improve competitiveness of SMEs in Tanzania. SMEs, on the other hand, may use the generated understanding to bloom and unfold their competitive potentials through appropriate use of BDS.

Important in this study is the context of Tanzania, a country whose economy is dependent on agriculture and its agribusiness processing activities are dominated by SMEs. Over a period of one decade, there has also been SME supportive BDS intervention in Tanzania under SCF through matching grants. This contextual background gives this study an impetus to be executed in Tanzania. To such stakeholders as TPSF, PASS, SIDO, and others, this study will provide a platform to enhance institutional innovation in organizing SME supportive and subjective programs in Tanzania.

Theoretical and Analytical Framework

Theoretical Background

Although various BDS support has been provided to agribusiness SMEs in developing countries, the SMEs are still challenged by a number of growth problems that are now characterizing SMEs in developing countries.[23] Generally, SMEs in a globalizing world have more or less similar characteristics[24] as well as challenges, benefits, and opportunities.[25] In efforts to overcome the SME challenges, others have raised their opinions on the need for innovation and creativity,[26] appropriate policy,[27] and intervention from the business sector support systems[28] as the potential solutions for improving SMEs in the fast-growing economies.

Despite the fact that objectives vary, different support programs argue that SME growth activities can be improved with robust interventions that focus on creating conducive environments for the SMEs to strengthen their activities. According to Agyapong,[29] this can be achieved through the private sector, as it is the main source of employment creation and economic growth. Provision of BDS (such as business planning, training, and market linkages) is what Rogerson[30] suggested may contribute to improving SMEs' performance in developing countries. As SME activities in most countries dominate the private sector, it is apparent that supporting the private sector in these countries translates to supporting SMEs for economic wide impact. Due to this contextual background, this study theoretically draws from SME, business planning, and BDS literatures as presented in the following sections.

In most cases, what we know about how SMEs behave is based upon empirical studies,[31] which carefully assessed SMEs and found out that they are mainly faced with lack of human resources and relational capital. Rogerson[32] indicated further that the following are additional characters that bind African SMEs:

- They have the sense of insecurity and lack influence in their environment. In this, Rogerson[33] noted that African SMEs are 'pioneers of development' as they manage to survive in hostile business environment.
- They tend not to have a clear market position for their products. Most do not use the formal retail chain structure; besides, they supply to the small retail stores or enterprises that are involved in further processing of their products.
- They are unable to take advantage of economies of scale and economies of scope (liability of smallness).
- They seldom are involved in promotional activities. Because they cannot afford advertising, they do marketing through word-of-mouth.

Due to the increase of demand of quality food products worldwide, SMEs are now shaping their focus toward a market-based approach.[34] From this approach, many challenges and opportunities are arising. Rogerson[35] argued that poor and inadequate infrastructure and information systems in developing countries are what constrain entrepreneurs to explore new opportunities. One of the major constraints is limited access to financial services. Although the growing microfinance services in some countries play the major role in serving microenterprises and small enterprises, most of the small businesses are still inadequately funded from the owners' equity or funds from private sources such as friends and family members.[36] Very few receive formal financial services from banks.[37] This tendency may have been attributed to high lending costs.

The increasing trend of retail chains such as supermarkets in developing and developed countries has created a concern of what consumers demand in terms of nutritional and dietary values in processed food products.[38] According to Henson et al.,[39] this is happening with growing food demand. High demand of processed food gives an opportunity for SMEs to produce and supply more. But safety and standard requirements have become another constraint that resulted into failure of SMEs to seize the food demand opportunity.

Mather[40] considered variation in the quality and uneven supply of raw materials (such as animal feeds and quality wheat) another set of challenges to food processing SMEs in Africa. These problems are caused by variable costs of inputs used for processing, which lead to difficult operation environment, and as a result, the cash flow of SMEs is affected. Other different constraints facing SMEs that hinder them from enjoying the promising opportunity of accessing international markets as identified by Edwards et al.[41] are lack of market information, poor R&D and extension services, lack of clarity institutions, slowness in exploiting entrepreneurial opportunities and lack of business knowledge, difficulties in acquiring appropriate inputs, and the burden of some government regulations.

Overseas markets that have strict entry requirements difficult for SMEs to penetrate are highly targeted by African governments or donor agencies for agricultural products exports, whereas regional markets are commonly ignored.[42] More importantly, SMEs in many cases lack the ability to capture relevant information needed to access foreign markets. Shepherd[43] pointed out that by supporting development of domestic markets, small-scale producers will gain an advantage supplying to the local consumers and at the same time benefit all the actors in the value chain. Biénabe et al.[44] found that smallholders are variably constrained when trying to access markets. These constraints include high transaction costs, information asymmetry, high risks due to production and marketing, barriers to entry, lack of human and social capital, and low bargaining power. However, Gengatharen and Standing[45] found that the most significant factors affecting SMEs success or failure are SME owner lack of innovation, ownership structure and governance, matching focus with their supporters, and understanding of the support programs.

Business Planning and the Performance of SMEs

It is equally important to consider factors that relatively promote or inhibit growth of SMEs. One such factor is business planning. Wong et al. noted in their study of small businesses that fewer small businesses have a business plan and training budget than do larger businesses.[46]

Morrison et al.[47] argued that the major factors like intentions, abilities, and opportunities of the owner or manager affects performance of small businesses. They explore an in-depth understanding of whether the activities listed in the business plan are implemented and how it affects performance of SMEs. In the same study, Morrison et al.[48] found out that 47.5% extensively used the business plan, whereas 21.3% made a little use of it and 31.2% did not use it at all. Conclusively, their study indicates that there is a possible relationship between the use of a business plan and the achievement of business growth.

Timmons et al.[49] noted that business planning is important to firms. On the other hand, they argued that in today's dynamic business climate, the plan is obsolete the moment it goes into the printer. So flexibility and responsiveness become critical skills for survival. They also noted that having a business plan does not automatically make the business successful—it is the opportunity, requisite resources, and the team to pursue it that will make a difference.[50]

Karlsson and Honig[51] spotted examples of successful businesses entrepreneurs who did not have business plans to start with, for example, Bill Gates, Steve Jobs, Michael Dell, and Calvin Clain, but as time passed and competition grew, they had to develop several strategies and plans to remain competitive.

Initially, Delmar and Shane[52] argued that business planning helps firms to perform development activities, make quick decisions, manage resources supply and demand, and turn abstract goals into concrete operational activities. Later in 2004, Delmar and Shane[53] referred to business planning as a kind of symbolic act written or prepared to please particular stakeholders. Similarly, Karlsson and Honig[54] found out both that firms used their business plans to gain legitimacy from the external actors and that there is a weak relationship between planning and implementation.

Business development projects must be grounded and shaped by market realities,[55] and organizations should not have predetermined models but rather sufficient knowledge and capacity in different intervention options to respond effectively to market constraints.

Business Development Support

Private sector development promotion plays a major role in its contribution to development,[56] and economic growth is well achieved by private sector. Lankford[57] similarly noted that private sector and market forces are highly perceived as drivers to economic growth required to reducing poverty. Since the private sector in many developing countries is crowded by SMEs and operates in poor condition, most donors have developed an interest concerning intervention to promote SME activities.

The Consensus in the 1990s about the development thinking in private sector[58] brought the new idea in the field of business development services. Committee of Donor Agencies[59] for small enterprise development created a new approach that is more market oriented and client led, specifically for BDS, called a *new market development paradigm*.

Miehlbradt and McVay[60] defined BDS as a wide range of services used by entrepreneurs to help them efficiently operate and grow their businesses with a broader purpose of contributing to economic growth, employment generation, and poverty reduction.

Recent evidence suggests that access to relevant business support can lead to development of formal and informal business in developing countries.[61] The services can be in terms of either financial services or business development services. Even though it has been proven that achieving sustainability in microenterprises is difficult compared to small and medium firms, BDS intervention in activities such as quality upgrading, marketing support, training, and improving market access might assist them. However, the USAID EDP program that directly supported BDS and SMEs proved that not all components performed well.[62] Similarly, BDS should neither be held responsible for the failure of SMEs nor should it claim responsibility for their success.

The Committee for Donor Agencies also supports the former view for Small Enterprises Development (CDASED), which observed that the supply of non-financial business services is essential to comprehend enterprise medium and long-term strategic issues.[63] Additionally, they noted that BDS include training, marketing assistance, advisory and consultancy services, promotion of business linkage, and information, technology change and transfer. Bear et al.[64] noted that the central task of BDS market development is to facilitate and that it requires relevant business experience to interact credibly to earn trust among the market players, understand business problems, and see valid project opportunities for market development.

Arroyo-Vázquez et al.[65] considered BDS as part of innovative and creative entrepreneurship support service that has to be provided by the universities, which again has to be jointly managed with the entrepreneurship encouragement. They suggested that universities should train not only entrepreneurs but also people who will offer support and advice to entrepreneurs.

Basic Principles of the BDS Approach

According to Caniëls et al.,[66] the key feature of new BDS approach suggests that services should be organized along commercial lines, and it requires indirect facilitation from NGOs, donors, and other developmental agencies that target BDS providers with sufficient technical assistance and incentives to launch new services. The diversification of activities provided should intend to help SMEs improve their businesses. Miehlbradt and McVay[67] identified BDS categories with examples of services under each category (see Table 13.1).

Figure 13.1 shows the whole chain of actors comprising the BDS facilitators (NGOs, donors, etc.). Donor funds are taken to the 'international facilitators'

TABLE 13.1 BDS Categories With Examples of Services

Market Access:	Training and Technical Assistance:
• market linkages	• mentoring
• trade fairs and product exhibitions	• feasibility studies and business plans
• market information	• exchange visits and business tours
• subcontracting and outsourcing	• management training
• marketing trips and meetings	• technical training
• market research	• counseling/advisory services
• packaging	• accountancy and bookkeeping
• advertising	

Source: Modified from Miehlbradt and McVay[68]

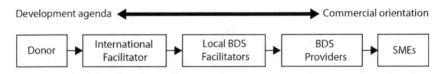

FIGURE 13.1 Chain of Actors in BDS Facilitation

Source: Modified from Caniëls et al.[70]

whose role is to promote good practice, initiate innovation, and develop new ideas. These international facilitators, in turn, finance projects in partnership with 'local BDS facilitators' in developing countries, of which are the actual suppliers of BDS services (BDS providers) to develop new services or products, setting standards, influencing government policies, and exploring new markets. Caniëls et al.[69] argued that the role of BDS providers lies in the actual service delivery itself and that BDS providers are on the supply side in direct contact with the SME clients.

However, Bergek and Norrman[71] argued that the most concern of business development services should be related to business development and training features, which include coaching and education related to business planning, leadership, marketing, and sales.

The Importance of BDS

In recent years, credit provision has been the major form of support, and the role of BDS support has been neglected, the main reason being the services are expensive with limited impact, are not sustainable and have uncertain paybacks, and tend to be supply driven.[72]

Since the 'discovery' of informal sector in 1970s, international agencies and governments supported farmers in different forms of support such as credit subsidies, technical support, training in business, training on how to identify market and have access to the market, and many others.[73]

In the beginning, BDS was focusing more on how the services should be offered rather than which specific services should be offered.[74] The importance of BDS as described by several authors is as follows:

- Provision of distinct service that an enterprise cannot generate internally; ease access to the required credit from the financial institutions.[75]
- Creation of networks among the business stakeholders to achieve the optimal outcome out of the suggested activities. For example, Ghobadian and Gallear[76] discovered that SMEs mistrust help from outside, and there is little interaction and information sharing among them. In the meantime, pressure is put on large firms to support SMEs or group of SMEs, through, for example, subcontracting networks, to provide a strong base for business linkages.[77]
- Promotion of innovation and entrepreneurial skills among small producers.[78]

Training, Counseling, and Networking for SMEs Development

SMEs' development depends on their ability to adopt profitable ideas and experiment to start or expand their businesses.[79] By recognizing this as important activity for business development, business training as a development tool is used increasingly by development organizations to uplift SMEs.[80] For example, YHUA scheme, which was funded by the European Commission (EC), found that high level of education and training provided to the employees of SMEs will provide them with the resources required to produce desired innovation.[81] It was also assumed that more innovation will bring more competition, creating more jobs and bringing more wealth to the economy.

Nieman[82] argued that the task of business service providers is to facilitate the delivery of efficient and high quality non-financial support services, which are training/education, counseling, and business planning. Further, he suggested that small business training must be closely related to small business environment and not based on the management of large enterprises, and that in order for training to be effective, it should be kept simple for small enterprises. Counseling is about empowering people to make fundamental decisions for themselves instead of solely accepting advice on what to do.[83]

For survival and growth of the firm, Rice[84] emphasized that there are resource gaps that need to be remedied through networking and counseling, which may be available through an affiliation between the service providers and SMEs. Developing and managing networking infrastructure is a significant function since most entrepreneurs lack credibility and a history of operation. Bergek and Norrman[85] argued that engaging in network mediation, which is considered beyond just networking, may establish information, knowledge, and expertise that are vital for the survival of new businesses and may also reduce the uncertainties entrepreneurs' experience. Westhead and Storey[86] studied the impact of management training and SMEs performance, and they concluded that some types of management training are effective in enhancing SME performance whereas others are not. However, Westhead and Storey[87] mentioned that small firms that have participated in management training have reported their businesses have derived some benefits from participating.

SME-BDS Interaction: Learning of SMEs in Relation to Skills Development and Goal Achievement

Having realized the importance or learning for small firms, Ram and Deakins[88] stated,

> We do not understand how entrepreneurs learn, yet it is accepted that there is learning experience from merely establishing a new enterprise. The learning process that is involved in business and enterprise development is poorly understood, yet programs have been devised and interventions are made in business development support. There is now a need for re-focusing research away from the emphasis on picking successful entrepreneurs or picking winners, to identifying key issues in the learning and developmental processes of entrepreneurship.

Therefore, it is equally relevant to consider the process in which learning is taking place.

Interaction between a client and a service provider is a very important factor for the success of the project.[89] Numerous studies have attempted to explain the theoretical models of the interaction can be regarded either as (1) the expert model whereby the client has less emphasis on solving problems and the consultant is seen as an expert who has access to knowledge base of a particular practice and dominates the relationship, or (2) social learning model whereby the client and consultant are active players in diagnosis (mutually dependent), problem-solving process and solution development, since it is believed that the client has valuable knowledge that needs to be incorporated also.[90]

For small businesses, learning may serve a purpose of optimizing current performance and performance in the long term as well as enhancing personal development.[91] St-Jean noted that learning in the small firms may have a big impact on how SMEs will in future learn how to solve their own problems, gain knowledge and skills, and have a better understanding on the environment they are working with, and perhaps increase sales or improve profitability.[92] BDS who provide support can offer a learning opportunity for SMEs by giving feedback and allowing individuals to learn and attempt the implementation of new ideas.[93]

One way for both parties to make the most out of intervention is through a proper learning process that involves SMEs and BDS providers. One question that needs to be asked is how the facilitation process from the BDS is taking part to help SMEs improve their businesses in the long term.

Learning style adopted in this study is based on the concept of the experiential learning cycle as it was structured by Heron.[94] In this, experiential learning cycle is conceptualized as a cycle consisting of four consecutive stages: (1) conceptual understanding, (2) imaginal understanding, (3) practical understanding, and (4) experiential understanding. It starts with conceptual understanding, where the trainer describes what is involved in experiencing the desired skill. Then they move to imaginal understanding, when skills are demonstrated where they can form an image of the sequence of behavior that manifest the skill. At the first two stages of the cycle, the facilitator takes responsibility for structuring the learning process by modeling the skills and describing the exercise. By doing this, the trainees will be guided to the practical skills and understand how to do it to bring an experiential understanding by practicing skills with other people. On the second cycle, feedback on the practice starts by returning the trainee to the conceptual understanding. Comments given reflect what the trainees go through in the practical and experiential understanding. This will lead to the improved imaginal understanding, where better image is built, then better practice, and so on. Figure 13.2 illustrates the cycle. Finally, trainees and facilitator come together to coordinate reviews for trainees' autonomous practice and feedback.

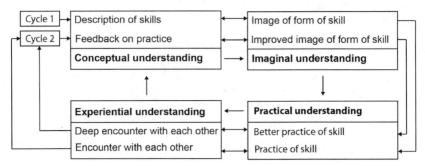

Figure 2: Experiential learning cycle (Source: Heron (1999))

FIGURE 13.2 Experiential Learning Cycle

Source: Heron[95]

The upper cycle represents the reflection phase and the lower cycle represents the action phase. Heron argued that going around the cycle several times enhances learning and improves interpersonal skills of both the service provider (facilitator) and the trainee. The benefits from such a learning situation can be neither immediate nor easily measurable, but they may be significant and eventually be reaped by SMEs themselves.[96] In a reviewed study of Zahra and George,[97] it was noted that dynamic capability pertaining to knowledge creation and utilization enhances a firm's ability to gain and sustain competitive advantage.

Van Gelderen et al.[98] argued that it is of crucial importance for entrepreneurs to master relationships with other business partners such as clients and suppliers, since entrepreneurial learning occurs through interaction with others. This argument supports the fourth stage of experiential learning cycle, which is better understood through encounters with other business actors. However, Kubr pointed out that mistakes happen in the early stages but it is part of the general learning process. He also argued that it is the consultant's task to minimize errors made in these stages.[99]

Analytical Framework

To identify the methodological and practical characteristics that may be responsible for significant variations in the findings, a detailed analytical framework was developed in an iterative process. The framework is developed on the basis of our understanding of theories and various mechanisms in this study that shaped the outcome of the concepts employed. The framework is built on the work of Miehlbradt and McVay,[100] who identified the types of BDS services and Heron,[101] who explained the elements of BDS facilitation determining the outcome which are SMEs focus. In other words, we assume that there is a link between BDS

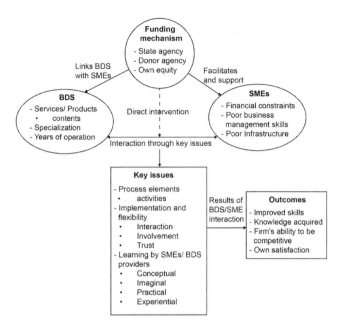

FIGURE 13.3 Analytical Framework

providers' knowledge ability and type of services that trigger specific consequences in the supported small firms' growth.

In this framework, BDS providers are viewed as the main facilitators, whose role is to promote and develop skills, knowledge, and capacity of small firms. The approach undertaken by the service providers has, to a greater extent, enhanced SMEs business growth. The key issues presented are based on the approach BDS providers take to address various matters to SMEs, the interaction of service providers with SMEs, implementation and flexibility on the planned activities, and learning based on the knowledge transferred from service providers to the SMEs. The outcome signifies the extent to which SMEs have improved their situations, resulting in a positive effect. Figure 13.3 illustrates the logic model underlying the analytical framework.

Research Methodology

The Research Design

The nature of the research questions in this study (i.e., what, how, and to what extent) called for research strategy that gave rich data to understand phenomena in their real-life context. The questions intended to uncover types of BDS, perception of the BDS, the extent of business plan implementation in the real-life activities of the SMEs, and the aspect of learning for SMEs as a result of receiving BDS services. In this situation, a researcher can hardly separate the context from the phenomena under study. According to Yin,[102] qualitative case studies are more suitable when phenomena under study can hardly be separated from their contexts. Silverman[103] asserted further that qualitative case studies explore what is going on in the real social environment and provide a holistic understanding of the context. With this background, this study employed qualitative case studies to identify type of BDS and established the perceptual understanding of BDS. Additionally, it employed a comparative analysis between the SME business plan and the actual activities of the SMEs to establish the extent of implementation adequacy of the planned SME activities.

According to Robson and McCartan,[104] case study is a strategy for doing research, which involves an empirical investigation of a particular contemporary phenomenon within its real-life context. Yin[105] asserted that this 'context' makes each case unique, thereby providing the opportunity to obtain different contextual information about the case. A case may, therefore, vary from situation to situation and may include individual, company, communities, departments, and so forth[106] The context that is under consideration in this study is that of BDS rendered to agribusiness SMEs in Tanzania through SCF framework. Thus, we treated each SME and BDS as units of analysis in an embedded multiple-case design.

Criticisms of the Case Study Research

Admittedly, we are aware of the ongoing scholarly criticisms about qualitative case study as a research strategy. Opponents of the case study criticize the strategy on the grounds that it lacks scientific rigor. According to Remenyi and Williams,[107] this critique is eminent perhaps because the aim of case study research is not to test any hypothesis. It is assumed that the use of subjective judgments during the data collection and analysis stage can render case studies construct invalid and unreliable.[108] Nevertheless, methodology contributors[109] have criticized the use of words 'reliability' and 'validity' as operational measures to judge the quality of qualitative research on the grounds that the words are more suitable for quantitative research. Instead, they developed four corresponding constructs for judging the quality of qualitative research including case study. Riege[110] called the four constructs test design: (1) confirmability, (2) credibility, (3) transferability, and (4) dependability.

According to Narteh,[111] confirmability assesses the extent to which interpretation of data is done in an objective and unbiased manner (i.e., whether the conclusions are the most reasonable ones from the data). Credibility involves the extent to which informants and peers approve the research findings. Transferability measures the extent to which findings confirm or reject a priori theory or similar research done within similar or different settings. Finally, dependability intends to assess the ability and consistency in the whole research process. The four constructs of test design in qualitative researches take the position of validity and reliability in quantitative researches, and we use the terms 'reliability' and 'validity' to refer to the four constructs.

To ensure validity of this study, the following undertakings were applied:

1   Refined and clear establishment of the research problems through presentations with peers. Suggestions from peers helped to shape the problem and research questions derived from it. Also, seminars with peers were used to define and establish the unit of analysis in order to focus the interview questions/topics.
2   Methodological triangulation, which according to Patton[112] require the combination of different methods and theories to study the phenomenon, was also employed in this study. For example, multiple sources of evidence were explored, that is, interviews with SMEs owners, BDS providers, and SCF official and additional information in terms of companies' documents.
3   Personal observation and response on reviews and feedback from the key informants were considered useful process of validation, having the respondent agree or disagree with what I gathered from them.

To ensure reliability of this study, the following undertakings were applied:

The use of interview guide and discussion with the key informants. During the interview, the respondents were recorded, the interviews were then transcribed, and some additional field notes were produced to support the data.

Study Area and Case Selection

This study involved a total of three SMEs and three BDS providers as case studies, one in Kilimanjaro region, one in Dar es Salaam and one in Kagera region, with two service providers from Dar es Salaam and one from Arusha (see Table 13.2). According to Yin,[113] replication logic underlying multiple-case study is that the cases must be carefully selected to predict either similar results (literal replication) or contrasting results (theoretical replication). In this study, we employed theoretical replication, using purposive sampling method so that diverse variation is covered and used to identify common patterns in the cases.[114]

The main selection criterion used were that (1) the case must be small sized, operating in dairy industry, and be under the framework of SCF; and (2) the case must be from different locations (northern, eastern, and western regions) due to presumably the differences in the accessibility of BDS services and availability of resources.

The case selection screening procedure was conducted during the fieldwork with the help from SCF officers. The qualified SMEs were contacted and briefed about the purpose of the study to have their consent prior to the site visits and interviews. At the end of an interview, SMEs were asked to mention service

TABLE 13.2 Company Overview Used for Case Study Selection

Case	1	2	3
Company Name	Profate Investment Ltd	West Kilimanjaro Dairy Products	DELCO Ltd
Region	Dar es Salaam	Kilimanjaro	Kagera
Town	Ilala	Sanya juu	Kyaka
Business sector	Dairy	Dairy	Dairy
Equity (% contribution)			
Owner equity	54%	39%	18.6%
Grant funds	46%	61%	81.4%
Year of establishment	1993	2000	2005
Markets			
Regional	X		X
National		X	
First contact to SCF:	2011	2010	2009
Size total matching grant (Tsh)	145,630,000/=	73,505,000/=	96,667,800/=
Number of BDS providers involved in grant	1	4	1

providers they have been working with at least in areas where the proposed activity was completed. The service providers were contacted by telephone and briefed about the study the same way as SMEs.

Both primary and secondary data were used in this study, and they were collected using document analysis and key informant interviews and direct observation. Documents including SMEs' business proposals for funding, progress reports of funds implementation, funds application templates, and BDS providers' profiles were analyzed for each case study. These documents were used to complement and supplement data obtained from the interviews. Key informants including SME owners, BDS providers, and a SCF officer were interviewed. BDS providers identified types of service inputs they provide to SMEs and their way of approaching SMEs problems. On the other hand, SMEs, which received BDS support, gave their perception or views on the services they received with regards to development of their products and market access improvements. The SCF officer was once interviewed to give a general overview of the SMEs and BDS providers involved in the project. SCF officials were also consulted to give guidance on the selection of cases in addition to providing documents such as business plans and progress reports for further evaluation of the cases.

Semi-structured interviews were conducted to the key informants selected, except for SCF officials whose interview was unstructured. Interviews were flexible to allow new questions to be raised following what the interviewee had said, and they were also allowed to ask any questions concerning the study or any matter that arose. Generally, interview content comprised general background information of the companies and information about the themes identified in research questions.

Our own observation of some of the SMEs activities and production sites visits provided additional information and evidence. I also had an opportunity to visit points of sale and taste their products.

Data Collection Tools

The tools used for data collection were mainly interview questions guidelines, a voice recorder, and notes taken at the field. According to Yin,[115] an interview is one of the most important sources of information when doing a case study. Most of the questions from the interviews were open ended, which gave respondents a chance to freely express their opinions, knowledge, and understanding of the matter in a conversational manner. Some of the questions were closed ended, which were set to clarify a specific situation explained in open-ended questions.

The voice recorder was used under the permission of the interviewees after the plan for transcription was made clear to them. It was previously made clear to them because the use of an audio device may distract the informants and, in turn, the quality of information given.

Data Analysis

Qualitative data are hard to analyze. Because of this, Miles[116] described qualitative data as an attractive nuisance. In the literature, much space often is given about data collection methods but little space is given for data analysis. This has created a challenge for researchers about how to move between the amount of raw data collected and the conclusion drawn from the data. According to Narteh,[117] this view was echoed by Miles and Huberman,[118] who observed that in data analysis one cannot ordinarily follow how a researcher went from 3,000 pages of field notes to the final conclusion. To deal with this challenge, Eisenhardt[119] and Miles and Huberman[120] proposed a framework for qualitative data analysis that involves data reduction, data display, and conclusion drawing. This study adapted the framework by Miles and Huberman[121] in analysis of the collected data. The data were reduced and displayed and the conclusion drawn in an iterative way to answer the research questions of this study.

Triangulated materials were employed to enrich the contextual background of this study and to contribute to drawing conclusions on the research questions. A comparative analysis of the actual SME activities and the planned activities was undertaken to establish the extent of implementation of the SMEs' business plans.

Data Presentation and Analysis

This section presents the information collected from semi-structured interviews with small and medium enterprises of dairy sector that were supported by SCF in Tanzania, their correspondent BDS providers, and business manager from SCF.

Some additional information came from business proposals submitted to SCF by SMEs interviewed and personal observation from the field.

The following themes were analyzed to explore how they might influence the overall performance of SMEs after receiving business development support services:

- Types of BDS services provided
- The kind of approach BDS providers use to deliver services
- Perception of SMEs on the services they receive
- Implementation and flexibility of SME plans
- SMEs' learning experience with BDS providers.

The collected data are presented in terms of case description (general description of the enterprise and the facilitating SCF project, challenges, and opportunities) and cross-case presentation (comparative analysis identifying relationships of various patterns among the cases). Case description for two companies and SCF project are presented in this section.

Data Presentation

Case 1: Profate Investment Limited—PIL

Background

PIL is a registered limited company in the milk processing and marketing sector. It is situated at Segerea area in Ilala district, Dar es Salaam. It started as a family enterprise in 1993. At first, it was meant to support and increase the family income, but later, the owner expanded the scope of production by recruiting more milk producers to supply large volumes of milk so that they can increase the sale volumes.

The vision as expressed by the company *is to become the leading cheese processor and marketer of other dairy products in Tanzania* and its mission statement is *to increase milk market share by ensuring quality, quantity, and standard of the products to the final consumers.*

The company's turnover is approximately 18 million Tanzanian shillings, with the capacity of milk collected and processed standing at 75,311 liters per year.

Production

The main products produced by this company are pasteurized milk, cultured milk (both full cream and skimmed milk), mozzarella cheese, feta cheese, halloumi cheese, and ghee. Operationally, the company collects fresh milk from numerous small-scale suppliers and processes the milk into the aforementioned products. The products are subsequently marketed in a number of domestic markets. Milk collection takes place mainly in two collection centers, where suppliers deliver the milk daily. Upon delivery, the milk is tested, and when accepted, further processing follows. On average, the amount of milk collected and processed per month amounts to 6,000 liters, but it varies during the high and low seasons. The capacity of the company is slightly underutilized due to various technical challenges like absence of appropriate technology for cheese processing, difficulties in monitoring milk collections, and shortage of milk processing equipment.

Firm Organization

The business owner has a long practical experience with the dairy industry in Tanzania, and she holds a post-graduate diploma in International Business and Management. The company has eight employees, four women and four men (see Figure 13.4). Occasionally, the company receives assistance from professional consultants, mostly concerning business development services.

Marketing Organization

PIL mainly sells milk in Dar es Salaam, although it is planning to expand its market range to reach more customers in the country through improving a large number of milk suppliers, product promotion, and the use of different pricing strategies. Currently, the firm is facing a major challenge in the domestic market, which is flooded by imported milk products, in addition to a serious lack of availability of milk product packaging materials, leading to high production costs, as packaging materials have to be purchased from Kenya, South Africa, or India.

The Buyers

Since its expansion, the firm is collecting more milk, processing the milk, and selling the milk to the nearby factory and to the loyal customers through two company sales points: retail shops and supermarkets in Dar es Salaam.

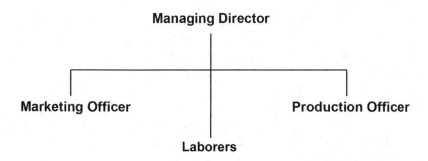

FIGURE 13.4 Organization Structure of PIL

Dairy Processing

Despite the challenges in the industry, the company has experienced remarkable growth. According to the business owner, the sales have increased, but the firm's capacity to satisfy the market demand is still low. Besides, they also face difficulties in relation to business management skills, financial management, and ICT utilization as well as suppliers' group organization. All these challenges have to be properly addressed for the company to meet its full production potential.

Involvement With the Project

Through its association with SCF project, PIL was linked to various business service providers. Through the SCF intervention, PIL has received a 54% contribution from the matching grant. The grant was used mainly for capacity building activities such as organization of small dairy holders for milk quality trainings, acquisition of processing technology, and market research.

BDS Intervention

The aim of the matching grant was to improve overall business performance and competitiveness. Through the use of BDS support, the grant has helped PIL to conduct market research, develop its own brand, improve labels and packaging materials, and create the company website. In addition, PIL has been able to participate in various training sessions, trade fairs, and exhibitions. These have, to a good extent, developed the business and taken it to a better place. For example, there are now acquired reliable sources of quality milk from suppliers, more appealing products now than before brand development was done, and a remarkable increase in the number of customers.

Case 2: West Kilimanjaro Dairy Products—WKDP

Background

West Kilimanjaro Dairy Product (WKDP) is a company that processes and markets dairy products such as cheese, ghee, and butter. The company started operating in 2000 before it was legally established under the Business Registration and Licensing Agency in Tanzania in the year 2008. It is grouped under the category of small businesses, and the owners are mainly family members who are a husband and a wife who assists in record keeping. The company is situated at Sanya Juu, Siha District in Kilimanjaro region. The owner has more than 8 years' worth of experience in the business, although he started working in the dairy farm where he gained the knowledge of producing cheese.

Production

The company's main produce is cheese, ghee, and butter, although the owner is intending in the future to expand his business into fresh milk and yogurt processing. As of December 2009, the amount of cheese produced was 51.6 tons. An average of 1,700 liters of milk is collected daily from peasant farmers during the peak seasons and about 700 liters during the low seasons. Currently, he is dealing with mushroom business as a part of a non-milk production line; however, it is practiced in a very small scale. Even with an increase in production and sales, WKDP has not yet met the increasing demand of cheese in the market.

Market Organization

The company's major customers are tourist hotels and tour operator companies mainly in Arusha, Moshi, Tanga, and Dar es Salaam. WKDP has opened more than 13 outlets for their products in those regions. Efficient road systems near the company's area simplify accessibility of material collection and distribution of products. The business service mentioned that the enterprise has a reliable source of milk supply because it is attached to various cooperatives and farmers' associations.

Involvement With SCF Project

The matching grant received from SCF-DANIDA project through the assistance provided by BDS services was 39% contributed by WKDP and 61% by SCF itself. Funds provided by SCF have played a major role in WKDP, enabling the enterprise to engage in BDS services for capacity-building intervention in different ways. Among the services were market survey, product standards improvements, development of attractive packaging and promotion of materials and labels, and overall business skills improvement.

BDS Intervention

The support provided for WKDP was meant to help face the challenges encountered in the market, although it seemed that it was doing well in the local market, despite the fact that it has never undertaken any market survey. So the services offered were meant to realize more opportunities in the market, regionally and nationally, in addition to improving the product quality. There have been several trainings he attended for milk processing technique in addition to participating in various trade exhibition events in Tanzania that were made known to the owner. BDS has also intervened in areas such as branding and product labeling and packaging material quality improvements. This has been done so as to attract more new customers. Other challenges like financial support for production investment and poor business management skills have also been addressed for support in this enterprise. Since BDS has intervened, WKDP has been able to explore more opportunities and improve business skills in various ways.

SCF Project Description

Small and Medium Enterprise Competitiveness Facility (SCF) was sponsored by DANIDA under the Business Sector Program Support III (BSPS III). SCF entered its second phase in 2008, which ended in 2015. The first phase (2005–2008) focused on helping agribusiness small and medium enterprises (SME) in Tanzania adding value to products and finding new markets. In its second phase, SCF was more concentrated on assisting SMEs in their efforts to develop domestic and international growth opportunities in food processing and food marketing. The support was generally aimed at improving product quality through improved packaging materials and labels, acquiring quality certification and barcodes, outsourcing new and better technologies, developing products; finding potential buyers through export negotiations, and supporting import substitution initiatives. SCF also advised and mentored SMEs on branding and rebranding and market positioning, and offered guidance on pricing policies.

A limited number of sectors have been given priority due to either their potential growth in sales and productivity or need for technology utilization. These sectors include dairy, edible oilseed, honey, processed fruits and vegetables, red meat, cereals and grains, snacks, and prepared meals. The targeted markets are export markets, food retailer stores (supermarkets and groceries) based in Tanzania, and food service companies (hotels, airlines).

The SCF Project Process

Tasks are performed using the SCF project cycle application procedure (see Figure 13.5), which has to be completed within 30 days from the submission of the concept note to the matching grant approval. Interested beneficiaries submit concept notes to be assessed and processed by SCF only when eligibility criteria are fulfilled. Business managers will, therefore, visit the site of the applicant to inspect the business environment and see whether the SME is qualified for the next step of the matching grant proposal writing. Business managers circulate the concept to the team, together with the comments and preliminary recommendation. Upon successful submission of the concept note, business managers forward the proposal format and invite the client to submit a proposal. If the concept note is not within the scope of SCF, the note is rejected and business managers counsel the applicant on alternative options.

SCF clients are expected to submit the proposal within 30 days after the invitation. Business managers maintain contact with clients during the proposal

Developing Agribusiness SMEs in Tanzania **265**

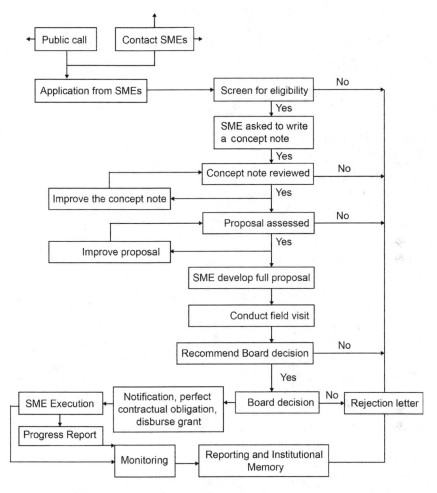

FIGURE 13.5   SCF Application Process Flowchart

writing process and, if called for, may link them to a BDS provider for assistance to develop the proposal. Business managers ask for and receive feedback from the international advisor and/or the director on proposal. If accepted by the management, the director forwards the proposal to the Board, and if declined, the director forwards to Board for endorsement.

The proposal is finally recommended for Board review and decision. Following the approval of the proposal, the applicant is informed about clarifications of contractual agreements and disbursement of the matching grant funds. Before authorization of transfer of money by the director, business managers introduce the accountant and the monitoring and evaluation consultant to the client and sets the stage for longer-term relations. Accountant and monitoring and evaluation consultant brief client on SCF requirements on funds management.

Data Analysis

BDS Service Provision

Types of Services Provided

The BDS providers are mainly engaged in providing consultancy services, technical advice, and training in areas related to entrepreneurship, international trade development, market survey/research, feasibility studies, events organization, brand development, and supply contract management. BDS providers differ in areas of specialization as well as years that they have been in operation in such kind of business. BDS 1 and BDS 2 stated that they are covering different discipline of businesses, whereas BDS 3 is mainly based on dairy sector. It was observed that the BDS industry is still low in Tanzania since the interviewed service providers have been in operation for fewer than 5 years.

What we observed from a small number of those who were interviewed is that common services, which were provided to them, are market research and brand development. Another service is events organization, which aims to promote SMEs' product, most of the time during the trade fair and trade exhibition events across the country. Business skills–related training, workshops, and seminars also seemed to take a great part of the support services. However, the services received by SMEs were aligned to SCF support requirements, so there is no wide-ranging chance of receiving other forms of support that SMEs expressed they needed. Most of what SMEs needed includes intensive capital good investment and access to advanced technological equipment. Although it is clearly shown that SCF supports outsourcing new technologies, SMEs still are experiencing a problem in accessing better equipment to support technology utilization. There is, therefore, a discrepancy between the services provided and the real-life need of the entrepreneurs.

An interesting remark was made when the interviewed SMEs stated that SCF is the one that usually arranges for training, seminars, and workshops. This again contrasted with what BDS providers have stated about their involvement in this activity. The fact that the mentioned services are mostly offered by SCF and not initiated by the service providers may be because of limited amount of financial resources or the split roles played between SCF and the service providers.

The overall response to this question revealed that BDS providers have emphasized different levels of intervention in these services. For example, BDS 3 required an up-front assurance that he can have room to monitor the implementation for the solution he offers to SMEs. Meanwhile, BDS 1, for example, considers after-care services as one of the major components in service he delivers, and he offers it for free, contrary to the rest of the interviewed BDS providers, who deliver only when their clients derive demand from it and when clients are bearing the costs.

Type of Clients and Their Relationship

The targeted clients are mostly non-government organizations (NGOs), government projects, international organizations, multinational companies, donor-fund projects, and individual business entities. Therefore, SCF project can be directly linked to these consultancy firms in a sense that they recommend SMEs to work with them or indirectly related to them when SMEs get to choose their own service providers. Figure 13.6 shows the link between SMEs relationship with SCF project, BDS providers, and the intermediary person who happened to be involved with SMEs before SCF intervention or engagement with service providers. The role of the intermediary person as how it was observed on SME 2 and BDS 3 cases, is to advise, mentor, and link the SMEs to various business development programs, which is the same as how it would be with the normal service provider except that they may have direct or indirect linkage with SCF and service providers of their clients.

Turning now to the experimental evidence on the most problematic areas facing SMEs in Tanzania, BDS providers had different opinions (See Table 13.3).

On average, money seemed to be the most problematic area for the SMEs' expansion, because many financial institutions have difficult conditions attached to the loans. Next to monetary problems are managerial problems, whereby service providers and small business owners lack managerial skills to run their businesses and their education level is low. Analysis showed that SCF has intervened

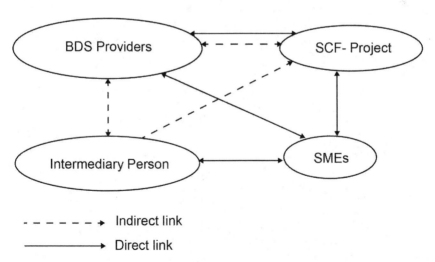

FIGURE 13.6 The Relationship Between SMEs, BDS Providers, and SCF Project

268 L.-B. V. Lema and D. W. Ndyetabula

TABLE 13.3 BDS Ranking on the SMEs Problematic Areas

Problematic Areas	BDS 1 Ranking	BDS 2 Ranking	BDS 3 Ranking
Managerial	1. Managerial	1. Managerial	1. Monetary
Monetary	2. Monetary	2. Monetary	2. Machines
Marketing	3. Marketing	3. Material	3. Motivation
Motivation	4. Machines	4. Marketing	4. Managerial
Mental	5. Material	5. Machines	5. Marketing
Machines	6. Mental	6. Motivation	6. Mental
Material	7. Motivation	7. Mental	7. Material

Source: Adapted from Kubr[122] and own elaboration based on data collected

in these areas to a large extent, but SMEs still have not been able to sustain themselves financially. On the other hand, SMEs reported significant changes in the way they operated the businesses before and after BDS support.

Regarding machinery problems, service providers and SMEs indicated that it is a big problem and argued that more flexibility is needed to support capital investment. Further analysis showed that SMEs do not get support to acquire capital goods under SCF intervention. Perhaps there are many other different government or private projects that are directing their support toward capital investment, but SMEs do not take a chance to explore those opportunities.

The Approach BDS Providers Use to Deliver Services

This study has been able to demonstrate different approaches taken by BDS providers to deliver the services. The approaches might differ at some points; however, all three consultants are seemingly following similar approaches (see Figure 13.7). In all the cases, clients are being attached by the government projects, donor funds projects, or NGOs, although it occurred that sometimes clients are recommended by other clients to work with a particular BDS provider, as mentioned by BDS 1 and BDS 2.

The method followed by the service providers starts from going into a mutual understanding of the concepts to be worked on, discussing and understanding what is the problem. The service provider with his or her client goes through the company's preliminary details by doing business synopsis. In this stage, the client and the service provider get a chance to explain to each other on one hand, what needs to be assessed, and on the other hand, the advisory service. The expected outcomes from both sides are made clear, and the service provider may get a chance to visit the client's production site before he or she starts to address the problem. Afterward, they write down terms of references and enter into a contractual agreement between them. Depending on whether the client has already been into a relationship with his or her BDS provider prior to the engagement, the BDS provider may also start from developing a concept note, request letter, and business proposal for funds solicitation.

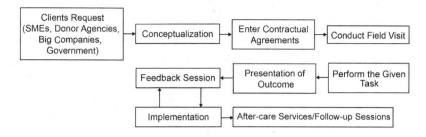

FIGURE 13.7 The General Approach Taken by BDS Providers

Once funds have been acquired, the service providers conduct field visits, which can either be for market survey, brand development, business training, and workshops, or any other requested activity. In all the three cases, SCF plays the role of facilitation to monitor that expected outcomes are accomplished by the SMEs. Some of the service providers, like BDS 2, for example, requires at least one staff person from the enterprise to participate in part of the fieldwork exercise so that he or she can have a feeling of what is happening on the ground.

In most cases, outcome presentation and feedback sessions go back and forth. This can be done through class presentation or a normal conversation between the service provider and the client, where the service provider presents the outcome for the activity, which has been completed. Then feedback is drawn after the presentation session, whereby questions are answered and the way forward to implementation is given. During the implementation phase, service providers may or may not take part depending on the kind of task given or solution provided. Here is where the SMEs have to put in practice what has been delivered by the service providers and the service providers too have the role of overseeing how they implement it. Thereafter, service providers can wind up with follow-up services, where they can be advised and guided whenever needed.

After interviewing BDS providers and analyzing SCF model during fieldwork, I realized that BDS providers have minor differences on approaches of delivering these services. SCF approach seemed to have a higher repercussion on SMEs, compared with other BDS approaches. BDS 1 placed more emphasis on after-care services, in which he believes sustainability can be ensured, whereas BDS 3 insisted on having an agreement to be given room to monitor implementation of the delivered results, so that funds are not inappropriately utilized and also to protect the image of the company against other potential clients and stakeholders.

SMEs Perception on BDS Services

All the interviewed SMEs agreed upon understanding the importance of BDS after receiving the services though they used to know little about service provider. However, according to the SMEs, service providers did little in creating networks and interaction among the business stakeholders as a way to achieve the optimal outcome; rather, in most cases, it was powered directly by SCF project. The reason for this is not so clear, but it might be related to the fact that service providers are more focused on the assigned tasks and failed to interact with their clients, limiting amount of funds to support extra activities beyond the approved planned activities. The results obtained from the fieldwork showed that in all cases, SMEs said that cost of the services are relatively high and they would not be able to pay for them if it were not for the support received from SCF project.

The most striking result emerging from data is that SME 2, for example, mentioned that he did not see any immediate effect on orders from the customers when the market survey report was finally presented to him. Literally, he was not satisfied with service provision because he felt like he was not part of it. The analysis showed that other SMEs' response to this situation was that they wanted BDS providers to be more involved during and after the implementation phase.

SMEs Plans Implementation and Flexibility

One of the conditions for fund application at SCF project is to submit a workable business proposal. However, it seemed to be a different case on Tanzanian SMEs, because findings of this study indicated that money is the significant barrier to developing a business plan in the first place. Interesting outcomes concerning this matter arose when interviewing service providers and SMEs. For example, SME 1 mentioned that even when the proposed activities were accomplished as planned, it is still difficult to keep up with demand in the market; meanwhile, the correspondent service provider mentioned that they consider competition while solving the tasks for their clients. Service providers should attempt to address the weaknesses and create ability for small firms to develop and recognize business opportunities to improve organizational capacity while implementing the proposed plans. Apparently, service providers have indicated that SMEs' request funds for activities for which they do not know its significance, and thereafter it becomes difficult to maintain the standard of their business after receiving business support.

SCF project conducts monitoring and evaluation after the completion of each phase to ensure that expected effects are observed and improvements have been made in areas where SMEs needed development support for their businesses. One unanticipated finding was that all the interviewed SMEs felt that BDS providers hardly take part in the implementation stage and that there was no commitment from the service providers on involvement on implementation, feedback, and after-care services. The finding was unexpected and suggests that service providers should focus more on the level SMEs' individual requirements rather than the facilitating agency to improve the overall outcome of their businesses.

Learning in Small Firms

Learning is an important tool for an organization to grow. When interviewing SMEs and service providers during the fieldwork, we discovered there are different ways in which the learning aspect is brought into play between SMEs and their business environment.

SMEs reported to have learned through different ways when working with BDS providers. BDS providers, on the other hand, have used different approaches to improve SMEs' skills, knowledge, and competence.

Learning has been made possible through participation in different training sessions, seminars, and workshops organized by either SCF project or service providers. Some of the SMEs have even had a chance to do training outside the country, which helped them to have different experiences and gain knowledge on how others are operating in the same line of business they are in. During seminars, SMEs have chances to share and discuss their experiences, which is a way to learn from each other and improve their networks. It was also mentioned that trade fair events helped them to learn by getting customers' feedback and networking with other shareholders. In other ways, SMEs indicated that they learned more through implementation process. Different skills have been reported to be acquired by SMEs through their involvement with service providers. Generally, there has been an improvement on customer handling, record keeping, communication techniques, and development of their own business plans.

When service providers were asked whether they consider SMEs' learning important, the response was quite interesting. First, they expressed the belief that most SMEs are not aware of BDS services, which makes it difficult to understand the importance of these services. Another concern is that SMEs' educational backgrounds are poor and makes the learning process complicated. It is hard for SMEs to develop necessary documents because of either the language barrier or poor business skills.

Against all these difficulties, service providers have established various ways to ensure that SMEs are gaining knowledge, skills, and competence when working with them. For example, BDS 3, who specializes in dairy business development, stated that some of his clients have reached the optimal level of knowledge absorption by applying the BDS knowledge from the services he delivers. One individual stated that listening to clients' opinions and discussion with them helps them realize their potential by involving them when solving problems. There was also a comment that SMEs start to learn from the first engagement, by participating in discussions and feedback sessions with their customers. To some SMEs, they reach an optimal level of knowledge absorption where the service provider requires them to employ a permanent person to assist them in daily business operations.

Turning to the experiential learning circle elements, SMEs stated that SCF has been more involved on improving personal skills and enhancing deep encounters with other actors in the sector. In the intervening time, service providers have been doing more on conceptual understanding where they describe skills to SMEs and invite their ideas prior to solving the problem. It has also been observed from the data that SMEs experience a linear learning model and rarely in a circular way, as how it was previously described in the theories. However, with SCF project, SMEs have chances to attend trainings and trade fair events, where they learn how to better practice the skills they have been taught and have a chance to discuss and get feedback on different matters concerning their businesses.

It was initially considered that BDS providers are the main source of knowledge and skills development and creating competence to SMEs. What is interesting about the findings for this theory is that while in other cases it was believed that a BDS provider is an expert of all, meaning that any opinion coming from him is valid, in some cases, one was not satisfied with the service provided. The reason for this contrast may be explained by the relationship service providers have had with their clients. The latter expressed that initially SCF project selected a service provider for him and that he was not happy about it. At the same time, the service provider mentioned that they were not so sure about the intention of the SME owner over the funds allocated for that particular activity. The analysis for this study showed that it is important to highlight the level of trust between the two parties, who are working together.

Discussion

Introduction

This section gives the discussion of the study in relation to the data and analysis previously presented. The reader may find it cumbersome to draw a line of demarcation between the sections, but the chapters are purposefully separated to give room to the comparison of the findings of this study to other previous studies.

BDS Service Provision

The findings for this category are similar to the key features Miehlbradt and McVay[123] identified under BDS services. The analysis of this study shows that the services provided are not directly tailored toward the needs of the particular industry. It can be argued that service providers' specialization and the years of experience in the industry improves the outcome of the service they are delivering to the small firms. Even though service providers mentioned that SMEs' request for business development services of which they do not know its implication, these findings cannot be extrapolated to all SMEs. For example, SME 1 and SME 3 were fully aware of BDS services, whereas SME 2 proclaimed that he did not know about the services and he was initially approached by the project staff simply because he was popular in the market. Lack of knowledge of the service provided by SMEs may influence the tendency of fund misappropriation because they channel their request to match the project requirements and focus less on their business requirements. It is somehow difficult to explain this result, but on the other hand, SMEs have expressed major challenges in their businesses, which are not supported by SCF project. This may imply that the support provided by SCF project was supply driven. This created a negative influence on SMEs to appreciate the value of the services. Apparently, this is consistent with the finding of Dawson and Jeans,[124] which showed that BDS support is neglected when it tends to be supply driven.

The Approach BDS Providers Use to Deliver Services

The particular characteristic of SCF intervention is similar to what Caniëls et al.[125] suggested in that the services provided should be aligned into commercial line and that BDS requires indirect facilitation from developmental programs. SCF's role is to facilitate small food processing firms by financing BDS providers to assist SMEs in areas where they need improvements.

After interviewing BDS providers and analyzing SCF model during fieldwork, we realized that BDS providers have minor differences on approaches of delivering these services. SCF approach seemed to have a higher repercussion on SMEs, compared with other BDS approaches. BDS 1 placed more emphasis on after-care services to ensure sustainability, whereas BDS 3 insisted on having an agreement to be given room to monitor implementation of the delivered results so that funds are not inappropriately utilized.

In reference to experiential learning cycle structured by Heron,[126] we learn that the cycle enhances learning and improves service providers' and trainees' (SMEs) interpersonal skills, followed by the provider several times. This learning cycle can be explained in two different scenarios in this study. First is on the approach taken by the service providers and second, it can be used to explain the learning experience for SMEs when interacting with the service providers. The latter will be elaborated in the subsequent sections.

It was observed that service providers do not directly start with the description of the skills, instead start with familiarization between themselves, the client, and the enterprise, like how it was emphasized by Kubr[127] in that in early stages, the check-up routine should be followed to identify potential problems in SMEs. This has at least happened for all the cases interviewed, where conceptual understanding comes after contractual agreement. The service providers in all cases have proved the importance of involving their clients in some of the exercise more in a participatory way of doing things as how it appears in all stages of the experiential learning cycle.

One of the issues that emerges from these findings is that SMEs have had encounters with each other through intervention with SCF and not through their service provider. SCF has been a platform where SMEs can experiment with interaction with other actors in the industry and build strong relationships with each other as how it was described in the third element of the experiential learning cycle by Heron.[128] The reason for this is not so clear, but it might be related to limited availability of resources as mentioned by BDS 1, awareness of the role of service providers, or poor relationship among the service provider and the firm owners.

The findings of this study support the ideas of Nikolova et al.[129] that theoretically regarded interaction models being either an expert model or a social interaction model. Interviews with BDS providers have shown them to behave in the same fashion. Depending on the level of problem-solving process, there were parts in which service providers were acting like an expert and dominated the relationship simply because they have access to knowledge based on particular aspects, and on the other hand, service providers were actively involving the SME clients in solution development, since it was believed that they too have valuable knowledge to be incorporated.

SMEs Perception on BDS Services

All the interviewed SMEs agreed upon understanding the importance of BDS after receiving the services, though they used to know little about service providers. SMEs' understandings on the importance of BDS agree with the studies of Sievers and Vandenberg,[130] Ghobadian,[131] Biggs and Shah,[132] and Dawson and Jeans.[133] However, according to the SMEs interviewed, service providers did little to create network and interaction among the business stakeholders as a way to achieve the optimal outcome; rather, in most cases, it was powered directly by SCF project. The reason for this is not so clear, but it might be related to the fact that service providers are more focused on the assigned tasks and failed to interact with their clients, limiting the amount of funds to support extra activities beyond the approved planned activities.

Dawson and Jeans[134] pointed out that the role of BDS is neglected for the reason that the services are expensive. The findings of this study support the previous research in the sense that in all the cases SMEs admitted that cost of the services is relatively high and they would not be able to employ them if it were not for the support received from SCF project. This is evident in Tanzanian context, since many SMEs have hardship in accessing finance. Besides, they do not see the immediate impact when practiced in their businesses. Case 2 SME can set a good example for this, because he mentioned that he did not see any immediate effect on orders from the customers when the market survey report was finally presented to him.

SMEs Plans Implementation and Flexibility

Prior studies have noted the importance of business planning in relation to business performance. One of the conditions for fund application at SCF project is to submit a workable business proposal, just like how it was argued by Timmons et al.[135] that flexibility and responsiveness of business planning are the critical skills for survival. However, it seemed to be a different case on Tanzanian SMEs, because findings of this study indicated that money is the significant barrier to developing a business plan in the first place.

Interesting outcomes concerning this matter arose when interviewing service providers and SMEs. For example, case 1 SME mentioned that even when the proposed activities were accomplished as planned it is still difficult to keep up with demand in the market; meanwhile, the correspondent service provider mentioned that they consider competition while solving the tasks for their clients. Service providers should attempt to address the weaknesses and create ability for small firms to develop and recognize business opportunities to improve organizational capacity while implementing the proposed plans. This appears as how it was mentioned in the literature review by Morrison et al.[136] that factors like ability and opportunities of the owners affect the performance of the small firms.

Another important finding was that service providers mentioned that SMEs request funds for activities for which they do not know its significance, and thereafter it becomes difficult to maintain the standard of their business after receiving business support. This result supports the previous research by Karlsson and Honig[137] that firms use business plans to achieve legitimacy from the external actors and noted that there is a weak relationship between planning and implementation.

Morrison et al.'s[138] study about understanding the relationship between business plan implementation and its effects on business performance cannot be directly related to the situation of SMEs supported by SCF project. The project conducts monitoring and evaluation after the completion of each phase to ensure that the expected effects are observed and improvements have been made in various areas of their businesses. One unanticipated finding was that all the interviewed SMEs felt that BDS providers hardly take part in the implementation stage and that there was no commitment from the service providers on implementation, feedback, and after-care services. The finding was unexpected and suggests that service providers should focus more on the level SMEs' individual requirements rather than the facilitating agency to improve the overall outcome of their businesses.

Learning in Small Firms

The importance of business development support can be recognized when the SMEs have successfully adopted the ideas to develop or expand their businesses. The main components from the experiential learning cycle build up the basis for this section's discussion: conceptual understanding, imaginal understanding, practical understanding, and experiential understanding. This can closely be related to the approach service providers use to deliver services. In this study, participation was found to be the main source of learning. Those who have participated in training have observed changes in their business. This finding accords with the earlier observation of Westhead and Storey,[139] which showed that SMEs derive benefits from participating in training. Being involved and participation in various activities aiming to improve their business has shown significant effect on SMEs' performance, and this has influenced trust between the actors, which can spur good relationship and learning among them. However, this study has been unable to demonstrate a clear outcome of those who expressed that they have not been fully involved in the support process by their service providers since, on the other hand, they have stated to have seen remarkable outcomes on different areas of intervention.

According to Heron,[140] going through every component in a cycle of learning several times improves interpersonal skills. This result supports the previous point even though SMEs have noted that SCF project and service providers are more involved in some of the phases than others, they saw their skills improved and behavior changing during the whole time they have been involved in the process.

Findings have also shown that SMEs network has improved since involving themselves in BDS services. The present finding seems to be consistent with other research, which found that networking may establish information, knowledge, and expertise that are necessary for small firms' survival.[141] Networking is made possible because SCF project or service providers organize events, business training sessions, and seminars, which gives an opportunity to come across different actors who are necessary for SMEs' establishment of knowledge, information, and expertise.

The analysis showed that the ability of SMEs to learn and implement activities involving BDS services results in their competency to perform sustainably and favorably in the dynamic business environment. This is a concept of absorptive capacity in agreement with Zahra and George.[142]

Conclusion

The purpose of the present study was set to answer the main research question: How does intervention through business development support and affect the performance of SMEs engaging in agro-food processing and marketing? This research question was addressed using embedded multiple-case design to study the effect of business development support intervention on the performance of SMEs engaging in agro-food processing and marketing. Three SMEs and three service providers under SCF intervention framework participated. The main focus was on types of BDS services provided, models BDS providers use to deliver services, perception of SMEs on the services they receive, implementation and flexibility of SME plans, and SMEs' learning experience with BDS providers.

A purposive sampling method was used to select the cases, which took into account diverse variation of cases so as to identify common patterns. The cases involved are SMEs engaging in processing and marketing of dairy products supported by SCF project and their correspondent business development support service providers. The data collected for the study were gathered from semi-structured interviews, company documents such as business proposals, and progress reports obtained from SCF project database. Some of the additional information came from observing the actual situations in the field. Short reports for each case were obtained during data analysis for undertaking the within-case cross-case analyses. The prepared cross-case display was used to develop the analysis of this study guided by the theories constructed in the earlier chapters.

This study has shown that generally those SMEs that are engaged in SCF business development support intervention have remarkable success in their businesses. Through the intervention and involvement with business development service providers, SMEs have been able to gain new knowledge, skills, and capabilities necessary to compete in the domestic market. However, many significant findings emerged from this research, which leads to the following conclusion:

> As it was highlighted in the literature, business development services should be demand driven and not influenced by the supply side. Even though service providers mentioned that SMEs do not understand the implication of the services they are requesting, it was clear that their focus was on different problems rather than the ones they have been supported with. It is also difficult to come into the conclusion that these SMEs have not benefited from these services, because they showed that there have been changes in their business before BDS service engagement.

This study has managed to explain the overall approach service providers take to deliver the services. The aim was to develop an understanding on the way services were delivered and how they contribute to SMEs' ability to address and face their own problems in the future. Another important focus between these two sections was on how the approach used by service providers enhanced learning on SMEs. Analysis showed that participation of SMEs on different stages of problem solving made it possible to acquire new skills and gain knowledge. All this depended on the level of SMEs' participation and BDS involvement in the process. Experiential learning cycle was used to explain relationship between the approaches used by service providers and what SMEs learn out of the process. It was found that SCF project has been the foundation of SMEs' learning experience in a sense that it is involving them more than service providers. The reason behind this occurrence is not so clear, but it might be related to limited availability of resources, awareness of the role of service providers, or poor relationship among the service provider and the firm owners. However, SMEs have indicated that they have acquired various skills and knowledge from the interaction between themselves, service providers, and SCF project but did not comment on their ability to compete fairly in the domestic market.

Regarding SMEs' perception on the business development service provided, results showed that SMEs understand the importance of BDS support, although it was difficult for them to realize immediate impact when practicing recommended actions on their businesses. They also felt like service providers should involve themselves more during the implementation phase and after the completion of the activity and emphasized that there needs to be a close relationship with the service providers. This is sufficient evidence to support the fact that SMEs do not learn more from service providers, but rather from the project. So SCF project should find a way of intervening more so that commitment can be observed from the service providers. However, a change in attitude and behavior toward the way they operate their businesses has been a significant credit to service providers by the SMEs. This is a good indication that besides their shortcomings that SMEs address BDS providers have been able to bring change in their mind-sets.

The most interesting finding to emerge from this section is that when some of the SMEs accomplish their proposed plans, they are still finding difficulties to catch up with the demand. This might have shown a weakness in the BDS intervention that needs to be addressed before long. It can as well be suggested that service providers should find a way to develop SME owners' ability and make them recognize opportunities to improve their businesses. The second finding for this section was that there needs to be more flexibility on the SCF project side, that the support should also be directed into capital investment where its biggest challenges lie. This finding suggested service provisions should focus on the SMEs' individual requirements rather than facilitators' to improve the overall outcome of the business.

SMEs' development and growth is a combination of many things, one of which is services, learning, and implementation of what has been received from the services providers. These services have to be appropriately delivered so that SMEs become capable of learning from them and implementing. Conceptually, the three dimensions are linked in the sense that SMEs need to learn from the interaction with the service providers and implement what they have learned. However, to receive the services, SMEs must be willing to learn and implement what they have been taught while service providers have good skills and education to deliver the support needed by the small firms.

Overall, the findings of this study suggest that there is a mismatch between the BDS intervention thrust put by SCF in the name of improving SME performance and the actual BDS desired by SMEs in Tanzania. Admittedly, the operationalization of the BDS intervention to SCF supported SMEs follows the classical theory-based BDS principles as discussed in this chapter. However, the mismatch does conceptually label such institutional support to SMEs as that of SCF more supply driven. This may explain the failure of most SMEs to grow. The implication of these findings is that although the BDS intervention may have a positive impact to improve and grow SME activities in developing countries, the needs for intervention should be demand driven.

Notes

1 Pascal Savioz and Manuel Blum, "Strategic Forecast Tool for SMEs: How the Opportunity Landscape Interacts With Business Strategy to Anticipate Technological Trends," *Technovation* 22, no. 2 (2002): 91–100.

2 Ibid.
3 Paul Collier and David Dollar, "Can the World Cut Poverty in Half? How Policy Reform and Effective Aid Can Meet International Development Goals," *World Development* 29, no. 11 (2001): 1787–1802.
4 Jonathan Dawson with Andy Jeans, *Looking Beyond Credit: Business Development Services and the Promotion of Innovation Among Small Producers* (London: Intermediate Technology Publications Ltd [ITP], 1997), www.cabdirect.org/cabdirect/abstract/19981805592.
5 Christian M. Rogerson, "In Search of the African Miracle: Debates on Successful Small Enterprise Development in Africa," *Habitat International* 25, no. 1 (2001): 115–142.
6 Dawson and Jeans, *Looking Beyond Credit*.
7 B.Y. Chang, M. J. Magobe, and Y. B. Kim, "E-Commerce Applications in the Tourism Industry: A Tanzania Case Study," *South African Journal of Business Management* 46, no. 4 (2015): 53–64.
8 Ibid.
9 Ibid.
10 Elina Eskola, *Agricultural Marketing and Supply Chain Management in Tanzania: A Case Study*, Vol. 16 (Dar es Salaam: Economic and Social Research Foundation, 2005).
11 B.Y. Chang, M. J. Magobe, and Y. B. Kim, "E-Commerce Applications in the Tourism Industry: A Tanzania Case Study," *South African Journal of Business Management* 46, no. 4 (2015): 53–64.
12 D. R. Olomi, "Opportunities and Challenges for Rural SMEs Development in Tanzania," in *Policy Dialogue Seminar Paper, Economic and Social Research Foundation*, ed. Donath Olomi (Tanzania: Economic and Social Research Foundation [ESRF], March 23, 2006).
13 Iddi Adam Mwatima Makombe, *Women Entrepreneurship Development and Empowerment in Tanzania: The Case Study of SIDO/UNIDO-Supported Women Microentrepreneurs in the Food Processing Sector* (Cape Town: The University of South Africa, 2006).
14 B.Y. Chang, M. J. Magobe, and Y. B. Kim, "E-Commerce Applications in the Tourism Industry: A Tanzania Case Study," *South African Journal of Business Management* 46, no. 4 (2015): 53–64.
15 Emmanuel K. Yiridoe and Vincent M. Anchirinah, "Garden Production Systems and Food Security in Ghana: Characteristics of Traditional Knowledge and Management Systems," *Renewable Agriculture and Food Systems* 20, no. 3 (2005): 168–180; Cheryl Doss, John McPeak, and Christopher B. Barrett, "Interpersonal, Intertemporal and Spatial Variation in Risk Perceptions: Evidence From East Africa," *World Development* 36, no. 8 (2008): 1453–1468.
16 Xinshen Diao and Paul Dorosh, "Demand Constraints on Agricultural Growth in East and Southern Africa: A General Equilibrium Analysis," *Development Policy Review* 25, no. 3 (2007): 275–292.
17 Richard Ogutu-Ohwayo and John S. Balirwa, "Management Challenges of Freshwater Fisheries in Africa," *Lakes & Reservoirs: Research & Management* 11, no. 4 (2006): 215–226.
18 Tamara Bekefi, "Tanzania: Lessons in Building Linkages for Competitive and Responsible Entrepreneurship," UNIDO and Kennedy School of Government, Harvard University, 2006.
19 Tamara Bekefi, "Tanzania: Lessons in Building Linkages for Competitive and Responsible Entrepreneurship," UNIDO and Kennedy School of Government, Harvard University, 2006; B. A. Malangi, "State of the Art: Review of the Informal Sector in Tanzania, 1990–1999," International Labour Organization and Ministry of Industry and Trade, SME Section, Turin, 2000; and Etienne St-Jean, "Mentor Functions for Novice Entrepreneurs," *Academy of Entrepreneurship Journal* 17, no. 1 (2011): 65.
20 Andrew Dorward et al., "Institutions, Markets and Economic Co-Ordination: Linking Development Policy to Theory and Praxis," *Development and Change* 36, no. 1 (2005): 1–25.

21 Kurt Larsen, Ronald Kim, and Florian Theus, "Agribusiness and Innovation Systems in Africa," World Bank Publications, 2009. https://elibrary.worldbank.org/doi/pdf/10.1596/978-0-8213-7944-8.

22 Marshall Bear, Alan Gibson, and Rob Hitchins, "From Principles to Practice: Ten Critical Challenges for BDS Market Development," *Small Enterprise Development* 14, no. 4 (December 2003): 10–23.

23 Christopher M. Mahemba and Erik J. De Bruijn, "Innovation Activities by Small and Medium-Sized Manufacturing Enterprises in Tanzania," *Creativity and Innovation Management* 12, no. 3 (2003): 162–173.

24 Abby Ghobadian and David N. Gallear, "Total Quality Management in SMEs," *Omega* 24, no. 1 (1996): 83–106.

25 Virginia Barba-Sánchez, María del Pilar Martínez-Ruiz, and Ana Isabel Jiménez-Zarco, "Drivers, Benefits and Challenges of ICT Adoption by Small and Medium Sized Enterprises (SMEs): A Literature Review," *Problems and Perspectives in Management* 5, no. 1 (2007): 104–115.

26 Marina Van Geenhuizen, Nurul Indarti, and Danny P. Soetanto, "Knowledge Acquisition and Innovation: Potentials for Upgrading of Very Small and Small Firms in Furniture Manufacturing in Indonesia," *International Journal of Foresight and Innovation Policy* 6, no. 4 (2010): 207–224.

27 Allan Gibb and Jun Li, "Organizing for Enterprise in China: What Can We Learn From the Chinese Micro, Small, and Medium Enterprise Development Experience," *Futures* 35, no. 4 (2003): 403–421.

28 Jacob Levitsky, "Support Systems for SMEs in Developing Countries," Small and Medium Enterprises Programme Discussion Paper (Vienna: United Nations Industrial Development Organization, 1996), www.clusterobservatory.in/articles/Article%20No.%2049.pdf.

29 Daniel Agyapong, "Micro, Small and Medium Enterprises' Activities, Income Level and Poverty Reduction in Ghana—a Synthesis of Related Literature," *International Journal of Business and Management* 5, no. 12 (2010): 196–205.

30 Christian M. Rogerson, "In Search of the African Miracle: Debates on Successful Small Enterprise Development in Africa," *Habitat International* 25, no. 1 (2001): 115–142.

31 Abby Ghobadian and David N. Gallear, "Total Quality Management in SMEs," *Omega* 24, no. 1 (1996): 83–106; Adrian Haberberg and Alison Rieple, *Strategic Management: Theory and Application* (London: Oxford University Press, 2008); Charles Mather, "SMEs in South Africa's Food Processing Complex: Development Prospects, Constraints and Opportunities," Working Paper 3–2005, Trade and Industrial Policy Secretariat, 2005; and Christian M. Rogerson, "In Search of the African Miracle: Debates on Successful Small Enterprise Development in Africa," *Habitat International* 25, no. 1 (2001): 115–142.

32 Christian M. Rogerson, "In Search of the African Miracle: Debates on Successful Small Enterprise Development in Africa," *Habitat International* 25, no. 1 (2001): 115–142.

33 Ibid.

34 Ibid.

35 Ibid.

36 Milan Kubr, *Management Consulting: A Guide to the Profession* (Geneva: International Labour Organization, 2002).

37 Tamara Bekefi, "Tanzania: Lessons in Building Linkages for Competitive and Responsible Entrepreneurship," UNIDO and Kennedy School of Government, Harvard University, 2006.

38 Estelle Biénabe et al., "Linking Small Holder Farmers to Markets: Lessons Learned From Literature Review and Analytical Review of Selected Projects," *Agritrop*. World Bank, Washington, DC 2, 2004, 84–138.

39 Spencer Henson, Ann-Marie Brouder, and Winnie Mitullah, "Food Safety Requirements and Food Exports From Developing Countries: The Case of Fish Exports From

Kenya to the European Union," *American Journal of Agricultural Economics* 82, no. 5 (2000): 1159–1169.

40 Charles Mather, "SMEs in South Africa's Food Processing Complex: Development Prospects, Constraints and Opportunities," Working Paper 3–2005, Trade and Industrial Policy Secretariat, 2005.

41 Nelson Edwards, Matt Tokar, and Jim Maxwell, "Agribusiness Development in Sub-Saharan Africa: Optimal Strategies and Structures," Technical Paper, no. 83 (1997), http://pdf.usaid.gov/pdf_docs/pnacb834.pdf.

42 Ibid.

43 Andrew Shepherd, "Approaches to Linking Producers to Markets: Review of Experiences to Date," Agricultural Management, Marketing and Finance Occasional Paper, Food and Agriculture Organization of United Nations, Rome, 2007.

44 Estelle Biénabe et al., "Linking Small Holder Farmers to Markets: Lessons Learned From Literature Review and Analytical Review of Selected Projects," *Agritrop*. World Bank, Washington, DC 2, 2004, 84–138.

45 Denise E. Gengatharen and Craig Standing, "A Framework to Assess the Factors Affecting Success or Failure of the Implementation of Government-Supported Regional E-Marketplaces for SMEs," *European Journal of Information Systems* 14, no. 4 (2005): 417–433.

46 Cecilia Wong et al., "Management Training in Small and Medium-Sized Enterprises: Methodological and Conceptual Issues," *The International Journal of Human Resource Management* 8, no. 1 (1997): 44–65.

47 Alison Morrison, John Breen, and Shameem Ali, "Small Business Growth: Intention, Ability, and Opportunity," *Journal of Small Business Management* 41, no. 4 (2003): 417–425.

48 Ibid.

49 Jeffry A. Timmons, Stephen Spinelli, and Yinglan Tan. *New Venture Creation: Entrepreneurship for the 21st Century*, Vol. 4 (Burr Ridge, IL: Irwin, 1994).

50 Ibid.

51 Tomas Karlsson and Benson Honig, "Judging a Business by Its Cover: An Institutional Perspective on New Ventures and the Business Plan," *Journal of Business Venturing* 24, no. 1 (2009): 27–45.

52 Frédéric Delmar and Scott Shane, "Does Business Planning Facilitate the Development of New Ventures?" *Strategic Management Journal* 24, no. 12 (2003): 1165–1185.

53 Frédéric Delmar and Scott Shane, "Legitimating First: Organizing Activities and the Survival of New Ventures," *Journal of Business Venturing* 19, no. 3 (2004): 385–410.

54 Tomas Karlsson and Benson Honig, "Judging a Business by Its Cover: An Institutional Perspective on New Ventures and the Business Plan," *Journal of Business Venturing* 24, no. 1 (2009): 27–45.

55 Marshall Bear, Alan Gibson, and Rob Hitchins, "From Principles to Practice: Ten Critical Challenges for BDS Market Development," *Small Enterprise Development* 14, no. 4 (December 2003): 10–23.

56 Lau Schulpen and Peter Gibbon, "Private Sector Development: Policies, Practices and Problems," *World Development* 30, no. 1 (2002): 1–15.

57 Bruce Lankford, "Irrigation Improvement Projects in Tanzania; Scale Impacts and Policy Implications," *Water Policy* 6, no. 2 (2004): 89–102.

58 Lau Schulpen and Peter Gibbon, "Private Sector Development: Policies, Practices and Problems," *World Development* 30, no. 1 (2002): 1–15.

59 Jacob Levitsky, *Business Development Services: Review of International Experience.* Intermediate Technology Publications, 2000. https://openlibrary.org/publishers/Intermediate_Technology_Publications

60 A. O. Miehlbradt and Mary McVay, "Developing Commercial Markets for Business Development Services: 'Are "How-to-Do-It" Recipes Possible?'" *Seminar Reader of the Third Annual Seminar* (Turin: International Labour Organization, September 1, 2003, [2002]).

61 Merten Sievers and Paul Vandenberg, "Synergies Through Linkages: Who Benefits From Linking Micro-Finance and Business Development Services?" *World Development* 35, no. 8 (2007): 1341–1358.

62 Bruce Lankford, "Irrigation Improvement Projects in Tanzania; Scale Impacts and Policy Implications," *Water Policy* 6, no. 2 (2004): 89–102.

63 Ibid.

64 Marshall Bear, Alan Gibson, and Rob Hitchins, "From Principles to Practice: Ten Critical Challenges for BDS Market Development," *Small Enterprise Development* 14, no. 4 (December 2003): 10–23.

65 Mónica Arroyo-Vázquez, Peter van der Sijde, and Fernando Jiménez-Sáez, "Innovative and Creative Entrepreneurship Support Services at Universities," *Service Business* 4, no. 1 (2010): 63–76.

66 Marjolein C.J. Caniëls, Henny A. Romijn, and Marieke de Ruijter-De Wildt, "Can Business Development Services Practitioners Learn from Theories of Innovation and Services Marketing?" *Development in Practice* 16, no. 5 (2006): 425–440.

67 A. O. Miehlbradt and Mary McVay, "Developing Commercial Markets for Business Development Services: 'Are "How-to-Do-It" Recipes Possible?'" *Seminar Reader of the Third Annual Seminar* (Turin: International Labour Organization, September 1, 2003, [2002]).

68 Ibid.

69 Marjolein C.J. Caniëls, Henny A. Romijn, and Marieke de Ruijter-De Wildt, "Can Business Development Services Practitioners Learn From Theories of Innovation and Services Marketing?" *Development in Practice* 16, no. 5 (2006): 425–440.

70 Ibid.

71 Anna Bergek and Charlotte Norrman, "Incubator Best Practice: A Framework," *Technovation* 28, no. 1 (2008): 20–28.

72 Dawson and Jeans, *Looking Beyond Credit*.

73 Ibid.

74 Merten Sievers and Paul Vandenberg, "Synergies Through Linkages: Who Benefits From Linking Micro-Finance and Business Development Services?" *World Development* 35, no. 8 (2007): 1341–1358.

75 Ibid.

76 Abby Ghobadian and David N. Gallear, "Total Quality Management in SMEs," *Omega* 24, no. 1 (1996): 83–106.

77 Tyler Biggs and Manju Kedia Shah, "African SMES, Networks, and Manufacturing Performance," *Journal of Banking & Finance* 30, no. 11 (2006): 3043–3066.

78 Dawson and Jeans, *Looking Beyond Credit*.

79 Bailey Klinger and Matthias Schündeln, "Can Entrepreneurial Activity Be Taught? Quasi-Experimental Evidence From Central America," *World Development* 39, no. 9 (2011): 1592–1610.

80 Ibid.

81 Stuart Macdonald, Dimitris Assimakopoulos, and Pat Anderson, "Education and Training for Innovation in SMEs: A Tale of Exploitation," *International Small Business Journal* 25, no. 1 (2007): 77–95.

82 Gideon Nieman, "Training Entrepreneurs and Small Business Enterprises in South Africa: A Situational Analysis," *Education+Training* 43, no. 8/9 (2001): 445–450.

83 Milan Kubr, *Management Consulting: A Guide to the Profession* (Geneva: International Labour Organization, 2002).

84 Mark P. Rice, "Co-Production of Business Assistance in Business Incubators: An Exploratory Study," *Journal of Business Venturing* 17, no. 2 (2002): 163–187.

85 Anna Bergek and Charlotte Norrman, "Incubator Best Practice: A Framework," *Technovation* 28, no. 1 (2008): 20–28.

86 Paul Westhead and David Storey, "Management Training and Small Firm Performance: Why Is the Link So Weak?," *International Small Business Journal* 14, no. 4 (1996): 13–24.

87 Ibid.

88 Monder Ram and David Deakins, "African-Caribbeans in Business," *Journal of Ethnic and Migration Studies* 22, no. 1 (1996): 68.

89 Natalia Nikolova, Markus Reihlen, and Jan-Florian Schlapfner, "Client–Consultant Interaction: Capturing Social Practices of Professional Service Production," *Scandinavian Journal of Management* 25, no. 3 (2009): 289–298.

90 Timothy Devinney and Natalia Nikolova, "The Client–Consultant Interaction in Professional Business Service Firms: Outline of the Interpretive Model and Implications for Consulting," Paper. Draft Version Presented at The University of New South Wales, New South Wales, 2004.

91 Marco Van Gelderen, Lidewey van de Sluis, and Paul Jansen, "Learning Opportunities and Learning Behaviours of Small Business Starters: Relations With Goal Achievement, Skill Development and Satisfaction," *Small Business Economics* 25, no. 1 (2005): 97–108.

92 Etienne St-Jean, "Mentor Functions for Novice Entrepreneurs," *Academy of Entrepreneurship Journal* 17, no. 1 (2011): 65.

93 Marco Van Gelderen, Lidewey van de Sluis, and Paul Jansen, "Learning Opportunities and Learning Behaviours of Small Business Starters: Relations With Goal Achievement, Skill Development and Satisfaction," *Small Business Economics* 25, no. 1 (2005): 97–108.

94 John Heron, *The Complete Facilitator's Handbook* (London: Kogan Page, 1999). http://cds.cern.ch/record/1151364.

95 Ibid.

96 Ibid.

97 Shaker A. Zahra and Gerard George, "Absorptive Capacity: A Review, Reconceptualization, and Extension," *Academy of Management Review* 27, no. 2 (2002): 185–203.

98 Marco Van Gelderen, Lidewey van de Sluis, and Paul Jansen, "Learning Opportunities and Learning Behaviours of Small Business Starters: Relations With Goal Achievement, Skill Development and Satisfaction," *Small Business Economics* 25, no. 1 (2005): 97–108.

99 Milan Kubr, *Management Consulting: A Guide to the Profession* (Geneva: International Labour Organization, 2002).

100 A. O. Miehlbradt and Mary McVay, "Developing Commercial Markets for Business Development Services: 'Are "How-to-Do-It" Recipes Possible?'" *Seminar Reader of the Third Annual Seminar* (Turin: International Labour Organization, September 1, 2003, [2002]).

101 John Heron, *The Complete Facilitator's Handbook* (London: Kogan Page, 1999). http://cds.cern.ch/record/1151364.

102 Robert K. Yin, *Case Study Research: Design and Methods* (Thousand Oaks, CA: Sage Publications Ltd., 2009).

103 David Silverman, *Doing Qualitative Research: A Practical Handbook* (Thousand Oaks, CA: Sage Publications Limited, 2013).

104 Colin Robson and Kieran McCartan, *Real World Research* (New York: John Wiley & Sons, 2016).

105 Robert K. Yin, *Case Study Research: Design and Methods* (Thousand Oaks, CA: Sage Publications Ltd., 2009).

106 Bedman Narteh, "Knowledge Transfer and Learning: The Case of Danish-Ghanaian Strategic Alliances," paper, Department of Business Studies, Faculty of Social Sciences, Aalborg University, 2006.

107 Dan Remenyi and Brian Williams, *Doing Research in Business and Management: An Introduction to Process and Method* (Thousand Oaks, CA, Sage, 1998).

108 Howard S. Becker, *Writing for Social Scientists: How to Start and Finish Your Thesis, Book, or Article*, 2nd ed. (Chicago: Guides to Writing and Publishing, 2016).

109 Bedman Narteh, "Knowledge Transfer and Learning: The Case of Danish-Ghanaian Strategic Alliances," paper, Department of Business Studies, Faculty of Social Sciences,

Aalborg University, 2006; Andreas M. Riege, "Validity and Reliability Tests in Case Study Research: A Literature Review With 'Hands-On' Applications for Each Research Phase," *Qualitative Market Research: An International Journal* 6, no. 2 (2003): 75–86; and Colin Robson and Kieran McCartan, *Real World Research* (New York: John Wiley & Sons, 2016).

110 Andreas M. Riege, "Validity and Reliability Tests in Case Study Research: A Literature Review With 'Hands-On' Applications for Each Research Phase," *Qualitative Market Research: An International Journal* 6, no. 2 (2003): 75–86.

111 Bedman Narteh, "Knowledge Transfer and Learning: The Case of Danish-Ghanaian Strategic Alliances," paper, Department of Business Studies, Faculty of Social Sciences, Aalborg University, 2006.

112 Michael Quinn Patton, *Qualitative Research* (New York: Wiley Online Library, 2005). http://onlinelibrary.wiley.com/doi/10.1002/0470013192.bsa514/full.

113 Robert K. Yin, *Case Study Research: Design and Methods* (Thousand Oaks, CA: Sage Publications Ltd., 2009).

114 Matthew B. Miles and A. Michael Huberman, *Qualitative Data Analysis: An Expanded Sourcebook* (London: Sage Publishing, Inc., 2014).

115 Robert K. Yin, *Case Study Research: Design and Methods* (Thousand Oaks, CA: Sage Publications Ltd., 2009).

116 Matthew B. Miles, "Qualitative Data as an Attractive Nuisance: The Problem of Analysis," *Administrative Science Quarterly* 24, no. 4 (1979): 590–601.

117 Bedman Narteh, "Knowledge Transfer and Learning: The Case of Danish-Ghanaian Strategic Alliances," paper, Department of Business Studies, Faculty of Social Sciences, Aalborg University, 2006.

118 Matthew B. Miles and A. Michael Huberman, *Qualitative Data Analysis: An Expanded Sourcebook* (London: Sage Publishing, Inc., 2014).

119 Kathleen M. Eisenhardt, "Building Theories From Case Study Research," *Academy of Management Review* 14, no. 4 (1989): 532–550.

120 Matthew B. Miles and A. Michael Huberman, *Qualitative Data Analysis: An Expanded Sourcebook* (London: Sage Publishing, Inc., 2014).

121 Ibid.

122 Milan Kubr, *Management Consulting: A Guide to the Profession* (Geneva: International Labour Organization, 2002).

123 A. O. Miehlbradt and Mary McVay, "Developing Commercial Markets for Business Development Services: 'Are "How-to-Do-It" Recipes Possible?'" *Seminar Reader of the Third Annual Seminar* (Turin: International Labour Organization, September 1, 2003, [2002]).

124 Dawson and Jeans, *Looking Beyond Credit.*

125 Marjolein C.J. Caniëls, Henny A. Romijn, and Marieke de Ruijter-De Wildt, "Can Business Development Services Practitioners Learn From Theories of Innovation and Services Marketing?" *Development in Practice* 16, no. 5 (2006): 425–440.

126 John Heron, *The Complete Facilitator's Handbook* (London: Kogan Page, 1999). http://cds.cern.ch/record/1151364.

127 Milan Kubr, *Management Consulting: A Guide to the Profession* (Geneva: International Labour Organization, 2002).

128 John Heron, *The Complete Facilitator's Handbook* (London: Kogan Page, 1999). http://cds.cern.ch/record/1151364.

129 Natalia Nikolova, Markus Reihlen, and Jan-Florian Schlapfner, "Client–Consultant Interaction: Capturing Social Practices of Professional Service Production," *Scandinavian Journal of Management* 25, no. 3 (2009): 289–298.

130 Merten Sievers and Paul Vandenberg, "Synergies Through Linkages: Who Benefits From Linking Micro-Finance and Business Development Services?" *World Development* 35, no. 8 (2007): 1341–1358.

131 Abby Ghobadian and David N. Gallear, "Total Quality Management in SMEs," *Omega* 24, no. 1 (1996): 83–106.
132 Tyler Biggs and Manju Kedia Shah, "African SMES, Networks, and Manufacturing Performance," *Journal of Banking & Finance* 30, no. 11 (2006): 3043–3066.
133 Dawson and Jeans, *Looking Beyond Credit*.
134 Ibid.
135 Jeffry A. Timmons, Stephen Spinelli, and Yinglan Tan. *New Venture Creation: Entrepreneurship for the 21st Century*, volume 4 (Burr Ridge, IL: Irwin, 1994).
136 Alison Morrison, John Breen, and Shameem Ali, "Small Business Growth: Intention, Ability, and Opportunity" *Journal of Small Business Management* 41, no. 4 (2003): 417–425.
137 Tomas Karlsson and Benson Honig, "Judging a Business by Its Cover: An Institutional Perspective on New Ventures and the Business Plan," *Journal of Business Venturing* 24, no. 1 (2009): 27–45.
138 Alison Morrison, John Breen, and Shameem Ali, "Small Business Growth: Intention, Ability, and Opportunity" *Journal of Small Business Management* 41, no. 4 (2003): 417–425.
139 Paul Westhead and David Storey, "Management Training and Small Firm Performance: Why Is the Link So Weak?" *International Small Business Journal* 14, no. 4 (1996): 13–24.
140 John Heron, *The Complete Facilitator's Handbook* (London: Kogan Page, 1999). http://cds.cern.ch/record/1151364.
141 Anna Bergek and Charlotte Norrman, "Incubator Best Practice: A Framework," *Technovation* 28, no. 1 (2008): 20–28.
142 Shaker A. Zahra and Gerard George, "Absorptive Capacity: A Review, Reconceptualization, and Extension," *Academy of Management Review* 27, no. 2 (2002): 185–203.

Bibliography

Agyapong, Daniel. "Micro, Small and Medium Enterprises' Activities, Income Level and Poverty Reduction in Ghana—a Synthesis of Related Literature." *International Journal of Business and Management* 5, no. 12 (2010): 196–205.

Arroyo-Vázquez, Mónica, Peter van der Sijde, and Fernando Jiménez-Sáez. "Innovative and Creative Entrepreneurship Support Services at Universities." *Service Business* 4, no. 1 (2010): 63–76.

Barba-Sánchez, Virginia, María del Pilar Martínez-Ruiz, and Ana Isabel Jiménez-Zarco. "Drivers, Benefits and Challenges of ICT Adoption by Small and Medium Sized Enterprises (SMEs): A Literature Review." *Problems and Perspectives in Management* 5, no. 1 (2007): 104–115.

Bear, Marshall, Alan Gibson, and Rob Hitchins. "From Principles to Practice: Ten Critical Challenges for BDS Market Development." *Small Enterprise Development* 14, no. 4 (December 2003): 10–23.

Becker, Howard S. *Writing for Social Scientists: How to Start and Finish Your Thesis, Book, or Article* 2nd ed. Chicago: Guides to Writing and Publishing, 2016.

Bekefi, Tamara. "Tanzania: Lessons in Building Linkages for Competitive and Responsible Entrepreneurship." UNIDO and Kennedy School of Government, Harvard University, 2006.

Bergek, Anna, and Charlotte Norrman. "Incubator Best Practice: A Framework." *Technovation* 28, no. 1 (2008): 20–28.

Biénabe, Estelle et al. "Linking Small Holder Farmers to Markets: Lessons Learned from Literature Review and Analytical Review of Selected Projects." *Agritrop*. Washington, DC: World Bank, 2, 2004, 84–138. http://agritrop.cirad.fr/524030/.

Biggs, Tyler, and Manju Kedia Shah. "African SMES, Networks, and Manufacturing Performance." *Journal of Banking & Finance* 30, no. 11 (2006): 3043–3066.

Caniëls, Marjolein C.J., Henny A. Romijn, and Marieke de Ruijter-De Wildt. "Can Business Development Services Practitioners Learn from Theories of Innovation and Services Marketing?" *Development in Practice* 16, no. 5 (2006): 425–440.

Chang, B.Y., M.J. Magobe, and Y.B. Kim. "E-Commerce Applications in the Tourism Industry: A Tanzania Case Study." *South African Journal of Business Management* 46, no. 4 (2015): 53–64.

Collier, Paul, and David Dollar. "Can the World Cut Poverty in Half? How Policy Reform and Effective Aid Can Meet International Development Goals." *World Development* 29, no. 11 (2001): 1787–1802.

Dawson, Jonathan with Andy Jeans. *Looking Beyond Credit: Business Development Services and the Promotion of Innovation Among Small Producers.* London: Intermediate Technology Publications Ltd (ITP), 1997. www.cabdirect.org/cabdirect/abstract/19981805592.

Delmar, Frédéric, and Scott Shane. "Does Business Planning Facilitate the Development of New Ventures?" *Strategic Management Journal* 24, no. 12 (2003): 1165–1185.

Delmar, Frédéric, and Scott Shane. "Legitimating First: Organizing Activities and the Survival of New Ventures." *Journal of Business Venturing* 19, no. 3 (2004): 385–410.

Devinney, Timothy, and Natalia Nikolova. "The Client-Consultant Interaction in Professional Business Service Firms: Outline of the Interpretive Model and Implications for Consulting." Paper. Draft Version Presented at The University of New South Wales, New South Wales, 2004.

Diao, Xinshen, and Paul Dorosh. "Demand Constraints on Agricultural Growth in East and Southern Africa: A General Equilibrium Analysis." *Development Policy Review* 25, no. 3 (2007): 275–292.

Dorward, Andrew et al. "Institutions, Markets and Economic Co-Ordination: Linking Development Policy to Theory and Praxis." *Development and Change* 36, no. 1 (2005): 1–25.

Doss, Cheryl, John McPeak, and Christopher B. Barrett. "Interpersonal, Intertemporal and Spatial Variation in Risk Perceptions: Evidence from East Africa." *World Development* 36, no. 8 (2008): 1453–1468.

Edwards, Nelson, Matt Tokar, and Jim Maxwell. "Agribusiness Development in Sub-Saharan Africa: Optimal Strategies and Structures." Technical Paper, no. 83, 1997. http://pdf.usaid.gov/pdf_docs/pnacb834.pdf.

Eisenhardt, Kathleen M. "Building Theories From Case Study Research." *Academy of Management Review* 14, no. 4 (1989): 532–550.

Eskola, Elina. *Agricultural Marketing and Supply Chain Management in Tanzania: A Case Study*, Vol. 16. Dar es Salaam: Economic and Social Research Foundation, 2005.

Gengatharen, Denise E., and Craig Standing. "A Framework to Assess the Factors Affecting Success or Failure of the Implementation of Government-Supported Regional E-Marketplaces for SMEs." *European Journal of Information Systems* 14, no. 4 (2005): 417–433.

Ghobadian, Abby, and David N. Gallear. "Total Quality Management in SMEs." *Omega* 24, no. 1 (1996): 83–106.

Gibb, Allan, and Jun Li. "Organizing for Enterprise in China: What Can We Learn from the Chinese Micro, Small, and Medium Enterprise Development Experience." *Futures* 35, no. 4 (2003): 403–421.

Haberberg, Adrian, and Alison Rieple. *Strategic Management: Theory and Application.* London: Oxford University Press, 2008.

Henson, Spencer, Ann-Marie Brouder, and Winnie Mitullah. "Food Safety Requirements and Food Exports from Developing Countries: The Case of Fish Exports from Kenya to the European Union." *American Journal of Agricultural Economics* 82, no. 5 (2000): 1159–1169.

Heron, John. *The Complete Facilitator's Handbook*. London: Kogan Page, 1999. http://cds.cern.ch/record/1151364.

Karlsson, Tomas, and Benson Honig. "Judging a Business by Its Cover: An Institutional Perspective on New Ventures and the Business Plan." *Journal of Business Venturing* 24, no. 1 (2009): 27–45.

Klinger, Bailey, and Matthias Schündeln. "Can Entrepreneurial Activity Be Taught? Quasi-Experimental Evidence from Central America." *World Development* 39, no. 9 (2011): 1592–1610.

Kubr, Milan. *Management Consulting: A Guide to the Profession*. Geneva: International Labour Organization, 2002.

Lankford, Bruce. "Irrigation Improvement Projects in Tanzania; Scale Impacts and Policy Implications." *Water Policy* 6, no. 2 (2004): 89–102.

Larsen, Kurt, Ronald Kim, and Florian Theus. "Agribusiness and Innovation Systems in Africa." World Bank Publications, 2009. https://elibrary.worldbank.org/doi/pdf/10.1596/978-0-8213-7944-8.

Levitsky, Jacob. *Business Development Services: Review of International Experience*. Intermediate Technology Publications, 2000. https://openlibrary.org/publishers/Intermediate_Technology_Publications.

Levitsky, Jacob. "Support Systems for SMEs in Developing Countries." Small and Medium Enterprises Programme Discussion Paper, United Nations Industrial Development Organization, Vienna, 1996. www.clusterobservatory.in/articles/Article%20No.%2049.pdf.

Macdonald, Stuart, Dimitris Assimakopoulos, and Pat Anderson. "Education and Training for Innovation in SMEs: A Tale of Exploitation." *International Small Business Journal* 25, no. 1 (2007): 77–95.

Mahemba, Christopher M., and Erik J. De Bruijn. "Innovation Activities by Small and Medium-Sized Manufacturing Enterprises in Tanzania." *Creativity and Innovation Management* 12, no. 3 (2003): 162–173.

Makombe, Iddi Adam Mwatima. *Women Entrepreneurship Development and Empowerment in Tanzania: The Case Study of SIDO/UNIDO-Supported Women Microentrepreneurs in the Food Processing Sector*. Cape Town: The University of South Africa, 2006.

Malangi, B. A. "'State of the Art' Review of the Informal Sector in Tanzania, 1990–1999." International Labour Organization and Ministry of Industry and Trade, SME Section, Turin, 2000.

Mather, Charles. "SMEs in South Africa's Food Processing Complex: Development Prospects, Constraints and Opportunities." Working Paper 3–2005, Trade and Industrial Policy Secretariat, 2005. www.smmeresearch.co.za/SMME%20Research%20General/Conference%20Papers/SMEs_South_Africa_food_processing.pdf.

Miehlbradt, A. O., and Mary McVay. "Developing Commercial Markets for Business Development Services: 'Are "How-to-Do-It" Recipes Possible?'" *Seminar Reader of the Third Annual Seminar*. International Labour Organization, Turin, September 1, 2003 [2002].

Miles, Matthew B. "Qualitative Data as an Attractive Nuisance: The Problem of Analysis." *Administrative Science Quarterly* 24, no. 4 (1979): 590–601.

Miles, Matthew B., and A. Michael Huberman. *Qualitative Data Analysis: An Expanded Sourcebook*. London: Sage Publishing, Inc., 2014.

Morrison, Alison, John Breen, and Shameem Ali. "Small Business Growth: Intention, Ability, and Opportunity." *Journal of Small Business Management* 41, no. 4 (2003): 417–425.

Narteh, Bedman. "Knowledge Transfer and Learning: The Case of Danish-Ghanaian Strategic Alliances." Paper. Department of Business Studies, Faculty of Social Sciences, Aalborg University, 2006.

Nieman, Gideon. "Training Entrepreneurs and Small Business Enterprises in South Africa: A Situational Analysis." *Education+Training* 43, no. 8/9 (2001): 445–450.

Nikolova, Natalia, Markus Reihlen, and Jan-Florian Schlapfner. "Client–Consultant Interaction: Capturing Social Practices of Professional Service Production." *Scandinavian Journal of Management* 25, no. 3 (2009): 289–298.

Ogutu-Ohwayo, Richard, and John S. Balirwa. "Management Challenges of Freshwater Fisheries in Africa." *Lakes & Reservoirs: Research & Management* 11, no. 4 (2006): 215–226.

Olomi, D. R. "Opportunities and Challenges for Rural SMEs Development in Tanzania." In Policy Dialogue Seminar Paper, Economic and Social Research Foundation, Donath Olomi, ed., Economic and Social Research Foundation (ESRF), Tanzania, March 23, 2006.

Patton, Michael Quinn. *Qualitative Research*. New York: Wiley Online Library, 2005. http://onlinelibrary.wiley.com/doi/10.1002/0470013192.bsa514/full.

Ram, Monder, and David Deakins. "African-Caribbeans in Business." *Journal of Ethnic and Migration Studies* 22, no. 1 (1996): 67–84.

Remenyi, Dan, and Brian Williams. *Doing Research in Business and Management: An Introduction to Process and Method*. Thousand Oaks, CA: Sage, 1998.

Rice, Mark P. "Co-Production of Business Assistance in Business Incubators: An Exploratory Study." *Journal of Business Venturing* 17, no. 2 (2002): 163–187.

Riege, Andreas M. "Validity and Reliability Tests in Case Study Research: A Literature Review With 'Hands-On' Applications for Each Research Phase." *Qualitative Market Research: An International Journal* 6, no. 2 (2003): 75–86.

Robson, Colin, and Kieran McCartan. *Real World Research*. New York: John Wiley & Sons, 2016.

Rogerson, Christian M. "In Search of the African Miracle: Debates on Successful Small Enterprise Development in Africa." *Habitat International* 25, no. 1 (2001): 115–142.

Savioz, Pascal, and Manuel Blum. "Strategic Forecast Tool for SMEs: How the Opportunity Landscape Interacts With Business Strategy to Anticipate Technological Trends." *Technovation* 22, no. 2 (2002): 91–100.

Schulpen, Lau, and Peter Gibbon. "Private Sector Development: Policies, Practices and Problems." *World Development* 30, no. 1 (2002): 1–15.

Shepherd, Andrew. "Approaches to Linking Producers to Markets: Review of Experiences to Date." Agricultural Management, Marketing and Finance Occasional Paper, Food and Agriculture Organization of United Nations, Rome, 2007.

Sievers, Merten, and Paul Vandenberg. "Synergies Through Linkages: Who Benefits From Linking Micro-Finance and Business Development Services?" *World Development* 35, no. 8 (2007): 1341–1358.

Silverman, David. *Doing Qualitative Research: A Practical Handbook*. Thousand Oaks, CA: Sage, 2013.

Stevenson, Lois, and Annette St-Onge. *Support for Growth-Oriented Women Entrepreneurs in Tanzania. Programme on Boosting Employment Through Small Enterprise Development*. Turin: Job Creation and Enterprise Department, International Labour Office, 2005. www.tzonline.org/pdf/supportforgrowthorientedwomenentrepreneurs.pdf.

St-Jean, Etienne. "Mentor Functions for Novice Entrepreneurs." *Academy of Entrepreneurship Journal* 17, no. 1 (2011): 65.

Timmons, Jeffry A., Stephen Spinelli, and Yinglan Tan. *New Venture Creation: Entrepreneurship for the 21st Century*, Vol. 4. Burr Ridge, IL: Irwin, 1994. www.academia.edu/download/31162458/MBA-559-4.pdf.

Van Geenhuizen, Marina, Nurul Indarti, and Danny P. Soetanto. "Knowledge Acquisition and Innovation: Potentials for Upgrading of Very Small and Small Firms in Furniture

Manufacturing in Indonesia." *International Journal of Foresight and Innovation Policy* 6, no. 4 (2010): 207–224.

Van Gelderen, Marco, Lidewey van de Sluis, and Paul Jansen. "Learning Opportunities and Learning Behaviours of Small Business Starters: Relations With Goal Achievement, Skill Development and Satisfaction." *Small Business Economics* 25, no. 1 (2005): 97–108.

Westhead, Paul, and David Storey. "Management Training and Small Firm Performance: Why Is the Link So Weak?" *International Small Business Journal* 14, no. 4 (1996): 13–24.

Wong, Cecilia, et al. "Management Training in Small and Medium-Sized Enterprises: Methodological and Conceptual Issues." *The International Journal of Human Resource Management* 8, no. 1 (1997): 44–65.

Yin, Robert K. *Case Study Research: Design and Methods.* Thousand Oaks, CA: Sage Publications Ltd., 2009.

Yiridoe, Emmanuel K., and Vincent M. Anchirinah. "Garden Production Systems and Food Security in Ghana: Characteristics of Traditional Knowledge and Management Systems." *Renewable Agriculture and Food Systems* 20, no. 3 (2005): 168–180.

Zahra, Shaker A., and Gerard George. "Absorptive Capacity: A Review, Reconceptualization, and Extension." *Academy of Management Review* 27, no. 2 (2002): 185–203.

14

THE ROLE OF ICT PRODUCTS IN AGRICULTURAL AND AGRIBUSINESS VALUE CHAIN DEVELOPMENT IN TANZANIA

The Case of Tanga Fresh Limited

Abdallah Mmeta Yongolo, Anna Andrew Temu, and Daniel Wilson Ndyetabula

Introduction

It is recognized that there is a sudden development in information and communication technologies (ICT) around the world over the past few years. ICT has entered almost every segment of the society, and the trends show an increased penetration rate. The only difference comes between new ICT such as computers and mobile phones and old ICT such as radio, television, and landline telephones. The new technological innovations seem to bring about more technical efficiency in terms of development, including development in agriculture and agribusiness value chains.[1] Today, a mobile phone can do multiple functions such as receiving, processing, storing, and displaying text and sound together.

Since the end of 20th century, ICT advances have led to multiple convergences of content, computing, telecommunications, and broadcasting. They have brought about changes in other areas, particularly knowledge management and human resources development, which in one way or another enhance agricultural development and agribusiness in Third World countries such as Tanzania. Since the 1990s, telephone service in Tanzania was mainly dependent on the fixed line and was very unreliable. The Tanzania Telecommunication Company (TTCL) provided the service, especially in large cities. However, from 1994, mobile phone technology started to improve. It has impacted the way business is conducted, and it has facilitated learning and knowledge sharing. For example, there is hitherto a resurgence of well-organized information flows among agribusiness value chain beneficiaries worldwide. Value chain actors are empowered in ways that have redefined value chain governance.

ICT has grown to a key factor in socio-economic development and has been associated with successes in agricultural value chain governance and upgrading. Access to relevant information and knowledge seem to have changed in the agribusiness value chain upgrading processes due to advances in ICT. It has improved efficiency and productivity, increased access to market opportunities, and increased potential agricultural development. As a result, ICT products, particularly those associated with mobile phone technology, have been considered so vital that in most developing countries, including Tanzania, it has been incorporated in the agribusiness value chain development and socio-economic development strategies.

The mobile communications technology has quickly become the world's most common way of transmitting information and services in the developing world. Given this dramatic change, mobile applications in general, and mobile applications for agricultural and rural development, in particular, hold significant potential for advancing agriculture and agribusiness development in developing countries. They provide the most affordable ways for millions of people to access information, markets, finance, and governance systems that were previously unavailable to them.

Some developing countries such as Tanzania consider agriculture the backbone of their economies because agriculture accounts for more than 25% of their gross domestic product (GDP) and employs more than 75% of the workforce. Agricultural activities in Tanzania are dominated by small-scale farmers who are numerous, inadequately educated, and facing such challenges as the lack of extension services, access to credit for inputs and, more importantly, lack of market information for both farm inputs and outputs. Reliable information and knowledge on various agricultural issues such as input and output markets, payment settlement systems, and extension services are very important for improving value chain activities. In this regard, access to and use of ICT facilities is the cornerstone to the commercial orientation and inclusion of most small-scale farmers in value chain activities. Effective access and use of agricultural market information through ICT facilities by small-scale farmers transform subsistence smallholding into improved, commercial, and rewarding small-scale farming.

Much as information technology contributes to the growth of world's communication, it also equally contributes to the governance and upgrading of agricultural and agribusiness value chains.[2] In Africa, it is believed that ICT can contribute to fast agricultural and agribusiness value chain development if it is refocused to expand the level of productivity and exposure to marketing activities.[3] Given their superior position in facilitating spread of information, ICT facilities have largely been used in various agribusiness marketing strategies. In Tanzania, for example, a number of agribusiness initiatives and private agribusiness firms use mobile phones and other ICT facilities to share market information, settle transactions, and market agricultural products. It is argued that these new developments have largely contributed to agribusiness value chain efficiency.[4] However, digital divide is still a challenge. Most small-scale farmers are excluded in relevant access and use of ICT facilities in agribusiness value chains. Against this background, the current study was designed to assess the role of ICT products in agribusiness value chain development using Tanga Fresh Limited (TFL; a milk processing company operating in the dairy subsector) as a case study. The chapter identifies systems used by ICT service providers and assesses their impacts on value chain governance and upgrading activities. In articulating the role of ICT, this study identifies the bottlenecks to effective use of ICT products in agribusiness value chains.

The reminder of this chapter is organized as follows: After the introduction is the literature review underpinning the agribusiness value chain construct and the role of ICT facilities in upgrading value chain activities. This section is followed by study methodology and discussion of the findings. The last section of the chapter presents conclusion and recommendations.

Literature Review

Over the past two decades, ICT in Africa has experienced the fastest growth in the global telecommunications market, especially due to the rapid growth of the mobile telecommunications sector. Studies have shown that ICT play a significant role in a country's development, and the strategic application of ICT in the agricultural sector, which is the largest economic sector in most African countries, offers the best opportunity for economic growth and poverty alleviation in Tanzania. The main objective of this study was to assess the role of ICT products in agricultural and agribusiness value chain development in Tanzania.

African countries have been characterized by a number of years' worth of unfruitful attempts to shift from the agricultural sector. On the basis of Western experience, the developing countries are struggling to push their economies through the transformation of their secondary depended sector and to decrease reliance on the primary sector. However, these economies remain predominantly agrarian, with the sector accounting for roughly 15% of the continent's GDP, employing 90% of the rural workforce and 60% of the total labor force (urban plus rural), contributing as much as 40% of export earnings, and providing over 50% of household needs and income.[5]

The share of agriculture in GDP in many African countries is much smaller, often 30% or less, indicating low productivity levels in the sector.[6] Despite the role played by agriculture in development in Africa, agricultural production and yields have lagged far behind those in developed countries over the past few decades. This poor sectoral performance, to a greater extent, has been attributed to underutilization of improved agricultural technologies, which has remained relatively low in developing countries since the 1970s.[7] It should also be noted that a critical force in transforming agriculture in countries such as China and Korea was the investment in transport and communications infrastructure, especially ICT, apart from their emphasis on agricultural research and extension, irrigation systems, and storage facilities, which are essential factors for raising productivity and increasing income for the poor.[8]

Although agriculture and natural resources are deemed to continue to be the key drivers of Africa's economic growth, it is the application of modern technologies that is considered to have the most significant impact on the growth trajectories of most African economies. This being the case, countries have identified ICT as an important component in moving the countries' subsistence-based economy to a service-sector-driven, high-value-added information and knowledge-based economy that can compete effectively in the global market.[9]

Value Chain Approach explains the full range of activities needed to bring a product through the different stages of production. As such, value chains include the vertically linked interdependent processes that generate value for the consumer.[10] A value chain analysis provides a convenient framework to study the impact of economic, technological, and institutional changes through global marketing chains and distribution of the incidence of those impacts and any gains arising from them between participants at different production and marketing stages.[11]

Value chain is a specific type of supply chain, where the actors actively seek to support each other so that they can increase their efficiency and competitiveness. They invest time, effort and money and build relationships with each other to reach a common goal of satisfying consumer needs so that they can increase their profit. The author defined actors as those involved in producing, processing, trading, or consuming a particular agricultural product, which includes direct actors who are commercially involved in the chain (producers, traders, retailers, consumers) and indirect actors who provide financial or non-financial support services such as bankers and credit agencies, business service providers, government, researchers, and extension staffs.

Value Chain Analysis extends the traditional supply chain analysis by locating values to each stage of the chain. The term 'supply chain' is used to encompass every activity involved in producing and delivering a final product, from the suppliers to customers. The primary focus of supply chains is thus on cost and efficiencies in supply, whereas value chains focus more on value creation, innovation, product development, and marketing.[12]

Value chain actors are those involved in supplying inputs, producing, processing, trading, or consuming a particular agricultural product. They include direct actors who are commercially involved in the chain (input suppliers, producers, processors, traders, retailers, consumers) and indirect actors who provide financial or non-financial support services, such as bankers and credit providers, business service providers, government, researchers, and extension agents.[13]

The use of ICT in agribusiness value chain and delivering of agricultural extension service in Tanzania was criticized to be ineffective and inefficient. Various literatures established that reasons for such ineffective use of ICT for agricultural and agribusiness value chain developments in Tanzania are due to lack of effective and reliable network systems.[14]

In attempts to boost and eliminate the problem for the development of agriculture and agribusiness value chain in Tanzania, several strategies have been established. One is the policy reforms, which are intended to decentralize delivery of agricultural extension services to local authorities so as to enhance the whole process of agribusiness value chain and agricultural development at large. Decentralization intended to ensure that more farmers, especially smallholder farmers, have access to effective agricultural extension services to enhance production for value chain development.[15] Some of these reforms include the Agriculture and Livestock Policy, National Agriculture Extension Programme, and Agricultural Sector Development Programme. However, these reforms failed to convert the agriculture and agribusiness value chain in the country.

Many studies conducted on the impact of ICT in agriculture and agribusiness value chain reveal that the effective use of appropriate ICT tools can strengthen the whole process of the value chain in agriculture and supplement the current agribusiness value chain system for a better life of the majority stakeholders—stakeholders along the value chain.[16] From the literature review, the use of ICT for agricultural development seemed to be not as effective as it was expected. Thus, this study tries to fill the gap by identifying the possible mechanisms to intervene in the use of ICT so as to enhance the agricultural sector in the country.

Agronomic and Marketing Information in Agribusinesses

The role of market information in facilitating efficiency and performance as well as equity in agribusiness value chain development is widely acknowledged in Tanzanian societies nowadays.[17] Accurate and timely market information enhances market performance by improving the knowledge of market actors. An equal balance of knowledge provides a more equal distribution of the gains from efficient market price formation. Presence of and access to ICT helps farmers in a number of ways. Traditional media and new ICT have played a critical part in disseminating important information to rural people in a way they manage to increase their potential and income as well.[18]

For example, the prepaid recharge helps mobile phone subscribers to use text messages across distances that would otherwise take days to travel, hence changing life for the better.[19] The use of mobile phones and messaging technology helps farmers in the country to get access to valuable agronomist, market, and other relevant data. Studies in Kenya show that available information on agronomist and market prices for seed cotton strengthened farmers' position when bargaining with traders.[20]

Again in Kenya, vegetable farmers tried to reinforce radio and television broadcasts to announce prices fixed by the government for horticultural staffs, and they managed to step ahead, as some of the local radios later started to announce the prices of other vegetables as indicated by the respective authorities.[21] Studies in Kenya showed that an Internet network among farmer organizations had increased farmers' incomes by providing information about crop status, weather, global market prices, and training.[22]

The literature also shows that information made available to traders, including big companies, reduces the price difference across markets. Kenya and Rwanda, for example, realized that the available information between exchanging agencies helps to reduce price differences in the marketplaces, though studies show that in most of the East African Countries, this has not yet been realized.[23] Moreover, it is realized that the adoption of mobile phones by fishermen and wholesalers in Tanzania has been connected with a sudden reduction in price dispersion and adherence to the price stability and price list provided by the given authorities.[24] In his three-country study (India, Tanzania, and Mozambique), Jensen found significant correlations between telecommunications and indicators of agribusiness value chain and socio-economic development as well.[25] Thus, ICT-related products can enhance agricultural development and agribusiness value chain by facilitating knowledge management.[26] Potential partners in agricultural sector may take full advantage of ICT to accelerate productivity and generate more income by adopting new technologies, including new varieties, adding value and marketing their products. Timely access to market information via communication networks also helps farmers make well-informed decisions about what crops to plant and where to sell their produce and buy inputs.

The adoption of modern industrial inputs in agricultural production relies on the information and communication infrastructure. The use of ICT products has contributed positively and significantly to output and productivity for development of agribusiness value chain in most of the Southern Saharan Countries.[27] However, literatures have alerted about the likely negative impact of ICT on the rural poor and disadvantaged groups if not well planned and implemented. ICT can result in the marginalization of economically disadvantaged groups within both developing and even developed countries.[28] One of the reasons is that different communication methods and different information sources are valued differently by rural farmers.[29] Also policy and infrastructural issues play a key role in ICT adoption by rural farmers and by sex.[30] The big thing to consider is when, where, how, and which ICT should be used for which category of societies to enhance their agricultural and agribusiness value chain development.

Other studies show that most young people preferred to use mobile phones and computers; women preferred listening to the radio and watching television, whereas men preferred listening to news on both the radio and television, and watching football matches.[31] This suggests that as the ICT infrastructure grows and connectivity and hardware costs decline, the critical constraints are likely to be the development of an appropriate policy and institutional environment for the creation and delivery of information and knowledge to the end users.[32] Thus, identifying suitable ICT for a specific rural segment is a thing to consider.

Research Methodology

Study Area

This study was conducted in Morogoro and Tanga regions (see Figure 14.1). Selected districts were Morogoro Rural, Kilosa, Handeni, Korogwe, and Tanga Municipality. Each district was represented by 10 respondents who serve Tanga Fresh Limited milk processing factory to total 50 respondents. Both regions have a conducive environment for dairy cattle keeping, owing to the climatic condition in the respective areas.

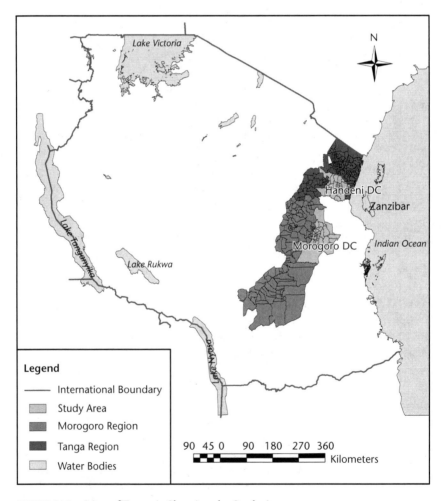

FIGURE 14.1 Map of Tanzania Showing the Study Areas

Population and Sample Size

The study population included all primary actors in agriculture and agribusiness value chain development in Morogoro region, based on the Growing Innovative Entrepreneurs (GIE) project objectives. The 50 respondents were randomly selected among the identified value chain primary actors. Apart from face-to-face interview, focus group discussion was also done to get in-depth and supportive information for the study. Key informants included ICT companies like Vodacom, Tigo, and Zantel and others included milk processors, government institutions, and NGOs.

Sampling Technique

In this study, the respondents and key informants across the agribusiness value chain were randomly selected and contacted in person for interviews that were conducted in the study area. Mobile companies such as Tigo and Vodacom were purposefully selected due to their products supporting agribusiness: Vodacom has M-Pesa, M-Pawa, and text messages on agribusiness and Tigo has Tigo Kilimo and Tigo Pesa. Since Tanga Fresh Limited has a special agreement with Vodacom concerning the e-payments for its customers, it was, therefore, selected for case study. Tanga Fresh Limited was selected on the basis of its contract with the Vodacom Company on the e-transactions through its product M-Pesa. The main aim was to find out whether e-payments brought more benefits to the farmers (Tanga Fresh Limited clients) than the cash payments, which had been in operation prior to the current (e-payment) system of payments.

Simple random sampling was employed to randomly select 50 farmers to accomplish the sampling frame from the study area with the assistance from the Tanga Fresh Limited officials and village and ward leaders. Ten respondents were selected from every targeted district of the study areas. Additionally, a stratified sampling technique was used in selection of farmers from various locations.

Service providers were used as key informants for whom a checklist was prepared so as to gather the intended information. Each service provider was provided with five checklists. Most of potential ICT service providers in Tanzania were included in this study after the identification process for ICT products used in the agriculture and agribusiness subsectors. The mobile phone companies, Airtel Tanzania, Vodacom Tanzania, Zantel, and Tigo were all consulted in this matter. Among the companies, Vodacom mobile company was selected due to its services that are related to agribusiness value chain development and the services that it performs for TFL customers. Cross section research design was used to collect data from the primary actors (representative participants of the Tanga Fresh Limited milk purchase program) of agribusiness value chain (farmers) in Morogoro and Tanga regions. Primary data were collected in Morogoro and Tanga regions using both semi-structured questionnaire and checklist.

298 Abdallah Mmeta Yongolo et al.

In an effort to draw valid results and conclusion, the data were collected, edited, verified, and coded with the aid of Statistical Package for Social Sciences (SPSS). Descriptive results such as means, frequencies, percentages, graphs, and ranges were generated and used to establish the relationship between variables, especially in terms of the contribution of ICT in agriculture and agribusiness value chain development in Tanzania and the general agribusiness value chain governance in the country.

Results and Discussion

Case Description

Tanga Fresh Limited is one of the leading milk processing plants in the country, which was established in 1996 in Tanga Region as a joint venture between FriZania cooperation from Friesland in Northern Netherlands and Tanga Dairy Cooperative Union (TDCU), a Tanzanian farmer cooperative. According to Africa Enterprise Challenge Fund (AECF), Tanga Fresh Limited has invested US$4.5 million in a new milk processing plant that has increased their capacity to process raw milk from 20,000 to 50,000 liters per day. The plant established the cooperative model, which organizes the collection of raw milk from smallholder dairy producers that ensures reliable daily supply of milk required for processing.

The history of Tanga Fresh Limited goes back to 1985, when the Dutch–Tanzanian bilateral program in smallholder dairy extension services was established. In this program, cross-bred animals were introduced to seven rural households. Through this aid program, farmers were taught how and encouraged to keep dairy cattle. In 1992, the program emphasized farmer's organization, milk marketing, and input supply, which led to the registration of the Tanga Dairies Co-operative Union (TDCU). As the number of participating farmers increased, milk production led to raw milk problems. In 1996, a group of Dutch farmers entered into a joint venture with TDCU to start Tanga Fresh so that branded milk could be sold in the market. At that time, the old record of 15,000 liters per day plant could no longer handle the volume and thus with new investments in an unused dairy building on a 20-acre parcel of land was acquired, followed by an adequate rehabilitation and equipping the plant with state-of-the-art machinery. The dairy farmers in Tanga Region organized themselves in primary societies that ran the milk collecting centers. The milk collectors are entrusted with receiving quality milk from the farmers, which is then chilled in bulk containers ready for transportation to the factory for the processing.

The M-Pesa System and How It Works

This service has been introduced in collaboration between TFL and Vodacom Tanzania through a special contract signed by the two parties. It is a kind of

Role of ICT Products 299

win-win contract, as no part pays anything for a sign, but each part has some kind of benefits. For example, Vodacom Tanzania benefits by having many transactions through farmers' payments, as every farmer is charged some amount of money as transaction cost for him or her to withdraw money from the mobile phone, and thus the mobile phone's company earn money in this way. TFL benefits by reducing not only operation costs but also the risks associated with the payment systems. For example, they managed to avoid theft, which could happen at a time they pay farmers by cash or during transportation of cash.

Tanga Fresh Limited opened a special M-Pesa account that enables them to deposit a huge amount of money. So when TFL wants to pay their farmers, the only thing they do is deposit the amount in the account to Vodacom Headquarters, then Vodacom confirms and verifies that the money has been deposited. After getting feedback from Vodacom about the deposition of money, TFL's finance department cross-checks the names of all farmers and the amount to be paid and approves the money to be paid. Then the database is sent to the IT department for payment. The IT department has a special program that enables them to have a single click to disburse money to all farmers at a time without regard to their numbers (see Figure 14.2).

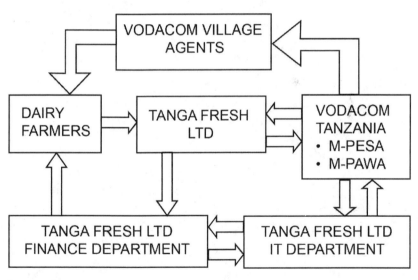

FIGURE 14.2 Relationship Between TFL and Vodacom M-Pesa System in Milk Value Chain

Setup of TFL's E-Payment Systems

Tanga Fresh Limited formerly used cash payments to its customers (dairy farmers and other milk sellers). This system ensured that farmers get paid in two installments so that they can afford purchasing of the facilities to handle dairy products. Despite the fact that farmers got direct cash from Tanga Fresh Limited, the system lacked confidentiality, as robbers knew that farmers were paid. In this regard, the events of farmers' hijack were rampant. Similarly, farmers had to spend a lot of time queuing in the bank to deposit cash received from TFL.

According to the findings through field observations, the use of e-payment systems was initiated to reduce inefficiencies in payments and provide timely payments to the customers. Tanga Fresh Limited established farmers' payment system through M-Pesa. Apart from the M-Pesa services, the company also had been paying farmers through their respective bank accounts for those who have the bank account and wished to be paid through banks. The Tanga Fresh Limited management decided to come up with this service so as to reduce operating costs, to avoid risks associated with the old payment system, including theft, and also to reduce farmer's disturbances in terms of time. With the new system of payment, farmers are able to get their money in a very short time after being approved by TFL. Since the system has been established, farmers are now able to get their money even when they are at home, unlike the time when farmers were supposed to go to milk collection centers for their money.

Farmers' Opinion on the Benefits New Payment System

The highest number of individuals whose payments were under M-Pesa and Banks show that M-Pesa and banks participated fully in the mobile money payment system (MMPS) and thus became important in the agribusiness development. Respondents' opinions on whether the system had brought them benefits shows that 90% benefited from the current system of payment (MMPS), whereas only 10% did not see the benefits from the cash payment system of the MMPS. Moreover, study findings (Table 14.1) show that 76% of the respondents agreed that the current system influences efficiency of local suppliers/farmers, whereas 24% respondents did not agree that the current system of payment influences efficiency to the local suppliers/farmers. The large number of the respondents who had benefited from the current system of payment implies that improvement in the system could bring dramatic positive changes in the dairy product business among the value chain actors.

Although e-payment is predominantly in use, the traditional cash payment is still used in villages in areas that do not have Vodacom mobile services because of a lack of mobile phone networks. Similarly, lack of use could be due to lack of confidence among the farmers on the effectiveness of the system. The next section describes the survey on farmers who were using e-payments.

Role of ICT Products **301**

TABLE 14.1 The E-Payment System Versus the Traditional Cash Payment System

Variable	Frequency	Percent
Payment system used by TFL prior to date on the local milk suppliers/farmers		
Manual payment systems(cash)	50	100.0
The current payment system used by TFL to facilitate payments is		
M-Pesa	2	4.0
M-Pesa and bank	48	96.0
Do you think this system (MMPS) is beneficial to you as a milk producer?		
Yes	45	90.0
No	5	10.0
Does the current system influence efficiency to local suppliers/farmers?		
Yes	38	76.0
No	12	24.0

Demographic and Socio-Economic Characteristics

Sex of the Household Head

Dairy cattle keeping businesses in selected districts were dominated by men. Dairy is a high-income-generating activity in the area, thus more likely male dominated. Seventy-eight percent of the respondents were men, whereas 22% were women (Table 14.2). Mongomongo (2014) observed that the majority of the productive economic activities is dominated by men, when it was found that 75% of the respondents were men, whereas 25% were women. These findings show that sex was an important demographic characteristic, because in Tanzanian social context, the matter of one's sex has implications on production, involvement in business, and access and control over resources within households.

Very surprisingly, milk was believed to be traded more by women than men both in Maasai and other tribes; however, Tanga- and Morogoro-selected districts were different, because in Arusha, milk is considered to pay less when compared with cattle, which is considered as men's business and, therefore, milk finds its way into women's ownership, whereas in Tanga and Morogoro, milk is men's business, as most of the milk sellers are not the dairy cattle keepers, but rather are the businessmen and businesswomen who have enough capital investment in business—something that is very rare among most of the females.

Age

From the findings presented in Table 14.2, 38% of the respondents were between 40 and 59 years old, whereas 32% were between 20 and 39 years old. Thirty

302 Abdallah Mmeta Yongolo et al.

TABLE 14.2 Demographic and Socio-Economic Characteristics

Variable	Categories	Frequency	Percent
Sex of the household head	Male	39	78.0
	Female	11	22.0
Age	20–39	16	32.0
	40–59	19	38.0
	> 59	15	30.0
Marital status of the respondent	Married	35	70.0
	Single	8	16.0
	Widowed	5	10.0
	Divorced	2	4.0
Education level of the respondent	No formal education	3	6.0
	Primary education	31	62.0
	Secondary education	11	22.0
	Post-secondary education	5	10.0
Occupation			
1. Primary occupation of the respondent	Wage employment	13	26.0
	Business	11	22.0
	Crop production	26	52.0
2. Secondary occupation of the respondent	Dairy cattle keeping	47	94.0
	Business	3	6.0

percent of the respondents were older than 59. Seventy percent of the respondents between 20 and 59 years old show that the majority of those who were engaged in the use of ICT in agriculture and agribusiness value chain in Tanzania are those who are more energetic than the older age individuals. This implies that the MMPS use in agriculture and agribusiness value chain has actors, most of whom are those younger than 60 years old. This concurs with the argument by Efraji (2011) that they are between 18 and 60 years old.

On the other hand, changes in technology had influenced farmers who used to supply milk to the Tanga Fresh Limited. When the milk processing company changed, clients had to adapt to the technology in issuing payments. It had been observed that there were many disadvantages associated with the traditional system of payments, and clients could not resist TFL's changes to mode of payment, as it is the only milk processor that is operating for which the farmers have built confidence in the milk value chain.

The Role of ICT Products in Agribusiness Value Chain Development

Study findings presented in Figure 14.3 show that ICT plays great roles in agribusiness value chain development. The roles include easy communication among

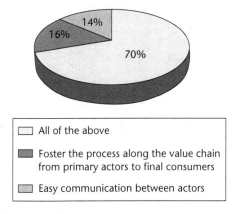

FIGURE 14.3   Roles of ICT in Agribusiness Value Chain Development

the actors (14.4%) and fostering coordination processes along the value chain from primary actors to final consumers (16.6%). On the other hand, 70.7% of the respondents reported that the most important role of ICT is easy communication among the actors and coordination among actors. As long as suppliers have supplied their milk to TFL, they needed not to go to TFL physically to queue for payment. This is very excellent according to respondent smallholder suppliers.

Products of ICT Important in Agribusiness Development

Study findings presented in Table 14.3 indicate that mobile phone applications and radio programs are the main ICT products that was reported to be used by 86% of the respondents, whereas 2% respondents reported using M-Pesa services as another ICT product. The highest percentage of the respondents who were aware of the ICT products used in agribusiness value chain show that ICT was not a new issue in the study area, implying that the products were in use by the majority, which may suggest its increased use for increasing profit gains among the actors.

These study findings (Table 14.3) indicate that there were several ICT-based services that had been in use by the respondents in the study area. These services included M-Pesa (62%), radio programs and M-Pesa services (10%), M-Pesa and bank services and other services like computer and Internet through banking systems (2%) and radio programs (2%). According to these results, M-Pesa services had been found to have been the major MMPS that were used by the majority. This suggests that improved efficiency use of ICT products in the development of agriculture and agribusiness could improve the well-being of the value actors' incomes and food security. On the other hand, use of Internet had been too low compared with other ICT-based services, which may suggest a low level of technical knowhow to use the related services and higher costs involved purchasing ICT hardware.

304 Abdallah Mmeta Yongolo et al.

TABLE 14.3 ICT Products That Promote Agribusiness Value Chain

Products	Frequency	Percent
M-Pesa services	1	2.0
Mobile phone applications and radio programs	43	86.0
I know nothing	5	10.0
Used both right	1	2.0
A list of ICT-based services that had been used		
M-Pesa	31	62.0
Not applicable	7	14.0
M-Pesa and radio programs	5	10.0
Radio programs	1	2.0
Computer and Internet through banking systems	1	2.0
M-Pesa and banks	5	10.0

Source of Initial Capital and Experience in Dairy Product Business

Study findings in Table 14.4 show that about 60% of the respondents' capital source is private, about 20% of the respondents indicated that TASAF contributed to their capital source, 16% sourced capital from formal credit institutions, and 2% obtained capital for dairy business from friends and informal credit sources. The largest number of the respondents whose capital source was own savings indicate that the majority of the dairy products value chain business actors had no access to formal credit institutions that could provide them with a reasonable amount of credit to run their business; this could be due to lack of collateral among the business persons that is required as bank loan/credit security. Dependence on informal financial capital sources is a drawback to business undertakings because informal sources of finance such as friends, family, business colleagues, clubs, associations, societies, or savings usually do not match the financial needs of an individual to the effective running of the business.

As indicated in Table 14.4, more than 60% of the respondents sell their milk to Tanga Fresh Limited, whereas 8% sell their milk to cooperatives. About 30% of the respondents sell their milk to both Tanga Fresh Limited and cooperatives. The largest number of respondents who used to sell dairy products to the company implies that TFL had been the leading company that had been the main market entry point for most of the milk suppliers within the study area.

Experience in any business undertaking increases efficiency and effectiveness in conducting the business, thus it was imperative to analyze how long the respondents had been in the dairy business within the study area. Findings show that 50% respondents had been in the business for more than 5 years, whereas very few had only 1 to 3 years of dairy businesses. The large number of the respondents who had a long time in the dairy business implies that many had

Role of ICT Products **305**

TABLE 14.4 Dairy Business Capital Source and Experience in Milk Business

Variable	Frequency	Percent
Source of capital for dairy product establishment		
Own saving	30	60.0
Family/friend	1	2.0
Formal credit	8	16.0
Informal credit	1	2.0
TASAF program	10	20.0
Where do you sell your milk?		
Tanga Fresh Limited	31	62.0
All of the above	15	30.0
Cooperatives	4	8.0
For how long have you been in the business?		
1–2 years	10	20.0
3–4 years	15	30.0
more than 5 years	25	50.0

enough experience in the business and that knowledgeable about the importance of MMPS in agribusiness development, as they had experience in the profits and benefits of the system when compared with the previous manual payment system that was in use.

Use of Funds Obtained From TFL in the Study Area

Figure 14.4 presents findings on various ways in which income generated from milk selling to TFL by dairy farmers was used. Findings show that 48% of the respondents used their money for supporting children's education by paying school fees, whereas 22% reported that they used the money for mixed household expenditure. The findings also show that children's school fees payments were the major issue that was reported by the majority, implying that benefits from milk value chain through MMPS increased access to important social services by the households involved in the dairy product value chain. This is because, through e-payments, people were able to save when compared with the cash payment system by which the farmer received a lump sum in cash and use the whole of it.

Proportion of the Income Saved and Spent

Study findings presented in Table 14.5 show that 84% of the respondents' income saving was between 0 and 20%, whereas 4% of respondents were able to save their income portion above 40%. On the other hand, expenditure was too high compared with saving. For example, according to the findings, 76% of the respondents

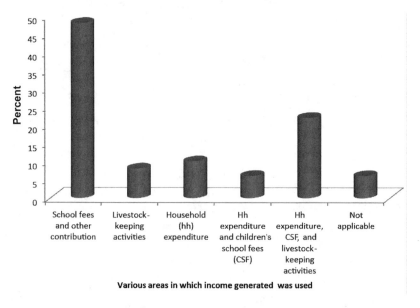

FIGURE 14.4 Income Use by Respondents

TABLE 14.5 Income Saving and Expenditure

Variable	Frequency	Percent
Income saved (%) as the result of using ICT		
0–20	42	84.0
21–40	6	12.0
> 40	2	4.0
Income spent (%) as the result of using ICT		
1–40	1	2.0
41–80	11	22.0
> 80	38	76.0

were found to have spent more than 81% of the income generated, whereas 2% were found to have spent 1% to 40% of their income.

The higher expenditure than saving implies that investment in the business was very low, since the amount that one saves indicates how much he or she can invest in the business undertaking. This is similar to what Kwai and Urassa (2015) found, in that 62.5% of the farmers in Mbozi District who were SACCOs members had savings less than TSh 100,000, implying that most did not save much, further implying that there was lack of adequate knowledge among the farmers on the importance of saving.

The Level of Use and Awareness of MMPS by Beneficiaries

Study findings in Table 14.6 show that 38% of the respondents were aware of the M-Pawa offered by Vodacom mobile company through its M-Pesa service, but about 62% did not know about this service. Though the service was well known to many respondents, findings indicate that 2% did not know if it was important to them, whereas only 30% know its importance. Additionally, there were 68% who were neutral about M-Pawa being important or not important. This implies that much was needed to be done in order to make it both well known in terms of its benefits and actually used by the stakeholders. With regard to the use of M-Pawa, only 4% of the respondents were able to tell that it is used as a bank, whereas 12% claimed that it stimulated the saving habit on the part of farmers; and another 12% claimed that it serves both banking and stimulation of the saving habits for farmers. Surprisingly, many 72% did not have a decision on its benefits. This implies the service might have been very new or somehow not new but not well promoted among the beneficiaries regarding its importance in business activities.

Perception of Primary Value Chain Actors on the Use of ICT Products

Findings in Table 14.7 show that 72% of the respondents have access to the MMPS applications to support their daily agribusiness activities, whereas 28% had no access to the same services in the study area. The large number of people who have access to MMPS applications indicates that MMPS applications were open to every individual who was in need and willing to access the services. Similarly, findings have shown that 86% of the respondents were able to use the services, whereas only 14% did not use them. This study's findings are in line with what

TABLE 14.6 Level of Awareness and Use of the MMPS

Variable	Frequency	Percent
Do you know M-Pawa?		
Yes	19	38.0
No	31	62.0
Is M-Pawa of important to you as farmers?		
Yes	15	30.0
No	1	2.0
Not Applicable	34	68.0
What is the importance of M-Pawa to you?		
Act like a bank	2	4.0
Stimulates farmers' habit to save	6	12.0
1 and 2 are correct	6	12.0
Not Applicable	36	72.0

TABLE 14.7 Perceptions on Access and Use of ICT Products

Variable	Frequency	Percent
Respondent had access to MMPS		
Yes (have access)	36	72.0
No (don't have access)	14	28.0
Respondent had used any of the MMPS		
Yes	43	86.0
No	7	14.0

was found by Kwai and Urassa (2015) in the study of the contribution of SAC-COs to an income poverty reduction in Mbozi District, where it was found that 77.5% of the respondents perceived well that the SACCOs contributed more to the income poverty reduction, which led to improving their standard of living in the rural farming communities.

Conclusion and Recommendations

Conclusion

The findings of this study have revealed that MMPS play a great role in agricultural and agribusiness value chain development in Tanzania, as it was found in the case of TFL. As the leading processing plant in the country, TFL has shown that through the use of MMPS in the payments of its customers, the operations come to be more effective. Thus, its efficiency in the provision of the services to the farmers/local suppliers can be improved more than if the previous local payment system was to be used. Various roles played by mobile phones included easy communication among the actors and fostering the process along the value chain from primary actors to the final consumers. Implying that, through mobile phones, there had been easy access to relevant information and knowledge to the agribusiness value chain actors that had made changes in the agribusiness value chain process and thus improved efficiency in service delivery and productivity among the producers as well as improved access to market opportunities by the farmers.

From the study findings, it is revealed that ICT has a number of products that value chain actors, especially the respondents, had accessed. These products include mobile phone applications from various mobile phone companies such as Vodacom Tanzania, Airtel, Zantel, and Tigo, among which Vodacom Tanzania is identified to be an important mobile phone company in milk value chain development due to its supportive services provided to TFL customers (dairy farmers and milk suppliers) through its M-Pesa and M-Pawa services. Findings have revealed that the majority of the respondents used the products offered by the Vodacom company through MMPS. Findings further revealed that M-Pesa services had been the major service that is depended upon by the majority, and thus suggesting improved efficiency use of MMPS in agribusiness value chain, which in turn could improve the well-being of the value actors' households' incomes and food security.

The use of M-Pesa services is favorable to most of the respondents because it saves time and ensures security and confidentiality of its customers, though it is accompanied by charges, which increase operational costs to its customers. Additionally, MMPS was preferred to the old manual payment system, as it increased income and scale of production and supplies among the farmers and local suppliers—the benefits that had increased the value chain actors' ability to meet expenses related to child education matters.

Findings have also revealed that the level of use and awareness of MMPS by potential beneficiaries in agribusiness value chain was very high, implying that MMPS brought more benefits than the old payment system. However, M-Pawa as the money saving Vodacom M-Pesa service is not being used by many, which may be due to lack of awareness of its importance as the result of lack of enough promotion campaign from its implementers, which implies that much needs to be done in order to make it both well known in terms of its benefits and actually used by the stakeholders, specifically the dairy farmers in the study area.

Finally, the findings revealed that perception of primary value chain actors on the use of ICT products in the daily activities was positive. A high proportion of the farmers have access to the ICT applications to support their daily agribusiness activities, which indicates that ICT has not been discriminative in use and access. Also, the majority of the respondents agreed that the current system does influence efficiency to local suppliers/farmers, which suggests a positive change in terms of income generation and wellness of households participating in dairy value chain associated with e-payments.

Recommendations

Because ICT products play great roles in agricultural and agribusiness value chain development in Tanzania as it was found in the case of TFL within the study area, the study recommends having strong public-private partnerships (PPP) for ensuring effective collaborations among TFL and other non-governmental organizations (NGOs) in finding ways of reducing the cost associated with using MMPS that will make the majority have access to and use MMPS. Though the initiatives of establishing MMPS by TFL were good, the company could have involved the government in order to be more effective and cover a large number of dairy farmers in the regions where TFL is operating.

Because use of MMPS could increase value chain actors' ability to save income and increase investing in dairy product production, processing, and marketing, the Vodacom Company should put more effort into n promoting its M-Pawa so that more people may be attracted to using it. Tanga Fresh Limited should make sure that whenever a new technology is introduced, the public and the government are well informed and involved in order to ensure high technology adoption. On the other hand, Internet technology use should be made common for local producers and suppliers of milk so that they can be in a better position to search for their products to market. The role of the government, NGOs, and financial institutions should be to reduce the costs involved in using the services by providing subsidies and reducing taxes on mobile phones, specifically smartphones. Additionally, banks should charge lower interest rates on the loans they advance to the producers and other actors to make them generate profits from their involvement in the milk value chain. There should be strategies for providing relevant education to the farmers on the use of Internet services through mobile phones. It is also recommended that M-Pesa service costs should be reduced to make the local suppliers/farmers continue using this service and make a profit that can sustain them to continue with their business in the dairy products industry.

This study recommends that more output-based research and projects should be done in the regions, creating a unit for output-based research on the use of MMPS in order to develop agriculture and boost agribusiness value chains. Research and project outcomes will bring in and strengthen both personal and institutional capabilities in terms of adapting to the modern technologies. Similar studies should be conducted in other areas of similar or different major income-generating activities to see the gaps associated with the use of MMPS in promoting agribusiness value chain. Such studies will be vital because the socio-economic and geographical environment differs from place to place.

Since milk agents face financial constraints, lack of milk storage facilities, and lack of market information on milk, there should be efforts by the stakeholders (government, NGOs, and processors) to make sure that the farmer or milk agents are directly linked to the buyers. Efforts should also be made to make sure that milk and MMPS are well advertised and enough promotion campaigns are made through the use of PPP collaborations.

Notes

1 Ahmed Tareq Rashid and Laurent Elder, "Mobile Phones and Development: An Analysis of IDRC-Supported Projects," *The Electronic Journal of Information Systems in Developing Countries* 36 (2009).
2 Temitope Waheed Oshikoya and M. Nureldin Hussain, "Information Technology and the Challenge of Economic Development in Africa," *African Development Review* 10, no. 1 (1998): 100–133.
3 Aarti Kawlra, "The Gender and Citizenship in the Information Society (CITIGEN) Research Programme," accessed August 6, 2017, http://gender-is-itizenship.net/resources/SOA_India.pdf.
4 Kerry McNamara, "Enhancing the Livelihoods of the Rural Poor Through ICT: A Knowledge Map," The World Bank, 2008, http://agris.fao.org/agris-search/search.do?recordID=US2012415552.
5 Sunil Sanghvil, Rupert Simons, and Roberto Uchoa, "Four Lessons for Transforming African Agriculture," *McKinsey*, April 2011, Accessed January 19, 2018, www.

mckinsey.com/industries/public-sector/our-insights/four-lessons-for-transforming-african-agriculture

6 AfDB, OECD, and UNECA UNDP, "African Economic Outlook 2012," Western African Countries African Development Bank. Dakar, Senegal. Accessed January 19, 2018. http://www.africaneconomicoutlook.org/en/countries/west-africa/cape-verde.

7 Aker C. Jenny, "Dial 'A' for Agriculture: Using Information and Communication Technologies for Agricultural Extension in Developing Countries," Tufts University, 2010.

8 AfDB, OECD, and UNDP, African Economic Outlook 2012, Western African Countries African Development Bank. Dakar, Senegal. Accessed January 19, 2018, http://www.africaneconomicoutlook.org/en/countries/west-africa/cape-verde/.

9 An Ansoms, "Striving for Growth, Bypassing the Poor? A Critical Review of Rwanda's Rural Sector Policies," *The Journal of Modern African Studies* 46, no. 1 (2008): 1–32.

10 Raphael Kaplinsky and Mike Morris. *A Handbook for Value Chain Research*, Vol. 113. (Ottawa: IDRC, 2001), www.prism.uct.ac.za/Papers/VchNov01.pdf.

11 Ibid.

12 Andrew Feller, Dan Shunk, and Tom Callarman, "Value Chains Versus Supply Chains," *BP Trends* (March 2006): 1–7.

13 Kaplinsky and Morris, *A Handbook for Value Chain Research*.

14 Camilius Sanga et al., "On Search for Strategies to Increase the Coverage of Agricultural Extension Service: Web-Based Farmers' Advisory Information System," *International Journal of Computing & ICT Research* 7, no. 1 (2013).

15 Barnabas Kapange and Po O. Box, "ICTs and National Agricultural Research Systems—The Case of Tanzania," Research and Development, Ministry of Agriculture and Food Security, 2004.

16 Sanga et al., "On Search for Strategies to Increase the Coverage of Agricultural Extension Service."

17 Peter G. Helmberger, Gerald R. Campbell, and William D. Dobson, "Organization and Performance of Agricultural Markets," 1981, http://agris.fao.org/agris-search/search.do?recordID=US2016214955.

18 A. Verhulst, "Lessons from Field Experience in the Development of Monogastric Animal Production," in *Proceedings of the Expert Consultation on Strategies for Sustainable Animal Agriculture in Developing Countries* (Rome, Italy: FAO, October 1991, 1992), http://193.190.239.98/handle/10390/4076.

19 Aloyce Menda, "ICT for Improved Crop Marketing in Rural Tanzania," *CROMABU*, 12, no. 10 (2005): 2009, Retrieved from www.Cromabul.ComOn

20 Mike Stockbridge, Laurence Smith, and H.R. Lohano, "Cotton and Wheat Marketing and the Provision of Pre-Harvest Services in Sindh Province, Pakistan," 1998, http://eprints.soas.ac.uk/id/eprint/9098.

21 Ibid.

22 UNDP, UNEP, "World Bank, and WRI (2000)," *World Resources*, 2001, 87–102.

23 Andrew W. Shepherd et al., "Marketing and Rural Finance Farm Radio as a Medium for Market Information Dissemination," 2001, http://agris.fao.org/agris-search/search.do?recordID=XF2016044670.

24 Robert Jensen, "The Digital Provide: Information (Technology), Market Performance, and Welfare in the South Indian Fisheries Sector," *The Quarterly Journal of Economics* 122, no. 3 (2007): 879–924.

25 Robert Jensen, "The Digital Provide: Information (Technology), Market Performance, and Welfare in the South Indian Fisheries Sector," *The Quarterly Journal of Economics* 122, no. 3 (2007): 879–924.

26 N.H. Rao, "A Framework for Implementing Information and Communication Technologies in Agricultural Development in India," *Technological Forecasting and Social Change* 74, no. 4 (2007): 491–518.

27 Klaus Hüfner, "UNESCO—United Nations Educational, Scientific and Cultural Organization," *A Concise Encyclopedia of the United Nations* (2009): 715–718, http://

312 Abdallah Mmeta Yongolo et al.

booksandjournals.brillonline.com/content/books/10.1163/ej.9789004180048.i-962.616/.

28 Wang Wensheng, "Bridging the Digital Divide Inside China," Annual Conference of the Association of Internet Researchers, October 13–16, Maastricht, NL, 2002. https://pdfs.semanticscholar.org/3c08/729afb44b49261b5cc09c83514957664016f.pdf.

29 Ibid.

30 Ibid.

31 Agnes Godfrey Mwakaje, "Information and Communication Technology for Rural Farmers Market Access in Tanzania," *Journal of Information Technology Impact* 10, no. 2 (2010): 111–128.

32 Temitope Waheed Oshikoya and M. Nureldin Hussain, "Information Technology and the Challenge of Economic Development in Africa," *African Development Review* 10, no. 1 (1998): 100–133.

Bibliography

AfDB, OECD, and UNECA UNDP. "African Economic Outlook 2012," Western African Countries African Development Bank. Dakar, Senegal. Accessed January 19, 2018. www.africaneconomicoutlook.org/en/countries/west-africa/cape-verde/.

Ansoms, An. "Striving for Growth, Bypassing the Poor? A Critical Review of Rwanda's Rural Sector Policies." *The Journal of Modern African Studies* 46, no. 1 (2008): 1–32.

Feller, Andrew, Dan Shunk, and Tom Callarman. "Value Chains Versus Supply Chains." *BP Trends* (March 2006): 1–7.

Helmberger, Peter G., Gerald R. Campbell, and William D. Dobson. "Organization and Performance of Agricultural Markets." 1981. http://agris.fao.org/agris-search/search.do?recordID=US2016214955.

Hüfner, Klaus. "UNESCO—United Nations Educational, Scientific and Cultural Organization." *A Concise Encyclopedia of the United Nations* (2009): 715–718. http://booksandjournals.brillonline.com/content/books/10.1163/ej.9789004180048.i-962.616/.

Jenny, Aker C. "Dial 'A' for Agriculture: Using Information and Communication Technologies for Agricultural Extension in Developing Countries." Tufts University, 2010.

Jensen, Robert. "The Digital Provide: Information (Technology), Market Performance, and Welfare in the South Indian Fisheries Sector." *The Quarterly Journal of Economics* 122, no. 3 (2007): 879–924.

Kapange, Barnabas, and Po O. Box. "ICTs and National Agricultural Research Systems—the Case of Tanzania." Research and Development, Ministry of Agriculture and Food Security, 2004. www.tzonline.org/pdf/ictsandnationalagriculturalresearchsystems.pdf, https://tanzania.go.tz/egov_uploads/documents/griculturalresearchsystems_sw.pdf.

Kaplinsky, Raphael, and Mike Morris. *A Handbook for Value Chain Research*, Vol. 113. IDRC Ottawa, 2001. www.prism.uct.ac.za/Papers/VchNov01.pdf.

Kawlra, Aarti. "The Gender and Citizenship in the Information Society (CITIGEN) Research Programme." Accessed August 6, 2017. http://gender-is-itizenship.net/resources/SOA_India.pdf.

Kimenyi, Mwangi S., and Nelipher Moyo. "Leapfrogging Development through Technology Adoption". *Foresight Africa* (2011): 13. Google Scholar. Accessed August 6, 2017. https://scholar.google.com/scholar?q=Kimenyi%2C+Mwangi+S.%2C+and+Nelipher+Moyo.+%22Leapfrogging+development+through+technology+adoption.%22+FORESIGHT+AFRICA+%282011%29%3A+13.&btnG=&hl=en&as_sdt=0%2C5.

McNamara, Kerry. "Enhancing the Livelihoods of the Rural Poor Through ICT: A Knowledge Map." *The World Bank*, 2008. http://agris.fao.org/agris-search/search.do?recordID=US2012415552.

Menda, Aloyce. "ICT for Improved Crop Marketing in Rural Tanzania." CROMABU 12, no. 10 (2005): 2009. www.Cromabul.ComOn.

Mwakaje, Agnes Godfrey, "Information and Communication Technology for Rural Farmers Market Access in Tanzania." *Journal of Information Technology Impact* 10, no. 2 (2010): 111–128.

Nyamba, Siwel Yohakim, and Malongo R.S. Mlozi. "Factors Influencing the Use of Mobile Phones in Communicating Agricultural Information: A Case of Kilolo District, Iringa, Tanzania." *International Journal of Information and Communication Technology Research* 2, no. 7 (2012).

Oshikoya, Temitope Waheed, and M. Nureldin Hussain. "Information Technology and the Challenge of Economic Development in Africa." *African Development Review* 10, no. 1 (1998): 100–133.

Rao, N.H. "A Framework for Implementing Information and Communication Technologies in Agricultural Development in India." *Technological Forecasting and Social Change* 74, no. 4 (2007): 491–518.

Rashid, Ahmed Tareq, and Laurent Elder. "Mobile Phones and Development: An Analysis of IDRC-Supported Projects." *The Electronic Journal of Information Systems in Developing Countries* 36 (2009). Google Scholar. Accessed August 6, 2017. https://scholar.google.com/scholar?hl=en&q=Rashid%2C+Ahmed+Tareq%2C+and+Laurent+Elder.+%22Mobile+phones+and+development%3A+An+analysis+of+IDRC-supported+projects.%22+The+Electronic+Journal+of+Information+Systems+in+Developing+Countries+36+%282009%29.&btnG=&as_sdt=1%2C5&as_sdtp=.

Sanga, Camlius et al. "On Search for Strategies to Increase the Coverage of Agricultural Extension Service: Web-Based Farmers' Advisory Information System." *International Journal of Computing & ICT Research* 7, no. 1 (2013). http://search.ebscohost.com/login.aspx?direct=true&profile=ehost&scope=site&authtype=crawler&jrnl=18181139&AN=90497025&h=m7A8uo0Ce25Jo%2BWr21RVm728nqYV3EUmBo9%2FnP3oA69AjcUZB2dVP96RPpKR5b3n7yZSqco%2F2HyE5CAqBtF%2Bng%3D%3D&crl=c.

Sanga, C. et al. "On the Development of the Mobile Based Agricultural Extension System in Tanzania: A Technological Perspective." *International Journal of Computing & ICT Research* 8, no. 1 (2014). http://search.ebscohost.com/login.aspx?direct=true&profile=ehost&scope=site&authtype=crawler&jrnl=18181139&AN=99022147&h=9q85OkIKjnGbyBEiWUaYDleIWKrs3zEHtaWfrTUEAbYotGwPCzGmwwxDr0hgwMTBGz6efGSt95WW4XlMxCITHA%3D%3D&crl=c.

Sanghvi, Sunil, Rupert Simons, and Roberto Uchoa, "Four Lessons for Transforming African Agriculture." *McKinsey*, April 2011. Accessed January 19, 2018. www.mckinsey.com/industries/public-sector/our-insights/four-lessons-for-transforming-african-agriculture

Shepherd, Andrew W., and others. "Marketing and Rural Finance Farm Radio as a Medium for Market Information Dissemination." 2001. http://agris.fao.org/agris-search/search.do?recordID=XF2016044670.

Stockbridge, Mike, Laurence Smith, and H. R. Lohano. "Cotton and Wheat Marketing and the Provision of Pre-Harvest Services in Sindh Province, Pakistan." 1998. http://eprints.soas.ac.uk/id/eprint/9098.

UNDP, UNEP. "World Bank, and WRI (2000)." *World Resources* (2001): 87–102.

Verhulst, A. "Lessons From Field Experience in the Development of Monogastric Animal Production." Proceedings of the Expert Consultation on Strategies for Sustainable Animal Agriculture in Developing Countries, FAO, Rome, Italy, October 1991, 1992. http://193.190.239.98/handle/10390/4076.

Vrasidas, Charalambos, Michalinos Zembylas, and Gene V. Glass, "ICT for Education, Development, and Social Justice." IAP, 2009. https://books.google.com/books?hl=en&lr=&id=AfwnDwAAQBAJ&oi=fnd&pg=PA85&dq=ITU.+(2006).+Online+statistics.+www.itu.int/ITUD/ict/statistics/+(accessed+September+10,+2015).&ots=R9DUDCIK-Z&sig=liz-6CV8QO7J7vfyrYJi627YE6I.

Wensheng, Wang. "Bridging the Digital Divide Inside China." Annual Conference of the Association of Internet Researchers, October 13–16, Maastricht, NL, 2002. https://pdfs.semanticscholar.org/3c08/729afb44b49261b5cc09c83514957664016f.pdf.

15

FRUIT-DRYING PROCESS TO ENHANCE AGRICULTURAL PRODUCTIVITY IN SUB-SAHARAN AFRICA

Hassimi Traore

Introduction

Fruit-drying processes worldwide have a deep cultural tradition. Their origins can be traced to early food drying and preservation practices in Mesopotamia and later to Middle Eastern countries. In many countries today, fruit drying focuses on specific types of fruit and represents years of historical experimentation supported by scientific experimentation. The combination of culturally based traditional approaches to fruit drying and scientifically based knowledge-building approaches related to fruit drying reflect the commercial importance of fruit drying itself to many countries marketing and exporting dried fruit such as figs, dates, and mangoes.

Small-scale food drying in African countries has traditionally been used to preserve food for home consumption and, in some cases, subsistence. Given increased production of fruit and related crops, many small family enterprises are turning to the use of family practices to market their excess production. Production of dried fruit is becoming an important enterprise for many African entrepreneurs. In some regions of sub-Saharan Africa, small clusters of fruit-drying ventures have cooperated to become economically viable and distribute their products regionally and even internationally under unique brand names. These efforts by the new age entrepreneurs and integrated clusters are becoming an integral part of African economies in Burkina Faso, Tanzania, and Ghana, among other countries. Much of the output from these operations is relatively small and specialized production of dried mangoes or other locally grown fruit. Traditionally, almost all the products are sun dried or air dried above ground or, in some instances, dried on cloths laid on the ground.

Some entrepreneurs working with industrial enterprises were able to develop specialized drying ovens suitable for drying fruit, herbs, and spices. However, power generation is limited in some parts of Africa and such drying equipment, mostly electric ovens, is still used only marginally. A limited number of ovens are fired by locally gathered fuel, but the efficiency of these ovens is very limited.

Cooperative efforts between entrepreneurs and non-governmental organizations (NGOs) have tried to introduce solar- and wind-powered energy to power more commercially viable drying equipment. However, there appears to be a knowledge gap between the manufacturers of fruit-drying equipment located abroad and practical application of the equipment by entrepreneurs in the rural African countryside. Accordingly, some locally minded African entrepreneurs are not interested in large-scale operations and perceive a limited use of small-scale drying ovens.

Large-scale fruit drying is a profitable commercial application in many parts of the world. Large-scale producers of dried fruit serve growing demand for dried fruit. Dried fruit producers work closely with engineering and manufacturing enterprises to develop more efficient drying equipment in order to supply growing demand. Large international manufacturers of drying equipment use scientific approaches to develop, test, and market equipment ideally suited for specific drying purposes and energy availability. Scientific testing of the equipment, based on the particular chemical composition of the fruit to be dried and the thermodynamic requirements of prevailing conditions, has produced optimal equipment for drying fruit in specific geographic regions of Africa. Although manufacturers of fruit-drying equipment are successful in selling equipment in parts of Europe, North America, and Australia, they are only marginally successful in selling equipment in sub-Saharan Africa. The lack of success is mostly due to economic conditions.

New age entrepreneurs in sub-Saharan Africa depend mostly on traditional approaches based on existing local technology to serve their local markets and develop competitive advantage in markets abroad—the emphasis on small-scale local production offers them an advantage in foreign markets. Strong markets abroad for dry fruit, mainly due to changing diets and consumption patterns, are driving increased production locally. Entrepreneurs have expanded their drying capacity and look for additional fruits to dry in response to foreign demand for dried fruit.

Entrepreneurs with experience abroad are introducing scientifically based drying procedures and controlling the entire process of drying and marketing dry fruit. Specifically, by retaining control over the entire marketing process, they can create better value for intermediate customers and the ultimate consumers abroad. These are significant technological developments that increase the economic efficiency and effectiveness of many recent entrepreneurial ventures. Instead of needing to discover new processes of fruit drying, African entrepreneurs can introduce more efficient and effective technology from abroad.

Fruit-drying enterprises, especially of mangoes, are becoming increasingly more important to West African economies, particularly Burkina Faso. The southern part of Burkina Faso is known for producing large quantities of mangoes. In earlier years, 35% to 50% of the mango crop was wasted due to lack of transportation, storage facilities, and preservation. In the past, these losses were considered a normal inefficiency of farming. At the same time, mango growers considered the market for fresh mangoes to be small.

By the 1990s, local entrepreneurs perceived drying mangoes as an opportunity to reduce the waste of fresh mangoes and an opportunity to create employment for the local labor force. Two early examples of enterprises drying mangoes are Groupe WAKA and Fruiteq, both located in Burkina Faso and active in European consumer markets.

WAKA means 'welcome' in the Moré language. As an entrepreneurial venture, Groupe WAKA was started in 2009 by Fogué Kouduahou, a Moscow-educated entrepreneur educated as a 'technical food processing engineer.' Since 2011, Groupe WAKA has used gas ovens to dry mangoes. Their largest market is in Germany, where they cooperate with MorgenLand, a local distributor.[1]

Fruiteq was established in 2005 as an exporting enterprise for several mango growers in Burkina Faso; today, it cooperates with mango growers in the Ivory Coast and Mali. Fruiteq's role in the mango marketing value chain is warehousing, storage, and transportation. Their warehouse is based near the town of Bobo-Dioulasso in Burkina Faso, around 800 km from the coast, where they collect, wash, sort, and pack the mangoes and ship them in cooled containers to Europe. Although Fruiteq is not directly involved with drying mangoes, it is very much considered as a facilitating intermediary in the entire Burkina Faso mango growing and marketing values chain.[2] Based on Fruiteq's success, external capital became available in 2008 from White Root Capital to finance growing fresh fruit and vegetables.

From a marketing management perspective, both enterprises are part of mango-growing clusters in Burkina Faso. Clusters such as these need to be emphasized more as the driving force behind an expanding mango growing and marketing industry in sub-Saharan African countries. However, most of the smaller mango-drying enterprises need assistance from qualified scientists to improve the overall efficiency and effectiveness of the entire consumer value chain not only for dried mangoes, but also fresh mangoes. Formation of industrial clusters is one of the important marketing management tools for improving entrepreneurial initiatives and marketing activities.[3]

Background

Burkina Faso is one of the poorest countries in the world, is landlocked, and has limited resources. Among the many difficulties the country faces is the very limited infrastructure—mainly, transportation capacity. The main paved roads joining the different cities are not well maintained and frequently cause fatal accidents. For instance, the 'National Route 1' from Bobo-Dioulasso to Ouagadougou is considered the main highway but it consists of only two lanes of traffic and is symbolic of transportation conditions in the country. Transportation of crops is hampered by bad road conditions; roads between villages are practically inaccessible in rainy season. Transportation of crops impacts the Burkina Faso economy the most since its main productive activity is agriculture. The southern part of the country, which produces most of the fresh fruit including mangoes, faces major transportation obstacles to delivering fresh fruit to the center and northern regions of the country.

Burkina Faso is one of the major mango-producing countries of West Africa, with an estimated production of more than 120,000 metric tons a year.[4] The mangoes produced are mainly marketed fresh and distributed nationally, regionally, and internationally. Storage and preservation of fresh mangoes are not adequate—35% to 50% of mangoes are wasted, at a huge loss to the economy.[5] New technology for drying mangoes was introduced in order to resolve this problem.

Similar problems with spoilage of mangoes are experienced in other West African countries. Recent expansion of drying mangoes offers a boost to the economies both in job creation and income. Dried mangoes retain their calories, carbohydrates, iron, and calcium as well as Vitamin A.[6] In addition, drying prolongs shelf life, preserves nutritional quality, and reduces the risk of contamination by toxic molds or other undesirable bacteria.

A recently published survey by the United Kingdom's Ministry of Foreign Affairs suggested a potential expansion of the EU market for dried mangoes.[7] The authors conclude that West African producers of dried mangoes should be encouraged to further enter the EU markets to reduce the dominant market position of Asian and South African producers. West African mango producers need to take a more aggressive competitive position in the EU market for dried mangoes.

In addition, the survey points out that the key competitors for dried West African mangoes are producers in Thailand, Philippines, and South Africa, in that order. Their highly competitive positions stem from production locations to processing sites; large industrialized and advanced drying technology; and longer experience in preservation, packaging, and marketing techniques. However, they also face weaknesses—their products are considerably and, in some cases, excessively sweet for EU consumers' tastes when compared with mangoes grown in West Africa. There seems to be a somewhat variable or seasonal supply of mangoes complicated by varying demands for transportation that increases shipping costs.

According to the survey, seasonal availability of mangoes in countries other than West Africa is clearly a problem. Consequently, mango variety crucially affects sweetness and subsequently marketability. From this perspective, West African mangoes are more competitive in EU markets. An example of problems of marketing mangoes in EU markets occurred in 2013 when Indian mangoes were banned from EU markets due to pesticide contamination and phytosanitary measures.

These developments suggest that West African producers have increasing opportunities to market their products, especially in EU markets. The primary reasons for their apparent advantages are the taste preferences for less sweet West African mangoes and proximity to the markets. Consequently, in order to compete more dynamically, West African mango growers and producers need improved drying technology, better pretreatment of mangoes, improved storage and transportation facilities, and closer distance between growers and processors.

The authors of the study made one observation that corresponds with local realities among West African growers and processors—the fact that wholesale and retail prices of West African mangoes tend to be lower than those from other parts of the world, but especially from South Africa and Asia. This single unexplored advantage indicates that West African growers and producers need to market their product better and be more direct, reliable, and professional in presenting superior products to EU markets. They must become more familiar with EU markets and match their product offerings to specific tastes of EU customers.

The Country

Burkina Faso is perhaps in the best position among the West African countries to benefit from demand for fresh and dried mangoes worldwide. Although Burkina Faso is one of the poorest countries in the world, it has the greatest economic and social growth potential; it is 274,000 sq km in size, situated in the center of West Africa, and has a dry tropical climate. The rainy season is from June to September, with average temperatures ranging from 25 to 30 degrees Centigrade. French is still the official language in the former French colony, although a multitude of regional languages are spoken. Burkina Faso is known in the region for a certain level of social stability, originating from the cultural diversity of its people with different ethnicities living together. The majority of the 18 million inhabitants (90%) make their living from farming but typically meet their own subsistence needs. Reforestation initiatives have improved ground and soil quality and stimulated diverse vegetation. The soil and climate conditions are ideally suitable for cultivation of mangoes, acacia, dates, baobab (the tree of life), and eucalyptus trees.

Commercial Dried Mango Business in Burkina Faso

A number of attempts have been made to improve mango-drying processes; most failed or were not totally suitable because of economic, technological, or social issues in Burkina Faso. The closest study of that was made by Mercer and Myhara.[8] In their book, the authors outlined in detail a process to improve the operation of commercially available mango dryers and described the entire mango-drying process from the perspective of a series of complex commercial initiatives. They pointed out that mangoes represent an important crop in many tropical countries, but drying mangoes as an entrepreneurial venture represents an ideal value-added opportunity in many economically and social challenged tropical countries. Burkina Faso is no exception; in fact, due to its price advantage, in addition to its emphasis on organically cultivated mangoes, dried mangoes could generate premium prices in markets abroad. These advantages can be accomplished through introduction of more advanced drying technology from abroad.

Drying Technology

Drying mangoes is a somewhat unique process. From a scientific perspective, it requires a precise combination of humidity and temperature. When mangoes are dried by the sun, an ideal place needs to be found where there is maximum exposure to the sun, but at the same time, the right humidity is also needed. Oven drying, due to its ability to control both temperature and humidity, is obviously less arbitrary. Most commercial mango-drying facilities use gas-powered ovens simply because of the size of the operations and economies of scale.

The mango-drying process consists of several steps. Organic mangoes are stored until completely ripe, then sorted for quality, peeled, and sliced. Sliced mangoes are dried in gas-powered ovens for approximately 12 hours. Ripe, dry mangoes can be very dark and have a sweet flavor and, by nature, do not require additional processing. The fundamental difference between the sun and oven-drying processes is that sun drying is done in batches, whereas oven drying requires large amounts of sliced mangoes. Some processing facilities use continuously moving steel belts, and the input and output sides of the continuous belt driers are automated and do not require manual handling.

Electric dryers are also used in drying mangoes. However, the cost of electric drying is high mainly due to the availability of electricity. There are frequent blackouts and other power disruptions. These can be avoided by using diesel-powered generators to generate electricity, which adds to the cost, contributes to air pollution, and defeats the purpose of organic production. That is why greater use of solar panels is ecologically preferred. Use of biogases is becoming increasingly common. The concern is over reduction of carbon dioxide (CO_2) emissions. Although both options are organically and ecologically preferred, they are costly and may place West African mango processors at a competitive disadvantage compared with their competitors abroad.

Most processing facilities operate under integrated quality management systems sometimes required by intermediaries such as MorgenLand in Germany, specifically organic standards Hazard Analysis and Critical Control Points (HACCP) or International Food Standard (IFS).[9] Such operational standards far exceed the normal operations and service in the present operating conditions and infrastructure in Burkina Faso.

Furthermore, dried organic mangoes are inspected for quality, packed in boxes, loaded into marine containers, and transported by train to the coast where the containers are loaded on ships for Germany. MorgenLand conducts a comprehensive incoming visual shipment inspection, organoleptic testing, and repackaging for deliveries to organic markets. Most dried mangoes are sold in Europe in 100- and 200-gram packages.

Cluster Approach

Due to the inherent characteristics of the mango-drying initiatives in Burkina Faso, cottage-type initiatives as well as initiatives by larger enterprises and formation of industrial-type clusters would be well suited to provide greater market position. Formation of regional or local industrial clusters is becoming an increasingly more viable approach to economic and social development and stimulation of growth among smaller enterprises. Cluster formation combined with marketing management approaches facilitates cooperation among smaller enterprises and organizes them into a series of sequential activities within a cluster that becomes economically and socially efficient and effective.[10] Smaller enterprises growing and processing mangoes in Burkina Faso are ideally suited for development of regional mango-drying and processing clusters.

This approach has recently been introduced in a workshop for major mango growers and processors in Burkina Faso. The workshop was held April 24–25, 2017, in Bobo-Dioulasso and organized by the United States Agency for International Development. Forty-five producers, processors, and exporters attended the workshop.[11] Bobo-Dioulasso was selected as the key venue for the workshop because 90% of Burkina Faso's fresh mango exports originate there and 70% of mangoes are processed in the region.

The main objective of the workshop was to focus on a regional collaborative effort to better address the opportunities and challenges facing the mango growing, processing, and exporting sector. The discussions focused on a regional collaborative or 'cluster' approach to address opportunities and challenges faced in expanding exports of dried and fresh mangoes.

At the end of the two-day workshop, organizers were interested in responses and feedback from the participants of the workshop. Responses and feedback were collected to further understand if the cluster approach would constructively benefit the expanding mango sector in Burkina Faso to become more active in exporting their products to major world markets. The following sample of responses are listed for purposes of soliciting more personal input into the entire process of exporting mango-based products from Burkina Faso. The responses are informative and provide a better picture of the cooperative issues dealing directly with commercial transactions and also the potential perceptual issues deeply rooted in the regional and local cultures:

1   'Mango industry in the region is relatively well developed, but many of the producers, processors, and exporters feel that they have reached the limit of what they can do alone.'[12]
2   'This meeting is so important. It gives us the chance to meet people from across the mango value chain and explain to them what our collective needs

as businesses are. . . . Here we are in contact with the transport sector, the government, producers. . . . We hope this meeting and the development of the mango cluster will help us solve problems together—for example, in the area of transport—that we face to get our products to the international markets.'[13]

3　'We can offer support, but it is up to you not only to work together to build on the already strong mango sector here, but to reap then the benefits of bringing together all the actors in this value chain to make this sector even stronger and build the economy of the Hauts–Bassins region.'[14]

4　'The international market is very demanding. . . . When we are dispersed, the importers can take advantage of you. Workshops like these can help us come together and defend our interests on the international markets.'[15]

5　'We are extremely proud of what the participants have accomplished over these two days, . . . Based on the work of the plenary meetings, the working group has identified objectives that the cluster needs to focus on and also identified activities that the cluster can get underway in short order. They can begin to work immediately now to improve the productivity and competitiveness of the mango value chains—together.'[16]

The results of the two-day groundbreaking workshop were summarized in four core objectives:

1　Double the export of fresh and processed mangoes from Hauts–Bassins over the next 5 years.

2　Reduce mango industry losses from 40% to 45%. (It was agreed that the current losses result mainly from fruit flies, poor handling, and incorrectly filled out certification papers, among other problems.)

3　Gather and disseminate knowledge about international markets, consumer preferences, and mango industry best practices.

4　Move toward establishing a cluster to achieve more competitiveness within the industry.[17]

The last core objective is the most important to the mango growing, processing, and exporting enterprises in the Hauts–Bassins region in Burkina Faso. The key concerns might be how potential clusters can be formed, who will manage them, and what marketing management philosophies each cluster will implement. These concerns require entrepreneurial talent that understands local economic and social conditions as much as the inherent managerial motivations of the growers, producers, and exporters.

Small Business, Dried Mangoes, and Impact on Their Country's Economy

Finding new market opportunities for mangoes, fresh or dried, is a complex challenge. Most mangoes are grown, produced, and exported by smaller enterprises often representing family ventures. Such operations have little knowledge of markets, especially markets abroad. Even for well-organized clusters, identifying markets throughout Europe, North America, or other parts of the world is very difficult and requires a great deal of international marketing know-how. Success in identifying and entering these markets is also a function of the product itself.[18]

Fresh mangoes are perishable; more export emphasis is placed on dried mangoes. Mangoes are a fruit that grows in many tropical countries on mango trees that are pervasive and abundant with enormous commercial potential for multimillion-dollar markets.[19] In Burkina Faso, most mango growers and processors are located around Bobo-Dioulasso, the second largest city, and the Ouagadougou region. This region is extremely important economically and socially for the growth of Burkina Faso. Most mango growers are internationally certified by entities such as Eco-cert and begin to harvest and ship their fruit in June.

Case I: The Groupe WAKA

The Groupe WAKA specializes in processing organic mangoes under strict hygienic regulations. WAKA's marketing strategy is to persuade small farmers to cultivate mangoes under organic standards and process them in accordance with these specifications so they can be exported. Five groups of farmers cultivate mangoes on an area of 300 hectares (approximately 741 acres). Several seasonal varieties are cultivated: Amelie variety is harvested in April and May and Brooks variety from beginning of June until late July. During these times, up to 200 workers, many of them women, harvest half-ripened mangoes that are transported via lorries (trucks) to processing facilities in Ouagadougou. Groupe WAKA opened the facilities in 2011 and since then maintains close commercial ties with German food distribution enterprises. A number of organic boutiques and grocery stores in Europe carry organically dried mangoes from Burkina Faso including Switzerland's Claro Suisse, Belgian Oxfam, French Solidar'Monde, Austrian EZA, and Italy's CTM in addition to several retail outlets in the Netherlands and Germany.

Case II: Fruiteq—Economic and Social Impact

An example of how important dried mangoes are to the economic and social infrastructure of Burkina Faso can be illustrated by Fruiteq.[20] Fruiteq is a private enterprise, located in Burkina Faso, that exports fair traded certified organic mangoes grown in Burkina Faso, Mali, and Ivory Coast. It has few competitors. Fruiteq is actively involved in community-based initiatives closely aligned with practices of social marketing. For example, the management of Fruiteq financed and built a house for village midwives in the community of Takaledougou where most of their employees live. Previously, women had to travel 15 km to reach the nearest health clinic. Now complications during childbirth have been reduced since there is a clinic in the community where they live. Fewer infants and mothers have died since the clinic was built.

The social impact of Fruiteq is further demonstrated by its financing of clean water wells in the villages of Banfora and Takaledougou. The wells provide drinking water for approximately 3,000 inhabitants who previously drank river water. Before the clean wells were available, women had to walk 3 to 5 km to obtain potable water during the dry season. Fruiteq also funded purchases of small diesel engines for the village of Takaledougou to produce electricity to power food processing equipment such as grinding mills and vegetable and nut oil presses. Such equipment provides useful time and energy saving tools for women who otherwise had to perform these processes manually.

Fruiteq is an excellent example of a cooperative enterprise, or an industrial cluster, very much integrated into the social space in the region including the regional health care sector. It provides ambulance service to 50,000 inhabitants in Banfora and the surrounding communities. The ambulance enables sick and injured people in the region to be transported to health centers in Bobo-Dioulasso and Ouagadougou, where they can get better medical care than is available in Banfora. A pharmacy was built and is run by villagers in Takaledougou to reduce the use of counterfeit drugs.

Fruiteq's operation and success has been the first research case study conducted in the mango growing, processing, and exporting sector in Burkina Faso. It provides a valuable practical example for entrepreneurs interested in forming clusters in other sectors of the Burkina Faso economy.

Case III: Female Entrepreneurship

As the mango-drying initiative is expanding and tends to be dominated by smaller and medium-sized enterprises, there are increasing opportunities for entrepreneurs to enter the value chain for fresh and dried mangoes. In order to enter the value chain, an entrepreneur needs minimal capital, the ability to identify and realize market opportunities, and especially understand potential markets. When the entire chain of marketing operations is examined from the West African entrepreneurial perspective, it reveals that most entrepreneurs are men. This does not mean that female entrepreneurs lack the knowledge or have the necessary propensity to face risk. It is not clear exactly what the reasons are, whether cultural, social, or economic.

However, there is anecdotal information available about a successful female entrepreneur who started a mango-drying business in the suburb of the capital city Ouagadougou about 10 years ago. She purchased and imported an oven processor from China in order to start her mango-drying operations, minimize capital expenditures, and reduce start-up risk. After 10 years of operations, her venture employs 90 seasonal workers, of which 85 are women and 5 are men. The main seasonal production period is from April to August. Her main export markets are France, Germany, Denmark, and other European markets. At the same time, this relatively small enterprise also supplies local and regional markets in Burkina Faso.

Although some female entrepreneurs in African countries prefer to remain anonymous, the numbers are increasing and can be found in the textile, personnel service, software development, and medical services sector, among other rapidly expanding social and economic sectors. Most female entrepreneurs received their educations abroad or received some specialized training abroad.[21] An increasing number of university programs on both the undergraduate and graduate levels are offering courses in entrepreneurship, but only a limited number are directed to female students.

Scientific Approach to the Mango Drying Operations in Burkina Faso

A mango-drying venture can be a complex initiative for many young entrepreneurs in any African country. Entrepreneurs need to fundamentally understand how risk-laden decisions are made—they need a decision-making framework. In addition, entrepreneurs need to structure or organize their initiatives in order to be able to control them. The most suitable framework for new ventures is marketing management. However, marketing management strategies need to be grounded in the scientific method. Ventures designed to dry mangoes or export fresh mangoes are not different. The entrepreneurial approach coupled with a decision-making process based on the scientific method provides an important foundation for any venture.

On the basis of well-established experience in the mango growing, processing, and exporting sector, it is possible to identify the critical factors that need to be considered in making decisions and structuring new ventures. A venture, or a new entrepreneurial initiative, needs a framework within which the entrepreneur has an opportunity to creatively develop the ventures—typically based on a comprehensive marketing plan. Each venture will most likely have a unique mission, structure, and decision-making approach. Nevertheless, some inherent factors are common to the mango growing, processing, and exporting process—some of these common factors are listed in Table 15.1.

TABLE 15.1 Burkina Faso Mango Prices by Quality and Market

Buyers	Type	Price to Producers, USD per kg.	Quality
Merchants ('Jula') for local consumption	'Carton mango'	0.04	Low, non-exportable
Processors for juice or dried mango	'Crate mango'	0.065	Medium, not exportable as fresh fruit; exportable if processed
Exporters	'Export mango'	0.19	High, exportable

Source: Rapid Impact Evaluation Fruiteq-Burkina Faso March 2013. RootCapital.org

Conclusion

The mango growing, processing, and exporting sector is extremely important for the economic and social development of many countries in sub-Saharan Africa. The abundance of mangoes offers entrepreneurial opportunities for many young entrepreneurs. Many successful initiatives in the mango growing, processing, and exporting sector are found in Burkina Faso, and the economic contributions in the sector are significant to the Burkina Faso economy. Even more significant are the social contributions made by some of the enterprises organized as industrial clusters or cooperatives as discussed earlier.

Enormous potential opportunities are still developing and becoming more specialized, including packaging, labeling, processing, and marketing branded products from specific localities or regions in sub-Saharan African countries. Entrepreneurs with appropriate understanding of the entire sector, including its international market potential, can benefit, grow, and innovate substantially as long as they make correct decisions and structure their ventures.

Notes

1 Groupe WAKA corporate literature available through MorgenLand, accessed August 23, 2017, www.morgenland.bio/organic-cultivation-projects/burkina-faso/?lang=en.
2 Fruiteq SARL corporate literature, accessed August 23, 2017, www.natureandmore.com/growers/zongo-adama-1.
3 George Tesar and Jan Bodin, *Marketing Management in Geographically Remote Industrial Clusters: Implications for Business-to-Customer Marketing* (Singapore: World Scientific Publishing Co. Pte. Limited, 2013).
4 West and Central Africa Council for Agricultural Research and Development, accessed August 28, 2017, www.coraf.org/en/2016/03/04/mango-drying/.
5 Pierre Gerbaud and Searce, "Reduce Competitiveness for Dried Mangoes," survey by CBI, published by Ministry of Foreign Affairs (UK) (no date).
6 Dried Mango Nutrition Information by ERIK ODOM, last updated April 15, 2015, accessed August 28, 2017, www.livestrong.com/article/48448-dried-mango-nutrition-information/.
7 Pierre Gerbaud and Searce, "Reduce Competitiveness for Dried Mangoes."
8 Donald G. Mercer and Robert Myhara, "Improving the Operation of a Commercial Mango Dryer," in *Using Food Science and Technology to Improve Nutrition and Promote National Development: Selected Case Studies*, eds. Gordon Robertson and John Lupien (Toronto: International Union of Food Science & Technology, 2008): Chapter 6.
9 Nicolas Canivet, *Food Safety Certification*, 2005, 20 and 29, ftp://ftp.fao.org/ag/agn/food/certification_programmes.pdf.
10 Tesar and Bodin.
11 Batamaka Somé, "Fruiteq-Burkina Faso," Rapid Impact Evaluation (report) From Root Capital.org, (Cambridge, MA: RootCapital, March 2013), accessed September 6, 2017, www.rootcapital.org/sites/default/files/downloads/root_capital_fruiteq.pdf.
12 Mango Cluster workshop targeted opportunities described by an industry assessment in Burkina Faso by the Trade Hub's Dr. Patrick Nugawela and Jean Bosco Dibouloni, who led the workshop with Mr. Martin Webber of J.E. Austin Associates, one of the Hub's core implementing partners.
13 'This meeting is so important. It gives us the chance to meet people from across the mango value chain and explain to them what our collective needs as businesses are,'

Fruit-Drying Process **327**

said Mr. Issaka Bougom, Chief Executive of Ranch du Koba, a Bobo-Dioulasso-based mango processor and exporter.

14 'We can offer support, but it is up to you not only to work together to build on the already strong mango sector here, but to reap then the benefits of bringing together all the actors in this value chain to make this sector even stronger and build the economy of the Hauts-Bassins region,' said Dr. Edouard Tapsoba, Permanent Secretary of the Presidential Investment Council.

15 'The international market is very demanding. . . . When we are dispersed, the importers can take advantage of you. Workshops like these can help us come together and defend our interests on the international markets,' said Mr. Yaya Kone of Sanle Sechage, one of the region's largest dried mango processors.

16 'We are extremely proud of what the participants have accomplished over these two days. Based on the work of the plenary meetings, the working group has identified objectives that the cluster needs to focus on and also identified activities that the cluster can get underway in short order. They can begin to work immediately now to improve the productivity and competitiveness of the mango value chains—together,' said Mr. Webber.

17 Conclusion report on the second day of workshop, the 12-person working group proposed concrete actions to the list of priorities and developed core objectives for the regional cluster.

18 Nicholas Dominic Cadbury, "When, Where, and How to Test Market," *Harvard Business Review*, May 1975, accessed September 6, 2017, https://hbr.org/1975/05/when-where-and-how-to-test-market.

19 "Mango," Wikipedia, last edited September 4, 2017, accessed September 6, 2017, https://en.wikipedia.org/wiki/Mango

20 Batamaka Somé.

21 Eyerusalem Siba, "Enabling Female Entrepreneurs and Beyond," The Brookings Institution, Washington, DC, *Africa in Focus*, July 25 (2016): 1.

Bibliography

Cadbury, Nicholas Dominic, "When, Where, and How to Test Market." *Harvard Business Review*. May 1975. Accessed September 6, 2017. https://hbr.org/1975/05/when-where-and-how-to-test-market.

Canivet, Nicolas. "Food Safety Certification". 2005: 20 and 29. ftp://ftp.fao.org/ag/agn/food/certification_programmes.pdf.

Gerbaud, Pierre, and Searce. "Reduce Competitiveness for Dried Mangoes." Survey by CBI. Published by Ministry of Foreign Affairs (UK) (no date).

Mercer, Donald G., and Robert Myhara. "Improving the Operation of a Commercial Mango Dryer." In *Using Food Science and Technology to Improve Nutrition and Promote National Development: Selected Case Studies*, Chapter 6. Eds. Gordon Robertson and John Lupien. Toronto: International Union of Food Science & Technology, 2008.

Siba, Eyerusalem. "Enabling Female Entrepreneurs and Beyond." *Africa in Focus*, July 25, 2016, 1.

Somé, Batamake. "Fruiteq-Burkina Faso," Rapid Impact Evaluation (report) From Root Capital.org. Cambridge, MA: RootCapital, March 2013. Accessed September 6, 2017. www.rootcapital.org/sites/default/files/downloads/root_capital_fruiteq.pdf.

Tesar, George, and Jan Bodin. *Marketing Management in Geographically Remote Industrial Clusters: Implications for Business-to-Customer Marketing*. Singapore: World Scientific Publishing Co. Pte. Limited, 2013.

INTEGRATION

Marketing management can provide the necessary tools and techniques needed to structure entrepreneurial initiatives and help entrepreneurs make better decisions. Marketing management as a strategic and operational philosophy provides a platform for innovative African entrepreneurs to build a sound social and economic public space where start-ups can introduce innovative approaches to the needs and wants of African consumers. In addition to entrepreneurial start-ups, smaller enterprises can grow into profitable larger enterprises, and consumers can organize their lifestyles around consumption patterns and social and economic awareness.

A number of African countries are moving from large-scale social and economic development projects to small-scale locally initiated entrepreneurial projects. Almost all of these projects are driven by technology, more specifically by telecommunication and the Internet. The combination of accessible technology, entrepreneurship, and consumer awareness of innovative products and services creates new lifestyles and greater participation of consumers in their environment. These new developments contribute directly to emergence of the new dynamic social and economic public space.

The new social and economic public space is the result of several internal forces in a number of African countries. Indigenous entrepreneurial initiatives offer products and services fundamentally needed by consumers and the public. Many of the new products and services are provided via telecommunication channels and the Internet as an increasing number of consumers have access to both. This is also possible because small-scale entrepreneurial projects deliver solar or wind power to remote areas where it was not available before. Local

330 Integration

entrepreneurs working with international satellite-based telecommunication operators make it possible for consumers to use mobile telephones for social and economic transactions.

The new social and economic public space in many African countries provides an opportunity for entrepreneurs and managers to introduce innovative products and services. Consumers' purchases and consumption of innovative products and services lead to new primary and secondary markets and subsequently to more entrepreneurial initiatives and additional enterprises. Socio-economic growth has become the necessary motivation for better consumer lifestyles and more stable social and economic environments.

Construction of the social and economic public space and resulting socio-economic growth is a function of three forces: (1) entrepreneurial dynamics, (2) public and private use of the Internet, and (3) telecommunication use and options. Entrepreneurial dynamics within the context of marketing management represent the fundamental initiatives needed to stimulate socio-economic growth. Indigenous entrepreneurial activities stimulate and motivate the necessary social and economic awareness, stimulate quality consumption options, and improve lifestyles of not only consumers but also the public. Private and public use of the Internet opens consumers' horizons beyond their immediate surroundings; consumers learn about new consumption options, social and economics possibilities, and new technologies. Introduction of the Internet alone dramatically changes individual lifestyles. Telecommunication options, particularly connectivity via mobile telephones, provide unprecedented possibilities to both rural and urban consumers by offering a window into another world. The possibilities include personal financial transactions, purchasing products and services even from remote locations, enhancing consumers' consumptions possibilities, and simply connecting with others, family and friends.

Social and economic public space is closely influenced by internal and external educational options. Many new entrepreneurial ideas result from educational experience. A sound educational foundation, combined with educational experiences based on the sciences and social and economic disciplines can motivate individuals to innovate, create, and act in the new social and economic public space. Entrepreneurial initiatives come from educational experiences obtained at home or abroad. Many individuals educated abroad return with ideas directly applicable to private and public needs at home.

Conversely, creation of social and economic public space contributes to creation of a technologically innovative pool of entrepreneurial talent. The dynamics and expansions of a social and economic public space produce additional opportunities for a new generation of entrepreneurs, start-ups, and small enterprises that grow into larger, often international, undertakings. The introduction of new technology requires a new generation of supporting entities—technology specialists, software developers, technical support specialists, a variety of engineers, and other support specialists. Introduction of new technology also requires support from more routine enterprises such as suppliers, fabrication shops, and manufacturers. These entities foster socio-economic growth and maintain environmental stability.

Socio-economic growth can be defined from two different perspectives. First is the economic component depicting the growth of an economy, employment, productivity, and economic stability. Second is social stability as a measure of social development of individual citizens and the public. From an economic perspective, social growth means measurable improvements in purchasing ability, consumption behavior, and lifestyles.

Economic growth among African countries is generally defined as an increase in the capability of an economy to produce products and services to benefit the public over time. Economic growth can be measured in nominal or real terms but must be adjusted for inflation. For economically and socially challenged African countries, economic growth is a proxy variable for formation of entrepreneurial activities, start-ups, small enterprises, and other activities producing employment opportunities, wages, tax revenue, and consumer markets. Economic growth is driven by consumers' abilities to purchase and consume products and services, define lifestyles, and contribute to society.

Social growth of individuals and the public is typically interpreted in African countries as social development. Some social and economic development specialists focused on socially and economically challenged countries suggest that development is perceived as the path to social growth. A systematic approach or plan for social development that leads to social growth is needed. Social growth is about increasing commitment to social norms that facilitate interaction of citizens and social stability. From an economic perspective, social growth focuses on aspects of education, health care and climate protection along with preservation of natural and non-renewable resources.

Many innovative entrepreneurial initiatives contribute to both social and economic growth because of the close relationship between social and economic growth. Entrepreneurial activities guided by marketing management philosophies bring about economic, structural, and market changes that initiate social changes. The main contributors to socio-economic growth, from an economic point of view, are (1) entrepreneurial start-ups that introduce economic, social, and technological changes; (2) small and medium-sized enterprises that provide platforms for social and economic expansion; and (3) private and public service providers that render the services necessary to assist entrepreneurs and managers in satisfying consumers and the public.

Marketing Management in Africa

Marketing Management Implications for Social and Economic Public Space and Socio-Economic Growth: An African Perspective

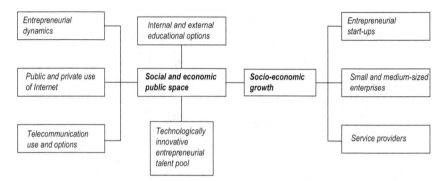

BIBLIOGRAPHY

Adisa, Toyin Ajibade, Issa Abdulraheem, and Chima Mordi. "The Characteristics and Challenges of Small Business in Africa: An Exploratory Study of Nigerian Small Business Owners." *Economic Insights—Trends and Challenges* III (LXVII), no. 4 (2014): 1–14.

African Economic Outlook: Sustainable Cities and Structural Transformation 2016, May 23, 2016. www.africaneconomicoutlook.orgaeo-2016-en.

Anderson, Christopher, and Yuliya Tverdova. "Corruption, Politics, and Attitudes Toward Government in Contemporary Democracies." *American Journal of Political Science*, 47, no. 1 (2003): 91–109.

Bagire, Vincent Amooti, and Juliana Mulaa Namada. "Strategic Management in Africa: Tracing Gaps in Sustainable Business Development." *Journal of Marketing Development and Competitiveness* 5, no. 7 (2011): 72–80.

Baker, Gill. "Zambia-Opportunity Knocks: A Stable Economy and Growing Middle Class Is Attracting International Banks to Zambia." *The Banker*, April 7, 2008. www.thebanker.com/World/Africa/Zambia/Opportunity-knocks.

Bischoff, Christine, and Geoffrey Wood. "Selective Informality: The Self-Limiting Growth Choices of Small Business in South Africa." *International Labour Review* 152, no. 3–4 (2013): 493–505.

Bratton, Michael, Robert Mattes, and Emmanuel Gyimah-Boadi. *Public Opinion, Democracy, and Market Reform*. New York: Cambridge University Press, 2005.

Chakiso, Cherinet Boke. "The Effect of Relationship Marketing on Customers' Loyalty (Evidence from Zemen Bank)." *Emerging Markets Journal* 5, no. 2 (2015): 57–70.

Coulter, J., and G. Onumah. "The Role of Warehouse Receipt Systems in Enhanced Commodity Marketing and Rural Livelihoods in Africa." *Food Policy* 27 (2002): 319–337.

Easterly, William. "The Middle Class Consensus and Economic Development." *Journal of Economic Growth* 6, no. 4 (2001): 317–335.

Faajir, Avanenge. "Effects of Market Infrastructure and Poor Access to Markets on Marketing of Grains in Selected States of Northern Nigeria, West Africa." *Journal of Business and Retail Management Research* 9 (April 2015): 110–118.

334 Bibliography

Gbadamosi, Ayantunji. "Consumer Involvement and Marketing in Africa: Some Directions for Future Research." *International Journal of Consumer Studies* 37 (March 2013): 234–242.

Glaub, Matthias E. et al. "Increasing Personal Initiative in Small Business Managers or Owners Leads to Entrepreneurial Success: A Theory-Based Controlled Randomized Field Intervention for Evidence-Based Management." *Academy of Management Learning & Education* 14, no. 1 (January 2015): 21–46.

Goetz, Stephan J. "A Selectivity Model of Household Food Marketing Behavior in Sub-Saharan Africa." *American Journal of Agricultural Economics* 74 (May 1992): 444–452. https://doi.org/10.2307/1242498.

Jones, David B. "State Structures in New Nations: The Case of Primary Agricultural Marketing in Africa." *The Journal of Modern African Studies* 20 (December 1982): 556–569.

Kharas, Homi. "The Emerging Middle Class in Developing Countries." Working Paper 285, OECD, Development Center, 2010. www.oecd.org/dev/emea/.

Knaup, Horand, and Jan Puhl. "Africa's Growing Middle Class Drives Development." *Der Spiegel*, July 2, 2012. www.spiegel.de/international/world/africa-s-growing-middle-class-drives-development-a-842365.html.

Kshetri, Nir. "Institutional and Economic Foundations of Entrepreneurship in Africa: An Overview." *Journal of Developmental Entrepreneurship* 16, no. 1 (2011): 9–35.

Madsen, Tage Koed. "Successful Export Marketing Management: Some Empirical Evidence." *International Marketing Review* 6, no. 4 (1989): 41–57.

McDade, Barbara E., and Anita Spring, "The 'New Generation of African Entrepreneurs': Networking to Change the Climate for Business and Private Sector-Led Development." *Entrepreneurship & Regional Development* 17 (January 2005): 17–42.

Morris, Michael H., Minet Schindehutte, and Raymond W. LaForge. "Entrepreneurial Marketing: A Construct for Integrating Emerging Entrepreneurship and Marketing Perspectives." *Journal of Marketing Theory and Practice* 10, no. 4 (2002): 1–19.

Munemo, Jonathan. "Entrepreneurship on Developing Countries: Is Africa Different?" *Journal of Development Entrepreneurship*, 17, no. 1 (2012): 1–12.

Mutch, Thembi. "The Rise of the Middle Class in Africa." *New Africa* (February 2012): 38–39.

Obayelu, Abiodun Elijah, Aisha O. Arowolo, Bolatito Ibrahim Shakirat, and Caroline Oluwakemi Oderinde. "Socioeconomic Determinants of Profitability of Fresh Fish Marketing in Ogun State, Nigeria." *International Journal of Social Economics* 43, no. 8 (2016): 871–883.

Owusu, Richard Afriyie. "Project Marketing to Africa: Lessons from the Case of IVO Transmission Engineering and Ghana's National Electrification Scheme." *Journal of Business & Industrial Marketing*, 17, no. 6 (2002): 523–537.

Oyewole, Philemon. "International Tourism Marketing in Africa: An Assessment of Price Competitiveness Using the Purchasing Power Parities of the IC." *Journal of Travel & Tourism Marketing* 16, no. 1 (2004): 3–17.

Ramachandran, Vijaya, and Manju Kedia Shah. *Minority Entrepreneurs and Form Performance in Sub-Sahara Africa*. Paper No. 86, Washington, DC: World Bank, Regional Program on Enterprise Development, June 1998 (Revised April 1999).

Singbo, Alphonse G., Alfons Oude Lansink, and Grigorios Emvalomatis. "Estimating Farmers' Productive and Marketing Inefficiency: An Application to Vegetable Producers in Benin." *Journal of Productivity Analysis* 42 (October 2014): 157–169.

Tweneboah-Koduah, Ernest Yaw, and Nana Owusu-Frimpong, "Social Marketing Communications on AIDS: Views of Implementers in Ghana." *The Journal of Business Diversity*, 15 (December 2015): 91–101.

Weatherspoon, Dace D. "The Rise of Supermarkets in Africa: Implications for Agrifood Systems and the Rural Poor." *Development Policy Review*, 21 (May 2003): 333–355.

WEBPAGES

Webpage name	Webpage address
3M Worldwide	www.3m.com
Abbott Laboratories	http://abbott.com
Africa Business Pages	www.africa-business.com/
Africa Health Placements	www.ahp.org.za/
AfricaRenewal	www.un.org/africarenewal/
Africa to Africa	http://africatoafrica.org/
African Business Magazine	www.africanbusinessmagazine.com/
African Clean Energy	www.africancleanenergy.com/
African Entrepreneur Collective	www.africanentrepreneurcollective.org/
African Entrepreneurship, The Case Foundation	www.caentr.org/ and https://casefoundation.org/
African Entrepreneurship Award	https://africanentrepreneurshipaward.com
African Epicure	www.africanepicure.com/
African Gourmet	www.africangourmet.us/cooking-tools.html
African Marketing Confederation	www.africanmc.org
Africa's Young Entrepreneurs	https://ayeonline.org/
Alliance for a Green Revolution in Africa (AGRA)	https://agra.org/
ARAHA	www.araha.org
Asante Africa Foundation	https://asanteafrica.org/
Ashoka—Social Entrepreneurship	www.ashoka.org/
Baxter	www.baxter.com
BRAC USA	www.bracusa.org
Construction Tanzania	www.tanzaniainvest.com/construction
Consumer Advocacy Centre Ghana	www.cacghana.org/

COPEC Ghana—Chamber of Petroleum	
Develop Africa	www.developafrica.org
Digital Ghana, Consumer Rights	https://digitalghana.org/complaints-enquiries/consumer-rights/
Eco Agriculture Partners	www.ecoagriculture.org/
Entrepreneurship in Africa	http://couldyou.org/initiatives/entrepreneurship/
EU-Africa Relations Africa	www.consilium.europa.eu/en/policies/
European Union External Action Africa	https://eeas.europa.eu/diplomatic-network/development-and-cooperation-europeaid_en
Financial Times	www.ft.com/
Forbes	www.forbes.com
Generac	www.generac.com
General Electric Renewable Energy, Wind Turbines	www.gerenewableenergy.com
GlobalGiving Foundation US	www.globalgiving.org
Goal Zero Generators	www.goalzero.com/heavy-duty
Grundfos	www.grundfos.com
Harvard Business Review	https://hbr.org/
Hualien Pumps	www.hualienpumps.com.tw/
Independent Journalism	www.tol.org/
Indiegogo Pumps	www.indiegogo.com/
International Food Policy Research Institute	www.ifpri.org/
Joint Development Associates	www.jdainternational.org/
Lifewater Organization	https://lifewater.org/
Lilly	www.lilly.com
Management Strategies for Africa	www.msforafrica.org/
Matter	www.matter.ngo/
McKinsey & Company	www.mckinsey.com
Merck	www.merck.com
Michigan State University, African Study Center	www.africa.isp.msu.edu
Mike Berry Associates	http://mikeberryassociates.com/
Modern Agriculture	https://modernag.org/
National Agricultural Library	www.nal.usda.gov/topics
National Institutes of Health	www.nih.gov
Organic Farmer Training	www.learngrowconnect.org/
Pathfinder International	www.pathfinder.org/tanzania
Protected Areas Management in Africa	https://courseware.epfl.ch/courses/course-v1:EPFL+protected-areas+2017_T3/about
Pumpmakers Solar	https://pumpmakers.com/en
S C Johnson & Sons	www.scjohnson.com
Self Help Africa	https://selfhelpafrica.org
Serving Entrepreneurs	www.edwardlowe.org/
Siemens, Wind Turbines	www.siemens.com/
Smart Electric Power Alliance	https://sepapower.org

Social Entrepreneurs	www.trwellsfoundation.org
Spark Entrepreneurship	www.spark-online.org
Successful Entrepreneurs in Africa	http://couldyou.org/
Tanzania Arusha Programs Overseas	www.abroaderview.org/
Tanzania Microfinance	www.fivetalents.org/
Tesla Srl Pumps	www.teslasub.it
Umeå University, Umeå School of Business and Economics	www.usbe.umu.se
United Nations Environmental Protection Program	www.grid.unep.ch
University of Wisconsin-Whitewater, College of Business and Economics	www.uww.edu/cobe/
University of Wisconsin-Whitewater, College of Letters and Sciences	www.uww.edu/cls
US Agency for International Development	www.usaid.gov
US Department for Energy National Renewable Energy Laboratory	www.nrel.gov
Vestas	www.vestas.com/
Which Are the Best B2B Portals in Africa?	www.quora.com/Which-are-the-best-B2B-portals-in-AFrica
Wind Energy Technologies	https://energy.gov/eere/wind/
Wristsponsible Water Brands	https://wristsponsible.com/
WSP USA	www.wsp-pb.com/en/

INDEX

acculturation 219, 222
AdminCard 187
Africa 2, 10, 16, 21–25, 27–31, 33, 35, 41, 47, 75–82, 84–88, 92–93, 100, 105–106, 119–127, 132–133, 136–138, 141, 143–148, 152, 175, 179, 181–182, 190, 195, 197, 207, 209–217, 224–229, 231, 235, 237, 243, 247, 261, 291–293, 298, 310, 315–316, 318–319, 326, 332
African Economic Outlook (AEO) 81–82
Africa Enterprise Challenge Fund (AECF) 298
agrarian areas 79–80
agribusiness value chain development 295, 302
agro-processing 245, 276
Airtel 148, 297, 308
airtime 139–140, 142, 147–148
alum 191
aluminium (aluminum) 163
anthropologist 183
anthropology 64–68, 94
arable land 25, 28, 32–34, 81
arbitrators 110
artisan fishing communities 40
ATMs (ATM) 134
audience 96–97, 99

banking 10, 119, 123–124, 126–128, 133–134, 139–143, 149, 171, 186, 191, 211–212, 303–304, 307
barriers 75, 79, 134, 146, 165, 248

Base of the Pyramid (BoP) 180, 183, 194
Berbera, port 40–41, 47, 52–55, 59–60, 62–68
Blue Ocean strategy: ICT 142
boat owners 40–41, 50, 62
bootstrapping 87, 160
borehole 183, 190
Burkina Faso 24, 315–316
business development service 277
business planning 246, 248, 251–252, 274, 281, 286
business to business marketing 16, 106–116

cartels 188
cattle 80, 296, 298, 301–302
cellular telephone 4, 93, 133, 137, 195–197
chemistry 10, 175, 177, 181, 192–193, 316
climate 5, 10–11, 13, 78–79, 92, 111, 171, 178, 187, 248, 319, 331
cluster 73–74, 76, 80–83, 87, 321–322, 324, 326
clusters, in Africa 3, 16–17, 74–76, 80, 82–83, 88, 127, 315
cluster theory 73, 80
coastal 40, 44–45, 47, 52, 230
competitiveness 75, 80–81, 83, 108, 110, 244–246, 262, 264, 293, 322
component parts 108, 110, 114
connectivity 4, 132, 138, 176, 182, 195–196, 295
consensus 28, 62, 92, 97, 104, 249

340 Index

consortium 76
consumer attitudes 209–210
consumer behavior 8, 153, 208–209, 214–215, 217, 226, 229
consumer ethnocentrism 209, 213
consumer satisfaction 1, 8, 209, 211
corporate social responsibility (CSR) 77
country-of-origin effects 209, 213
crime 42, 48, 52, 54, 64, 67, 128
currency 13, 27, 133, 147

Danish International Development Agency (DANIDA) 47–49, 51, 59–60, 65, 74, 77, 80, 83–84, 87, 187, 237, 245, 263–264
delivery 92, 98, 100–101, 103, 105, 107–108, 122, 128, 176, 182–183, 190, 194–195, 197, 251–252, 261, 294–295, 308
dietary adjustments 94
dietary values 247
dried fruit 315–316
Drinkable Book 176, 179
drought 47

East Africa 64, 76, 129–130, 146, 182, 228, 231, 234–237, 279, 286, 295
econometric 38, 208
economic growth, Africa 13, 22–35, 126–127, 136, 143, 175, 208, 215, 224–225, 243, 246, 249, 292–293, 330–332
electronic payment system 125, 141
emerging trends 50
encryption 184
engineering 3, 108–109, 111, 121, 180–182, 190–191, 197, 316
engineers 10, 181, 186, 191, 331
entrepreneur 5, 8, 11–12, 48, 82, 103, 106, 160, 165, 167, 195
entrepreneurial orientation 150, 153, 155–158
entrepreneurship 3, 16, 48, 82, 95, 114, 136, 159, 165, 168, 171, 176, 244, 250, 252, 266, 325, 329
equipment 2, 4, 107–109, 112, 114, 190–191, 226, 261, 266, 316, 324
export 35, 75–76, 243, 264, 292, 322–325

FairFishing 40–42, 47–49, 51, 55–56, 59–60
farmer 295, 298–300, 305, 310
farming 124, 127, 291, 308, 317, 319

farms 76, 80, 233–234, 291
filters 180, 184
financial services 135
financing 160, 162–164, 167–170
fisheries 42, 44, 51–53, 60
fishermen 50
fishing 40–41, 43, 45, 47–49, 51, 53, 55, 57, 59
food retailing 225
foreign aid 21–26, 29–35, 74–75, 77
foreign direct investment (FDI) 21, 25–26, 28, 32–33, 35, 78
fresh water 175
fruit 15, 17, 315–316, 318, 322–323, 325
Fruiteq 317, 323–327
fuel 5, 178, 316

General Agreement on Tariffs and Trade (GATT) 79
generalized method of moments (GMM) model 33
globalization 28, 75, 83, 133
global positioning system (GPS) 183, 193
Global System for Mobile Communications (GSM) application 195
gravity-driven membrane (GDM) 210
gross capital formation (GCF) 25
gross domestic product (GDP) 25, 27–33, 119, 133, 136, 147, 207, 224, 243–245, 291–292
gross fixed capital formation (GFCF) 28, 31–33
groundwater 175, 184–185
Groupe WAKA 317, 323
growing middle class 225, 236
Grundfos 82, 176, 182–187, 189–191, 194

health care 3–4, 15–16, 23, 32, 37, 92–95, 98–101, 103, 105, 109, 124, 331
horticultural 294
human capital 9, 11–12, 22, 25–27, 34, 122

incremental innovation 151
information and communication technologies (ICT) related products 120, 122–124, 128, 136, 138, 142, 295
International Monetary Fund (IMF) 76
international retailers 207, 225–229, 234–235, 237
Internet 3–5, 8–10, 15–17, 73–75, 81, 83, 91–93, 97–98, 100–101, 103, 106–107, 112, 116, 136–138, 146, 184, 186, 195, 295, 303–304, 310, 329–330

Index **341**

Internet of Things (IoT) 195, 199, 204
inventory 7
irrigation 188, 292

Kenya 24, 76, 79, 100, 115, 120, 124–126,
132–134, 138, 140–143, 146–148,
175–178, 182–183, 185, 187–189,
194–195, 226, 228–229, 231, 234,
238–239, 261, 294–295

liability 170, 247
LIFELINK 176, 182–191, 194–195
LifeStraw 176–179, 181
low-income 21–22, 24, 29, 31–35, 120,
133, 177, 214, 235–236

machine-to-machine (M2M) 176, 182, 195
mango dryers 317, 319–321, 325
mango growers 317, 319, 321, 323
maritime 52, 57–58
marketing 1–17, 73–75, 92–101, 104–105,
107, 126–127, 149–150, 153, 176, 182,
193–194, 197, 207–211, 213–217,
224–227, 229, 235–237, 245, 247–251,
260–261, 264, 268, 276, 291, 293–295,
298, 309, 315–318, 321–326, 329–331
marketing management 1–3, 5–13, 15–17,
73, 75, 115–116, 215, 238–239, 317,
321, 322, 325
marketization 50, 62
market orientation 150, 153
microeconomic foundation 83
middle-income 21, 24, 29, 31–35, 128, 224,
226, 236
mobile money 17, 123–124, 126–128, 133,
135, 138, 141, 146–153, 191, 300
mobile penetration 132
mobile phone networks 123, 132, 300
mobile phones 122, 124–125, 140–141,
147–148, 150, 153, 183, 186, 194,
290–291, 294–295, 308, 310
modernization 46, 102, 228
MoMo 196–197
money transfer 120, 126, 133, 138, 141,
147–148, 186, 191
M-Pesa 120, 124–126, 132–135, 138–143,
146–150, 186, 194, 297–301, 303–304,
307–310

Nanofilter 176, 180–182
nanomaterials 180–181
natural resources 21, 24–25, 27–28, 35, 81,
83, 87–88, 108, 195, 293

North Atlantic Treaty Organization
(NATO) 45
nutritional values 247

One Belt One Road initiative (OBOR)
79–80
outsourcing 250, 264, 266
Oxford Water Network 195

penetration 74, 83, 99, 124, 126, 132, 134,
136, 193, 229, 290
piracy 40–45, 48–49, 51–62, 183
processors 293, 297, 310, 319–321,
323, 325
products 1–17, 23, 73, 78, 81–82, 91–93,
95–96, 104, 106–115, 127, 138, 142,
146, 148, 150–152, 159, 169, 171, 184,
209–216, 226, 228, 230, 233–235,
243–245, 247–248, 251, 258–264, 276,
290–293, 295, 297, 299–305, 307–310,
315, 318–319, 321–322, 326, 329–331
public needs 330
pumps 182, 186, 190, 195–196
purchase decisions 142, 209–211
pyramid 81, 183

quality of infrastructure 25, 31–33

radical innovation 83, 150–151, 153
raw materials 79, 108, 247
regional 3, 23, 41, 44, 58, 74–75, 78,
80, 82–83, 103, 105, 109, 127, 136,
184–185, 228, 244, 248, 258, 319,
321, 324
rejection 55, 94, 123, 214
remote 5, 8, 10, 14–15, 17, 76, 82–83, 98,
103–105, 124, 166, 180, 182, 184, 194,
197, 329–330
renewable resources 114, 331
repair 188–189, 194, 196–197
retail 4, 124, 126, 133, 138, 140–142,
210–212, 224–228, 231–232, 234–237,
247, 261, 319, 323
revenue 28, 35, 40–41, 47, 54, 57, 98, 139,
141, 175, 178, 185–186, 190, 193, 331
revolution 124
radio frequency identification (RFID)
182, 186
risk 6, 9, 11, 41–42, 44–45, 49–50, 54–56,
60–61, 77, 119, 121, 123, 125, 140, 146,
151–152, 160, 165–168, 170, 179, 186,
224, 248, 299–300, 318, 324–325
risk-taking 151

342 Index

robotics 182
rural business 149

Safaricom 125–126, 133, 136, 138–143,
 146–147, 153, 157, 186
sales 15, 74, 99, 112–113, 149, 153, 175,
 181, 183, 191, 214, 225, 251, 253,
 261–264
sanitation 175–177, 180, 193, 195
satellite 184, 195, 330
scalability 193
science 85, 101–102, 128, 176, 180, 197
sea 28, 40, 42, 44–48, 52, 55
security 42–45, 48–52, 54, 58–61, 125,
 149–150, 160, 194, 197, 212, 216,
 303–304, 309
sensors 182, 195–196
service-dominant logic 150, 152–153
service innovation 123
service quality perceptions 209, 211
small and medium enterprise 244, 259, 264
smartphone 146, 151, 197, 226, 310
social marketing 10, 15, 92–93, 95–101,
 104–105, 218, 323
societal issues 97
solar 3–5, 10, 14–15, 76, 81, 86, 107, 115,
 148, 183–184, 190–191, 316, 320, 329
Somaliland 40–62
stability 2, 5, 9, 13, 82, 128, 193–194, 295,
 319, 331
stakeholders 43, 58, 61, 128, 194, 227,
 244, 246, 249, 251, 269, 274, 294, 307,
 309–310
storage facilities 293, 310, 317
strategies 1, 6–8, 12, 15, 17, 48–49, 78–79,
 82, 97, 112–113, 115, 123, 126–127,
 142, 176, 194, 207, 214–217, 224,
 226–227, 235, 244, 246, 248, 261, 291,
 294, 310, 325
structural elements 2, 12, 26, 82, 97,
 179, 194
structure 5, 8–9, 12, 76–77, 120–121,
 135, 138, 146, 160–161, 184, 247–248,
 325–326, 329
subcontracting 250–251
sub-Saharan Africa 23, 78, 88, 105, 120,
 132, 136, 141, 175, 181, 195, 197, 207,
 217, 315–317, 326
suppliers 74, 81–82, 91, 107–110, 112,
 114, 149, 227–228, 232–237, 251, 254,
 260–262, 293, 300–301, 303–304,
 308–310, 331
supplies 107–108, 233–234, 309, 324
survival 58, 168, 211, 244, 248, 252,
 274, 276

sustainability 26, 138–139, 182–183, 185,
 187–188, 190, 249, 269, 273
sustainable activities 27, 34, 76, 80–81, 85,
 88, 121–122, 138, 143, 152, 175–176,
 178–179, 181, 185, 187, 190, 194–195,
 207, 251
Sustainable Water, Energy and
 Environmental Technologies Laboratory
 (SWEETLab) 195
systematic approaches 9, 12, 99, 110, 127,
 208, 331

Tanzania 3, 24, 29, 93, 100, 103, 105,
 125, 141, 147–148, 159, 162, 180–181,
 195, 197, 210, 225, 228–232, 234–237,
 243–246,, 256, 259–264, 270–271, 273,
 278, 290–299, 302, 308–309, 315
taxes 92, 236, 310
technical issues 21–22, 47, 107, 110, 112, 152,
 176, 182–183, 185, 188, 190–191, 193,
 250–251, 261, 266, 290, 303, 317, 331
technological resources 1–7, 11, 13–16,
 73, 79, 93, 108–110, 113, 226, 266, 290,
 293, 316, 319, 331
technologies 9, 23, 45, 48–50, 55, 74,
 107–108, 112, 114, 126, 128, 133, 136, 152,
 195, 264, 266, 290, 292–293, 295, 310, 330
telecommunication 3–5, 8–10, 15–17, 93,
 98, 128, 137, 147–148, 290, 329, 330, 332
telemedicine 182
telephones 4, 10, 13, 91, 93–94, 133, 147,
 290, 330
testing 8, 112, 177–179, 181, 185, 190, 194,
 197, 316, 320
theory 15, 26–27, 73, 80, 102, 123, 152,
 161, 164, 226–227, 256, 272, 278
The Straw 176–177
trade 23, 27, 34, 52, 75–76, 79, 87, 92, 104,
 121, 142, 160, 208, 232, 236, 245, 250,
 262–263, 266, 271–272
TradeWater 190
training 2, 4–5, 21–22, 26, 44, 46, 48, 55,
 85, 100, 103, 152, 181, 183, 188, 190,
 194, 212, 234–235, 246, 248–252, 262,
 266, 269, 271, 275–276, 295, 325
transactions 7, 10, 107–108, 123–125,
 140–141, 143, 149, 184, 291, 297, 299,
 321, 330
transportation systems 21, 94, 115, 193,
 298–299, 317–319

United Nations (UN) 44, 74, 77, 78–80,
 175, 193
United Nations Capital Development
 Fund (UNCDF) 47

urban areas 92, 107, 119, 124, 126, 134, 175, 182–183, 185, 190, 192, 210, 213–214, 216, 226, 229, 232, 292, 330
urbanization 78, 81–82, 126

value creation 12, 98, 150, 152–153, 293
vandalism 183
VendorCard 187
ventures 7–8, 73–74, 87, 92, 106, 159–161, 163, 182, 315–316, 323, 325–326

Vodacom 147, 297–300, 307–309
Vodafone 125–126, 138–140, 148–149

water 4, 10, 15, 17, 44, 50, 58, 104–105, 107, 115, 149, 168, 175–198, 210, 296, 324
Water Missions International (WMI) 190, 191, 193
World Development Index (WDI) 28
wealth 79, 120–121, 252

youth 52, 54, 214